Off The Beaten Track
SPAIN

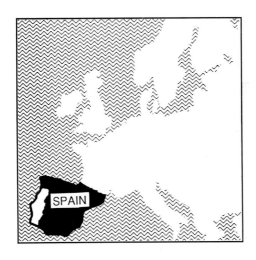

*Off the Beaten Track*

# SPAIN

Barbara Mandell • Roger Penn

MOORLAND PUBLISHING

The Globe Pequot press

Published by:
Moorland Publishing Co Ltd,
Moor Farm Road West, Ashbourne,
Derbyshire, DE6 1HD England

ISBN 0 86190 494 X (UK)

The Globe Pequot Press,
6 Business Park Road,
PO Box 833, Old Saybrook,
Connecticut 06475-0833

ISBN 1-56440-296-7 (USA)

First published 1990, Reprinted 1992
Revised 2nd edition 1994
© Moorland Publishing Co Ltd 1994

Cover photographs: Ronda, Costa del
Sol (*MPC Picture collection*)

Black and white illustrations have been
supplied by:
Editorial Everest SA; Gonzales Byass;
M. Gray; R. W. Penn; J. A. Robey;
Spanish Tourist Office.

Colour illustrations have been supplied
by:
Editorial Everest SA; M. Gray; R. W.
Penn; J. A. Robey.

Printed in Hong Kong Ltd by:
Wing King Tong Co Ltd

**Note on Maps**
The maps for each chapter, while comprehensive, are not designed to be used
as route maps, but to locate the main
towns, villages and places of interest.

British Library Cataloguing in Publication Data:
A catalogue record for this book is available from the British Library.

Library of Congress Cataloging-in-Publication Data
Mandell, Barbara
  Off the beaten track. Spain/Barbara Mandell, Roger Penn. — Rev. 2nd ed.
    p. cm.
  Includes Index.
  ISBN 1-56440-296-7 (USA)
  1. Spain — Guidebooks.  I. Penn, Roger. II. Title. III. Title: Spain.
DP14.M25 1994
914.604'83 — dc20

93-10704
CIP

# Contents

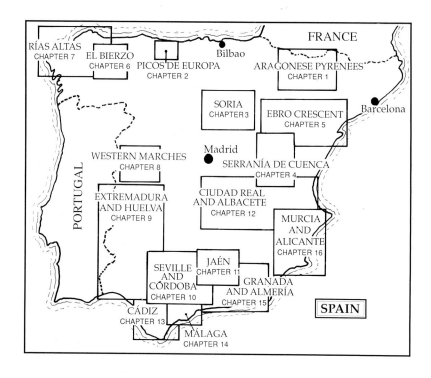

RÍAS ALTAS
CHAPTER 7

EL BIERZO
CHAPTER 6

PICOS DE EUROPA
CHAPTER 2

Bilbao

FRANCE

ARAGONESE PYRENEES
CHAPTER 1

SORIA
CHAPTER 3

EBRO CRESCENT
CHAPTER 5

Barcelona

WESTERN MARCHES
CHAPTER 8

Madrid

SERRANÍA DE CUENCA
CHAPTER 4

PORTUGAL

EXTREMADURA
AND HUELVA
CHAPTER 9

CIUDAD REAL
AND ALBACETE
CHAPTER 12

MURCIA
AND
ALICANTE
CHAPTER 16

SEVILLE
AND
CÓRDOBA
CHAPTER 10

JAÉN
CHAPTER 11

GRANADA
AND ALMERÍA
CHAPTER 15

CÁDIZ
CHAPTER 13

MÁLAGA
CHAPTER 14

SPAIN

## Museums and Other Places of Interest

Wherever possible opening times have been checked, and are as accurate as possible. However, during the main holiday period they may be extended. Conversely, outside the main season, there may be additional restrictions, or shorter hours. Local tourist offices will always be able to advise you.

Generally all churches, and abbeys and monasteries still in use, are open every day, except during services. You should remember that these are places of worship as well as historical monuments, so dress and conduct should be appropriate.

# Introduction

Western Europe is a continent of great diversity, well visited not just by travellers from other parts of the globe but by the inhabitants of its own member countries. Within the year-round processes of trade and commerce, but more particularly during the holiday season, there is a great surging interchange of nationalities as one country's familiar attractions are left behind for those of another.

It is true that frontiers are blurred by ever quicker travel and communications, and that the sharing of cultures, made possible by an increasingly sophisticated media network, brings us closer in all senses to our neighbours. Yet essential differences do exist, differences which lure us abroad on our annual migrations in search of new horizons, fresh sights, sounds and smells, discovery of unknown landscapes and people.

Countless resorts have evolved for those among us who simply crave sun, sea and the reassuring press of humanity. There are, too, established tourist 'sights' with which a country or region has become associated and to which clings, all too often, a suffocating shroud — the manifestations of mass tourism in the form of crowds and entrance charges, the destruction of authentic atmosphere, cynical exploitation. Whilst this is by no means typical of all well known tourist attractions, it is familiar enough to act as a disincentive for those of more independent spirit who value personal discovery above prescribed experience and who would rather avoid the human conveyor belt of queues, traffic jams and packed accommodation.

It is for such travellers that this guidebook has been written. In its pages, no more than passing mention is made of the famous, the well documented, the already glowingly described — other guidebooks will satisfy the appetite for such orthodox tourist information. Instead, the reader is taken if not to unknown then to relatively unvisited places — literally 'off the beaten track'. Through the specialist

7

knowledge of the authors, visitors using this guidebook are assured of gaining insights into the country's heartland whose heritage lies largely untouched by the tourist industry. Occasionally the reader is urged simply to take a sideways step from a site of renowned tourist interest to discover a place  perhaps less sensational, certainly less frequented but often of equivalent fascination.

From wild, scantily populated countryside whose footpaths and byways are best navigated by careful map reading, to negotiating the side streets of towns and cities, travelling 'off the beaten track' can be rather more demanding than following in the footsteps of countless thousands before you. The way may be less clear, more adventurous and individualistic, but opportunities do emerge for real discovery in an age of increasing dissatisfaction with the passive predictability of conventional holidaymaking. With greater emphasis on exploring 'off the beaten track', the essence of Spain is more likely to be unearthed and its true flavours relished to the full.

*Martin Collins*
Series Editor

# 1 • The Aragonese Pyrenees

The mountains of the Pyrenees extend for 480km (298 miles) in an impressive chain from the Atlantic to the Mediterranean. They were intensely folded and pushed northwards in far distant geological time, so they are steeper on the French side than in Spain, where they descend gradually in steps to the Ebro valley. The region of the Aragonese Pyrenees lies in the centre of the range, between Navarra and Cataluña, in the north of the province of Huesca in Upper Aragón (the old kingdom has recently been reconstituted as an autonomous region). The highest peaks of the whole range are near the border with Lérida province (Cataluña), and include Aneto (3,404m) 11,165ft, and Posets 3,371m (11,057ft) rising amid the surviving glaciers of the ice moulded granite massifs of Maladeta and Posets. The larger part of the region is made up of limestone of the Pre-Pyrenees, sometimes massive with fine steep cliffs and escarpments which form long high *sierras* running east to west. However, the rivers flow north to south, so each valley is cut into compartments, sometimes broad and verdant, followed by sections of steep and narrow gorges. The heads of these valleys end in magnificent cirques (*circos*) with waterfalls, beech, fir and pine forests, giving scenery on a grand scale as in the Ordesa valley. Further south the landscape gradually becomes drier, and the hills are covered with evergreen oaks, pines and broom.

The high valleys were isolated for centuries, but earlier they were quite well populated, with independent political and pastoral communities having their own customs, folklore and traditional dress — some still exist as in the Ansc valley — and practising a form of transhumance, with large flocks of sheep. Others, like the Noguera Ribagorzana on the eastern edge of the region, were almost unknown until 1946, when they began to be exploited for HEP (hydro-electric power). However, most of the large artifical lakes like El Grado in the Cinca valley were inundated in the drier bare limestones and marls of the lower slopes. The HEP works in the upper valleys were well landscaped, with buildings in the traditional style of the High Pyrenees.

Isolated farms in the landscape are rare. The people live in villages and hamlets with picturesque stone, houses and slate roofs. Towns are small, but well distributed like Ainsa at the confluence of the Ara and Cinca rivers; Boltaña a little further west; Biescas on the Gállego; Benasque at the head of the Esera valley, and Campo midway up it. The largest places are Jaca, a pleasant old garrison town with an ancient cathedral, on the former pilgrimage route to Santiago de Compostela over the Puerto de Somport from France. Barbastro, almost out of the region southwards; and Pont de Suert, on the left bank of the Noguera Ribagorzana and in Lérida province.

The attractions of the region, with its rugged isolation and beauty, are many, and cover a wide range of interests. The national park of Ordesa and Monte Perdido, first established in 1918 and extended sevenfold in area in 1982, is outstanding. Walking in high forested valleys, climbing (all grades), caving in the limestone areas, some horse-riding and winter skiing are all there to be enjoyed. Several small places have swimming pools, there are thermal centres at Benasque and Panticosa, and it is possible to eat well at any restaurant, however remote. In the interior of the region there are innumerable opportunities for exploration away from the roads, as some of the area is still untrodden, especially in the southern limestone canyons, gorges and ravines of the Sierra de Guara. It must be said, however, that with the vast increase in cars in Spain, and in spite of greatly improved mountain roads, the road infrastructure is inadequate for the number of visitors. Since the intense summer heat in Spanish cities brings many visitors to the mountains it is inadvisable to visit the Pyrenees in August.

The Pyrenees form a distinct climatic divide, and the contrast can be quite dramatic when crossing the frontier on the high passes, from often damp and cloudy weather in France to sunshine and clear weather in Spain. The climate of Upper Aragón is sub-alpine in the high valleys, where the summers are warm, often well above 21 °C(70 °F). Autumn is the wettest season, with winter snowfall in December and January. Further south in the limestone *sierras* the summers are rather hotter: 24-30 °C (75-86 °F), the seasons have less rain and snow, and it becomes progressively more arid, with abundant sunshine. Occasionally quite fierce storms can occur at any time of the year, and snow can block the high passes. Another feature is the marked difference between sun and shade: the sunny slopes, known as *solanos*, are cultivated, even for vines in some areas.

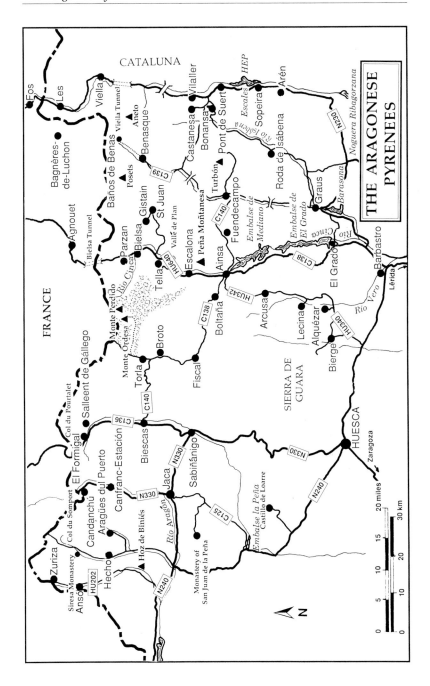

The High Pyrenees are much greener than is generally realised, with pure stands of black pine, silver fir, and rhododendrons high up, and fine beech forests on the limestone slopes of the western valleys and Ordesa, while the river valleys are clothed in poplars, larch and firs. And all around is a scented undergrowth of laurels, sweet briar, heather and broom. Forestry is important, and an immense programme of reafforestation was carried out in the years following the Civil War, especially on the drier deforested limestone *sierras* further south.

The wildlife of the region is in retreat, as in most mountain areas that have been opened up for skiing, climbing or increased tourism. HEP works have affected it far less, once the schemes were completed. Wolves and bears have gone, but some wild boars, beavers and a few pine martens remain, along with many badgers and foxes. Vipers are found on all south-facing slopes. Bird life, especially high up, is generally abundant: eagles, owls, vultures, sparrowhawks and crows plus the common European songbirds are here, but not many robins, nightingales, stonechats or swifts.

## Travelling to the Area

Access to the region, formerly difficult, is now much easier, with tunnels and new roads.

### From France by Road

From Bordeaux (Méringnac) airport: *autoroute* A63; N10 to Castets, then D947 to Oloron-Ste Marie, then N134 to Puerto de Somport (1,632m, 5,353ft) 281km (174 miles).
*Autoroute* A63 to Langon, D932/4 to Pau and Col de Portalet (1,794m, 5,884ft) 258km (160 miles).
From Toulouse (Blagnac) airport: N117 near to Lannemezan then D929 to Bielsa tunnel (1,820m, 5,970ft) (occasionally closed), 163km (101 miles).
N117 to St Gaudens, D8 to N125/N230 to Viella (Vielha) in Spain. 160km (99 miles).

### From France by Rail

Paris-Bordeaux-Pau. Oloron Ste Marie to Canfranc (tunnel) tri-weekly.

### Through Spain by Road

Zaragoza (Sanjurjo) airport: *autopista* A2/N330 to Zuera; N123 to

Huesca; then N240/C134 to Jaca. 162km (100 miles).
Barcelona (Prat) airport: A2/A7 to Lérida; N240 to Huesca, then as
above. 350km (217 miles).

**Through Spain by Rail**
From Zaragoza, Tardienta, or Jaca to Canfranc (also through train
from Madrid).

## The Eastern Margins of High Aragón

### Viella and High Ribagorzana

This is a convenient way of reaching the Aragonese Pyrenees, but as
it is the border between Aragón and Cataluña, there may be a few
language problems. However, both names will be given where
necessary.

After crossing the frontier from France, the route follows the
valley of the Upper Garonne (Garona), and N230 road to Viella
(Vielha). The landscape is very wooded and green, and really cli-
matically belongs to the French Pyrenees, as it actually would have
done, if the French signatories to the Peace of the Pyrenees in 1659
hadn't overlooked it. Then the route reaches Viella, the small capital
of the Val d'Aran, politically in Cataluña, but having a language of
its own — Aranès. This area has undergone a massive change after
centuries of isolation, and following exploitation for HEP and development for skiing, is now very tourist orientated, and much visited.
It was here that the famous speleologist, Norbert Casteret, investigated underground using coloured dyes to show that the source of
the great French river Garonne derived from a resurgence, and that
its waters came from the glaciers of the Maladeta massif in High
Aragón. Though now much developed, the beauty of the region
remains unaltered.

From Viella the route traverses the 5km (3 mile) long tunnel under
the massif, and opens out onto the high rock-strewn valley of the
Noguera Ribagorzana, now much developed for HEP. On the right
the valley ends in a cirque, with a waterfall, Cascada de Mulleres,
and higher up are some small lakes forming part of the river's source,
with a path leading to the Tuc de Mulleres (3,010m, 9,873ft). It is often
overcast and cloudy, and although the lower slopes are forested with
black pine and silver fir, the bare granite landscape of the cirque
looks rather grim and austere, but it is well worth exploring.

The road now descends into the valley, which becomes the
boundary between the province of Huesca (Aragón) on the right

bank, and the province of Lérida/Lleida (Cataluña) on the left bank. The river bed is a mass of boulders and rock debris, evidence of past storms. Soon the HEP lake of Baserca appears, and the power station of Senet, architecturally well in harmony with the landscape as most are in this area. Small cultivated fields of alfalfa and wheat can be seen flanking the great mass of stones in the wide river bed. Go past the hamlets of Senet, Bono and Forcat, in a greener landscape, until the large, pleasantly sited village of **Vilaller** is reached. The provincial boundary has a 'kink' to the west here, so it is in Cataluña, and all official notices are in Catalan. The church has a curious circular stone and brick bell tower. Further south an excursion can be made up a steep road on the right to Montanúy, an interesting old village with very tall houses built in varieties of local stone, which is set in the midst of a high, very fertile valley shoulder, well exposed to the to the sun and known as a *solano*.

Back in the main valley the small Catalan town of **Pont de Suert** comes into view. Although much expanded as an HEP company town, it has an attractive old quarter by the river. Just beyond begins the large HEP lake (*embalse*) of Escales, which is bordered by the N230 on the right bank, now in Aragón again, in a long corniche section with many tunnels. On the left, near the head of the lake, the ruins of the eighth-century monastery of Labaix can be seen, almost submerged, this being the final indignity the building suffered after its disestablishment in 1835.

At the southern end of the lake, which shines with a curiously beautiful green colour, is the village of **Sopeira**, and nearby at the foot of an immense cliff is one of the oldest and most famous monasteries in Aragón — Alahón. It is believed to have been founded in 643, and became a Benedictine institution. The oldest part now dates from 1123, having survived pillage by extremist Republican elements in the Civil War.

At the end of the gorge by the modern dam, the steps (*escales*), cut into the steep side before the road was made, can be seen. They were cut by the monks of Alahón, which gave the gorge and lake their name. From here the valley widens out into a well cultivated *huerta*, and some way along off on the right is the small town of **Arén**, with some very old and interesting architecture. There are arcaded plazas with balconied houses, and in the main plaza are rough square stone pillars of great age supporting large houses, showing how people lived in this isolated valley for many centuries before the recent great changes. An old castle is perched on the limestone ridge behind the town.

## The Isàbena, Esera and Benasque Valleys

The route now returns to the upper Ribagorzana valley, to where the road forks just before Vilaller. From the road junction, the route takes the C144 for a short way, climbing up to where, on the left, a side road (HU940) goes to the village of **Bonansa**. Here, especially in springtime, are very good views of the surrounding snow-capped mountains, with the prominent Pico de Llena (2,676m, 8,777ft) to the east. The valley of the river Isábena is now descended, but only in very recent years has this become a through route. This upper valley was always attractive in its isolation, and still has a charm, even now the new road passes through the gorge lower down, amid massive limestone crags. At the end of the gorge is the restored monastery building of Nuestra Señora d'Obarra, near the road to the village of Calvera.

The valley now opens out with the river bubbling over broad braided channels of stones, and at length past the villages of Serradúy and La Puebla de Roda. Off to the right, on a dominant site, is the medieval village of **Roda de Isábena**. Here, perhaps surprisingly, is an eleventh-century cathedral, with an old Bishop's palace situated on a well paved terrace. The cloisters are quite remarkable, of solid construction yet graceful, and in the chapel there are thirteenth-century frescoes. Outside, a short walk round the cathedral is interesting, revealing the pilasters of Lombard design (early Romanesque). Early in the year the visitor is quite likely to see large flocks of sheep being driven through the narrow alleys and streets past the cathedral at sunset. Originally Roda was the spiritual centre of the obscure Christian mountain state of Ribagorza, and in 1040 became part of the emerging kingdom of Aragón which, after the Christians had been forced back into the mountains, successfully repulsed the Moors from the Pyrenees. Hence the growth of the many monasteries and churches in the region. From Roda the distinctive shape of the isolated mountain of Turbón can be seen to the north, snow-capped and prominent in spring, while to the north-east and east the green Sierra de Serradúy and the river Isábena in its valley make a fine view.

Now the route returns upstream to the C144, which climbs up to a corniche amongst a verdant landscape of meadows and glimpses of the valley floors to the Collado de Fadas (1,479m, 4,851ft). On the way, off on the right, is a road (HU630) leading to the village of **Castanesa** at 1,500m (4,920ft), which until recently could only be reached by a steep mule track, and by jeep or landrover. This substantial settlement, with its large church, had all its flour brought on mule-back, but its redeeming feature (owing to its siting on a large patch of alluvium) was that it produced the best potatoes in the district. Before the paved road however, even the building of new houses did not stop the inhabitants from leaving. Although this area is in Aragón, many of the older people spoke a rough Catalan dialect mixed with Aragonese, but most could understand Spanish.

Just below the pass, before the village of Bisaurri on the winding road, there is a very fine view of the snowy peaks of the Maladeta massif: Aneto (3,404m, 11,165ft), and Pico de Maladeta (3,308m, 10,850ft). Then comes the descent to **Castejon de Sos** in the Esera valley. The more interesting part of this village, with its old houses and balconies, lies behind the wide main street. From here the C139 is joined, turning north to go up the Esera valley. This is wide and green with steep slopes, and the river flows fast and clear over its bed of granite boulders. Then the valley narrows by the hamlet of Sahún, and opens out to the HEP lake at **Eriste**. From here the massif of Posets can be explored by high paths, and Posets itself (3,373m, 11,063ft), the second highest Pyrenean mountain, can be climbed in just over 4 hours. The view from the summit is perhaps the finest in the Pyrenees.

Continuing upstream the ancient village of **Benasque** is reached, which, although remote, became a Roman *civitas*, which gave its name to the upper Esera. It has had a long history, from tenth-century Ribagorza, through Philip II, the Napoleonic and Carlist wars to the Civil War, including an earthquake in 1660, and an ambitious plan for a railway linking Paris with a port on the Ebro Delta in 1890! But it remained remote and little known until the 1960's, as Robin Fedden noted in his *The Enchanted Mountains*. When he was being shaved by a barber here, a man expressed a wish to see him, 'having never seen an Englishman'. Now enormous expansion has occurred, with cars and skiing overshadowing the ancient houses with their carved armorial bearings above the huge door-ways and courtyards, a reminder of when the nobility of Aragón, came here to escape the scorching summers of the plains. It is still a very interesting place to explore, and is also a climbing centre.

Further upstream on the right, a road leads to **Cerler** at 1,553m (5,094ft), now the skiing centre for the valley, and further on (the road is now above the valley floor), below on the right, is a large open meadow with scattered bushes, used for camping, and a road leading up to the thermal Baños de Benasque. These have been used since ancient times. The principal building was built in 1801 by the Duke of Alba for the use of local people, and is now owned by the Benasque municipality, who have added to and repaired the buildings, especially after they were burnt in the Civil War.

From here the whole of the upper basin of the Esera offers a vast area to explore. One possible excursion is up a side valley, the Río Literola, a fine torrent with rapids and wooded banks which is accessible from a new bridge. Take the road (C139) to its present terminus past a waterfall. At its end is a path that winds up through pines and clumps of irises, then across slopes covered with alpine flowers — harebells, yellow gentians and roses of Sharon — to some waterfalls on the Gurgutes stream. Going on higher, there are two grey-green cirque lakes with alpenrose growing nearby. Finally, go past a larger lake (Lago de Gurgutes) to arrive at the Pico de la Glera (2,496m, 8,187ft) on the French frontier.

Very large flocks of sheep (3-4,000), plus a few goats, are often seen on these slopes, for the best grass is high up, and transhumance is still active. The sheep come from the Huesca plains on an 8-day journey, and remain from mid-June to mid-September. They are grazed for mutton — always a good thing to eat in the Pyrenees.

Returning to the road, a path descends to the Esera which can be followed up the valley to the Puerto de Benasque (2,449m, 8,033ft), the lowest local pass into France which was much used in the Middle Ages by merchants, soldiers, smugglers and pilgrims to Santiago. This walk is good for a view of the glacial lakes, El Boum, in France at the pass itself, and a full scale view of the granite Maladeta massif with the highest peaks, which can be climbed from the refuge at **La Renclusa** (2,145m, 7,036ft) on its flanks.

Return now to near Castejon, to continue the route (C139) downstream of the Esera, which soon enters the Congosto de Ventamillo, an extraordinary narrow and very deep gorge with vertical limestone walls, for 3km (1³/₄ miles). With the river boiling below among the huge rocks, covered with spume, and a tangled vegetation of brambles, heather, ferns and moss clinging to the sheer sides, it is quite a remarkable sight.

After the gorge the valley opens out, and the small town of **Campo** is reached, off the main road. This is a most pleasant place with stables, granaries, old fashioned shops in its narrow streets, a church with a square tower, and a good restaurant — the Boyon. From here a road goes eastwards along a dead-end encircling southerly valley round the isolated limestone mountain of Turbón (2,492m, 8,174ft) whose shape is like a turban. The route follows the Lierp valley, through a semi-arid landscape of soft clays and marls heavily eroded into gullies and ravines. This is a miniature version of the South Dakota Big Badlands in the USA, so named because the pioneers found them difficult to cross.

However, the valley becomes greener as the road climbs to the village of Vilás de Turbón at 1,400m (4,592ft), with a good view of the mountain, and nearby is the source of the Aguas del Turbón, and a bottling plant. The waters can be tasted at a fountain in a little stone hut, with a statue and a tiled floor plus a silver tap and tumblers. Its taste is nondescript, but it is good for the kidneys, and well patron-ised by older people — there are two *fondas* (inns) here.

After this 'nature cure', return to Campo, and continue down the Esera valley to the junction of the C140. Here an excursion can be made further southwards, which at first presents a rather sombre picture of an arid landscape with hills furrowed by ravines. But past the village of Besians with its medieval bridge, and approaching the large HEP lake of Joaquin Costa, the benefits of irrigation can be seen. Orchards of fruit trees and vines are seen growing in a profusion of greenery, which contrasts with the previous aridity. Then comes the pleasant small town of **Graus**, where the valleys of the Esera and Isábena meet at the beginning of the plain of the river Cinca.

The medieval town on the edge of this Pyrenean region might perhaps surprise visitors by the wealth of its noble and interesting buildings. Note especially the beautiful Plaza Mayor, where old fifteenth- to eighteenth-century houses have sculptured frescoes, and brick arcades. One mansion in particular will surely arouse interest, being the house of the famous Inquisitor, Fray Tomás de Torquemada. Also in the old town are the Roman bridges of Abajo and Perarrúa, with a museum. Above the town, which lies at the foot of its great rock the Peña de Morral, is the famous sanctuary of Nuestra Señora de Peña.

Return northwards to the road junction with the C140 in the Esera valley and follow this road. After climbing to the Collado de Fora-dada (1,020m, 3,346ft), the route joins a river valley, with the Sierra de Ferrera in the background. Further on at Fuendecampo, amid green irrigated cultivation of vines and fruit, is some spectacular badland erosion. After this a distant view of an HEP lake is seen, and the Embalse de Mediano and the ancient mountain kingdom of Sobrarbe is entered. A short distance off on the left, by the shores of the lake, is the village of **Gerbe**, completely depopulated because of HEP works and becoming ruinous. A walk round it is interesting, because of its houses and the fine views of the mountains, Peña Montañesa and the distant Monte Perdido massif. Soon the old and delightful town of Ainsa is reached.

# Central High Aragón

## Ainsa and Sobrarbe

The small town of **Ainsa** at 589m (1,932ft) is well situated at the confluence of the Cinca and Ara rivers on a rocky promontory, and at the crossroads of transverse routes across the interior *sierras*, and northwards to France. It was the capital of the eleventh-century kingdom of Sobrarbe, the name still being used to denote the surrounding district. This pleasant place has two sharp contrasts: the old town above, now virtually a well preserved national monument, and the new town below, a commercial quarter grouped around the crossroads and known as 'Las Carreteras'. Ainsa has been called 'The Toledo of Aragón', and the old part certainly merits it. The visitor climbs up to an old walled and fortified town which has several fine gateways, particularly the Portal Alto, and then into a magnificent medieval Plaza Mayor with colonnades, behind which are houses with balconies, and cellars. One has been converted into a good class restaurant — Bodegas de Sobrarbe. At the western end of the Plaza is the old castle and fort, still being restored. The other end leads to one of the finest churches in the region — Santa Maria — begun in the eleventh century. It was restored in 1972-4, and is notable for its robust style, with a remarkable crypt, cloisters and tower. Much of the church treasure disappeared or was burnt in the Plaza during 1936-9. While much of Sobrarbe has become depopulated, Ainsa has grown, due to improved roads and the tunnel to Aragnouet in France.

The first route leaves Ainsa by the road to France (HU640). Just north of the town, the Cinca valley is particularly fine, with, on the right, the superb scarp of Peña Montañesa (2,291m, 7,514ft), then the valley narrows before **Escalona**, which has an information office for the national park of Ordesa and Monte Perdido. Here, on the left, one can enter a world of canyons, precipices, glaciated grottos, caverns and the various forms of karstic limestone erosion on the southern flanks of Monte Perdido. It offers much for the expert in caving and pot-holing, but also for the walker and for those who simply want to look, for there are old hamlets and churches too. Until recently the area was hardly known.

The route in is by paved forest track (HU631) to San Urbez, then on foot up the Añisclo canyon, which is within the park. This gorge has interesting sub-mediterranean vegetation, and because of thermal inversion, the higher areas have holm oaks, whilst lower down it is mixed: olives and figs growing up to 900m (2,952ft), with beech, firs, and on the river banks ash and maple, where it is colder. The hinterland of this wild area, mainly outside the park, contains much to explore — the gorges of the Rio Yesa and Rio Arirés for example — but very tough walking is necessary. The track which returns to the main road (HU631) is very narrow, and passing is hazardous.

The route continues on past the hamlet of Santa Justa to another road on the left that goes up to the village of Tella. This is also steep, and very narrow, with many hairpin bends but a good surface. But before climbing to Tella, another area can be explored. This is the valley of the Río Yaga, with the gorges of Escuain in the upper part reached by a paved track, narrow with a poor surface, to the settlement of Revilla. This gorge has a similar forest pattern to Añisclo. The lower Yaga has the less frequently visited Miraval gorges, equally fine and rather mysterious, which are reached on foot from the hamlet of Miraval and a track off the road at Cortalaviña. To descend all these gorges special equipment is needed (like rubber canoes) and when the river levels are low, usually at the end of summer and the beginning of autumn, 4 x 4 vehicles are also advised to reach them. Just before the village of Tella is a dolmen, a vestige of pre-history, showing that these remote highlands have always been lived in. From here the view of mountain ranges and gorges is truly panoramic. **Tella** itself, at 1,384m (4,540ft) and sited around a *solano*, has an information office and four churches and hermitages. The first, San Juan y Pablo, is reached by a fine walk along a clifftop amid flowers and park-like bushes. It was consecrated in 1018 and has a crypt and interesting fonts. It was probably sited there due to lack of water in the original village, but the views all round are magnificent. The parish church of St Martin is very picturesque, with snapdragons on the roof, and lavender roundabout is being restored. The other two: Our Ladies of Rode Peña and Fajanillas, are semi-ruined and also isolated, and their siting seems to indicate a defensive lookout. The village's history is typical of the area: two families (twelve people) live there now, but others return at weekends and in the summer. They have had electricity for a long time (probably longer than many other parts of rural Europe). The village had a mill, cattle, sheep, pigs, potatoes, tomatoes, beans and rye. They hunted boar, rabbits and pigeons locally, and had a water problem due to limestone, but lived a tough, isolated and healthy life for centuries.

Back on the main road, continue to Salinas, and turn right up the Cinqueta valley (HU641), narrow and impressive, which opens out onto one of the most attractive but lesser known Pyrenean landscapes of green and gold hedged fields, forests higher up, and the villages of Plan, San Juan de Plan and Gistain. From **San Juan**, a long path leads to Las Granjas de Viadas, at the foot of Posets (3,371m, 11,057ft), a little known and wild area.

Return to the road towards France, which gradually climbs to the village of **Bielsa**. This once quiet mountain outpost has achieved prosperity on account of the tunnel to France, but in doing so has become a tourist frontier post, with souvenir shops, and terribly crowded narrow streets. From here the route penetrates the long, straight, glaciated Pineta valley, whose upper zone is in the national park, and which ends in an enormous amphitheatre — a cirque, *circo* or corrie. The flat floor is full of meadows and flowers like snapdragons, buttercups and mountain clover, and with waterfalls flowing down the impressive slopes of Monte Perdido the valley is very beautiful, and in consequence much visited. There is a *parador* here, and scope for many excursions of all kinds, especially up and around the cirque, through and above beechwoods, to remote side valleys, where alpine flowers, larkspur and iris bloom in profusion.

The route now rises to Parzan at 1,130m (3,706ft) and beyond, on the right, a long track leads up to the Lago de Urdiceto (2,360m, 7,741ft), and Puerto de Urdiceto on the French frontier at 2,403m (7,882ft). Then, along the main road, the route continues to the abandoned lead and silver mines of Parzán, and on the left the last valley, Barrosa, near the ruins of the old Hospital de Parzán. This ends in an impressive glaciated cirque, and is a wild and rocky region leading to the peak of La Munia (3,134m, 10,280ft). After this, return to Ainsa for the next stage.

### The Sierra de Guara

From Ainsa the HU342 is taken to Arcusa in southern Sobrarbe, which, although a fairly new road across a high plateau, has a poor surface. At **Arcusa** there are the remains of a castle tower on a large rock, dating from at least 1087, which formed part of the defensive line of Sobrarbe against the Moors. From here the road has a much better surface as it climbs to the Collado de Eripol (860m, 2,821ft). Past Bárcabo, the valley of the Vero can be seen by turning right on to a side road towards the village of Lecina. When a bridge over the river is reached, the visitor is once again on the threshold of the world of canyons and precipices.

Here a word of explanation may be necessary: These canyons, precipices, gorges, caves, and river reaches between sheer walls, of the vast limestone massif of the Sierra de Guara, were virtually unknown until a pioneer French journalist, Lucien Briet, visited and studied them in 1904-8, and later those of the Monte Perdido massif. He published his findings in Spanish in 1913. The region, a landscape of stunted pines and thorn bushes, with odd isolated hamlets and villages of which many are now abandoned, has been inhabited since well before Roman times. The main reasons for the *sierra* being literally off the beaten track, were a complete lack of roads, and only the frugal comfort of the village *fonda* or inn. With improved communications plus motor transport, these incredible natural features of limestone erosion, both above and below ground, have become better known, especially to those interested in pot-holing and caving, but there is nothing written in English about this area. The region is much larger than the Monte Perdido Massif, so there is a lot to explore further west and north, but only two will be described here: the Vero canyon, which is the best known and the most beautiful, and one further west, the Río Alcanadre.

The descent of the Vero can begin from the bridge, but for the first time visitor it is best to continue southwards on HU342. This route now climbs towards the Collado de San Capraiso (810m, 2,657ft). Beyond the col is a bridge with a good view of a gorge meander in a tributary of the Vero. The route continues through the village of Colungo (now HU340) to another bridge across the Vero at the camp site: 'Camping Rio Vero'. Here a walk upstream can begin from the bridge, either wading through the shallow water or walking the bank by bamboo grass. Then, at a Roman bridge, the canyon really begins. At length a disused HEP dam is reached, and afterwards, up through a canebrake, the ancient village of Alquézar and its castle can be seen towering above, and the full beauty of the canyon is realised. Soon a pool, too deep to wade, is reached, and any further progress has to be by swimming or rubber canoe. If this possible, the passage of the canyon is enlivened by the birdsong of thrushes and redstarts, and high overhead perhaps an imperial eagle. Eventually a concrete walkway is reached, though part of it is not in good condition, and progress beyond it needs equipment, like ropes.

Back at the disused dam, there is a steep path leading upwards to the village of **Alquézar**, on its incredible site. The original *Castrum Vigetum*, of the Visigoths became a Moorish *alcázar*, and after its capture in 1070, was transformed into a collegiate church of which the cloister is particularly interesting. The village under the castle ramparts is attractive, with narrow alleys and vaulted passages converging on to the Plaza Mayor surrounded by arcades. From Alquézar it is possible to descend to the river Vero again by a route via the Barranco de Fuente (ravine), and a winding path which goes down to the bridge of Villacantal, traditionally Roman, opposite the steep limestone walls of the canyon. From here is a glimpse of the far longer upper part of the Vero with its resurgences, grottos, rocky debris and subterranean passages. Across the bridge, a path leads through a side ravine, which after a while opens out, and on the left at the base of a puddingstone (conglomerate) cliff, is a grille protecting the prehistoric grotto of Villacantal, discovered in 1978 and subsequently investigated by the University of Zaragoza. Some 200m (220yd) further on the left, at the end of the cliff, is another grille through which animal paintings can be seen, believed to be perhaps 4,000 years old. This walk from Alquézar takes about $1^1/_2$) hours. On returning to the HU340, continue the route to Bierge via Adahuesca, and from there northwards to a small HEP station by a bridge over the river at the lower end of the Alcanadre canyon. The canyon is very long, and the two-day descent of it involves the use of rubber canoes or swimming, and ropes. However, the first part from here can be walked along a corniche route on the left bank, amid rushes and fishermen, for this is a trout stream, which also contains the common barbel. The river in this first stretch is deep, but later becomes shallow and easily paddled through to cross to the right bank, but always keep close to the stream, because the corniches are of conglomerate, and rather friable. The meanders can be cut by passing through the bushy banks. This first section to Puntillos takes about 2 hours, and further upstream the birdlife is abundant and colourful with species like bee-eaters (green, blue and yellow), hoopoes (black and white, pinkish brown with crest), swallows and cuckoos. From Puntillos it is possible to return by climbing out of the gorge, walking to the HU332 road, and then to the bridge and HEP station. This is only a foretaste of the immense possibilities of exploration in this region, but the descent of these canyons does need time and thought. The deep gorges provide a zone of refuge for many species including deer, badgers and boars, and in the *sierra* (because of the decline in shepherds) the bands of wild goats are descended from the domestic flocks. In late summer, around the pools in the gorges, are snakes such as montpellier (venomous only to its prey), and the viper (which swims, and has been largely exterminated by walkers), and also the common toad which grows much larger here.

The return to Ainsa is made by a longer and more scenic route. From Bierge, go southwards to the main N240 Huesca-Barbastro road, and turn left, on through the hedged, fertile wheatlands of the Somontano to **Barbastro**, which can be bypassed, but the early sixteenth-century cathedral, seat of the old bishopric, is worth seeing.

Then the route follows the course of the Cinca northwards to the impressive dam of El Grado and the beginning of the large HEP lake (*embalse*) of the same name. Then the road, now C138, swings away from the lake and climbs towards Naval and Alto de Pino (857m, 2,811ft), with many bends and curves for some 30km (18$^1/_2$ miles), through a picturesque countryside of terraces, small gorges and villages with tall square towers perched on the crests. At length the beginning of another lake is seen, Embalse de Mediano, with the village of **Samitier** off to the right. From the village church a path winds up to a limestone crest at 856m (2,808ft) where there are the remains of an ancient castle and church built about 1030. This, once more, is the little known ancient frontier of Sobrarbe. The road continues its winding way northwards, with occasional glimpses of the lake, and finally to Ainsa. This run is at its best on a summer evening, when the well surfaced road often has little traffic.

### The National Park of Ordesa and Monte Perdido

From Ainsa the route goes westwards on the C138, arriving shortly at **Boltaña**, a town often overlooked, perhaps because of its commercial appearance along the main road. Off it, however, the old town is really a very interesting place with alleys, and renovated buildings in good condition, particularly the one made into a public library, and its old castle on a rock above the town. Continuing along the Ara valley the route comes to the gorge of Jánovas, where there is a most curious example of limestone erosion. Long parallel lines of what appear to be walls reach down to the river, which in reality are erosion remnants of rock. Then the valley widens out, and further on is the abandoned hamlet of La Veilla with a picturesque suspension footbridge across the Ara. The road turns north into the mountains, and the very pretty, but often crowded village of Broto appears in its valley. Onwards to the attractive village of **Torla**, usually full of tourists, but somehow retaining its charm, especially in the small restaurant, 'La Brecha'. Outside the old quarter, the Hotel Bujarelo is also a good place to eat, but this is the gateway of the most frequented valley in the Pyrenees, and probably the most beautiful, noted for its floral variety, and the richness of its fauna.

It is **not** advisable to visit this area in August, or even in the last half of July, for it becomes insufferably crowded, and movement by car is hazardous and frustrating. Also, before May and after September, access is often limited by snowfall. However, there is a great range of moderate walking, mountain walking, climbing, and exploring possibilities of all kinds, and the region is very interesting

*The church at Linas de Broto*

geologically.

Ordesa is a huge glaciated canyon, which lies parallel to the main axial zone of the Pyrenees and the limestone massif of Tres Sorores (Three Sisters), containing the third highest Pyrenean peak, Monte Perdido, which reaches to 3,351m (10,991ft). The valley is carved out of enormous folded limestone strata, with 1,000m (3,280ft) slopes, on which are grey, red and ochre coloured bands of rock. This huge canyon, with two fine hanging valleys plus waterfalls on the north side, ends in a wide cirque (Soaso). Being open to the west, Ordesa is cooler and more humid, which gives magnificent beech forests, along with silver fir, Scots pines and larches, with flowers like irises, azaleas, yellow arnica, violets and mountain thrift. The carline thistle grows on heights up to 2,800m (9,184ft) whilst the edelweiss, which is really a limestone flower, is found on the highest peaks in the area. A pleasant mountain trout stream, the Río Arazas, flows along the valley floor.

There are many walks, but one which takes in a good spread of different features and views, (but is long, taking 7-8hrs), starts from the parking place at the end of the road into the park from Torla, then goes along the valley to **Soaso**. Come first to a waterfall (El Abanico — the fan), then, on going nearer the river, notice potholes, and the river flowing between undercut limestone walls. Carry on through

*Ordesa*

beech forests, with, on the right, a torrent (Tobacor) plunging down the valley sides, a fall of 80m (262ft). Then, further upstream comes a long stepped fall, 'Gradas de Soaso', and after this the valley opens out onto a flat grassy area, which ends with the river Arazas tumbling down the slopes of the Monte Perdido massif in a fine horsestail fall. Here, there is a path up the cirque face that leads to the refuge at **Goriz** (2,160m, 7,085ft), from which it is possible to climb Monte Perdido, the highest limestone peak in Europe. The climb from the refuge is tough, but can be achieved in half a day — the most difficult factor is the weather, which can change rapidly and make a normal steep path highly dangerous. Also leading from this refuge is a whole series of paths spreading out above the steep slopes of the canyon, giving scope for exploration, and descending down into the valley floor by means of *'clavijas'* (pitons) — not for those suffering from vertigo!

Back at Soaso, the route returns above the valley by the Faja de Pelay. This path gradually rises to almost 2,000m (6,560ft), giving magnificent views. The word *faja* here means a mountain path or traverse formed by the freeze-thaw process of eroding weaker bands of rock through fissures and splitting them into fragments. From this walk the whole prospect of the valley unfolds, first the Cirque de Cotatuero coming into view, then the Cirque de Carriata with the incredible rocky face of Tozal del Mallo (2,280m, 7,478ft). Finally the descent into the valley floor is made by the steep Senda de Cazadores (Hunter's Path), returning from there to the starting point.

Alternatively, the Faja de Pelay can be continued beyond the Senda de los Cazadores upwards to the Sierra de las Gutas, and then via the Puerto Diazas (2,247m, 7,370ft), and the Hermitage de Santa Ana, giving a superb panorama over the Broto valley, before returning to the valley floor at the Puente de Navarros or alternatively Torla itself.

Just outside the park's limits, at Puente de Navarros, is a forested walk up the Ara valley to Bujarelo (1,326m, 4,349ft). From there a steep path climbs to a refuge, and then via the Col de Boucharo (2,270m, 7,446ft) to the Cirque de Gavarnie in France. The fauna of Ordesa seems now to be at higher levels, no doubt due to the increase in the number of visitors. But protected species like the Sarrio (Pyrenean chamois), Bucardo mountain goat (there are only thirty left), marmots (from France), and green lizards can be seen, along with water creatures such as the otter, Pyrenean desman , a kind of water rat or shrew, and the Pyrenean salamander. As for birds of prey, the golden eagle, griffon vulture and the nearly extinct lammergeier often fly over the park, but one of the joys of walking in the region is the butterflies. The beautiful isabella, the orange fritillary, red admiral, clouded yellow, marbled white and peacock are seen all around, but the small 'Ordesa Blue' once very common, seems now to be rare.

Other walks in the valley are to the cirques of Cotatuero and Carriata, famous for their waterfalls and one to the 'Copos de Lana' (flecks of wool) falls (250m, 820ft) at Cotatuero. Each takes about 4 hours.

## Western High Aragón

### The Gállego valley, Aragón valley and Jaca

From Torla the route goes westwards by turning right onto the C140, a corniche road, with the scarps of the Sierra de Tendeñera, over 2,800m (9,184ft) high on the right. Soon a very fine large church appears on the left at **Linás de Broto**, with an interesting old reconstructed porch and, unusual for Spain, an adjacent graveyard, giving the appearance of an English country church. Then over the Puerto de Cotofablo (1,423m, 4,667ft) with its long narrow tunnel and winding road, and finally a sharp descent to the pleasant town of Biescas set in the wide Tena valley (Río Gállego).

**Biescas** lies on the busy route from France via the Col du Pourtalet to Huesca and Zaragoza, but from here an excursion can be made to **Balneario de Panticosa** via the upper Tena valley (C136), past the HEP lake of Bubal to a road on the right (HU610), through the steep and dark gorge of the Escalar. During the passage through the gorge the rocks change from limestone to the schists and granites of the axial zone, which are emphasized when the gorge opens out to a towering austere cirque. The thermal station at 1,639m (5,376ft) has a wide reputation for its sulphurous and radioactive waters. It is encircled by trees, contrasting with the bare steep slopes of the Picos del Inferno (3,076m, 10,089ft). The village is attractive, with a curious church having thick supporting columns, full of gold statues, old books and paintings plus an interesting gallery. Panticosa is also a ski centre, claiming the best natural circuits in Spain.

After the turn for Panticosa the frontier road goes by a corniche amid fir trees, and a tunnel, to **Sallent de Gállego** set in green slopes, with streams, and dominated by the very fine isolated granite peak of the Peña de Foratata (2,343m, 7,685ft). Sallent is a noted trout fishing and climbing centre. Further on lies El Formigal at 1,500m (4,920ft), a ski station with a restaurant on the pistes at 2,040m (6,691ft).

Back at Biescas the route descends the wide valley of the Gállego, and before reaching the industrial town of Sabiñanigo, turns westwards (C134) to climb gently to the town of **Jaca**, first capital of the old kingdom of Aragón. Sited on a river terrace of the Río Aragón, and dominated by the limestone scarp of the Peña Oroel (1,769m, 5,802ft), it has been a fortress town since 195BC, defending the road to Gaul, and later against the Moors in the eighth century, when the women and girls of Jaca helped defend the city. It was a crossroads town between the Pilgrim's road to Santiago de Compostela, and the old route from Béarn to Zaragoza used by French crusaders to the Ebro, and Arab merchants to France. Although expanded, this small cathedral and garrison town keeps its character, and is a good centre.

A wander around the town can take in the churches of Carmen

*Jaca cathedral*

(Plateresque), and Santiago (eleventh century), along with the Casa Consistorial (1545), and Jaca's thirty-eight restaurants, enough to suit all tastes. It is also one of the few places in the region with a railway station. The cathedral, built in the eleventh century and now restored, was the first of the Romanesque style in Spain. If the exterior appears rather severe and overshadowed by other buildings, the interior is a revelation, with its graceful decorated columns, friezes, and side chapels. There are a number of buildings well worth seeing, like the Benedictine monastery at the end of the Calle Mayor, containing a reformed church, and a carved stone sarcophagus of the daughter of Ramiro I (eleventh century) with human and animal figures. The fortress (*ciudadela*), headquarters of the Military Command, can be visited, but the hours are brief. It dates from 1592, but was not completed until the early seventeenth century. It takes the form of a pentagon, with a moat and an impressive arched entrance gate. Inside are a patio, garden, archways, and a chapel. Recently restored, it gained a diploma of merit from the prestigious Europa Nostra association.

Northwards from Jaca, along the frontier road (N330), parallel with the railway is **Villanúa** with limestone caves, galleries, and an underground river. They can be visited, but the going is tough, with descents of 18m (59ft) by rope, then up an underground cliff, and several hours are spent beneath the surface, but it is an interesting and unusual excursion. Further on is the frontier station of Canfranc and the railway tunnel to France, and beyond are the ski centres of Candanchú and Astún, near the crest line.

Southwards from Jaca are two places which could well represent Christian and military Aragón. The route (N330) is taken to Bernués past the Peña Oroel to a right-hand turn (HU230), which leads to the new monastery of San Juan (seventeenth century, ruined by Suchet [Napoleon's troops] in 1809, but now restored), and then climbs up to Balcón de Pirineo, from which there is superb view of the mountains. From the new monastery, descend to the old monastery of San Juan de la Peña. At 1,220m (4,002ft) this is considered to be the most significant monument in Aragón. Founded in the ninth century, it became a symbol of Christian resistance to the Moors by the kings and nobles of Aragón and Navarra, and the robust architecture of the council room, the primitive lower church with its unique twelfth-century sculptured and decorated cloisters between cliff and precipice, covered by natural vaulting, dramatically illustrates this.

From the monastery, the route returns to the N330, and continues on to join the Río Gállego, and later the N240 road, where the river now flows past some massive high red ochre cliffs of conglomerate, known as Los Mallos, to the village of Ayerbe. Here the route turns left on to HU311 leading to the village of Loarre, and then after 4km ($2^1/_2$ miles) further on, by a narrow winding road, is the most important Romanesque fortress in Spain. Built against the Moors on a beautiful and rocky site by Sancho Ramirez, king of Aragón and Navarra, it has a thick wall with round towers and two doorways, and then a massive square keep superimposed on the crag itself, with a vaulted stairway. In 1096 it became a monastery, with a church (having arches at two different heights) placed on a barrel vaulted crypt. This remarkable building was completed in the twelfth century. The panorama which unfolds whilst walking around the walls covers an immense area, including the Ebro basin.

### The Hecho and Ansó Valleys

The route now returns to the N240, which is taken northwards to Puente la Reina in the Aragón valley, and then by the HU210 up the Hecho valley. This, and its neighbouring valley of Ansó, were relatively closed communities for centuries following the small kingdom of Aragón's resistance against the Moors. Until recently their religious festivals were very closely connected with their own distinct costumes. Ironically, the setting up of the Spanish *autonomas*, which has made some regions turn inwards, has increased the rate of development and tourism here, and there is a very grave danger of the area and its customs being spoilt by a concentration of visitors, which the local road network is also inadequate to cater for. The route next mounts the Hecho valley as far as Santa Isabel, where it turns right up the Osia valley to the village of **Jasa**. Here the *casa abadía* (abbey) and the church are interesting buildings, and in the local *ayuntamiento* (town hall) a married woman's dress, typical of the region can be seen — they vary greatly according to the ceremony, and whether she is married or single. Then on to **Aragües del Puerto**, where there is a fine church in baroque style. Here, on the flanks of the Sierra de Maito, it is well forested, especially with beech, common in these western high valleys, where the axial range is lower and open to Atlantic influences. The paved forest road continues up the valley to pinewoods and meadows by the river. It is possible to explore further up the valley beyond the roadhead, but the path is non-existent. If the river bed is low or dry this can be followed up to the high, wild, rocky limestone slopes of the Sierra de Bernero. However, remember that a sudden summer storm can turn the river bed into a raging torrent. From Aragües there is track northwards via the Lizara valley, and past the peak of Visaurin (2,670m, 8,758ft), going further on to the lake of Estanes near the French frontier, but it is difficult.

Returning to the main valley road the small town of **Hecho** is reached, a place that has been preserved, and reconstructed, and about twenty new dwellings built in the traditional style. The town has narrow streets, and austere, dark grey little squares, rather higgledy-piggledy, with the church in the centre. The shops are in the same style. Two traditional bakers stand opposite each other, selling large round loaves, and the others are small corner shops, with some butchers and bars. This is a place to stroll around and savour.

Onwards from here is **Siresa**, set in a narrow valley with stone houses. The lintels of the windows are white and they have tiled roofs, and traditional chimneys, which contrast with the imposing ancient Augustinian monastery of San Pedro, built in the ninth century, and reformed in the eleventh. The tall church was also built at this time, and has arcaded walls with solid buttresses, and an interesting interior with fifteenth-century altar pieces. The key can be borrowed from the last house before the church.

The valley now narrows considerably, and enters the well named Boca de Infierno (Devil's Mouth) which is a dozen kilometres (about $7^1/_2$ miles) of gorge with many rough tunnels and few passing places. Then comes the fine beech forest of Oza, and the upper valley of the Río Aragón Subordán, opening out on to grassy river terraces covered with purple autumn crocus in late summer. The paved road ends here, and on going further upstream the hills close in again. Then, at the valley head, it widens once more, with the limestone peaks of the frontier *sierras* rising above the green landscape.

Coming back downstream to Hecho, the route now crosses the interfluve between the two valleys by taking the forest road to Ansó. Just after turning on to it, there is a fine view westwards, and then the road winds through a wild, but pleasant landscape to the Ansó. valley. The small town of **Ansó** is reached by turning right at the valley of the Río Veral. It is even more traditional than Hecho, the white-walled houses having distinctive chimneys covered by small shelters to avoid heavy snowfalls. It has a fine ornate fifteenth-century church, an eighteenth-century abbey house and a thirteenth-century fortified tower — all worth seeing. There is an interesting ethnological museum with fourteen traditional costumes (unique to Spain), and tools and equipment of an eighteenth-century shoe-maker and a shepherd. On a wall is list of names of those who fell in the Civil War, for here is a traditional corner of Spain, in keeping with the famous Requetés of neighbouring Carlist Navarra. The list is headed by José Primo de Rivéra, son of General Primo de Rivera (Prime Minister during the Monarchy) who was shot by the Republicans while in prison, and became a Nationalist martyr. A walk around the narrow streets confirms this. Its atmosphere is very tranquil, and there are small artisan workshops, with carpenters, and traditional bakers with the kindling stacked beside their ovens,

*Gorge of the Río Vero, the Aragonese Pyrenees*

*Ansó valley, the Aragonese Pyrenees*

*Ansó*

and a few old 'corner shops'.

Going northwards from Ansó up the valley, the road along the river is particularly beautiful, the river with its deep rocky pools, along with beech trees and meadows making the route very verdant. The summers are often very hot here, and these trees give welcome shade. Sometimes large flocks of sheep can be seen close together under them. The next place is **Zuriza**, which has a very good camp site and restaurant. After this the Río Veral divides into rocky ravine-like streams (Barrancos de Petrafich and Petrahama) with pot holes, both of which can be penetrated and explored.

The heads of all these valleys: Veral, Aragón, Subordán and Osia, can also be explored on horseback from Aragües del Puerto, where arrangements can be made with the municipality (Mancomunidad de Los Valles) for itineraries from 3 to 5 days between June and October. The traveller who chooses this form of transport can leave Aragües by the Barranco Santa Eulalia to the hamlet of Urdués, then to Hecho, and by a route bordering the Sierra del Vedao to Ansó. From here to Zuriza, where the camp site can be used overnight, and the horses stabled by arrangement with the forestry authorities (Mancomunidad Forestal Ansó-Fago). The next stage is more difficult because of the high altitude. Using the Barranco de Petraficha to reach a refuge at Tatxeras, follow cattle paths with caution, and then go over the Collado de Petraficha (1,958m, 6,422ft) to reach the military refuge at La Mina at the bottom of the Guarrinza valley (head of the Hecho valley). An alternative itinerary leaves Zuriza by the the other Barranco de Petrahama, turns left up the Barranco de las Eras, goes over the Paso de Ansotiello (2,015m, 6,609ft), and then on also to La Mina.

The return down the Hecho valley (Río Aragón Subordán) is via the forest of Oza, where there is a camp site, and horses can be left by arrangement at the stables of the Ayuntamiento de Hecho in the immediate vicinity. The return to Hecho is made via the Boca de Infierno, where, on account of the traffic, great care is needed, especially in the tunnels. However, a path can be taken on the left by a forest house, following the river and road through meadows via Siresa, and then to Hecho (and if necessary to Aragües).

The advantages of the horse over the motor car and walker in this rugged, but interesting and beautiful landscape, are considerable, and of course this was the mode of travel in this region of the Pyrenees for many centuries. In medieval times, there would have been many pilgrims travelling slowly over these mountains on their way to Santiago de Compostela.

The costumes worn in these valleys are very distinctive. They are no longer worn every day, or seen in the streets as they were until a few years ago, but are mostly worn now by people in groups taking part in folklore festivals, fiestas and religious celebrations. They vary considerably, but the principal colours seem to be green, white and red, the women having very long full green dresses with white puffed sleeves, a high collar and a large red gorget hung with gold and silver religious ornaments. They wear various red head-dresses, depending upon whether they are married or single. The men's costume is green shorts and waistcoat with white knee stockings and shirt, with a red sash and round black hat with a brim, not unlike that of the Austrian Tyrol.

The route southwards from Ansó down the Río Veral valley is wooded and picturesque, and near the end is the Hoz de Biniés, a gorge 3km (2 miles) long which leads to the cultivated plains. Here join the main N240 road, leading westwards to Pamplona, and southwards to Huesca.

# Further Information
## — The Aragonese Pyrenees —

## Activities

*The Eastern Margins of High Aragón*
**Graus**
Fiestas: 12-15 September, Santo Christo and San Vincente Ferrer, dancers *Caballet Furtaperas*, and songs *albadas* (morning seranades). Also *novillados* — bullfights with young bullfighters.

*Central High Aragón*
Fiestas: 4-8 September, N.S. del Puyeo, Jota (Aragonese dance), bullfights, pigeon shooting contests, 'flower battle', popular dances and sports.

*Western High Aragón*
**Jaca**
Fiestas: 1 May, historic victory over the Moors, cortège, 'paloteo' dance and *alarde*.
25 June, Santa Orosia, procession, dances and sports competitions.
25 July-15 August, summer festivities.

## Places of Interest

*Central High Aragón*
**Alquézar**
Collegiate church
Open: 10am-1pm; 5-7pm.

**Tella**
Rural Museum (with Information Office)
Open: May-September.

*Western High Aragón*
**Jaca**
La Ciudadela (fortress)

Open: 11am-12noon; 5-6pm.

Diocésan museum (cathedral cloisters)
Open: 11.30am-2pm; 4-6pm.

Monastery of San Juan de la Peña (South of Jaca)
Guided visits (3-4 hours) sunrise-sunset (torch advisable).

## Sports

*The Eastern Margins of High Aragón*
**Piragüismo (canoeing)**
On the hydro-electric power lakes of Escales, Sapeiro, Linsoles and El Grado; Río Noguera Ribagorzana, Río Esera, Río Isábena and Río Cinca.
Federal Licence needed from:
Club Nautico Gradense
Barranco 25
Graus

**Skiing**
Cerler (Benasque)
☎ (974) 55 10 12

**Climbing**
Refuge hut
La Renclusa
Open: July-September, guarded; at other times accessible in part.

*Central High Aragón*
**Piragüismo (canoeing)**
On the hydro-electric power lake Mediano and Río Cinca.
Licence from:
Club Atlético Sobrarbe
Ordesa 14
Ainsa

**Climbing**
Refuge hut
Goriz
Open all year.

*Western High Aragón*
**Piragüismo (canoeing)**
In hydro-electric power lakes
Bubal and Yesa; La Peña Río
Gállego and Río Aragón.
Licence from:
Club Deportes Valle de Tena
Urbanización Formigal
Sallent de Gállego

**Skiing**
Candanchú
☎ (974) 37 31 92

Astún
☎ (974) 38 30 34
Telex 58638 ASPNE.

Formigal (Sallent de Gállego)
☎ (974) 48 81 25
For snow information
☎ (974) 22 56 56 (Huesca)

**Fishing**
Coto Fluvial de Jaca: $7^1/_2$km
stretch Río Aragón.
Period: 3rd Sunday in March-end
of August.
Permits: *ayuntamiento*, Jaca.

**Tourist Information Offices**
The opening hours of Spanish
Tourist Offices and *Ayuntamientos*
(municipal authorities and town
halls) are normally 10am-1.30pm
and 4-8pm, but they vary from
place to place and are sometimes
irregular.

*The Eastern Margins of High Aragón*
**Benasque**
Avenida de los Tilos
☎ (974) 55 12 89

Centro de Iniciativia Turistica
Plaza Mayor 5
(Swimming pool and discothèque)

*Central High Aragón*
**Ainsa**
Tourist Office
Avenida Pirenaica (crossroads)
☎ (974) 50 07 67

Ayuntamiento
☎ (974) 50 00 02

**Barbastro**
Tourist Office
Plaza de Aragón
☎ (974) 31 01 50

Centro de Iniciativa Turistica
Argensola 26
Casa de Culutra

**Bielsa**
Ayuntamiento
☎ (974) 50 10 00/19

**Boltaña**
Ayuntamiento
☎ (974) 50 20 02

**Escalona**
(11km Ainsa, on the road to France)

**Huesca**
Plaza de Cervantes 522071
☎ (974) 24 33 61
Information about the National
Park of Ordesa and Monte Perdido

**Tella**
Information Office
Open: May-September.

**Torla**
Information Office
Calle Francia
☎ (974) 48 62 12

*Western High Aragón*
**Ansó**
Ayuntamiento
☎ (974) 37 00 03/21

**Aragües del Puerto**
Ayuntamiento
☎ (974) 37 50 26
Information on horseriding.

**Canfranc**
Tourist Office
Avenida Fernando el Católico 3
☎ (974) 37 31 41

**Fago**
Ayuntamiento
☎ (974) 37 00 96

**Hecho**
Ayuntamiento
☎ (974) 37 50 02

**Jaca**
Tourist Office
Avenida Regimiento Galicia 2,
Room 1
☎ (974) 36 00 98

**Jasa**
Ayuntamiento
☎ (974) 37 51 04

**Panticosa (Balneario)**
☎ (974) 38 71 61/2
Information for thermal station
and skiing.

# 2 • The Picos de Europa

The triple massif of the Picos de Europa forms the highest group of peaks in the Cantabrian mountains in northern Spain. They project majestically towards the sea from the main range, and run parallel only 30km ($18^1/_2$ miles) from the coast between Santander and Oviedo. Three provinces meet at the summit of the pyramidal peak of Tesorero (2,571m, 8,433ft) in the central massif: Oviedo to the north, León to the west, and Santander to the east, or, as they are now, the autonomous regions of the Principado de Asturias, Léon y Castilla and Cantabria, but to avoid confusion the provincial names will be used here.

This complex labyrinth of magnificent summits is contained in a rough triangle with its base towards the north. The western point, is Cangas de Onis (Oviedo), the eastern point, 54km ($33^1/_2$ miles) distant, is Panes (Santander), and the apex southwards near the small town of Riaño (Léon). This region was the cradle of the Spanish kingdom, for the decisive battle against the Moors took place at Covadonga in the western massif in 722, thus initiating the seven centuries long struggle of the *Reconquista* or Reconquest. This western area is now a national park, created in 1918. The name Picos de Europa is thought to have come from sailors and fishermen, who on seeing the jagged peaks regarded them as their first and last sight of Spain and Europe on their long voyages out into the Atlantic Ocean.

The Picos are perhaps the finest and most compact set of crests and pinnacles formed of hard Carboniferous limestone in all western Europe. It is a region of karst topography: underground rivers, resurgences, caves, gorges, steep valleys, and scanty pastures with thin soil. The mountain mass is carved into stupendous chasms, like those of the Cares valley, whose sheer walls often rise to 1,000m (3,280ft). Above these great gorges are meagre pastures, called *vegas*, which are often small plateaux or small alps, but not as fertile, where sheep, goats and even cows graze. They are intermingled with scree filled cirques, rock terraces, and finally sharp peaks with steep rock

PICOS DE EUROPA

Dirt Track – – – – – –
Path ..................

faces up to 500m (1,640ft), like the redoubtable smooth peak of the Naranjo de Bulnes (2,519m, 8,262ft), and although there are many in the region higher, it was not climbed until 1904 by Don Pedro Pidal, Marques de Villavicosia de Asturias, the founder of Covadonga National Park.

The upper mountain area is an impressive barren limestone landscape of a confused maze of peaks, huge round depressions called *hoyos* or sink holes filled with limestone debris, crevices, ridges and disappearing streams which reappear lower down as rushing torrents in green valleys, with trees and terraced fields. The region divides into three massifs: West (Cornión), Central (Urrieles) and East (Andara). The western is greenest, with lush grasslands containing the Peña Santa de Castilla (2,596m, 8,515ft), considered the finest summit in the Picos. The central area has the highest peaks (Cerredo 2,648m, 8,685ft), and is extremely complex. Appropriately known as the Central Knot, it is also much visited. The eastern massif has been much mined for manganese and zinc, and is not so often visited, but there are good peaks there too, like the long ridge of Morra de Lechugales (2,441m, 8,006ft). The people of the region are mainly pastoral, raising cattle and sheep, but in the summer are increasingly turning to tourism. In the Cabrales valley a dry traditional cheese (*Cabrales*) is made from a mixture of milk from ewes, cows and goats, which is fermented and cured in the natural limestone caves. The rich mineral deposits of Andara are worked by mining companies, reached over tracks by jeeps and Land Rovers, which can be hired.

The Picos were remote and unvisited, except by game hunters and zinc prospectors, and the upper mountain wilderness unknown, until a Spanish mining engineer, D. Casinado de Prado discovered it in 1845, followed later by French geologists and a British pioneer, John Ormsby. Many maps of the area are inaccurate, especially some of the heights, parts are still unmapped, and the inner labyrinth of peaks are nearly as difficult of access as they were in the 1930s. In contrast are the green, fertile valleys which surround the triple massif, giving points of entry into this mountainous centre. The tarmac roads are good, but narrow and crowded with visitors in the summer. The nearest large city is Santander, also a port, lying 90km (55 miles) eastwards on the coastal road N634. The towns and villages that surround the Picos can be grouped as follows:

On the north side along the base of the 'triangle', C6312 road (Oviedo), Cangas de Onis, is the largest town, former capital of the Asturian kings, and has an elegant Romanesqe bridge. Eastwards lies the Onis valley with the village and shrine of Covadonga, and the national park, then comes Arenas de Cabrales, a village resort at the entrance to the Cabrales valley and the gorge of the Cares. Further east is the large village of Panes, at the junction of C6231 with N621.

On the eastern side, the N621/S240/S242 (Santander and León), leads through the gorge of the Río Deva to Potes, a large pleasant village at the entrance to the Liébana valley, which is the most used and popular route of entry, leading to the Aliva valley and the cableway at Fuente Dé. After this comes Portilla de la Reina, a hamlet at the entrance to the Puerto de Pandetrave (1,561m, 5,120ft), a viewpoint and southern approach to the Valdeón valley. Southwards is the ruin of Riaño, a town that no longer exists, having been destroyed for a 20 years delayed irrigation scheme to put an end to flooding of the Río Eslar.

On the western side, along C637 (León and Oviedo) and northwards to the Puerto de Pontón, is the south-western approach to the Valdeón valley, along a fairly new road to what was, until recently, the most picturesque and unspoilt village of Posada de Valdeón. Then come Oseja and Soto de Sajambre, villages at the entrance of the gorge of the Río Sella. The climate of the Picos, which is both moun-

*The foothills of the Picos de Europa*

tainous and close to the sea, is humid temperate, which means that at times it is cloudy and rainy, but southwards it is appreciably drier. Spring and summer tend to have rain, but otherwise in July and August dense early morning mist occurs, then disperses, followed by a cloud blanket, with later clear evenings. It can be very windy between May and September. A late summer-early autumn feature is mist filling the surrounding valleys, but above 1,500m (4,920ft), there are clear skies and sunshine all day long. With annual precipitation of 1,500mm (60in), much falls as snow in winter and early spring. However, it is a very variable climate, with many places like Potes in a rain shadow, and so much drier, and the whole region can be very hot during high summer.

The Alpine flora of the upper mountain zone is generally sparse because of so little soil, but gentians flourish in the Andara massif, and the lower valleys are verdant with a great variety of trees such as walnut, chestnut, ash, lime, birch, hazel, alder and many wild fruit trees. As for wildlife, hunting has removed bears and wolves long ago, but *rebecos* (chamois) are widespread, particularly in the national park, due to a ban on hunting, and wild horses roam on the meadows in the Enol and Ercina lakes area. Otherwise the harsh landscape provides an unfavourable environment for the smaller mammals. However, high among the peaks and crags are large golden eagles and ptarmigan, but the imperial eagle is rarer; the larger rivers are full of trout, and salmon in those that flow to the sea.

The attractions of the Picos are many, but it must be understood that the valley roads end at the foot of enormous rock walls, and if visitors wish to see the magnificent views of the inner peaks, they must climb up. Those who go to the region perhaps fall into one of three categories:

**1** Climbers of all types from the experienced alpinist to the skilful novice, who may find that even in May and June, long stretches of snow and icy slopes might need axes and crampons, and that above 1,600m (5,248ft) the chances of finding running water are extremely rare.

**2** The mountain or fell walker, who needs to be cautious about paths and waymarking, be well-shod, carry a map, and perhaps a compass.

**3** The visitor who admires panoramas and good viewpoints, likes some walking, but if using a car to see the views, must also observe caution. For it must be realised that the entrance valleys are choked with car and coach-borne visitors in August, the roads are inadequate for the density of traffic, parking is always very difficult and sometimes impossible, and valley footpaths are uncomfortably crowded. The main reason for this, apart from the Spanish holiday season and the huge increase in mobility, is that the stifling summer heat in the main cities, particularly Madrid, draws people to the mountains. Many of them unfortunately have little interest in regions like the Picos, and are driving rather aimlessly around the narrow roads, so it is strongly advised *not* to visit this incomparable area in August. The Picos is one of those regions, which although well-known and popular with the Spanish is largely off the beaten track for visitors from other nations.

There is, however, plenty of scope for exploring the region at other times of the year, in the less visited Andara massif, from the top of the Fuente Dé cableway in the Liébana valley, and along the inner valleys like Valdeón, Dobra and Aliva.

## Travelling to the Area

### By Road

From France: Biarritz airport, *autoroute* A8 to Hendaye, then *autopista* A1 to Bilbao, thence (follow signs for Santander) N634 to Unquera, thence N621 to Panes and Potes.

From Madrid (Barajas) airport, *autopista* A2 to city, then A6 to Villacastin; NVI to junction of Valladolid road (N403) then Valladolid. Then N601 León road to LE211 junction, then to Cistierna and N621

N621 to Riaño (420km, 260 miles). Then either to Potes or C637 to Cangas de Onis.

From Bilbao (Sondica airport) to N634/621 to Panes (200km, 124 miles).

From Vitoria airport, *autopista* A68 to Bilbao, then to Panes (265km, 164 miles).

From England: ferry Plymouth to Santander (Brittany Ferries), N611 to Torrelevega, N634 to Unquera, N621 to Panes and Potes.

From North America: the best way is to fly direct to Madrid, then either by hire car or a domestic flight to Bilbao or Vitoria.

### By Rail
F.C. Cantabrico: Santander-Oviedo. With stations at Unquera, 12km ($7^1/_2$ miles) from Panes, 28km (17 miles) from Potes; Arriondas, 7km (4 miles) from Cangas de Onis (narrow gauge and slow, but scenically very interesting).

## The Western Massif (Cornión)

### The Covadonga National Park
This route starts from **Cangas de Onis**, a town amid an area of very ancient settlement, with a shapely Romanesque (twelfth-century) bridge over the Río Sella, in the form of a steep central arch flanked by two smaller ones. Quite close, in the Vega de Contraquil, is the chapel of Santa Cruz, built over a Bronze Age dolmen — probably the sixth or seventh such chapel, as the first was as early as AD437. In the town are the sixteenth-century palace of the Cortes (Asturian assembly), and the fifteenth-century parish church of Santa Maria, with its triumphal arch and three-storey bell tower, but it is mainly an eighteenth-century reconstruction.

Leave eastwards by the C6312, and a short distance along this road off on the left, over the Río Gueña, lies the the Buxtu cave of Solutrian and Magdalenian age (ranging from 20,000-8,000BC). Not many are allowed to visit it, however, in the course of a single day. A little further on the right is the O220 road to Covadonga, and after passing the village of La Biera, the park is entered, and the village and shrine of **Covadonga** reached, dominated by the impressive red basilica built between 1877 and 1901 by a German architect (Frasinelli) on the summit of the Montes de Cueto, in a style best described as a mixture of neo-Romantic and neo-Byzantine.

The shrine commemorating the famous victory over the Moors in 722 is even more impressively sited in a cave on the side of a huge

*The twelfth-century bridge over the Río Sella at Cangas de Onis*

cliff. Both of these places are much visited, and very crowded in the peak month of September. The route now continues along the O220 to the Mirador de la Reina, the first of many views over the park. The road then goes on to the Lago Enol at 1,070m (3,510ft), a lake without an outlet. From here, on the right, a road suitable for jeeps, but usable for cars, goes southwards for 3km (2 miles), then rises to a broad ridge (1,086m, 3,562ft), where cars can be parked on the right. From here the road deteriorates to a path, which reaches the Vega Redonda refuge at 1,560m (5,117ft). This is the easiest of the refuges to attain in the Picos($1^3/_4$-2hrs from car park). From here there are several excursions for mountain walkers: one giving a splendid viewpoint is to the Mirador de Ordiales at 1,691m (5,546ft). The path starts below the hut, and crosses the Río Jungumia valley on a waymarked route. Near the *mirador* is the tomb of Don Pedro Pidal, the national park's founder. The views are stupendous, including a sheer scarp edge that looks down on the Dobra valley 1,000m (3,280ft) below.

A tougher and much longer walk or scramble is along the main ridge of the Cornión massif to the Vega Huerta refuge (1,970m, 6,462ft), thought to be one of the finest high level walks in the Picos. It starts behind the refuge, and follows the main path up the valley to Llampa Cimera (1,830m, 6,002ft) then by the pillar of Porru Bulu (2,025m, 6,642ft). Next follow a good path left to the Collada de la

Mazada (2,030m, 6,658ft), then a winding traverse path below the peak of Torres de Cobolleda (2,438m, 7,997ft) zigzagging to the col of the Horcada del Alba (2,251m, 7,383ft), then a steep track to reach the col of Horcadas de Pozas (2,070m, 6,790ft). After this a descending traverse above the hollow of La Llerona, towards and below the needle of Aguja del Corpus Christi, to reach and cross the Vega Huerta saddle and thus the refuge. It would undeniably be a hard day's trek — 4 hours out and $3^1/_2$ back — but worth it.

Returning to Lago Enol, the route continues to the roadhead at a motel. From here a long path leads to the Ario refuge at 1,560m (5,117ft), going near Lago Ercina, pleasantly sited amid green pastures with wild horses grazing, and with a backdrop of the peaks of the two Peña Santas: de Enol (little: 2,478m, 8,128ft) and de Castilla (big: 2,596m, 8,515ft) — this last being the finest in the Picos. The path continues via the chalets of Ercina, Las Bobias, Redondiella, Las Reblagas, Las Lagos Hoyo and Las Compizas to the Jito Col, and then it is 10 minutes to the refuge (3 hours from the roadhead). There are some good mountain walks from here, in an area not well known, including one to the Vega Redonda, but it is trackless for half its way, although over easy ground, through a series of saddles in parallel ridges north-west to the Enol lakes (3 hours).

### The Defile of Los Beyos and Soto de Sajambre

This route also begins from Cangas de Onis southwards on the C637 following the Río Sella valley upstream. The first section, to the confluence, of the Río Ponga, is a typical deep verdant valley; at the confluence, the savage gorge of the Ponga is seen. Then the narrow 10km (6 miles) long defile of Los Beyos is entered, cut in exceptionally thick and massive Carboniferous limestone — a truly remarkable, beautiful and sunlit trench, with trees growing on the patches of calcareous debris.

On leaving the gorge, the road winds up to the Mirador de Oseja de Sajambre, with views of the mountain opposite: Najera (1,732m, 5,681ft). Then turn left, to enter a beautiful valley which has been called 'The Garden of Peña Santa', and then up to the pleasant village of **Soto de Sajambre**. From here is a grassy jeep track, possible for cars, to the refuge at Vegabaño 1,340m, 4,395ft (1 hour's walk from the village). From the refuge is a walk through very fine woods, crossing the Río Dobra to arrive at the Collado del Cueto, then continuing to the Collado de Frade, and crossing the Canal de Perra, (gully) and following the Camino de Burro trail to the Vega Huerta refuge at 2,080m (6,822ft), which is below the south face of La Peña

Santa de Castilla (3³/₄ hours from Vegabaño). This is a climbers' mountain, and if it is any consolation for those who have to remain at the foot, the view from the summit has been described as 'curiously unsatisfactory'.

## The Central Massif (Urrieles)

### Valdeón Valley

The south-western approach to this valley is from the Puerto de Pontón (1,290m, 4,231ft) on the C637, then the LE244 road to the Puerto de Panderruedas (1,438m, 4,717ft). Here awaits the Mirador de Piedrahita, where visitors can see from a 10 minute walk: Peña Santa; then the highest peak of all: Torre Cerredo (2,648m, 8,685ft); and the second highest, Llambrión (2,642m, 8,666ft). From this viewpoint, however, a long trail, the Camino de Burro goes up through wooded slopes eventually to reach the Collado de Frade (1,780m, 5,838ft), then the west side of the Torre de Cotalbin (2,193m, 7,193ft), a very good viewpoint, and then on to the Vega Huerta refuge (4¹/₂-5 hours from the car park at the Puerto).

The route from the Puerto descends on a fairly recent paved road down to **Posada de Valdeón**, originally one of the most unspoilt villages in all the Picos. The influx of visitors has altered this aspect somewhat, although out of the peak summer period it probably retains its charm. From the village there are several walks of all descriptions. The fine double tower of the Torre del Friero (2,445m, 8,020ft) can be climbed from the valley by going up the very steep Asotin ravine, and reaching the top from the east side. There is a shorter route from the west side, but the last few metres up a chimney are very difficult.

Another interesting, but a long and tiring climb, is up the Torre de Bermeja (2,393m, 7,849ft). This starts at Posada de Valdeón, crosses the Río Cares, becomes a steep trudge up to the first big rock barrier, and from there on zigzags up into a hidden valley, and eventually up a big gully called the Canal de Bufón to the summit (4³/₄ hours).

A less strenuous, but very verdant walk is from **Soto de Valdeón** following the Cares stream up to its headwaters on the Sierra Cebolleda. The southern approach to Valdeón is from Portilla la Reina (1,231m, 4,038ft) on the N621 road, up to the Puerto de Pandetrave (1,562m, 5,123ft). Here is a panoramic viewpoint over the three massifs, with in the foreground on the right, two peaks: Peña Remoña (2,247m, 7,370ft), and Torre de Salinas (2,446m, 8,023ft). From this col, there is a jeep track which crosses the Puerto de Valcavao

(1,782m, 5,845ft), then passes by a grassy summit, Alto de la Triguera (1,914m, 6,278ft) and then to Fuente Dé the road head in the Liébana valley. Continuing on the road to Valdeón, now metalled, but unclassified, the hamlet of **Santa Marina de Valdeón** is reached. From this hamlet there is a route to the Collado Jermosa refuge (2,046m, 6,711ft). The path goes up to the Collado de Valdeón (1,775m, 5,822ft), zigzags to the Canal de Pedavejo, then rises to the Collado de Remoña (2,030m, 6,658ft), and again zigzags down the north side, passing a forestal hut to reach the Vega de Liordes and Padiorna saddle. Then round Lago Cimero, climbing up to traverse under Llambrión (2,641m, 8,662ft), to the Collado de Jermosa refuge (4 hours from parking on the road above Santa Marina de Valdeón).

The road continues down into Posada de Valdeón, and is metalled further past La Llanos to the hamlet of **Cordiñanes**, and then to the Mirador del Tombo (866m, 2,840ft). This is marked by a statue of an isard (chamois), and has very good views at the beginning of the Cares gorge. The upper part here has a narrow single track down to the isolated hamlet of **Caín**, but this is frankly not advisable for cars. However, this first section down to Caín is spectacular in itself, and the rather primitive hamlet in a quite extraordinary setting, is the scene for *the* walk in Valdeón, the Garganta Divina, one of the most magnificent rock landscapes in all Europe. It is almost 12km (7$^1/_2$ miles) by a narrow path to Puente de Poncebos in the Cabrales valley. The first part of the downward descent (3 hours) of the gorge is surprisingly verdant with vegetation for such fantastically steep walls. The waters of the Cares are utilised for HEP by passing the main volume through a canal and seventy-one tunnels alongside and through the gorge, giving a total fall of 230m (754ft) for the power station at Poncebos. This was achieved quite early on when the path was made between 1916 and 1921.

## Cabrales Valley

This valley is approached from **Arenas de Cabrales** on the C6312, up the road O204 which follows the deep and narrow valley of the Cares, called the Garganta del Canal Negra (gorge of the black gully). The route arrives at the hamlet of **Camarmeña**, almost 'suspended' between precipices. There is a *mirador* here, up a steep winding path to a monument to the pioneer climbers, guides and victims of the Picos. The view is of the famous El Naranjo de Bulnes (2,519m, 8,262ft) — the orange refers to streaks on the north-east face), but as the Spaniards say: *'con permiso de las nieblas '* — 'with permission of the clouds', for it is often so.

From Camarmeña it is a short distance to **Puente de Poncebos,** where the Cares walk can be resumed. From here the track forks after the Jaya bridge (route to Bulnes), but the upper one is the route — a good walk along a limestone chippings path with exciting views of the gorge from high above it. Half way along there is a steep track down to a flimsy bridge, with an equally sharp ascent to a high meadow, cut and stacked for hay in 1987, with a farm building, which perhaps gives a glimpse of the former hard rural life here. One of the high gorge bridges nearer Caín, the Puente Bolín, is a shapely arched wooden structure with breathtaking views. The ascent from Poncebos takes about 5 hours.

From the Poncebos Hotel a route crosses the Jaya bridge over the Río Cares, and goes up by a path called the Salida de Bulnes following the valley of the Riega del Tejo to the quaint hamlet of **Bulnes,** built on two levels, the lower called El Castillo (castle) and the upper, El Pueblo (town). It is $1^1/_4$ hours from Poncebos, and has a small inn. The tiny picturesque church here, Our Lady of the Snows, is worth visiting, and one can record that Bulnes had 340 people in 1900, 95 in 1970, and now less than half that number. It is the natural entrance to the Central Massif, and the deep Bulnes valley runs up to the very foot of the Naranjo. However, this hard route is much used by climbing and intrepid walkers, and starts eastwards from Bulnes, and climbs up the incredible crevice of Balcosin gully, then to the Camburero ravine, next the gully of Jou Lluengu which gives vistas of the peak, tantalising because it seems interminable, and finally to the Vega de Urriellu, where the Julian Delgado Ubeda refuge is at 2,050m (6,724ft) ($4^1/_2$ hours). The peak, Naranjo, is the most famous not only in the Picos, but in all Spain, a giant limestone monolith with smooth faces, and as such is worth contemplating, even if not climbed.

From Poncebos a road of 12km ($7^1/_2$ miles) runs up the valley of the Río Duje, green and narrow, via the village of Tielve to the hamlet of **Sotres** a picturesque spot, regrettably spoilt by an overdose of visitors. However, it is an excellent centre for exploratory walks, and a jeep road leads to the Aliva refuge (1,667m, 5,468ft),via the Duje valley ($2^1/_2$ hours from Sotres). Also from Sotres is a route to Naranjo, via a mule trail going west from the jeep road to the Terenosa refuge (1,380m, 4,526ft), then a high level track from there to the Collado Vallejo (1,650m, 5,412ft), descending a steep gully and across trackless ravines to the foot of the Celada ravine near Naranjo (6 hours).

*Peña Vieja, the Picos de Europa*

*Cart drawn by cattle, the Picos de Europa*

*Cathedral façade, Burgo de Osma, Soria*

*Traditional dancers in the Liébana valley*

## The Liébana Valley

This is the popular entry route to the Picos, approached from Potes on the N621. **Potes** is a very pleasant small town with an agreeable atmosphere, perhaps due to its site and drier climate. The old wooden houses, with heraldic coats of arms, overlook the Río Deva, and there is an interesting town hall converted from the medieval Torre del Infantado. Nearby is another old tower, the fifteenth-century Torre de Orejón de la Lama, and with the ancient bridges (Puente San Cayetano), plus a famous Monday market, there is plenty to see and do here.

The valley is a wide tectonic depression surrounded by high peaks, and cut through by the Río Deva, with a series of side valleys, and although far north, its climate and landscape make it an enclave of Mediterranean cultivation. Here almonds, oranges, olives and vines flourish up to 300m (1,000ft), the valley floor has wheat and vegetables, whilst growing higher up are potatoes and maize — a little region of rich agriculture.

Drive along the valley (N621), and off on the left after 3km (2 miles), is the monastery of Santo Toribio, below Monte Viorna. Now Franciscan and transformed, its sixth-century foundation was followed by the Bishop of Astorga bringing a fragment of the true cross (in a sanctuary by the cloisters).There are also some valuable copies of illuminated eighth-century manuscripts. Nearby, at the hermitage of San Miguel, is a good viewpoint.

Continuing on the main route past the hamlet of Camaleño, is a turn to the picturesque village of **Mogrovejo**, in a rather fine mountain setting. The next village, **Cosgaya**, has good places to eat, and afterwards the hamlet of **Espinama** is reached, where a rough jeep route leads to the Aliva refuge (1,667m, 5,468ft, $2^1/_2$-3 hours walk). Then onwards to the end of the road at Fuente Dé (1,050m, 3,444ft), where visitors are confronted by the huge 800m (2,624ft) wall of a vast amphitheatre. At its foot is a *parador*, and a cable car station. Although it has brought too many visitors in its wake for the summer infrastructure to accommodate, this cableway has enabled climbers and mountain walkers to penetrate into the Central Massif. At the top, the Mirador del Cable at 1,843m (6,045ft) provides stupendous views, and a base for many walks and exploratory excursions. The Aliva refuge is reached by a jeep road via the Collada de Cavasobres (1,930m, 6,330ft, $^3/_4$ hour walk). The Peña Vieja (2,613m, 8,571ft) can be climbed by following the Vueltona road, then leaving it, and taking the path, which reaches the Collado de Canalona (2,420m, 7,938ft), then follows an ample path to the north-west face, with very good views from the summit ($2^1/_2$ hours or 3 from Aliva). However, the best summit for the mountain walker is undoubtedly the Pico Tesorero (2,570m, 8,430ft), as it lies in the middle of the Central Massif, and provides an excellent viewpoint. It is about 3 hours from the Mirador del Cable by the jeep road, Collada de Canalona junction, Horcados Rojos (narrow pass), the south side of Urrieles (2,501m, 8,203ft), and the saddle between here and the Pico Tesorero.

Return now to the Liébana valley. This area probably offers the most variety of lower level walking, with the many side roads, paths and attractive villages in a very verdant setting, plus what is most important — often sunnier and drier weather.

## The Eastern Massif (Andara)

### The La Hermida Gorge
From **Panes** the Deva flows in a green open valley, which narrows at Puente Llés to a deep gorge for some 20km ($12^1/_2$ miles), past **La Hermida**, a hamlet, where a steep rough road leads into the Andara massif. The defile extends to the small town of **Cillorgo-Castro**, which has some fine houses and a regional museum, north of Potes. The steep dark depths of the gorge preclude much vegetation, and its

*Pico de Valdecora (1,810m, 5,937ft) Espinama*

narrowness has caused a Spanish writer, Pérez Galdos to remark that it was not a gorge, but a gullet. The Río Deva has eroded the softer bands of rock so intensely that the gorge is that of a saw or zigzag. However, it has a reputation here for salmon fishing. Where it opens out towards the village of **Lebeña** on the left, is the small and very interesting ninth-century Mozarabic church of Santa Maria surrounded by trees and under rocky limestone heights. The bell tower and porch are at the back, and inside the vaulting of the naves is horseshoe shaped, and the columns are in Corinthian style.

## Andara

This massif, smaller and remoter, was exploited for minerals, chiefly zinc, in the last century, and a maze of tracks existed between the picturesque villages lost in the solitude of the mountains. Ox carts carried the zinc concentrates down from the Andara mines to the Río Deva, then by barge to the Ría Tina Mayor on the coast, and thereon to Belgium and other countries.

The massif is best penetrated from **Sotres** in Cabrales, by hired jeep down to a crossroads at Jito de Escarandi in Andara, then turning right with the view later of the Picos de Mancodiu (1,999m, 6,557ft), to arrive at the old mines of Mazrarasa. This area has become very attractive to British speleologists because of the numerous caves and chasms to explore and study. Here is a base for walking or climbing the principal peaks in the massif, which are mostly within the ability of good mountain walkers: Ingotable (2,230m, 7,314ft) and Evangelista (2,426m, 7,957ft). If the jeep road through the Andara mines area is taken to past the Providencia mine, a path leads to Pico de Samelar (2,227m, 7,305ft). These peaks, the nucleus of the massif, are in a huge rocky cirque. The road goes on to the mining area of El Dobillo (1,060m, 3,477ft), where the old furnaces which concentrated the zinc ore by roasting, can be seen. The road, or track, now goes to the Collado de Hoja (818m, 2,683ft), then the hamlet of **Beges**, and on to La Hermida in the gorge.

Take a left turn at the Jito crossroads, past the sheepfold of the Hoyo del Tejo (pit of the yew tree), Collado de Barreda (1,280m, 4,198ft), then Collado de Pirué, source of the Río Sobra, then via Portillas de Sobra to the hidden village of Treviso. This village is famous for its cheese, stronger than *Cabrales* and more fermented. From here one can go by the mineral road (on foot) by the torrent stream of the Urdón, passing the Balcón de Pilatos (645m, 2,116ft), with views above the gorge, and thus to the power station at Urdón in the La Hermida gorge. Trips by horseback to Treviso can be arranged from here. Another means of entry into Andara is from **Espinama** in the Liébana valley to the Aliva refuge, and from the road to this refuge, a path goes to the Collada de Cámara (1,653m, 5,422ft), where the main ridge can be reached, or a most ambitious traverse of the whole range undertaken (8 - 10 hours).

The Andara massif is little visited, there is much to explore, and it is really off the beaten track.

# Further Information

## — Picos de Europa —

### Activities

**Arenas de Cabrales**
Fiesta del Queso, last Sunday in
August; Romería de San Juan, 24
June.

**Bulnes**
Fiestas: San Pedro, 29 June; San-
tiago, 25 July; Our Lady of the
Snows, 8 August.

**Cangas de Onis**
Romería del San Antonio, 13 June;
Santiago (St James), 25 July.

**Covadonga**
Romería, 8 September.
Fiesta del Pastor (shepherds): Enol
lake, 25 July, with horseracing and
canoeing after Mass and meeting
of Shepherds' Council.

**Posada de Valdeón**
Fiesta de N.S. De Corña. Procession to sanctuary, 7-10 September.

**Potes**
Romería Ermita de la Salud, 2
July;Fiesta Ermita San Tirso (Ojeda
village), 30 August.

**Oseja de Sajambre**
Fiesta de N.S. Asunción and San
Roque, 15-16 August.

### Land Rover/Jeep Hire and Taxi Service

*Operate from:*

**Espinama** to Aliva refuge, and
further to Fuente Dé (top cable

station) and La Vueltona, and to
Pandetrave col.

**Fuente Dé** as above.

**La Hermida** to Andara mines.

**Sotres** to Aliva refuge and Andara
mines.

These trips are expensive unless
there are more than six people.

They also operate from Llanes (on
coast) by Rutasor Auda S Pedro 2,
☎ 40 14 58 for a minimum of five
people. Traversing Picos (round
trip); 'Triangle' route (Picos);
Central Massif and Eastern Massif.
The last two are for climbers and
mountain walkers.

### Maps

FEM Tres Macizos de los Picos
1:50,000, 1966

FEM Macizo Central 1:25,000, 1977

FEM Macizo Oriental 1:25,000, 1979

Map-guide del Macizo Occidental
1:25,000, J.R. Lueje, Editorial
Alpinal, 1982

Parque Nacional de la Montaña de
Covadonga 1: 30,000, Icona,
Madrid, 1979

Picos de E. Macizos Central y
Oriental 1:30,000 J. Malo Bilbau,
1974

The official IGC survey 1:50,000
maps are very old (sheets 55, 56, 80
and 81).

## Mountain Refuges

### Western Massif
(FEM — Federación Española de Montañismo)

Casa Municipal de Pastores (1,080m, 3,542ft), Covadonga National Park, Lago Enol. Thirty-five places.

Vega Redonda (1,560m, 5,117ft), open all year, sixty-eight places, FEM.

Vega Huerta (2,010m, 6,593ft), forestry hut, usually open, eight places.

Marques de Villaviciosa (1,582m, 5,189ft), open summer, otherwise key at Casa Municipal, thirty-six places.

Vegabaño (1,340m, 4,395ft), an *albergue* (youth hostel), locked except when warden is there, key at Soto de Sajambre Inn.

### Central Massif
(FAM — Federación Asturiana de Montañismo, Oviedo)

Collado de Jermoso (2,064m, 6,770ft), FEM, normally open in late summer, keys at Santa Maria de Valdeón/Potes chemist, twelve places.

Julián Delgado Ubeda (2,050m, 6,724ft), FEM, keys at Poncebos (inn), Posade de Valdeón (police) and Potes (chemist), forty places.

Terenosa (1,380m, 4,526ft), FAM, keys at Puente Poncebos (hostel), thirty places.

Aliva (1,667m, 5,468ft), open June-September, State Tourist Author-

ity, forty-six places (good restaurant).

There are no refuges in the Eastern Massif (Andara)

## Places of Interest

### Cangas de Onis
Cueva de Buxu: visits limited to maximum of twenty-five people per day.

Chapel and dolmen: key at tourist office.

### Covadonga
Visit to basilica treasure 10am-8pm (6pm in winter).

## Tourist Information Offices

### Arenas de Cabrales
Tourist Office
Carretera General (Main Road)
☎ 84 52 84

### Cangas de Onis
Tourist Office
Emilio Lara 2
☎ 84, 80 05/43

Ayuntamiento
Avenida de Covadonga
☎ 84 80 43

### Panes
Tourist Office
Calle Mayor
☎ 41 40 08

### Potes
Tourist Office
Ayuntamiento
Plaza del Capitán Palacios
☎ 73 00 06

# 3 • Soria

This is the least known of the provinces of Old Castile and reflects, even in the rapidly changing Spain of today, the older traditional image of castles and wide horizons of the Meseta. Soria was the springboard, along the fortified line of the river Duero, from which the Spanish gradually reconquered the country from the Moors in the tenth century.

The province lies in the north centre of Spain, and is part of the high plateau of the Meseta surrounded by the mountains of the Iberian Cordillera (mountain range). The softer rocks have been subjected to different patterns of erosion over an immense period of geological time, and have formed interesting variations of landscape on the Meseta. Far from being monotonous, there are many curious flat-topped hillocks, narrow canyons, broad valleys, and gently rolling hills; whilst in the Sierras de Urbión, formed of older crystalline rocks, there are forests, lakes, rushing streams, rocky crags and wide sweeping vistas.

The history of Soria goes far back to Roman times, with the remains today of the ruins of *Numancia* just outside the city of Soria, and a fine triumphal arch in the small ancient town of Medinacelli, 75km (46 ½ miles) south on the Madrid road. A vision of the *Reconquista* (Reconquest) is provided by the castles of Berlanga and Gormaz in the Duero valley, and the ruins of one in Soria city. But the inheritance that gave the province its greatest riches was the Mesta. This was a large group of sheep breeders who in the thirteenth century organised the transhumance of their animals with a right of way across the cultivated fields. All powerful by the sixteenth century, their privileges were curbed under Charles III in the late eighteenth century through fencing the lands, and by 1836 the Mesta was ended.

Soria had one of the five great stock routes — known as *canadas* — reserved for the huge flocks in the summer, from the dry pastures of far away Extremadura going to the greener slopes of the Iberian

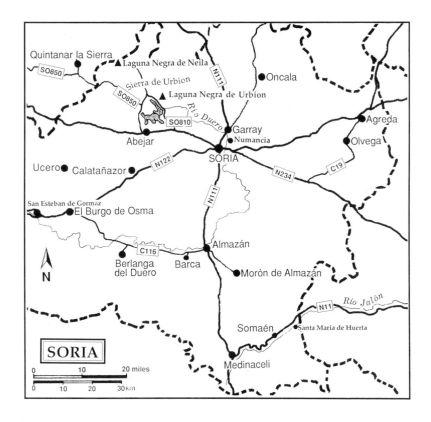

Cordillera. The prosperity of these sheep breeders has given Soria some beautiful buildings like the Old Custom House (Casa Nobiliaria).

The city, although small, is well situated on the river Duero, with a fine Gothic cathedral and many old churches, but the ecclesiastical jewel of the province is the small cathedral city of El Burgo de Osma, with traditional religious festivals, 56km (35 miles) south-west of the capital (N122). Another old town is Almazán 35km (22 miles) south (N111), and 51km (32 miles) eastwards lies Agreda, under the shadow of the Sierra del Moncayo (N122). In the Duero valley, overlooked by its great castle, is Berlanga de Duero with interesting buildings, and right in the south is Medinaceli, now little more than a large village, although it was once a fortified town, with the gorges of the river Jalón to the east.

Soria's climate is distinctly continental, but the worst extremes are to some extent modified by the effect of the Iberian mountains. However, the summers are very warm, above 20°C(68°F), often rising in July/August to 27°C (81°F) or more (in 1987 they were far higher). The winters are cold, 2°C (36°F) in January by day, while during the night temperatures often well below 0°C (28°F) are the rule. Rainfall is light 600mm (25in), and high summer is driest. Sunshine is ever present, and from April to September there are long bright days with 7 to 11 hours of sun daily. But summer storms, often with heavy hail, sometimes happen, and on occasions it can be very windy, especially during August. This climate has tended to make the people of Soria tough and resilient, which is a Castilian characteristic.

The province is attractive, because of its relatively unknown and unspoilt isolation. There are opportunities for walking and climbing in the *sierras*, particularly to the Laguna Negra, a glacial lake at 1,700m (5,576ft) in the Sierra de Urbión, and over the border in Burgos is the lake of Laguna Negra de Neila at 2,000m (6,560ft). The scenery of the Sierra del Moncayo is somewhat wild, bare and desolate, but none the less interesting. In all these areas there is good fishing in the lakes and rivers. On the Meseta the exploration of Soria city and the provincial towns can be a delight on account of their plazas, alleyways and old buildings with intriguing courtyards, and there are always restaurants, cafés and taverns to satisfy the inner traveller. But remember Spanish dining hours are very different from the rest of Europe — especially away from the tourist coasts, and they eat late, be it breakfast, lunch or dinner!

## Travelling to the Area

### By Road
From Madrid (Barajas airport) 220km (136 miles) via Medinacelli (NII), and N111.
From Barcelona (Prat de Llobregat) 470km (291 miles) via motorways A2/A68 to junction of N122, then to Soria.
From Bayonne-Biarritz airport 300km (186 miles) via Pamplona N121, motorway A15 to exit No 1 (Arguedas), then C101 and N122 to Soria.
From Zaragoza airport 180km (112 miles) via Calatayud (NII) or via Tarazona (A68).

### By Rail
Madrid (Atocha) to Soria 250km (155 miles).
Zaragoza to Castejón de Ebro then change for Soria.

# The Capital City
## and the Mountains and Lakes of Soria

The approach to **Soria** city from the east (N122), in the Duero valley is very pleasant. On the left is a steep hill, with the park and gardens of the old ruined castle now containing the modern *parador* from which there are superb views. Before continuing, turn sharp left on to a side road through a narrow archway and along a tree-lined walk besides the river to the eighteenth-century hermitage of San Saturio, with its grottos, perched on the river cliff giving remarkable views. Back along the road, on the right is the ancient monastery of the Knights Templars (now a church, San Juan) with the remains of its strange and beautiful cloisters. Cross the bridge over the Duero and climb up the hill on the right to see the large cathedral of San Pedro, really two churches, one twelfth-century with its cloisters and galleries, and the other sixteenth-century Gothic with a plateresque door, and a Flemish triptych inside.

Entering this small but lively city, it must be realised that for centuries, until a few years ago, it was one of the most traditional places in all of Spain. Now it has been overtaken by the modern European epidemic of expansion and tearing down of older buildings, plus growth of automobiles in its narrow streets. Nevertheless, one can wander around and see houses with glassed-in balconies, and verandahs redolent of old Spain.

It is best to start from the Plaza Ramón y Cajal (Tourist Office), and go down the Calle Caballeros, a street of notable old houses, taking in the church of San Juan de Rabanera. Then left to Calle Juan, right to the Calle de Aguirre, where one is confronted with the immensely long façade and imposing tower of the Palace of the Counts of Gómara. Peep into the patio and you have a glimpse of the Golden Age of Soria at the close of the sixteenth century. The building is now part of the government of the autonomous Community of Castile, an arrangement hardly desired by Castile, however eagerly demanded by less Spanish regions. (With so many *autónomas*, Spain is in danger of being over-governed — like Australia was.) Turn about and go along the Calle de Collado to Calle Aduana Vieja on the right, where the Old Custom House with its ornamental door surmounted by a balcony and a large coat of arms can be seen, yet another reminder of an opulent past. At the end of the street, on the right, is the fine twelfth-century church of Santo Domingo, with perhaps the best Romanesque façade in Soria, with its large circular window above a magnificent doorway. Inside its rich sculptures show influence from

*The palace of Condes de Gormaz, Soria*

Poitiers, because its founder Alfonso VIII married Eleanor of England who had inherited Gascony.

Outside, a visit to the park, Alameda de Cervantes, is worthwhile, and pleasant if it is hot. One large tree contains a bandstand amid its branches, and another overlooks a large patio with stone seats. You might see men playing 'Tanguilla', a game played for money, by skilfully throwing a metal disc nearest to a peg in the ground — it's not as easy as it looks! Nearby is the Numancia Museum with material found from the Roman ruins, and this is also the place to enquire about visits to the church of San Juan de Duero, and its cloisters. For exploring the streets of Soria, mid-afternoon is best, and avoid Thursday (market day).

The route now leaves the city by the N111 (Logroño road) to the village of **Garray**, and then a road leads up to the summit of a flat hill overlooking the Duero, where the ruins of *Numancia* are still being restored. This was a city reconstructed by the Romans after it had been burnt by its 8,000 Lusitanian citizens in 133BC, when the Romans were beseiging it, thinking to pacify the Iberian peninsula easily. It became an important Roman town surrounded by cultivated land, forests, and garrisons. Now, with a landscape of wide vistas and less trees, it all seems far off, until the eye catches the long line of poplars and alders along the Duero, and the importance of the site is realised. Return down to Garray, which is an interesting little village, with at the back, a lane leading up to an old hermitage, where the church itself seems to be invariably locked but there is a very good view over the Duero valley.

From Garray the C115 is taken across fertile countryside that is surrounded by snowy peaks, and is a prelude to the vineyards of La Rioja in the nearby province of Logroño. The route climbs to the Puerto de Oncala (1,454m, 4,769ft), and a short way on, off to the right, is the highland village of **Oncala**, where the old church has an extraordinarily rich collection of Flemish eighteenth-century tapestries — typical of unexpected treasures to be found in remote places. Continuing on the C115, **Yanguas** is reached in the valley of the Río Cidacos, amongst the spurs of the Sierra de Cameros. This is a hill town, once defended by its Moorish castle, and in the Plaza Mayor with archways are some splendid mansions.

From here, go back along the C115 until a side road (SO 640/630) on the left, which is followed through San Pedro Manrique and Magaña close to the Río Alhama with a fine castle, and then reaching the main road (N122), with the rather bare outlines of the Sierra del Moncayo as a backdrop, and turning left for some way, the town of **Agreda** comes into view, off the main road. Historically this was a fort on the frontier between Aragón and Castile, and is a surprise, as the landscape just behind it is very attractive with water meadows, poplar groves and fountains dating from the time of Charles III (1759-88). Inside the town is the old church of San Miguel built of multi-coloured local stone, having an impressive tower, and combining successfully two different styles — Gothic and plateresque. There is also the seventeenth-century convent of 'La Concepción' founded by Sister Maria-de-Agreda, the celebrated 'conscience' of King Phillip IV (1621-55), who thought himself responsible for the loss of Artois and Roussillon to France. Besides the churches, there is much to see, especially in the quarter known as Los Castejones, with its medieval watchtower and twelfth-century palace. Before leaving the town note the *bacalao* or dried cod factory, 200km (124

*Ruins of the Roman city of* Numancia

miles) from the sea, showing the importance of fish in the Spanish diet.

From Agreda, forays can be made into the Sierra del Moncayo, by taking side roads (SO382/3) up to the nature park of La Dehesa del Moncayo, and further to the highest point (2,313m, 7,587ft), via the sanctuary of Moncayo. This area was once mined for its minerals and is still worked sporadically.

Returning to Agreda the C101 road is followed by the flanks of the *sierra* to the village of **Olvega** in a fold of the hills. This is sheep country, and sometimes on a spring or early summer evening, a round-up of the flocks will be seen — a reminder of the great days of the Mesta. Then through isolated villages and the odd pinewood until the main N234 Soria road is reached. Turn right along this road, and off on the left are a whole series of isolated villages in river valleys joining the master stream of the region — the Duero.

After reaching Soria the N111 is taken again to Garray, but now the route continues on the N111, until on the left SO820 leads to the village of **Rollamienta**, where sometimes large flocks of sheep are penned for a period. There is a large church here, which is interesting for so small a place. The route continues by the SO820 through

Valdeavellano to Sotillo del Rincón, with the landscape changing gradually — more wooded, hillier and rock outcrops — as the approach to the *sierras* is made by the attractive valley of the river Razón. Soon the road turns south near a good viewpoint, and after El Royo the direct route to the Laguna Negra is reached. This passes a large open stretch of water, the HEP lake of La Cuerda del Pozo (the well-rope), and then climbs up through forests of Scots pine and black pine to a glacial lake set in a cirque of high rocky cliffs and waterfalls. Here is an area to explore — the headwaters of the Duero, with two other lakes, Larga and Helado, higher up amid beech and pinewoods, steep cliffs, and rockbound streams until the Pic de Urbión (2,226m, 7,301ft) is reached. This is an almost unknown mountain region.

Further exploration can be made by going over the Puerto de Santa Ines (1,753m, 5,750ft) on the SO831, and into the province of Logroño to the mountains of the Sierra de la Demanda. Or one can descend by a winding road past the peak of Congosto (1,824m, 5,983ft) to the SO850, then turn right, following the road over the Puerto de Hierro (1,135m, 3,723ft), that leads to **Quintanar de la Sierra**, a woodworking town in Burgos province. From there one can go up by a scenic winding road to the Mirador San Francisco (1,901m, 6,235ft), where there is a fine panoramic view over the area, and then on to the summit lake of Laguna Negra de Neila (1,951m, 6,399ft) — really a series of glacial lakes, and high enough to have alpine flowers like yellow oxalis, that blooms abundantly by the lake from May to October. For a direct return to Soria, after crossing the Puerto de Hierro, keep straight on until the main N234 Burgos-Soria road is reached. From the Laguna Negra in Soria, one can return to the capital by the direct route past the HEP lake and dam (SO810) to the N234, then left to Soria.

## Almazán and the Duero Valley

This route leaves Soria by the Madrid road (N111). Two kilometres (just over a mile) out on the right is a good camp site, Fuente de la Teja, open all the year round, with a restaurant and a swimming pool. A little further, on the left, is the village of **Los Rabanos**, near the wooded shores of a lake formed from the widened course of the Duero — a pleasant spot on a warm day. Returning to the main road, the route continues for a short way, then turns left on to a side road which passes through woods of pine and holm oaks. Soon it swings away from the river through Miranda de Duero, and Cubo de la

*Laguna Negra, Sierra de Urbión*

Solana, then rejoins it, and follows closely through dense pinewoods to the N111 again to reach the old town of **Almazán**.

This is a very pleasant little place, traditional and full of narrow streets, and alleyways. There are remains of Roman walls, and in the Middle Ages it was the scene of a power struggle between the kingdoms of Castile and Aragón, of which the three fortified gateways still left are a reminder. In the Plaza del Ayunamiento (Town Hall Square) is the fine twelfth-century church of San Miguel, with a cupola and dome, on which are carved stone reliefs of the martyred St Thomas of Canterbury. This may seem curious, but twelfth-century Europe had one Church, and in spite of distance, communication was maintained. Over the way is the sixteenth-century palace of the Counts of Altamira, with a classical façade. Behind are balconies opening on to the river far below and in the middle of the plaza is a statue of a sixteenth-century learned man, one Diego Traynez, brooding over it all.

From Almazán the route follows the C116 along the quiet and rural Duero valley, and after a short way, a turning on the left leads to the hamlet of **Barca**, where there is an ethnological museum. The route continues along the valley, close to the railway, but the only sounds heard are the croaking of the frogs in the marshes, and the prolific bird life of plovers, warblers, and above, the usual hovering kestrel. At length, take the SO104 on the left, to **Berlanga de Duero** on the river Torete. It is overshadowed by a magnificent and massive fifteenth-century castle on a hill with walls and solid ramparts, which was a fortress facing the Moorish south. It was used again in the Peninsular War (1809-14), and the Duke's Palace which faced the town, was burnt by the French army. All that remains is a skeletal façade, looking like a curtain wall fronting the castle. But the town has some fine houses and buildings, and is worth a wander round to see the 1526 Gothic collegiate church, with its chapels and painted altarpieces, then the sixteenth-century hospital, and other buildings of the past nobility. If the road is taken a further 8km (5 miles) to **Casillas**, there is an isolated eleventh-century Mozarabic hermitage, San Baudelio, with unusual frescos of hunting scenes and geometrical signs (some tenth-century examples are in the Prado, Madrid).

Returning to Berlanga, and the C116 via Hortezuela, the route bears left to Quintanas de Gormaz, turns left again to Gormaz by the river, with a ruined fortress from which there are fine views over the Duero. From here the route is through woods of maritime pine, from which is extracted resin for oil of turpentine. Then it enters the little city of **El Burgo de Osma**, once called 'La Bella Desconocida' (The Beautiful Unknown), as indeed it was for centuries. Even now, except at weekends when it is invaded by *madrileños* (it is only 200km, 124 miles, by road from Madrid), it remains quiet, traditional and has a reputation for good eating.

Although small, El Burgo de Osma is one of the oldest bishoprics in Spain, being founded by the Visigoths (sixth and seventh centuries). The cathedral was built through the centuries in a mixture of styles, starting with a Romanesque site; the main body (1232), consists of a Gothic apse, transept and chapter house. The cloisters are sixteenth-century Gothic with a decorated Renaissance choir. Finally a tall profusely decorated baroque tower, which can be seen from afar was added in the eighteenth century. All this, however, makes for a very fine, and complete building. Religious festivals are important here, and one worth seeing on the 16 August is that of the town's patron San Roque, with its procession of a flower-decorated image,

*The massive castle and walls at Berlanga de Duero*

girls in national costume, choirboys and the town band. But there are many other things to see — largely of the eighteenth-century baroque period. In the Plaza Mayor (1768) is the hospital of San Agustín with twin towers, and an imposing façade; all around are colleges and institutions like the old university of Santa Catalina (plateresque façade), the Bishop's Palace and the National College of Juan Yagüe. This is a place to walk around slowly, and have a good look!

From here an interesting exploratory journey can be made by going due north on the SO920 (San Leonardo road), which is verdant with orchards and cultivation until the Sierra de Cabrejas is approached. Then comes **Ucero** in a narrow valley, with the remains of an ancient monastery, and a gaunt castle ruin on top of a steep cliff, and beyond is a very fine view over the Río Lobos valley with high cliffs and green banks in a canyon. Once wild and unvisited, it has become the Río Lobos nature park, and is popular for local people at weekends for bathing and camping. Nearby the area opens up possibilities for exploring the canyon with its grottos and caves, and above the Meseta (plateau) of Ardal (1,213m, 3,979ft), with the escarpment of Galiana, which looks down on a chasm of 200m (650ft). Here is the most impressive landscape in the province.

Returning to El Burgo de Osma, the route continues down the Duero valley, but just outside the present town is a place called **Ciudad de Osma** — evidently an extremely ancient settlement, because there are remains here, in the form of mosaics, of the Roman town that was called *Uxama Argalae*. After this, and soon on the left off the main road (N122), is the old fortified village of **San Esteban de Gormaz**, with its large ruined castle on a hill, and its church perched on rocks. The place has an interesting old mill and river bridges, and with large grain elevators denotes a tradition of milling, as this has been wheat country for centuries.

Further along the valley, off on the right, is the valley of the Río Madre de Rejas with a striking landscape typical of the Castilian Meseta with wide horizons and skyscape. But visitors are advised, when walking in a reserved hunting area (*coto de caza*), to observe caution, if it happens to be in the open season.

Continuing along the N122, there is a sharp contrast between the bright green of the Duero *huerta*, and the dry farming either side of the road. The steep river banks on one side of the river are very green during May and June with conifers and other trees. Finally, our last castle appears, partly restored, at **Langa de Duero**, which has some fine houses with balconies, and an old church.

The return to Soria is made direct on the N122, continuing along it beyond El Burgo de Osma. This is a fine scenic road with good views over the forests, as the road climbs, and at **Calatañazor**, off on the left up a steep hill, there is an authentic medieval village high amid the castle ruins. The old parish church is detached from the village, and from this high point there is a good view over the countryside below.

Return to the main road, which continues to climb to Villaciervos (1,179m, 3,867ft), and then just east of here, on the left, appears a magnificent limestone scarp, before the road descends to Soria city.

## Southern Soria

This route goes south-east from Almazán on the C116, and along the valley of the Río Morón to the delightful small town of **Morón de Almazán** — a place of elegant architecture in the sixteenth-century plateresque style. Essentially Spanish, its name is from *platero*, a silversmith, as the decoration was fine but at the same time solid, like the craftsmen's work in silver, gold or jewellery. Thus, along with the Renaissance, the Golden Age of Spain began.

Here in the Plaza Mayor the buildings to see are the church tower with its storeys marked by flowery friezes and the old town hall with an ancient pillory, but many others are worth a good look. The route then climbs up through a pinewood, past Valtueña, and near the

HEP lake of Monteagudo to the main Madrid road (NII), just inside
Zaragoza province. Then, turning right along the NII for 7km (4
miles) and inside Soria once more, on the left is the ancient Cistercian
monastery of Santa Maria de Huerta founded in 1162. Like many
others it flourished for centuries, adding differing architectural
styles to enoble the building, only to be dis-established in 1835, and
fall into ruin. But in 1930 the monks returned and now one can see the
building, shown by the monks themselves. It is still partly ruined, but
the thirteenth-century Gothic vaulting in the refectory, and the
kitchen with its enormous chimney is outstanding. The cloisters at
ground level also have elegant vaulting, whilst the upper storey has
splendid florid plateresque decoration. One unusual item is the
preserved cope, gloves and boots of the twelfth-century Archbishop
of Toledo. Finally, on leaving, look at the splendid gateway with its
imposing pediment, and then peer through it at the approach to the
church, with its fine Romanesque door, and above it the magnificent
rose window. In the spacious precincts of the monastery are *huertas*,
*bodegas* (wine cellars), storehouses and cultivated fields. Back on the
NII, the route continues westwards along the Río Jalón valley to
Arcos de Jalón, with its bullring, and at the village of **Somaén** the
gorges of the Jalón begin. These are cut into red ochre-coloured
sandstone with cliffs that tower as much as 200m (650ft) above the
river. The main road winds through the gorges to **Medinaceli**, off on
the right sited high up on a small plateau.

This small place, known to the Romans as *Ocilis*, was important
in the second and third centuries, and has left as a witness a fine
triumphal arch with three gateways — unique in Spain. From it there
is a sweeping view southwards over the Jalón valley, the distant
white patches being salt works or *salinas*, giving their name to the
village of Salinas de Medinaceli. The town was the Medina Selim of
the Moors and they fortified it, and in the centuries that followed
patrician houses were built along with churches and convents. The
most interesting of these was the sixteenth-century Gothic college of
Santa Maria, but there is also an eighteenth-century palace of the
Dukes of Medinaceli. Now the town is quite small, and its brilliant
history is only seen in its buildings.

To complete this triangle of routes the N111 is taken northwards,
but a diversion can be made to a palaeontological museum, south of
Ambrona on the SO133, and the N111 rejoined north of Medinaceli.
The route on to Almazán climbs to the Alto del Minguete through a
pinewood, and descends to Almazán, and then on to Soria via the
Alto de Lubia through a vast forest of pines. Thus this glimpse of a

little known Spanish province of 'silver hills, grey slopes and mauve rocks, where the Duero winds round Soria like a cross-bow' as Antonio Machado, the poet of Soria wrote — has come to an end.

# Further Information
## — Soria —

## Activities

### Almazán
*Fiesta:* San Pascual Bailón, 17 May. A semi-burlesque person, El Zarrón, accompanied by groups of dancers.

### San Pedro Manrique
*Fiesta:* Paso del Fuego, June 23-5. People walking barefoot on red hot coals; San Juan pilgrimage: part of same fiesta.

### Soria
*Fiesta:* San Juan or de la Madre de Dois, from the first Thursday following 24 June. Bullfighting.  ·

### Vinuesa
*Fiesta:* La Pinochada, día de San Roque,16 August. 'Battle' between youths and married couples with pine branches, commemorating an earlier encounter between the two villages of Covaleda and Vinuesa.

## Places of Interest

### Burgo de Osma
Cathedral: enquire priest at 1 Plaza de la Catedral to see San Pedro de Osma's tomb, chapter house and archives and manuscripts in the museum.

### Santa Maria de Huerta
Monastery
Open: 9.30am-1pm, 4.30-7pm (3.30-6pm in winter).

### Soria
*Numancia* Museum
Open: 10.30am-1.30pm, 3.30-6pm (winter); 10am-1.30pm, 4-9pm (summer).

*Numancia* Roman Ruins
Open: 10.30am-1.30pm, 3.30-sunset. Closed 1 January, Good Friday, Easter, 1 and 12 May, 25 December.

## Tourist Information Offices

### Almazán
Ayuntamiento
Plaza Mayor
☎ 30 04 61

### Burgo de Osma
Ayuntamiento
7 Plaza General Franco
☎ 34 01 07

### Soria
Tourist Office
Plaza Ramón y Cajal 2
☎ (975) 21 20 52
Open: 10am-1.30pm, 4-8pm.

# 4 • The Serranía de Cuenca

The rather remote province of Cuenca in New Castile is the link between the Meseta, and the distant shores of the Mediterranean Sea, and the city of Cuenca perched on its stupendous rocky site is the link between La Mancha, and the mountains of the Serranía or the Iberian Cordillera. Cuenca is an ancient city of Roman origin, but the nearest Roman ruins are at Valeria, 35km (22 miles) due south on the CU712 side road. The city itself is in two parts — old and more recent. The old city is at the end of a high spur of rock between the green waters of the wide Río Júcar in a narrow defile of red cliffs, with trees on one side, while on the other the slim ribbon of its tributary, the Río Huécar, flows through the wider defile of a verdant *huerta*, far below the apparently precariously built houses.

Cuenca has been called the improbable city, not only for its justly famed *casas colgadas* or hanging houses, but for others that are perched with artistic precision like nests. In some, one storey is in a street, and eleven storeys lower the same house overlooks the river in a parallel street. Yet others are so tall, that they have been nick-named *rascacielos* or skyscrapers, after their American counterparts. One writer has even insisted that Cuenca has a passion for dizziness!

However, as with many old Spanish cities, Cuenca has some beautiful buildings, a Gothic and Renaissance decorated cathedral, and many fine churches among its tangle of narrow side streets and alleys. Much of Cuenca's glory is in the past, however, when it was the largest diocese in Spain, and produced some famous churchmen like Cardinal Gil Alborniz, who in the fourteenth century, restored the Pope to Rome after his captivity in Avignon.

The Serranía covers the north-eastern third of the province, and is a hilly and mountainous region largely of Cretaceous and Jurassic limestone, similar to the Causses region of the Massif Central in France, but not so barren or bleak. Much of this landscape is trenched by *hoces* or defiles, and *torcas* or dolines (sink holes). There are also chaotic groups of huge strangely carved blocks of limestone, which reach their zenith in the Ciudad Encantada or Enchanted City 35km

(22 miles) north of the city of Cuenca. All these features are caused by the erosion of thick layers of limestone, and are splendid examples of karst landforms, but strangely unknown or ignored by geographers and geomorphologists of the world who dwell at length upon karst landscapes in the West Indies or China. The region is quite well provided with rivers, as well as spectacular resurgences of limestone streams, and the river Tagus (Tajo) rises in the bordering *sierras* (mountain ranges) with the Teruel province. It is a well-wooded landscape with pines, tall black poplars and the graceful white variety, whilst the floors and lower slopes of the gorges have deciduous woods of trees like limes and ash. The province is noted for its fine trees.

Apart from Cuenca city, the towns and villages in the region are small. Along the valley of the Río Júcar north-east of Cuenca on the CU913 lie the villages of Villalba de la Sierra, near the gorge of the Devil's Window. Further on is Uña, a pleasant little place with its small green lake, and higher in the *sierras* at 1,283m (4,208ft) is Tragacete, famous for its trout fishing. South of this region is the Sierra de Valdemeca, with some remote hamlets leading to the main N420 Cuenca-Teruel road 61km (38 miles) from the city, where there is the small ancient town of Cañete with its castle and old walls — a traditional outpost of old Spain.

Northwards through the *sierras* is the picturesque village of Beteta perched above a deep valley, and then through a gorge and spectacular scenery to Vadillas, leading to the *balneario* (spa) of Solan de Cabras. Finally through a gorge to the old town of Priego noted for the growing and drying of osiers, and its nearby famous ancient convent. The attractions of the region as a whole lie in the variety of things to see in a relatively small area. The city of Cuenca, old and with intriguing and interesting architecture, is not far from, and in complete contrast to the curious natural features of the limestone landscape. Added to this are the many gorges, wooded valleys, waterfalls and river resurgences of a relatively unknown mountain region.

There is a great deal to explore in and around the capital city, with the two river valleys and defiles, and also in the northern part of the Serranía, which has recently been made more accessible by forest roads and tracks along the Teruel border, where the source of the Tagus is found at 1,623m (5,323ft) in the Montes Universales. Some of the towns and villages too, like Cañete and Priego, are worth a good wander round, as they are not often visited from outside Spain.

The climate of Cuenca is continental, in spite of its altitude, being

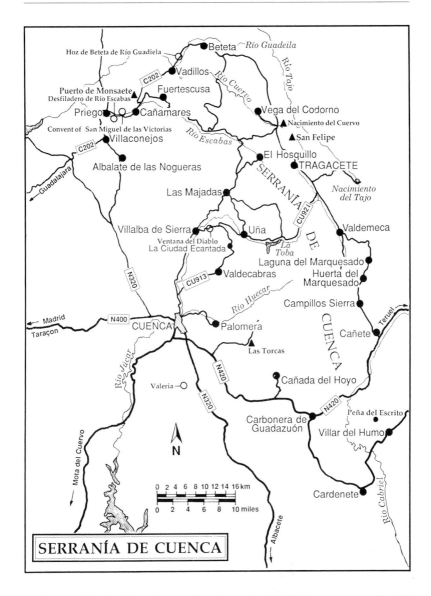

SERRANÍA DE CUENCA

influenced by La Mancha, rather than the Mediterranean, so that it is generally rather dry, with most rain in the spring, and the occasional storm. July is the warmest and driest month with 22°C+ (72°F+) average rising to 30°C+ (86°F+), with low humidity, and only 19mm ($^3/_4$in) of rain. This warmth extends well into late autumn, but the higher parts of the Serranía have snow in January and February, and the winter is generally cold, dry and sunny.

# Travelling to the Area

## By Road
From Madrid (Barajas) airport A2 into city, then M30 ring, then A3/ NIII road to Tarancon; then N400 to Cuenca, about 180km (112 miles).
From Valencia airport NIII to Minglanilla, then CU504 to Almodóvar del Pinar, then N320 to Cuenca, 209km (130 miles) or via Motilla del Palancar NIII/N320, 221km (137 miles).

## By Rail
From Madrid (Atocha) 2hrs 37min via Aranjuez, 210km (130 miles).
From Valencia (Termino) 2hrs 54min, 203km (126 miles).

# The City of Cuenca and Vicinity

## Old Cuenca City — Ciudad Antigua
This is a place to walk round slowly, not only because there is much to see in a small space, but because its spectacular site offers so many fine views that one needs to stop quite often and look.

From the central square — Plaza Mayor de Pio XII — the cathedral draws attention at once. It is thirteenth-century Gothic-Anglo Norman, and unique in Spain. Inside, the body of the church has three naves, with a beautiful triforium (gallery above nave and transept), and a double girola (portion of nave round the presbytery). The later works, mainly of the sixteenth century, include the high altar and very fine ironwork in the choir. In the transept is the incredible 1546 Renaissance decorated Jamete arch, and in the main sacristy is perhaps the most appealing work of all: *The Dolorosa (Our Lady of Sorrows)* by Pedro de Mena. The Church Treasure is really a small museum, and can be visited. Outside, the façade has lost some of its former elegance, as it partially collapsed in 1902.

From the cathedral down the Calle Obispo Valero is the adjoining Bishop's Palace with an interior patio, rather plain and sober, and the important diocesan museum containing paintings by El Greco, David, a fourteenth-century Byzantine diptych and rare Royal Cuenca carpets and Flemish tapestries. Beyond are the justly famous fourteenth-century *casas colgadas* perched on a rocky promontory, with beautiful wooden balconies, apparently opening out into space. Believed to have been a royal summer residence, they now house a typical *mesón* (inn), and the unique museum of abstract art of many famous Spanish painters (Chillida to Zóbel). To the right in the

Casas colgadas *(hanging houses)*, Cuenca city

adjacent Barrio de San Martin are also the curious *rascacielos* (sky-scraper houses) overlooking the Hoz de Huécar. In front of the *casas colgadas* is the archaeological museum, sited in an old grain store or *almudi* (from an ancient Castilian measure of about 4,000l) contain-ing palaeolithic and Roman material from Valeria. Returning to the Plaza Mayor, the *ayuntamiento* (town hall) is worth a look for its 1762 baroque façade, and then a walk through some of the old streets is enjoyable, starting with Calle Santa Maria Ayala to Plaza Merced to the Calle de Alcaza, where there is the Torre de Mangana. This was an old Arab fort, and is now the municipal clock tower, from which there is a good view. Go across the Plaza del Carmen to the church of San Felipe Neri, and down the narrow Calle de los Caballeros turning right into Calle Moreno, and from the Calle del Peso, there is a panoramic view over the old city.

## Las Hoces (The Defiles)

On each side of the rocky spur, a road along the river gives superb views including the hanging houses. Taking the Hoz de Júcar first, start from the Plaza Mayor in front of the *ayuntamiento*, pass by Calle Severo Catalina, where there is a historic house in the form of a museum (Museo Zabala), containing a library, furniture and paintings of the period of great architecture in Cuenca. Then down to the old church of San Miguel, which is now an auditorium of religious music (important during Holy Week),with a good view over the Hoz, continue to the Ronda del Júcar, and descend to the Plaza de los Descalzos, the courtyard of a Franciscan convent, and a hermitage in a very peaceful setting amidst trees. A further descent reaches the river, then over by the Puente de los Descalzos to the poplar-lined bank along the green waters of the Júcar, where the views will be well worth the effort.

For the longer Hoz de Huécar return to the Ronda, and go left along it, with a good view of the Júcar valley, to the seventeenth-century octagonal church of San Pedro, in the Calle Trabuco, and if wished, to the old castle. Then taking the pleasant old alley of the Calle Julián Romero, with its steps and landings, the cathedral is reached again. Pass by the *casas colgadas* and down a ramp on the side of the cliff, and so on to the Puente San Pablo, giving an interesting view of the *casas colgadas*, with the *huerta* of the Huécar far below. But when the ramp is descended to the road along the Hoz, the views are stupendous. The road following the river can be taken to the end of the defile, taking a left turn on to a winding road in the direction of the San Jerónimo convent. Soon afterwards on a curve to the right, there is a remarkable sight of the high rocks of the valley, and in the distance the houses of Cuenca. One can return to the old city by the gate in the ancient wall.

## Las Torcas de Los Palancares

This route leaves the city by the N420 Teruel road, and after 11km (7 miles) turns left on to the Los Palancares forest road. Then it crosses the railway east of Cuenca, and continues on for another 10km (6 miles), keeping straight, to Las Torcas amid an open pine forest. Las Torcas in Spanish means 'deep hollow places in the earth', but these are somewhat different, being a series of twenty-five sink holes or solution depressions in dolomitic limestone varying from 50 to 70m (160 to 230ft) in diameter with considerable depth, some being inaccessible. The most probable explanation for these is underground erosion of the layers of thick limestone by solution, and there may exist at depth a system of caverns, although some people think surface erosion or solution created them by rainwater going underground through the joints. But the rainfall of Cuenca is not heavy, only about 600mm (22-3in). However, whatever the cause, they are interesting natural features, and have been given fascinating names: Las Mellizas (twins), El Medio Celemin (half measure), La Llanilla (little plain one) and La Escaleruela (little staircase). Some refer to people, as Tio Agustín (Uncle Augustus), and some are obscure: El Lobo (wolf) and La Novia (bride or fiancée). This last mentioned may be the first to be seen — it is quite impressive. Some of these depressions have quite large trees growing in them, far down on the level floor.

### La Ciudad Encantada and Ventano del Diablo (The Enchanted City and the Devil's Window)

This route leaves Cuenca by the CU921 road to Villalba de la Sierra, and on reaching the Salto de Villalba there is a fine waterfall used for HEP. Then the road climbs to what is, in effect, a hole in the limestone overlooking the impressive gorge of the Río Júcar, and its green waters far below — the 'Devil's Window'. After this the route continues along to a side road on the right, CU913, which leads to La Cuidad Encantada. It is perhaps one of the most impressive, extraordinary, and relatively little known examples of limestone erosion in Western Europe. The limestone strata here amid clumps of pine trees, has been carved into a series of fantastic shapes, and figures almost capricious, which gives the impression of an abandoned city with streets, squares, arches and bridges. Some of these have been named accordingly, a lancet shaped arch in a thick wall of rock is called El Covento (the convent). Most striking is a huge isolated pedestal of rock over 12m (39ft) high, known simply as El Tormo Alto (the high tor or steep rock). Yet others have caught the imagination with names like El Puente Romano (Roman bridge), La Foca (the seal), El Elefante (elephant), El Tobogán (the toboggan), and a wide flat expanse of rock criss-crossed with joints and crevices is known as El Mar de Piedra (sea of stone). This in geographical terms is a splendid example of a limestone pavement, and along with the other residuals are features of advanced karst topography or landscape. There has been some surface erosion by frost, wind and rain, but almost certainly the main agent has been underground solution of the limestone, leaving these curiously shaped great masses of rock as remnants. The site has been declared a national monument, and covers 20sq km (7$^1/_2$sq miles).

Return to Cuenca by continuing along the same road past the village of Valdecabras, and at length rejoining the CU921 road to the city. Just before crossing the bridge over the Júcar, the sixteenth-century church of La Virgen de la Luz on the right hand, may be visited to see the high altar, and the fine plateresque porch. If one continues over the bridge and along the avenue on the left to the bridge over the Río Huécar, there is a fine riverside walk along the Calle de los Tintes (both sides). Before leaving the city, mention should be made of Semana Santa (Holy Week) and its processions, with the sacred music competitions held in the church of San Miguel.

## The Serranía de Cuenca

### The Sierra de Valdemeca and Cañete

This route leaves the city by CU921 and continues on to the village of **Uña**, and its small picturesque green lake. From here there is a walk to a look-out called the Mirador de Uña, giving very fine views over the rocky valley of the Júcar, and Uña with its lake. This lake is good for fishing, and at an inn called Hospederia La Luguna, it is possible to eat well, especially trout. There is one unusual feature of this part of Cuenca in that it draws butterfly collectors from outside Spain for the abundance of the large blue isabella species of butterfly found here.

On to the Embalse da la Toba, which is a really attractive sheet of water with its high cliffs and wooded shores. Many of these HEP lakes look artificial, but this one doesn't. Then go along the valley past Huélamo to a road junction taking the obtuse right hand turn into the Sierra de Valdemeca. This route to the village of Valdemeca is through the pretty wooded Valdemeca valley, and shortly after the village, the right turn is taken and the road climbs through the *sierra* and pinewoods to join a valley road to the village of Campillas Sierra. Beyond here the road is bordered with much cultivation until the old town of **Cañete** is reached on the main N420 road to Teruel. This is another of these old Spanish towns that has seen a great deal of

*The eroded rocks of La Ciudad Encantada*

history. It was important during the Middle Ages, as the remains of its castle, and some extensive walls still show. These fortifications again served in the Peninsular War against the French, and as late as the mid-1800s Cañete was the operational base for the Carlists against Isabella II. The best view is from a sanctuary by a path marking the stations of the cross, up from the *hostería* just outside the town. In Cañete itself the Plaza Mayor is especially interesting, with its houses and colonnades, and in the Calle de Muralla there is a magnificent rose tree with orange-pink blooms. There are some new buildings, but the spirit of old Spain remains, and nightingales can be heard singing in the poplar trees.

From here the route returns to the Sierra de Valdemeca, but not quite by the same road. When the road forks after Campillos Sierra, the right hand turn is taken to Huerta del Marquesado with scattered pine trees, and then from there to Laguna Marquesado is a winding road with a very pleasant small lake, apparently very good for trout fishing, and reputed to be the finest in the province, which is why, along this valley of the Río Campillos, it seems to be strictly controlled. After this the road climbs very sinuously through pines and scrub into the *sierra* with higher open meadows. It is in this area that one can hear that rather rare bird in northern Europe, the nightjar. From this very green and pleasant upland, one descends to the village of Valdemeca once more.

## The Serranía
After this the route continues to the CU921, which is taken northwards to a T-junction, and the right hand route followed, which climbs up through a wooded landscape to the Puerto de El Cubillo (1,620m, 5,314ft). Beyond here on the left is a track to La Mogorrita (1,866m, 6,120ft) a new skiing area. If the road is followed onwards to a junction, and the left turn taken, it leads eventually to the Nacimiento del Tajo — the source of the river Tagus, almost in the neighbouring province of Teruel.

Returning to the CU921 the route continues through a landscape of rough limestone pastures, scrub oak, hawthorn and gorse in the upper Júcar valley to the resort of **Tragacete**, renowned for fishing. The local Hotel Gamo is a good place to eat. The route goes on further through meadows and pine trees to Alto de Vega (1,490m, 4,887ft), with a large recreational area, and an unguarded camp site. Here a good car and caravan park, stone shelters and picnic tables are provided, and a large, excellent tourist map sign. Here too, flourish species of alpine flowers growing in abundance: wood anemones, blue viper's bugloss, with bright blue alpine columbine. From here it is but a short distance to one of the showpieces of the Serranía — the Nacimiento del Cuervo — the source of the river Cuervo. This comes from a resurgence, and pours over 30m (98ft) high limestone ledges festooned with moss, forming shining threads of cascades, with a whole spectrum of colours, at its best in late afternoon. The entire area is surrounded by luxuriant vegetation, and pine forests, providing some interesting exploratory walks.

Returning to Alto de Vega, a road leads along the valley of the Cuervo to a *sierra* village, **Vega de Codorno**, where there is a grotto which is lit for the first 200m (656ft). Back at Alto de Vega again, the route goes on further northwards over a recently paved road through a landscape which becomes progressively rough and barren, and then later somewhat abruptly changes to pinewoods and meadows. After a large stretch of *sierra* the route reaches a T-junction and the village of Masegosa, and turning right continues to the old village of **Beteta**, with a ruined castle. This village, which has some very picturesque old houses with balconies and wooden pillars, overlooks a deep valley or *arroyo*, which has a cultivated flat floor with trees. This leads to the Hoz de Beteta, an extraordinary, rich,

*Nacimiento del Cuervo*

wooded limestone gorge of the Río Guadiela, with deciduous trees, especially limes or linden trees, growing on the floor and the lower slopes, whilst conifers climb up the steep sides. Here too, is a small unlikely power station sited at Fuente de Tilos (fountain of the limes) — the whole area is swathed in rich vegetation, with an immense variety of plants.

The route (now the C202) goes on past a very old isolated house with a plaque stating that Don Quixote stayed there on his passage through the gorge, and at the end of the defile is the small industrial town of Vadillos. From here a road leads up the valley of the Río Cuervo, through another gorge with luxuriant vegetation ending in a huge amphitheatre, and the *real balneario* or royal spa, Solán de Cabras, whose medicinal waters have long been famous. Returning to Vadillos the route continues to **Cañizares**, a pleasant little village. After this the road climbs steadily to the spectacular Puerto de Monsaete (1,156m, 3,792ft), termed the 'Balcony of Cuenca' and then a sharp descent brings the route to the valley of the Río Escabas, and the village of Cañamares.

From here the route divides, and leaves the C202 for CU903 and goes via La Frontera to **Villaconejos de Trabaque**, which has an interesting small artisan works for the manufacture of furniture (tables and chairs) made from osiers. Continue to **Priego**, an ancient town in the osier growing region, which has a factory for making fishing rods. In the church, and on the façades of several houses with coats of arms, an echo of past glory is found by the town's connection with the Battle of Lepanto (1571), and Count Fernando Mendoza, the steward or *majordomo* of Don John of Austria. Priego was very much an area of *hidalgos* (old nobles). From Priego the route takes the C202 once more, and on leaving the town past small tight plantations of osier beds, vines and olives a turning on the left mounts to the old convent of San Miguel de las Victorias, on a terraced site with tremendous views overlooking the gorge of the Río Escabas. A visit is interesting for the baroque statues by Manuel Carmona.

Returning to the C202, the route now goes through an extremely narrow defile of the Río Escabas, called the 'Estrecho de Priego' — the 'Strait of Priego' to Cañamares again, and retracing part of the route along the valley goes on past osier beds, fields of poppies and clover to Fuertescusa. The route then rejoins the valley of the Escabas, which becomes narrow and gorge-like, rising slowly through the *sierras*, with many green lizards running across the road. Here the timber is much exploited, and the route arrives at a wooded, unguarded camp site and refuge in the vicinity of Poyatos. There is a river bridge here, and it is a good place for walks and exploring the district.

On to the Casa Forestal de Tejadillos, where the road forks, and our route now goes southwards into the forested highlands of the Sierra de las Majadas, and off on the left is a road leading to the national park of El Hosquillo. This is a sanctuary for the brown bear, an animal once widespread in Spain, but now confined as a wild creature to very small areas in the Cantabrians and the Pyrenees. Although normally nocturnal, they can sometimes be seen during the day in this very quiet area. Other animals such as deer and mouflons or wild sheep may be observed there also, in what must simply be a paradise for them.

After some kilometres back on the main forest road, with the landscape becoming more open, off the road on the left is Los Callejones de las Majadas or 'the narrow lanes of Majadas'. This is a limestone formation somewhat similar to La Ciudad Encantada, but not nearly so well known, in Spain. As the name implies, it is a series of huge limestone blocks forming narrow paths between walls of rock, and quite spectacular, covering a fairly large area. From here the route reaches the village of Las Majadas, where another forestal road forks on the left. And at this point it offers a choice of three different routes back to Cuenca city.

*Cutting and loading osiers, Priego*

**1** Keep straight on by a very winding wooded road, which gradually descends to Villalba de la Sierra, and then take the CU921 direct to Cuenca.

**2** Take the left hand forestal road, which after a short way divides into two routes: the right hand one, southwards, on a not very well surfaced forest road, leads directly to the gorge of the Júcar, above Uña, then to Cuenca on the CU921.

**3** The left hand route eastwards, although a much longer way, is very interesting as it passes through forests of oaks and conifers, then open limestone country in the heart of the Serranía. This area has much scope for exploring and walking. Then it turns south, and along here the unusual sight of cattle grazing in between pine trees may be seen. At length it emerges by the HEP lake of La Toba, giving good views from a small corniche, and then joins the CU921, and so to Cuenca via La Toba and Uña.

## The Southern Serranía — Cañada del Hoyo and Villar del Humo

For the last two routes, start from Cuenca. Taking the N420 Teruel road over the Puerto de Rocho (1,150m, 3,772ft), then turning left to **Cañada del Hoyo.** Near here are further *torcas* (solution depressions), but they are different, for of the seven, five have been converted into lakes, scattered amongst the pinewoods — an unusual, but fine sight. The final route is of a rather different nature. Since the discovery of the Altamira cave paintings in Santander province in 1879, there had been no further discoveries of note, but in recent years several have been investigated. For example Villacantal (see Aragonese Pyrenees chapter), as well as very recently in Cuenca, a province full of natural caves and isolated rock formations. After returning to the N420, the route continues to the village of Carboneras de Guadazaón, then turns right on the CU501 to Cardenete, parallel with the railway line. Then left at the village on a winding route through pinewoods to Villar del Humo.

Some distance from here is 'La Peña del Escrito' (The Rock of Writing), which is a national monument. Here is 'La Peña del Toro' (Bull's Rock) and others, which are palaeolithic rock paintings in red of bison, boars, bulls, horses and archers.

# Further Information
## —— The Serranía de Cuenca ——

## Activities

### Cuenca City
*Fiestas:* San Mateo, mid-September, and 24, 25, and 31 December.
*Semana Santa* (Holy Week). Processions from Palm Sunday to Easter Sunday. 'Camino del Cavario' (Road to Calvary), early on Good Friday, is outstanding, with crowds mocking Christ, trumpets and drums.

## Places of Interest

### Cuenca City

### Cathedral
Treasure (El Tesoro)
Open: daily 9am-1.30pm and 4.30-7.30pm summer. Winter to 6.30pm.

### Diocésan Museum
Open: Tuesday to Friday 11am-

2pm and 4-6pm, Saturdays 11am-2pm and 4-8pm; Sundays 11am-2.30pm. Closed Mondays.

### Casas Colgadas (Museum of Abstract Art))
Open: as for Diocésan Museum, except Sundays closes at 2pm. But also closed on: 1 January, Maundy Thursday, Good Friday, and Fiesta de San Mateo in mid-September and 24, 25 and 31 December.

### Cuenca Museum (Archaeological and Bellas Artes)
Open: Tuesdays-Saturdays 10am-2pm and 4-7pm. Sundays and holidays: 10am-2pm. Closed Tuesdays.

### Casa-Museo Zabala
Open: Saturdays 5-7pm, Sundays 11am-1pm. Free admission.

## The Serranía

**Ciudad Encantada**
Open: all day.

**Convent of San Miguel de las Victorias (Priego)**
To visit, ask the caretaker.

## Transport

**Rail**
RENFE station
☎ 22 07 20
Stations at Palancares (Las Torcas) and Cañada del Hoyo

**Buses**
There are a number of bus companies, but hardly anything through the Serranía.

To Cañete by Empresa La Rapida
Avenida República Argentina 13
☎ 22 27 51

To Priego by Empresa Alsina
Avenida Reyes Católicos 9
☎ 22 04 96

To Beteta by Empresa Campi SA
Calle Cayo Concersa 4
☎ 22 14 65

## Tourist Information Offices

**Beteta**
Ayuntamiento
1 Plaza Mayor
☎ 31 80 01

**Canete**
Ayuntamiento
2 San Julian
☎ 34 60 01

**Cuenca City**
Corner of Calle Fermin Caballero and Calle Dalmacio Gardía Izcara
8, 1st floor
☎ 22 22 31
Difficult to park (one way street), approach on foot.

**Priego**
Ayuntamiento
1 Plaza Generalisimo
☎ 31 01 01

**Tragacete**
Ayuntamiento
1 Trinquete
☎ 28 90 02

**Uña**
Ayuntamiento Secretaria
1 Plaza Constitucion
☎ 28 13 01

# 5 • The Ebro Crescent

This is not a region, but a series of places and remote areas linked by the common thread of the basin of the river Ebro and its tributaries — Spain's greatest and most powerful river — rising in the Cantabrian mountains, then receiving much water from the Pyrenees, and finally flowing via a delta in to the Mediterranean.

This 'crescent' contains a large part of the old kingdom of Aragón, some territory fought over savagely in the Civil War, modern HEP works, and places rarely visited by people from outside Spain.

The nature of the landscape shows variation and contrast from the vines and olive groves on the clay hills of the Iberian mountains fringing the basin, through the broad trough of the Ebro with its terraces, the green irrigated *huerta*, and the desert of Los Monegros. Then the lower Ebro cuts through the massif of the Catalan mountains to reach the fertile delta, and flow into the Mediterranean Sea. The towns and villages of the crescent show differences in site, situation, and purpose as well.

Begin with the ancient town of Calatayud on the Río Jalón, then to the equally ancient thermal baths of Alhama, and a diversion southwards to the village of Nuévalos, which has the superb water gardens of the Monasterio de la Piedra, next to the old walled town of Daroca. Then, leaving the hills for the Ebro terraces and Cariñena, famous for its vineyards, continue to the Civil War ravaged ruins of Belchite, and Caspe on the Ebro itself, with its HEP works. Now northwards to Los Monegros, almost a desert, with its salt outcrops, and back to the new town of Mequinenza, with its restored castle, and ancient abandoned town below it at the confluence of the Ebro and Segre rivers, and a curiously unknown area southwards. On to Alcañiz, famous for its olive groves and sweets made of almonds, and a group of villages centered around Hijar which celebrate Holy Week (Semana Santa) in an unusual fashion with drums. The rugged terrain of Teruel province has now been reached, the scene of extremely fierce and bloody fighting in the battle of the Ebro in July

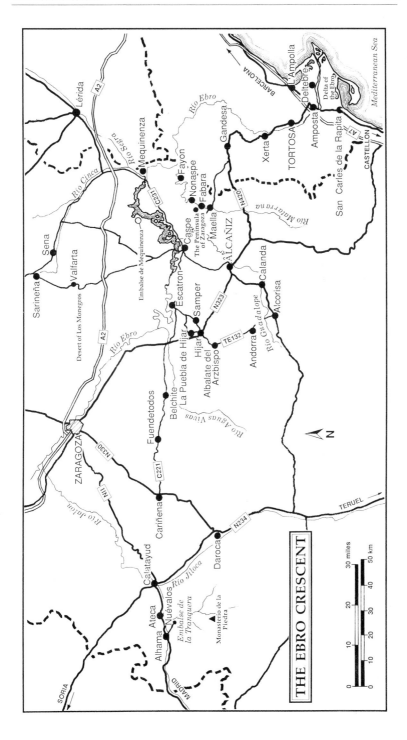

THE EBRO CRESCENT

1938. Then to Gandesa, in the Catalan province of Tarragona, and through the gorge section of the river by the village of Xerta to the cathedral city of Tortosa on its banks, then Amposta, a bridge town, and so to the delta. Here is the town of Deltebre, and the Natural Park, with the old royal port of San Carlos de Rapita, now rejuvenated, on the south side.

The attractions of this crescent are in its variety of places and small regions, with the remoteness and unvisited aspect of some of them. Most are not in the itinerary of the average visitor to Spain, and so they demand a rather different approach to completely understand their points of interest, which might appear at first sight to be slightly obscure. This of course, gives great scope for exploration of each place and area, offering sharp contrasts like the water gardens of the Monasterio de la Piedra, with the ruins of Belchite, not to mention being in a real European desert like Los Monegros. Further downstream is the gorge of the Ebro, which is very different from the fertile delta, the greatest area of wetland in Catalonia, where the wildlife bears comparison with the Camargue (Rhône delta), and Coto Doñana (Guadalquivir marshes).

The climate of the Ebro crescent is basically that of the river Ebro basin or depression, but there are differences in the climates of the hills of the Iberian mountains or Cordillera, Teruel, and again in the gorge and delta of areas of the river Ebro.

*The Ebro Basin or Depression*
This climate is extremely continental and very dry, with only 300mm (12in) of rain per year — often even less in Los Monegros. However, it is very sunny, with fairly long and hot summers (25-31 °C/77-88 °F), but winters can be cold (3 °C/37 °F), and if there is such a thing as a wet month, it might be May, with 45-50mm (1.8-2in) of rain. The northwest winds in the winter, the '*Cierzo*', sometimes bring a cold mist over the river's course.

*Fringing Iberian Sierras*
Less warm in summer, slightly more rain (500mm/20in), winters colder, and slightly less sunny — a climate rather like Soria.

*Teruel Province*
Generally similar to the Ebro Depression, but occasionally very cold in the winter, with frosts.

*Tortosa and the Delta of the Ebro*
Hot summers (30 °C/86 °F), warm damp autumns (September

*Calatayud*

61mm/2.4in rain), mild winters (11°C/52°F), and warm springs. Mediterranean maritime climate.

## Travelling to the Area

### By Road
From Zaragoza airport to Calatayud, direct by NII (Madrid road) 87km (54 miles).
From Madrid (Barajas) airport direct (NII) to Calatayud 192km (119 miles).
From Barcelona (Prat) airport to Tortosa and Delta, *autopista* A2 direct. 160km (99 miles).

### By Rail
Zaragoza (El Portillo) direct to Calatayud 96km (60 miles). 54min.
Madrid (Atocha) direct to Calatayud 242km (150 miles). 2hrs 31min.
Barcelona (Sants) to/from Tortosa 168km (104 miles) 1hr 44min.

## Calatayud, Alhama and the Monasterio de Piedra

**Calatayud** is a more interesting town than it looks, surrounded by rather arid hills in the valley of the Río Jalón. Although the name of the town is Arabic in origin — Kalat Ayoub — a little to the east are the remains of the Roman city of *Bilbilis,* on the imperial highway that ran from Zaragoza to Mérida. Here the famous writer, Martial, known for his witty epigrams, was born in AD43. Moreover, Calatayud has two elegant Moorish bell towers which are prominent in the skyline of the town. The first is that of the collegiate church of Santa Maria, octagonal in shape, and one of the best in the Moorish region of Aragón. With its fine geometrical designs it is typical of the Moorish-influenced architecture of Aragón in the sixteenth century. In complete contrast is the Renaissance main doorway, as is the interior of seventeenth-century baroque. The other fine bell tower rises from San Andrés church. This is a town where one may eat well: fresh vegetables from the nearby *huertas*, meat with a sauce of peppers and tomatoes (*en chilindrón*), eggs cooked with asparagus, garlic and parsley, and marzipan chestnuts are typical products of Aragonese cooking.

Fourteen kilometres (9 miles) upstream along the valley on the Madrid road, **Ateca** is reached. This seems to be the image of what a medieval village should look like, for it is strung round a hill, which culminates in the parish church of Santa Maria, the remains of a castle, and a clock tower. The Casa Consistatorial is also worth looking at, with its wide arched porch.

Another 14km (9 miles) along the road, brings the traveller to the ancient and picturesque small town of **Alhama de Aragón** on the banks of the Río Jalón, where its thermal waters at 35 °C (95 °F) are transparent, colourless and odourless, and come forth from Cretaceous rocks. They were known to the Romans as *Aquae Bilbilitanae,* from their city a few miles away, and are beneficial for a long list of maladies, among which rheumatism is prominent.

From here, leave the main road by the Z410 side road, and by a corniche alongside the HEP lake of Tranquera, which contrasts with the dry red soil of the area. Then the village of **Nuévalos** comes in to view with its site, with a commanding panorama of the Piedra valley and the lake. Along the road are the remains of a monastery, with a large tower set in a rough stone wall, known as 'El Torre del Homenaje', where traditionally monks who had committed a fault were placed, along with others living within the monastery walls. Further on is a magnificent gateway in a rather ruinous state, still with statues and armorial bearings carved above the entrance. But inside is a revelation. By a quirk of nature the arid plateau, with little vegetation, hides a green and luxuriant oasis, fed and maintained by the Río Piedra. This tranquil site was seen by the Cistercian monks, and in 1194 they built their monastery here, as they had done in similar

*Waterfalls at Monasterio de Piedra*

tranquil valleys all over Europe since their foundation in 1098 at
*Cistercium* or Citeaux, a village near Dijon. The monastery flourished
amid water and verdant tranquility until 1835, when it was disestab-
lished and began to fall into ruin. The various arms of the Río Piedra
form many waterfalls and cascades, and in the later nineteenth
century the proprietor, Don Federico Muntadas, improved a tangled
forest growth into a superb water park and garden. Paths, steps,
bridges and tunnels are laid out, and the visitor can take different

routes guided by red or blue arrows. The impressive waterfall of the 'Cola de Caballo' (horse's tail), which falls 53m (174ft) has a *mirador* or lookout at the top, from where it is possible to go down behind the fall to the Iris grotto, and see the plunging waters close to, through a hole in the rock. The numerous cascades and falls have names like Cascada Iris (rainbow), from the reflection of late afternoon sun; and Cascada Fresno (ash tree). The terrain being limestone, is very suitable for ash trees, if there is enough moisture. The intermingling of waterfalls, trees and plants is of extraordinary harmony and can hardly be equalled in Europe. More fanciful are the Baño de Diana, and Cascada Caprichiosa, but the lake, Lago de Espejo (mirror lake) at the foot of the towering red cliffs with its clear waters full of fish is a sight for much contemplation. The route finishes with a visit to the monastery ruins and restored buildings, consisting of the kitchen with its many chimneys, the refectory and the cloisters. After leaving the monastery the route goes back to Calatayud on the C202, where there is a viewpoint on the left over the valley and an HEP lake not far from Nuévalos. At Calatayud the route takes the main N234 south-eastwards over the Puerto de Villafeliche to Daroca.

## Daroca, Cariñena and Belchite

**Daroca** lies just south of where two main roads meet (N234/N330), and from the main road itself, the town is almost hidden in a basin between pine covered hills.

Around the crests of these enclosing hills are the town's encircling walls, more than 2km (1$^1$/$_4$ miles) long, now broken and crumbling in places, but solidly maintained until the sixteenth century. There were originally many towers and turrets, and two fortified gates remain: Puerta Alta (upper) and Puerta Baja (lower) or the west gate, which still has the shield of Charles V upon it. From above the view is of a myriad of reddish roofs and many church or bell towers pointing upwards producing, with the reddish soil round about, a kind of terracotta landscape.

In the Middle Ages Daroca had a great reputation for craftsmen, and their work is still to be seen in the town, which contains some fine buildings. Pride of place is given to the Colegiata Santa Maria, in the Plaza de España, built in medieval times, but transformed in the fifteenth and sixteenth centuries. By the side of the bell tower is a large flamboyant Gothic doorway, and inside the church this Gothic style continues with the nave, but added to it are Renaissance ideas in the form of a cupola in the transept. The side chapels contain some

*Daroca*

fine decorative work, notably *azulejos* (blue tiles), made locally and
displayed on the altar pieces. One of these (fifteenth century) is of
particularly fine multi-coloured alabaster, with careful detail, of
English craftsmanship. As already noted, the connection between
medieval Spain and England was closer, in spite of distance and
difficult communications, than is often realised. This is a very fine
building, and well worth spending some time seeing. Two other
churches of merit are San Miguel and Santo Domingo, each in their
own small plazas. The first should be seen for its twelfth-century
door, and both for their bell towers. There is also plenty to see just
wandering around the narrow alleys: the houses with their dormer
windows, the many unexpected small plazas, and then by walking
the length of the Calle Mayor, which runs from the Puerta Alta to the
Puerta Baja, where nearby in the Avenida del Carmen is another fine
tower. Daroca also has a curious legend of the Holy Cloth, which
arose in 1239 following an attack by the Moors on a Christian camp
during the celebration of Mass. The chalice and paten were subsequently hidden, but on retrieving them, the cloth which they were
wrapped in was found to have an imprint of blood. Three towns

claimed the precious relic: Calatayud, Daroca and Teruel. The Holy
Cloth was therefore put on a mule, which was set free, and tradition
has it that the mule headed for Daroca, and died crossing the Puerta
Baja.

On leaving Daroca the route takes the main N330 road on the
right, continues past the village of Mainar, turns left onto the Z133
side road over the Puerto de Mainar (990m, 3,247ft) to Codos, and
then turns right on to the C221, to cross the scenic Sierra de Algairén
by the Puerto de Aguarón (1,048m, 3,437ft) where, on descending the
eastern slopes, the vineyards of Cariñena begin. Past the shrine on
the left of Nuestra Señora de las Viñas, and the village of Aguarón to
Cariñena itself. Cariñena is a pleasant little wine town full of *bodegas*
(wine cellars), and produces a white wine (yellow in colour), Monte
Duray, which can be thoroughly recommended. The tall, slim elegant tower of its medieval parish church looks out over the surrounding vineyards, which have fruit and almond trees amongst
them. The vines extend in all directions along the roads, and the route
eastwards, the C221, is no exception, up on the flat clay hills bordering the Ebro valley. After some kilometres of vines, a pine forest is
reached with the village of Villanueva de Huerva, where on the right
the Huerva valley leads to Tosos and Aguilón, two villages famous
for wine. The route continues to the isolated medieval village of
**Fuendetodos**, where in a humble house the great painter, Goya, was
born in 1746. The house, which can be visited, is much as it was in his
childhood, a kitchen and living room with rustic farmhouse chairs.

Beyond Fuendetodos the road, after a wide bend, passes by a
scrubby wooded hill on the right, with a most striking isolated
building. It looks Byzantine, with its cluster of five turrets, and for a
moment, aided by the spacious landscape, one could imagine oneself
in old Russia. In reality it is the large shrine of Nuestra Señora del
Pueyo in a medieval Aragonese style. A little further on, and the
ruins of **Belchite** are reached. A turning on the left leads to the new
settlement, and ahead is the extensive relic of the Civil War, including the convents, churches and buildings left just as they were after
the battle in 1938. Belchite was a town of 4,500 people, with very fine
mudéjar architecture. Accounts of the battle are obscure, but the
following is an eye-witness account by an inhabitant: The Río Aguas
Vivas formed a small barrier to the east, with the Nationalist forces
in an evacuated seminary. Republican batteries on a nearby hill
shelled the town, including the parish church, where nuns were
looking after the wounded. The Republicans then shelled the other
church — turned into a dance-hall by the Republican Government in

peace time — and the battle was over, a Republican victory.

The route goes on to the N232, and turns left to Azaila. Before turning left to the C221 again, look southwards across the Meseta: in spring, it is a colour contrast of green growing corn, terracotta soil, blue sky and white clouds. Rejoin the C221, and take it to Escatron, and the river Ebro in its wide terraced valley. At **Escatron** it is possible to cross the river, and see a ruined monastery — Monasterio de Rueda. The C221 road now continues to Chiprana, where the large HEP lake Embalse de Caspe begins, and soon the town of Caspe is reached.

## Caspe, Los Monegros, Mequinenza and Hijar

The town of Caspe is at the end of one HEP scheme, and the beginning of the next, that is the enormous lake created from the river Ebro, and now called El Mar de Aragón (Embalse de Mequinenza). However, Caspe is a good base for several excursions in interesting and unusual landscapes. The town itself has some good buildings, including the church, the castle, and the Casa Barberán y Consistatorial (municipal council).

### Los Monegros

This route takes the C230 northwards from the town, crossing the Ebro by a large dam, then through the rather dry looking landscape on the left bank followed by woodland as the road climbs towards Bujaroz on the main Lérida-Zaragoza highway NII. From here a side road (HU832) is taken — the route has crossed into the province of Huesca — to the semi-desert of Los Monegros, with low hills, tufted plants, and even the odd isolated tree. At first sight one might say that some other parts of Spain look like this, but the marked feature of the climate here is winter dryness. The two driest months of the year are January and February, which are even drier than July and August with their shimmering heat. Then comes the village of Valfart, and from here onwards is a vast space northwards and eastwards with virtually no roads, tracks and habitations, but there is sparse vegetation, and even some dry farming and cultivated fields. For a canal runs right into the centre of the region, fed not from the Ebro, but from far north (70-80km, 40-50 miles away) from the Embalse de Sotonera, which is fed in turn by the Río Gállego from the Pyrenees, although there is not always water in it.

In recent years there have been international trials for four-wheel drive vehicles held here, something after the style of the great Cali-

fornian variety in the USA — 1,000km (620 miles) non-stop without
pauses or servicing, for as the Aragonese say: *'En Los Monegros no hay
puertas'* ('In the Monegros there are no gates'). For a more tranquil
experience it is a pleasure to camp here in summer, with a starry sky
overhead, and the climate during spring and autumn can be very
pleasant, with abundant sunshine. But the climatic downturn in
Europe has had its repercussions in Spain too. Apart from the fearful
heat in 1987 when absolute maximum temperature records standing
for many years were broken, there was torrential rain in this region
in November 1982, and the rivers Segre and Cinca to the east burst
their banks with disastrous results.

The route continues northwards to Sariñena after crossing the
Canal de Monegros. Here is contrast indeed, for turning right on to
the C1310 one follows the *huerta* of the Alcanadre valley, down past
the hamlet of **Sena** where a track on the right leads to the ruins of the
Sigena monastery on the banks of the river itself. At length following
the river, a right turn is taken on to the HU860 southwards, and after
leaving irrigated fertility, Los Monegros is crossed once more to
reach the NII at Candasnos. Here the route is by the HU710, and after
some distance the traveller will be surprised by the landscape, for
although in a wild dry area, its appearance is at times quite green,
with pasture and some woodland. The grass covered white limestone hills may remind visitors of the extreme north of Scotland, or
even perhaps chalk scenery in France. The road winds through dry
valleys, reaches the C230, and then goes on to Caspe.

## Mequinenza and the Peninsula of Eastern Zaragoza
From Caspe this route takes a new road, the C231, which passes
through a landscape surprisingly interesting for its contrasts, and
which was very difficult of access before. The first part is quite wild
and rocky terrain along the ravines and gorges of the bordering hills
close to the wide sinuous waters of the Ebro 'lake', but is unusual to
see the many barley and wheatfields amongst the rocks. The road
then passes near a wide open stretch of water and cuts across an
enormous bend of the river through wild and hilly country to eventually pass near a huge dam, later crossing the river to reach
Mequinenza.

**Mequinenza** is very old and very new. It is strategically sited at
a very important place — the confluence of the Ebro and the combined waters of the Pyrenean rivers Cinca, Segre, Nogueras Ribagorzana and Pallaresa. So it is not surprising that a large castle was
built by the Moors 130m (426ft) above the town on the huge tabular

hill that borders the river here. The town below was of ancient origin, probably Roman *Octogessa*, then *Hictosa* of the Visigoths, and later either from a Berber tribe *Miknassa* or Greek origin *Mikununcia* to Mequinenza! Both town and castle have suffered the vicissitudes of time and history. In 1149 it was conquered by Alfonso II of Aragón, the castle becoming a baronial residence, then later a palace of the Marquis of Aytona (sixteenth century). After this it was a fort on the frontier between Aragón and Catalonia and used by the Spanish army, then it suffered attack by the French in the Peninsular War, and after a siege surrendered (Mequinenza appears as a battle honour on the Arc de Triomphe in Paris). It held out against the Carlists, and saw active service during the Civil War in the battle of the Ebro. Ultimately it was restored by the state HEP company ENHER about 1950. Today it is a fine sight, surrounded by pine and cypress trees in its superb position, and can be visited at certain times. Mequinenza itself was an important river port for grain and coal in barges until a few decades past. Now there is a complete metamorphosis, as the town has been abandoned, and a new one built on the banks of the Río Segre. There is an interesting innovation here in that the stretch of water at the actual confluence is termed 'campo de regatas', evidently where river events are held.

From here, return to Caspe by a little known route called the Peninsula of Eastern Zaragoza. Take the Z720 to the village of Fayón, where there is a new town and a hermitage, N.S. del Pilar, in a district of olive groves. Then return to the Z720, and continue to Nonaspe, at the confluence of the Ríos Matarraña and Algas in a verdant *vega* (fertile plain) contrasting with the high, bare and scrubby riverside hills. Here is an eighteenth-century classical style hermitage, La Virgen de dos Aguas, set in a paradise of vegetation, which has briar patches, rushes, a hundred cypresses forming a 'walk', a dozen gigantic pines and silence. The Moorish castle is being rehabilitated, and the church is worth seeing.

Onwards now to Fabara, a place that has one of the best and least known Roman buildngs, the first-century mausoleum, now a national monument. Here also is the granary or cornloft of the Princess of Belmonte, a fine building with arcades, being converted to the Casa Consistatorial. The church here is strange, being late Gothic, restored eighty years ago, and appears to have crenellation, but is a noble building all the same. Finally the route Z720, along the valley of the Río Matarraña, reaches the town of **Maella**, which has much to show. The *ayuntamiento* is an unusual, but fine piece of architecture. It is in two parts, the lower being the ancient palace of the

Counts of Aranda (fifteenth century), fortified and battlemented over one of the gates to the medieval city, and originally part of the outer wall. This building also had battlemented towers, and from between these a very fine seventeenth-century clock tower arose, forming the upper part. This has ornamental friezes of blue tiles below the cornices, the tower itself being quadrangular, then octagonal, and finally circular, making the entire structure harmonious visually. The old castle and the walls too, are well worth a good walk round.

Now join the C221 to Caspe. Although the traveller may have noticed olive groves in this region, the terrible frosts of 1970 forced many of them to be replaced, near Caspe with maize and alfalfa (lucerne grass), and with peach trees at Nonaspe, using modern techniques of irrigation.

### The Route of the Drums: Híjar to Alcañiz

In many parts of Spain the church and festive calendar reaches its climax in *Semana Santa* (Holy Week), and in Baja Aragón and Teruel it is celebrated in a singular manner, the origin of which is obscure. Briefly it consists of processions, parades (*tamborradas*), and concourses of mass drum beating in a small region, with as many as a total of 10,000 drums taking part. The people wear black costumes with hoods. It began in the late seventeenth century, but the origin is thought to be from parishioners stamping their feet on the church benches in the final office of the darkness of Good Friday, symbolising the earthquake before the crucifixion of Christ.

The region is rough quadrilateral, based on the small town of Híjar in Teruel province, and the route leaves Caspe by the C221 and after Escatron takes the Z703/TE703 to La Puebla de Híjar, then retracing to meet the TE702 to Samper de Calanda, and then to Híjar. From here the route follows the valley of the Río Martin (TE110) via the villages of Urrea de Gaén, then Albalate del Arzobispo, keeping left on the TE132 to the small town of Andorra, then TE130 to the town of **Alcorisa**. Here there is a procession on Palm Sunday, and also an enactment of the Passion on Good Friday afternoon. From Alcorisa the main road, N420, is taken to **Calanda**, the birthplace of Luis Buñel, the film producer, who made the film *Nazarín* using drums for a background, as did the producer Carlos Saura, who included '*tamborradas*' in his famous film *Pepperment Frappé*. Here they wear purple and black costumes. From Calanda the route goes to Alcañiz, a town described in the next section of the 'crescent'.

*El Tormo Alto, La Ciudad Encantada, the Serranía de Cuenca*

*Hoz de Huécar, city of Cuenca, the Serranía de Cuenca*

# Alcañiz to the Lower Ebro, Tortosa and Amposta

## Alcañiz

Here is a prosperous town in the midst of fertile *huertas* and olive groves on the banks of the Río Guadalope, in Teruel province. The most outstanding building is the baroque collegiate church of Santa Maria la Mayor with its great door. Inside, the spaciousness of the building is remarkable, as is the height of the columns capped by projecting cornices. Almost as impressive, sited on a flat hill above the town is the castle (twelfth century), which was the seat in Aragón of the religious and military Order of Calatrava (New Castile), founded in 1158 for defence against the Moors. But much of it is eighteenth-century reconstruction, with vestiges of earlier times, including thirteenth-century murals, an equilateral arched arcade, a Gothic chapel, and now refurbished as a state *parador*. The real glory of the town, however, is the magnificent Plaza España, with a high Gothic gallery (*lonja*), and the façade of the Renaissance *ayuntamiento*. Here some of the activity of *Semana Santa* takes place, the penitents in their tall white hoods and scarlet cloaks. In Alcañiz, there are processions throughout the week, including those with drums. The town is famous for its marzipan sweets, but much of its prosperity is based upon an old and very important high quality soap industry. The final thing to see here is an impressive waterfall on the Río Guadalope.

From Alcañiz the route continues through well cultivated countryside on the N420. After the olive groves the landscape becomes wilder as one crosses into the Catalan province of Tarragona. This is the terrain of the terrible and bloody battle of the Ebro in July 1938, when the Republicans attempted to stop the Nationalists driving towards Valencia. They crossed the river at Tortosa, but could not advance very far — it was almost a repetition of the trench warfare of 1914-18. Then the Republicans threw men in recklessly, leaving 150,000 dead before finally being repulsed by the Nationalists. Some 6km (4 miles) west of Gandesa is a viewpoint from where the Nationalists directed the battle, with a memorial and a shrine, which has unfortunately been defaced and desecrated, but the view remains. The route continues through **Gandesa**, a small town set in a fertile region of vines, fruit and olives, and then strikes southwards (C221/N230) to meet the Ebro at the village of Xerta. Here the river flows through a fine gorge cut through the softer secondary rocks of the Catalan mountains. The route, now by the river, is very picturesque, but the road is extremely winding until the ancient city of Tortosa is reached. The contrast here between the limey soil of the hills, and the intense greenness of the valley *huerta* is quite extraordinary. The soil on the hills, retained by stone walls, produces olives, but down below protected from the sea winds by cypress trees, flourish oranges, peaches, maize and vegetables. **Tortosa** was originally Roman, then Visigothic, later captured by the Moors in 714, but reconquered by Ramón Berenger IV, the Aragonese king of the House of Barcelona. It was important as it guarded the only bridge in the region. Now it is a Catalan city, its cathedral having an unfinished baroque façade which hides the pure Gothic style of construction that took 200 years to complete between 1347-1547. Inside, the Catalan style appears rather plain and sober, but one of the side chapels has a large fourteenth-century triptych of carved wood describing the life of Christ. Outside, adjoining the cathedral, is the Bishop's Palace, with a very pleasant large fourteenth-century patio, and a straight staircase alongside an arcaded gallery with slender columns.

From Tortosa there is a choice of routes down the river Ebro. The right bank is the more pleasant route leading to Amposta, with its three bridges in the vicinity of the town. The first is a concrete motorway bridge, carrying the *autopista* A7 to Valencia; the next, leading to the town itself, is a slender, elegant suspension bridge, built 1915-19 and rebuilt after the Civil War; and the third carries the main N340 Barcelona-Valencia highway, built to replace the second, and to bypass the town.

**Amposta**, also a Roman city, which vanished after the second Punic War (218-201BC), was the headquarters of the Knights Hospitaller of Aragón in 1154, which organised the economic life of the Ebro delta. The ruined castle was abandoned as early as 1466 by John II (of Aragón) because of the 'innumerable throng of vipers and wolves', and then the city suffered constant attacks by the Barbary pirates. Now it has the Montsià Museum of Natural History, rice cultivation and early settlement; also an interesting market. However, by far the most attractive place is the suspension bridge itself, from which one can have good views, upstream of the mountains, and downstream a panorama of the delta. This is the most fascinating natural feature, and also the most interesting, intense, and controlled man-made development of the region.

## The Delta of the Ebro

The deltas of the great Mediterranean rivers are regions of supreme value for three main reasons: firstly, the richness of agricultural

*The Río Ebro at the Xerta gorge*

production; secondly, the wildlife found there; and thirdly, the preservation of the unaltered coastal countryside. It is true that the Mediterranean coastal lands, have been subjected to much alteration over thousands of years of human activity, but it is only since the

1950s that they have had such intense occupation as to cause large areas to be almost completely spoiled, and natural features almost submerged under a flood of concrete and tarmac. Therefore, it is only in the deltas that there are large areas of dunes, lagoons and saltings covered with their natural vegetation. These areas are also the last refuge of a special fauna, and need to be conserved to keep the correct environment for migrant birds. The Ebro delta is not only a unique landscape in Catalonia, but in all Spain, as only the marshes of the Guadalquivir approach it in similarity, and they are of a different type, with Atlantic climatic conditions.

The origin of the delta goes back some thousands of years, when the Catalonian coastline was similar to what it is today, but the level of the sea was much lower. The Ebro then forced a passage to the sea from what was a lake region in the Iberian depression, but the real development of the delta began with the rise in sea level after the end of the last glacial period. Then followed two stable stages, when the delta was built up, first in the late Old Stone Age, and the second in the New Stone Age, when the sea was about 5m (16ft) below its present level. But its present appearance only began some 2,500 years ago (at the beginning of Iberian civilisation). The level has remained unchanged, but the shape has altered considerably. In the fifteenth century, the river had several mouths. In recent times (1937), heavy floods caused the Ebro to open a new outlet further north, from which it has never returned to the original eastern mouth. Since 1946 the eastern side has been eroding, and the western side filling up. Until 1940, 20 million tons of silt were carried down the river annually, but now most of it is deposited in the calm water above the HEP and irrigation dams, and only about 3 million reach the delta.

The delta climate is humid and mild, with dry gusty north-westerly winds in the winter blowing aross the rice fields and dry reeds making it rather desolate. During the remainder of the year, the winds most frequent are 'sea breezes', caused by warm land and a cooler sea. The rain-bearing wind is the *levanter* (east wind) often chilly. A cold north wind (*tramontana*) blows sometimes also, but it is uncommon. Rainfall is very variable, on average about 5-600mm (20-4in), but it can be halved or doubled in some years. At present it is rather dry. Temperatures are equable for Spain: January minimum 10°C (50°F), August maximum 27°C (80°F). Frosts are rare.

The flora is specialised, being found in plant communities like the salt marshes, and strangely, caused local quarrels as they are rich in soda, and were used for making soap and glass for centuries. The

*An old house in the Ebro delta*

dunes rise above the marshes, and have some colourful plants like sea daffodils, yellow harrow and some rare plants not generally found in Spain. The reed beds contain sedge, reedmace and large bindweed with huge white flowers, and the river banks have a woodland of white poplars high up, and willow lower down. Other trees are alder, ash, elm, plane and eucalyptus. A species of honey-suckle is found with yellow loosestrife, and where the influence of the sea is stronger, the woods thin out with tamarisks and oleander. The rice fields provide a special vegetation of pondweed, bladder-wort and water lilies — which can sometimes cause problems if they invade the irrigation canals.

The fauna has such a wide range of habitats, that only a brief mention can be made here. Leeches were so common that they were exported in their thousands annually. There are mosquitos of course, but fewer now through spraying. Malaria had been endemic here earlier. Shellfish are common, like cockles, prawns, crayfish and the American river crab. Amongst the reptiles and amphibians are slow-worms, montpellier snakes, grass and water snakes, marsh frog, painted frog and toads — all of which are less common now further north in Europe. Many species of lizards are seen scampering about the beaches. Fish are abundant, but some species such as sturgeon and lampreys have declined, while others are new arrivals, like river pike and black bass, due to the varying salinity of the many channels, ponds and outlets, but mullet, carp, sea bass and eels are very common. The larger mammals have disappeared, but wild boar and badgers are seen occasionally, and only rabbits, foxes, weasels, brown rats, voles and shrews are common, with some otters and hedgehogs.

But the glory of the wildlife in the delta are the clouds of birds of many species. Not only is it the home and breeding ground of aquatic birds, ducks, gulls and landbirds, but it is an essential stop-off on the flight paths of the migratory birds. These are best seen in the autumn, especially in October and November. Some species of interest are northern shoveler, Eurasian wigeon and thousands of mallard. The red-crested pochard nests here — a threatened species, except in Iberia. Waders like sandpipers, plovers, snipe, curlews, oyster catchers, and avocets are common in the winter. Colourful birds of the heron family, grey and purple are often seen, and a typical delta sight are the cattle egrets feeding in the rice fields. Small nesting birds live here too, like flycatchers, wrens, and species one would expect to find: reed buntings, and warblers with their suspended nests and loud song. Swallows in May are everywhere — evidence of the many insects. Larks and sparrows are here in large numbers, unfortunately hardly helping the delta farmers. As for birdwatching in the delta, many species are relatively tame, and providing the watcher keeps still, easy to identify.

Until relatively recently the population of the area was not stable: some seasonal sheep herding, fishing, hunting, and the extraction of salt and soda seem to have been the main uses of the delta. Then, out of the many attempts to make the Ebro navigable, with the creation of a ship canal and the new port of San Carles de la Ràpita, in 1780 came the economic revolution of rice growing in the nineteenth century, and subsequent creation of new villages, and expansion of settlements around the old farmhouses. Today nearly 50,000 people live and work in the delta, or on the edge of it.

In order to reconcile agriculture, fishing, wildlife and tourism (mainly to seaside towns and beaches), and it seems also, due to local popular interest, the Catalonian Government (Generalitat) created the Ebro Delta Natural Park in 1983. It consists mainly of a seaward belt, including special protected areas of enclosed water, Buda island and the mouth of the Ebro. Outside this area, south of the Ebro are the national game reserves, and on Punta de la Banya, a national game sanctuary.

## Amposta — Sant Carles — Sant Jaume — Amposta
### (southern or right-side of delta)

This route leaves Amposta by the N340 road which runs parallel to the old navigation canal (Canalet Marítim). On the way one passes L'Enclusa farm, where there are old locks that were used for regulating the water level and working a mill. Nearby is the old Forgeron farm, which was fortified against the Barbary pirates, with some of the first oak trees planted in the delta. Then the small, lively, pleasant port of **Sant Carles de la Ràpita** is reached. The port, planned by Charles III and laid out in a grid iron pattern, never succeeded, but it is important for fishing, and it is interesting to see the fish auction at about 6pm. This is reflected in the number of fish restaurants like the unpretentious Bar Gavilan in the nice little Plaza España, which serves delicious small shellfish. If one climbs up to the Sagrat Cor (Cerro de la Guardiola, 116m, 380ft) past the municipal stadium at the back of the town, there is a fine view over the delta. The route goes now to **Poblenou** (Villa Franco del Delta) past smallholdings to the L'Encanyissada lagoon by a bridge, where on the left is a game reserve, and one can see the traditional *pantena* method of fishing, with a long elaborate platform of nets. Poblenou was a new peasant settlement built in 1947, on the lines of the 'Badajoz Plan', with low white houses, bordered with palms and oleanders. Then keeping on past the La Tancada lagoon on the left (yet another game reserve), stretching away across the bay is the *tombolo* of El Trabucador (neck of sand), with a fine beach leading to the game sanctuary of Punta de la Banya.

This spot faces the open sea, soon Eucalyptus is reached, and from here is a walk to Els Muntells, a new village. Onward to the delta town of **Sant Jaume d'Enveja**, where maize fields are ploughed by mules, which, though expensive, are thought to be cheaper and better than a tractors. It seems that about 100 are left in the delta. Frogs can be heard everywhere, and the town is full of bicycles at the end of the school day — as it is so flat, it is the best way of getting about. The Casal de Sant Jaume is worth a visit, with a bar and a museum. Along the bank are three public ferries across the Ebro to Deltebre, and one can get a view of Gràcia island whilst crossing the river.

From Sant Jaume the route follows the river road to the old village of Balada with its huge oleander. From Balada the road is taken back to Amposta between the river and canal, and here on the highest land in the delta are fruit orchards and fields of artichokes.

**L'Aldea — Deltebre — mouth of the Ebro — Camarles —
L'Ampolla (northern or left side of the delta)**
From Amposta the N340 is taken to the old town of **L'Aldea**, an area
of intense and careful cultivation, with a twelfth-century hermitage
(now rebuilt), which is an impressive group of buildings. The route
then goes across the rice fields towards Gràcia island. Their appearance depends on the time of year. In winter they are dry and brown,
covered with old weed; in spring they are ploughed, sowed and
turned into lakes; with summer the bright green turns to gold. They
are under water until September. Approach the town of **Deltebre** by
the former settlement of Jesus i Maria. From the river bank there is a
good view of the Ebro, with the woods and orchards of Gràcia island,
which can be visited by ferry. Into the town itself, which is in the
middle of the delta and very pleasant with patios, gardens, trees and
flowers all mixed up with the buildings. Here is the visitor's centre
of the natural park, and the Cambra Arrossera de la Cava (rice co-
operative), where rice, fruit and vegetables can be bought. La Cava
was the other old town absorbed to make Deltebre in 1977. To the left
the prominent line of plane trees along the canal are for retaining the
banks.

The route goes out now to the mouth of the river, and the service
area of the natural park. A boat can be taken here to the lagoons of
Buda Island, and El Garxal where the river meets the sea. After this,
one can go to the new town of Riomar by the beach and open sea,
where groups of fishermen with special nets might be seen, wading
quite far out for small shellfish and cockles. From here, go right along
the coast road to the fishing port of L'Ampolla, or across the delta to
**Camarles**, where there are some old, rather ruinous defence towers.
All along the base of the delta are large fields of artichokes. From
Camarles, L'Ampolla can be reached via a side road that goes past
part of the old coastline. **L'Ampolla** is a more traditional delta fishing port, with the fishermen arranging their nets and traps in the
street, and the usual interesting fish auction in the evening.

# Further Information
## — The Ebro Crescent —

### Activities

**L'Aldea**
Fiesta: 21 April (Fiesta Mayor) and
14-21 August (Assumption and
San Roc).

**L'Ampolla**
Sea Festival: 16-20 July (Virgin of
the Carme).

**Amposta**
Fiesta: 14-21 August (Feast of the
Assumption).

Agricultural Fair: 8 December.

**Balada**
Fiesta: 10 July.

**Camarles**
Fiesta: 24-9 July (St James).

**Fabara**
Traditional dances, El 'Polinario'
(mixture of Catalan *sardana* and
Aragonese *jota*) 15-18 August,
Plaza Mayor.

**L'Hostal dels Alls**
Fiesta: 5-12 August (Our Lady of
L'Aldea).

**Lligallo del Ganguil**
Fiesta: 24-8 June (St John).

**Maella**
Dancing *la jota* at Monastery de la
Trapa, Easter Monday.

**Muntells**
Fiesta: 9-15 August (St Lawrence).

**Nonaspe**
*Romería* (pilgrimage) to hermitage
Virgen de Dos Aguas, first Sunday
in September.

**Poblenou** (Villa Franco del Delta)
Fiesta: 18 August.

**Sant Carles (Sant Carles de la
Rapita)**
Fiesta: 25 July-1 August (St James).

*Semana Santa* (Holy Week) processions are also held widely throughout the region.

### Places of Interest

**Amposta**
Montsià Museum
Open: weekdays 11am-2pm, 5-8pm;
Sundays and holidays, 11am-2pm.

**Monasterio del Piedra**
Monasterio de Piedra
Open: sunrise to sunset.

**Tortosa**
(Note: this is a Catalan speaking
city, but Spanish and sometimes
English are understood. All signs
are in Catalan. Regional ☎ 977.)

Cathedral
Open: only during hours of religious offices.

College San Luis
Open: 10am-2pm, 5-9pm. Closed
Sundays and holidays.

Museo y Archivos Municipal
1 Plaza España
☎ 44 15 25

## Tourist Information Offices

**Alcañiz**
Urbanización Santa María
Casa Consistatorial
Plaza de España
☎ 83 02 61

**L'Aldea**
Town Council
☎ 45 00 12

**Amposta**
Ayuntamiento
2 Plaza España
☎ 70 00 57/10 25

**Belchite** (new town)
Ayuntamiento (Alcadia)
☎ 83 00 03

Ayuntamiento
14 Dieciocho de Julio
☎ 83 00 35

**Calatayud**
Ayuntamiento
1 Plaza España
☎ 88 13 14

Casa Cultura
Plaza Comunidad
☎ 88 16 73

**Camarles**
Town Council
☎ 47 00 07

**Caspe**
Centro de Iniciativas Touristicas
8 Arcos del Toril
☎ 63 01 34

**Daroca**
Centro de Iniciativas Touristicas
Casa Consistatorial
2 Plaza España
☎ 80 03 12

**Deltebre**
Visitors' Information
Ebro Delta Natural Park
Plaça del 20 Maig (Town Hall)
☎ 48 10 63

Town Council
☎ 48 05 87

**Híjar**
Centro de Iniciativas Touristicas
Casa Consistatorial for *Semana Santa* information.

**Samper de Calanda**
Centro de Iniciativas Touristicas
Plaza de España 2 for *Semana Santa* information.

**Sant Carles (Sant Carles de la Rapita)**
Ayuntamiento
Plaza Carlos III 13
☎ 74 00 51

Tourist Office
Gdor Labadie 2
☎ 74 01 00

**Tortosa**
Ayuntamiento
1 Plaza España
☎ 44 00 00

# 6 • El Bierzo

T his region lies in the extreme north-west of the ancient province of Old Castile, and in the west of the province of León (now the autonomous region of Castilla-León). It forms a large basin lying between the mountains of León and the Galician massif, and in far distant Mesozoic times (150 million years ago) it was a huge lake surrounded by mountains, and when the level fell through earth movements, masses of alluvium were banked up against these mountains. This was to be profoundly significant in the later historical period.

It was settled during the Bronze Age, about 2000BC, evidence of which was a megalithic fertility token found at Noceda, in the hills north of Bembibre. This primitive *Bérgida*, an ancient region which gives its name to El Bierzo, remained as it was, until the arrival of the Romans, who exploited the minerals of the region, particularly alluvial gold, in massive opencast mining operations. In the early Middle Ages the Knights Templars were active here, and the pilgrimage routes to Santiago passed through the region. Later, in the fifteenth and sixteenth centuries, the Inquisition had its seat in the hermitage of San Pedro in the Sierra del Teleno. The modern period has seen greater exploitation of the minerals in the Carboniferous rocks, especially anthracite and iron, along with the Río Sil, the main river, being developed for HEP. In the extreme north-west of the region, the Sierra de Ancares has been made a natural park.

All these things have left their mark on the landscape of El Bierzo, which makes it an extremely interesting area to visit. It also has a variety of scenery, which is verdant with meadows, vineyards and orchards, as well as old villages and isolated monasteries in the hills and mountains. It is an outpost of old Christian Spain, and physically a very compact region with its limits well marked geographically.

Towns are mainly along the line of the Madrid-La Coruña road NVI, and the largest is the capital of the region Ponferrada, on the Río Sil, with an old Knights Templars castle, and some good buildings. Villafranca, west of Ponferrada is a very pleasant small town, at the confluence of the Ríos Burbia and Valcarce, with gardens, old churches and a *parador*. Cacabelos on the Río Cua, is a town in a rich agricultural region amid vineyards, and orchards with a wine co-operative. Toreno is a small mining town in the Sil valley north of Ponferrada, and east of Ponferrada just off the main NVI is Bembibre, a small industrial town on the Río Tremor, but old in history, and famous for an author Enrique Gil y Carrasco, and his novel *El Señor de Bembibre*.

The attractions of this region are many, but they are sometimes difficult to define or describe. Not least is the fact that, although it is scenically and historically an extremely interesting area, it is not often visited. It is of course a gateway region, and with one of the principal highways of Spain (NVI), and a railway running through to Galicia, people tend to pass by, and not stop at the 'gate'. It has been a passage region before, being on the route to Santiago de Compostela, but whereas in modern times the 'pilgrims' whizz through, the pilgrims in the Middle Ages took their time, and many old churches and buildings in El Bierzo relate to the era of the famous pilgrimage. As one guide puts it: 'From Ponferrada to Villafranca is a delightful walk, 20km [12$^1/_2$ miles], crossing one of the richest regions in Spain ....'

The climate tends to be sub-continental on account of being surrounded by mountains, which shut off the influence of the sea even though it is not far distant. This means cold winters, with as much as 40 days of frost, but it rarely snows. It is a sunny climate, as the vineyards and orchards bear witness. Summers are warm, sometimes hot: August 28 °C (82 °F); autumns golden: October 19 °C(67 °F); and winters mild in the day: December and January 8 °C (46 °F), but cold at night 1.8 °C (34-5 °F); springs are moderately warm: April 17-18 °C (63-4 °F). Rainfall is also moderate, 600mm (23-4in), heavy in winter, December 89mm (3$^1/_2$in), and moderate in spring and autumn. Summer rainfall is light.

## Travelling to the Area

Although relatively far distant, access is direct from Madrid.

### By Road
From Madrid (Barajas airport) to Ponferrada. M30 ring to city, then NVI to A6, A6 to Jemenuño, then NVI to Ponferrada via Tordesillas and Astorga direct. About 400-20km (250-60 miles).
From France: Unless cutting across from Burgos via Palencia and

León, which needs good map reading, the best route is: Hendaye, *autopista* A1 to Bilbao and Burgos, join N620 at Las Huelgas Reales outside Burgos, take it to Vallodolid, then to Tordesillas on the NVI, then Ponferrada. 584km (362 miles).(French frontier.)
From Irun/Hendaye to Ponferrada 614km (381 miles).

### By Rail
Madrid (P. Pio) to Ponferrada 548km (340 miles).

## Las Médulas and Lago Carrucedo

This is a route which should surprise the visitor in two senses, the landscape he or she sees, and the history behind it. Starting from Ponferrada, take the road to Carrucedo, which is the old road to Orense and Vigo in Galicia, but still numbered N120, and for the first few kilometres runs down the valley of the Río Sil. This is very green, with irrigated orchards and vines, and then the road swings away from the river through the village of Villalibre de la Jurisdicción, and after passing Priaranza del Bierzo the meadows are left behind, and the road climbs. At Santalla there is a turning to the left, leading to the village of **Borrenes**, but before the village take a path up to the ruined castle of Cornatel perched on a steep rocky hump. This has seen much history and, it seems, legends also, for it is where the author of *El Señor de Bembibre* set his story. The view from here is a fine panorama, with cultivated slopes in the foreground, the lake of Carrucedo in the middle distance, and the snow capped mountains of Galicia in the background. You might notice a dam at one end of the shining blue waters, and thus think immediately that this is an artificial lake. So it is, but not made by modern Spaniards, for it is the product of the immense gold mining operations of the Romans in the first century AD.

Returning now to the N120 road, just before the village of Carrucedo, a turn on the left is taken that leads to the village of **Orellán**. This has a picturesque little church, with a slate roofed porch, and a stone façade plus bells, the whole of which is ivy covered. From the village there is a wide, but very rough winding road for 2km ($1^1/_4$ miles) that leads to the *mirador* of Orellán, where there is a view which is unique in the world. Stretching in serried ranks are the bright orange coloured denuded peaks which are not ruins but the result of a vast opencast goldmining enterprise, that may be the biggest in history. It certainly rivals anything the Russians have done on the river Lena in Siberia, or even the deep mining in the South African Rand.

The original masses of gold bearing alluvium were formed against the mountains stretching from this region (Las Médulas) eastward to Castropodarme, and north-west to Villar de Acero. The Romans utilised the rivers Sil, Cua and other streams by bringing water from great distances, one by a tunnel from the mountain El Teleno (2,185m, 7,167ft). Then Las Médulas were pierced with great precision by tunnels in a circular formation, with sluices that were opened and shut alternately. The water then circulated under hydro-static pressure at great speed, sending the material to three places, the gold being obtained in the form of fine dust by the old traditional 'Golden Fleece' method of using sheep's wool. Pliny (who had been the administrator of the mines of north-west Iberia) said 20,000 Roman libras (7.2 tons or 230,800oz) of gold per year were extracted from these mines. A modern estimate is that 300 million tons of material had to be removed, probably needing 80,000 slaves daily to do it, guarded by the Roman army. The lake of Carrucedo was formed from the damming up of the water needed. It is estimated that over 500 tons of gold were exploited here — a colossal amount.

*Las Médulas, the result of Roman gold mining*

The name 'Médulas', derived from the Latin *metalla*, means a mine.

Finally, between 1940 and 1945, a German company exploited the Río Sil for gold, but how much they mined is not really known.

From the *mirador* a return is made to the N120, and the lake of Carrucedo. This lake has given rise to all kinds of legends of hidden treasure, nymphs, water sprites, and drowned cities, and can be crossed by the modern dam. But the real treasure in it is probably the fish and eels, the latter made into delicious pies or pasties.

## Compludo and The Pilgrim's Road
### (Camino de Santiago)

From Ponferrada the road to Molinaseca is taken, LE142, by leaving the city along the Avenida del Castillo, and turning right. Then 6km (4 miles) further on through the valley of the Río Miruelos with vine covered hills, is the small town of **Molinaseca**, a place very much connected with pilgrims as one of the old routes to Santiago, came in here. The Santuario de las Angustias was the building that received them, but its doors had to be reinforced with iron, as the pilgrims tore strips or splinters off them, as if they were precious relics! The bridge that leads into the town is a noble structure with flying buttresses, and dates from the Middle Ages. The parish church of San Nicolás is also a fine large building, and the main street, Calle Real, keeps its special medieval character, with a stone cross recalling the pilgrims' era. The town is famous for its *chorizos* or pork sausages.

A further 6km (4 miles) on, with the road climbing, is **Riego de Ambros**, high above the river with steep slopes, and on the actual pilgrim's road from Astorga. Here is a good inn, and an interesting church. The road continues, now high in the hills covered with broom bushes and occasional chestnut and beech trees, to **Acebo**, rather a primitive place once, whose picturesque houses have slate roofs with straw and are tightly grouped together. In the church there is a fine altar called the Santiago Apostol.

From here the route turns right, down a hill, and along a steep corniche road into a deep valley, which is reminiscent of Scotland, a Devon combe, or a valley in the Cévennes. At the bottom, after this long sharp descent, cross over the Río Miruelos into a verdant valley with really luxuriant vegetation of beeches and poplars contrasting with the bare scrub of the hills. A short way along is a wooden sign 'Ferraria de Compludo' (old spelling for modern *herrería* meaning ironworks). Vehicles must be parked (there is not a great deal of space) and you have to walk some way along a path on the river bank. Then the primitive ironworks themselves appear.

This is a most fascinating and extremely interesting working example of a medieval water powered ironworks. The story behind it goes back far in time to the nearby village of Compludo, where in the seventh century a young hermit San Fructuoso, founded a monastery, dedicating and developing the 'Regula Monachorum' and 'Regula Communis' (Monastic and Communal Rules), which were to be the basic canons of monastic life. The ironworks were probably employed by the monastery, and the Compludo ironworks is testimony to the agrarian and monastic economy of the Middle Ages. It was a primitive Bierzo industry complementing rural work by producing tools, ploughshares, hoes and pitchforks. The works were built outside the village at the entrance to the valley, and are sited on a natural rock base, surrounded by very pleasant woods of poplars, walnuts and chestnut trees. The water comes from the confluence of two streams: Ríos Miruelos and Miera, which is led to a stone pound, and works a toothed wooden water wheel. This in turn operates a heavy wooden beam with a drop hammer attached. All

*Los Cristales, La Coruña city and port*

*Vegas de Coria, in the Río Hurdano valley, the Western Marches of Spain*

*The statue of Francisco Pizarro, Trujillo, Extremadura*

*Molinaseca, Camino de Santiago*

the gearing and cooling water channels are made of old walnut wood hardened with stone and bound with thick bands of iron. There may have been a smelting furnace as well at sometime or other, but now a furnace using water powered bellows is used for heating the bar iron itself, prior to forging. An old local saying gives a clue to the age of the works, which referred to pilgrims to Santiago, and local harvesters or reapers who happened to be passing by, taking the road through Acerbo:

*'Caminante, si en la noche cuando te acerques a Compludo, oyes unos truenos intensos, que parecen salir de las montañas, no temas, es el martillo de la Herrería.'*

'Traveller, if in the night near Compludo, you hear heavy thunder, which seems to come out of the mountains, have no fear, it's the hammer of the ironworks.'

It is interesting that there was a water powered ironworks here so early, Spain being a pioneer in this respect. They gradually spread across Europe, but didn't reach England (Yorkshire), until the late fourteenth century — well over 250 years later. It is also remarkable that it has survived until modern times, having obviously been maintained with care, especially in recent years.

From the ironworks, go to the village of **Compludo**, set in its deep vale, to see the place that was the cradle of Spanish monasteries, and whose founder San Fructuoso, afterwards became the metropolitan

Archbishop of Braga in Portugal. The name of the village is thought
to derive from the pre-Roman *Compleutica*, then the Roman *Com-
plutum*. There is an old church, but all that remains of the monastery
is the *solar* or site. This is undoubtedly an extremely ancient settlement, worth walking around, and up the slopes to admire the scenery of the valley. It is possible to return to Ponferrada from Compludo, via **Salas de los Barrios**, which has a sixteenth-century
church, San Martín, with three naves, and a Romanesque door. The
village had Roman remains, including an altar from a temple of
Mercury, and carved stone blocks. But the road to it is unpaved from
Compludo, and very dusty in dry weather.

## Peñalba de Santiago and San de Montes

From Ponferrada this route leaves from the Avenida del Castillo, due
south on the LE161, the road to San Esteban de Valdueza, crossing
over the railway line and the Río Tremor, and climbing almost at
once, with good views. At San Esteban the road divides. It is easy to
make a mistake here, as the LE161 — the better road — is the right
fork to Villanueva de Valdueza. However, after several bends with
the road mounting higher and higher, this 'wrong' road reaches the
summit of a lofty peak, Guiana (1,850m, 6,068ft), where there is a
radar station, doubtless the reason for the good road. It is lonely and
windswept, but with magnificent views all round, so in a way is
worth the detour.

Taking the correct fork (left from Ponferrada) the route continues
along the valley of the Río Oza on a very wooded road to the village
of **Valdefrancos**. This is a delightful place and has an air of subdued
activity, with old men sitting about, others tending their vegetable
plots and haymaking, plus hens and chickens running about. There
is an old church, and a picturesque ruined bridge over the Río Oza.
The name of this village relates to an old settlement of French people,
whose houses are built above the road.

The route goes on through a leafy valley full of chestnut trees,
oaks, mountain scrub and the flowing stream, until it reaches San
Clemente, a village with a church which has a stone crucifix in front
of it. From here onwards, the road is narrow, and deceptive, as it has
occasional wide spaces which disappear into the increasingly sharp
curves, blind bends and consequent poorer visibility, so it deserves
caution. At length one arrives at **Peñalba de Santiago** sheltered between high mountains, its grey stone houses, with slabs of slate on
their roofs seeming to grow out of the ground. There is a magnificent

*Valle de Silencio*

old church here of original Mozarabic construction built between 931 and 937 which has quite a history about it. Viewed from a distance it appears almost merged with the other buildings, but for the height of the belfry rising distinctively. Inside, however, is one of the finest examples of Spanish church architecture. A single nave with double horseshoe-shaped arcades supported by marble columns with Corinthian capitols. The main door is very fine with twin horseshoe-shaped arches being supported on three columns, and is described in many books on the subject as being geometrical, aesthetic and having equilibrium. Certain authorities confirm that it is geometric and aesthetic, but disagree about the equilibrium. They maintain that the left arch is different. The reason given is this: the Knights Templars have been mentioned as being active during the Middle Ages in El Bierzo, and it is asserted that they reformed this church, and in doing so altered the arches. The left is negative, and the right positive. The Templars' symbol of the cross was the Greek letter Tau

(T), but in El Bierzo their symbol was a cross (at an angle of 40°), with alpha-omega, and the right arch is a perfect omega (Ω), but not seemingly the left.

Peñalba de Santiago is a most peaceful place, and the neighbouring vale is called: Valle de Silencio ('The Silent Valley'), as all noise is absent, due perhaps to the caves. The founder of the church, San Genadio, is reputed to have been a hermit in one of them and this has since been closed with a grille, and made into a chapel. For whatever reason, Peñalba has known tranquility for over a thousand years.

From here, go back to a turn on the left leading to the monastery of San Pedro de Montes; the road was formerly difficult, but now it is much improved. Very rich and dense vegetation with walnut and chestnut trees surrounds the surviving buildings. The original monastery was the second foundation of San Fructuoso, being restored in 895 by San Genadio, later Bishop of Astorga, and the church is twelfth-century Romanesque. The monastery was said to be rich in the seventeenth century, and in much favour with kings and popes, but disputed its territory with the Knights Templars of Ponferrada. It was rebuilt in the eighteenth century with a splendid façade, being then Benedictine (black monks), but the whole of this interesting building in a superb setting is now rather ruinous, although it is being restored. The adjoining hamlet has some old houses and is worth a walk round. On leaving the hamlet there are the remains of the hermitage of Santa Cruz, with carved stone inscriptions of Visigothic design in the doorway, surmounted by a stone cross with the omega and alpha symbols. The cross appears to be at 40°.

## Ponferrada, Cacabelos and the Sierra de los Ancares

### Ponferrada

Although a commercial and industrial city, Ponferrada has an old foundation, and some interesting buildings. The origin of the name stems from a bridge built across the Río Sil in 1082, to help the pilgrims on their way to Santiago, which was reinforced with iron, and called *Pons Ferratus*. The castle is one of the best examples in Spain of the military architecture of the Middle Ages. Most of it was built in the twelfth and thirteenth centuries. It belonged to the Knights Templars, and was at one time their most important castle the world over. At this point a note on their activities in Bierzo is perhaps apposite. They were connected in the Middle Ages with the iron industry, and the mineral deposits of coal and iron here in Bembibre, Toreno, Fabero and Villablino were used by the Templars to make arms, and to search for suitable places to make them. They

*The castle at Ponferrada*

were poor, with a fervent Christian faith, and all economic wealth was used for churches, cathedrals and the protection of pilgrims. They chose sequestered places like Compludo, which may be one of their foundations, for they made ploughs as well as arms.

An order of monks, the Cenobites, lived in the castle, and it was also used as a palace. Subsequently it passed to the Conde de Lemos, after the dissolution of the Order of Templars in 1312, and later to the Crown. It is impressive, although sober, but very large, extending over 8,000sq m (2 acres), forming an irregular pentagon with the north-west side above the Río Sil, and the south-west side dominating the bridgehead. There are two distinct styles in this great fortress: Romanesque and Gothic. Nearby in the Plaza del Temple is the seventeenth-century church of San Andrés, with a famous thirteenth-century 'Cristo de las Maravillas', and baroque retable. Off the Avenida del Castillo, in the Calle Comenador is the Basilica de Nuestra Señora de la Encina (1577), with a fine tower (1614). This is the patroness church of the city, with a Gothic sculpture *Our Lady of the Oak*, officially recognised as such in 1958 by Pope Pious XII. The church is full of very fine carvings, paintings and decorated work.

Ponferrada was once a walled city, but all that remains now is a very impressive gateway, and a bell tower with a clock, in the Calle Isidro Rueda, and alongside is the ancient guildhall (Consistatorio), one of the earliest in Spain built by Philip II, but now fallen from grace and used as a prison. The actual guildhall in the Plaza del Ayuntamiento, is an interesting building with an arcaded entrance, and a long balcony above it, right along the façade, built in the colonial period of Carlos III. For the steam railway enthusiast there is the station of the MSP, Minero Siderdúrgica de Ponferrada, an industrial concern that works trains to Villablino via the Sil valley. Until recently they operated a passenger service, by what was a most picturesque route. The journey by car is not nearly so interesting, but there is still the odd locomotive in steam in the yards. Ask permission first before entering though.

From the city the route leaves by the very straight old main road, formerly the pilgrim's route to Santiago, and continues to the wine village of Camponaraya, and then through vineyards to **Cacabelos**. This small town is in the midst of vineyards and cherry orchards. The cherries form the basis of a local drink mixed with *aguardiente* (brandy), which is quite strong. The wine of El Bierzo is considered the best of the wines of León. There is a type known as Blanquiazul de El Bierzo ('White and Blue'), quite notable, but the reds and amber coloured wines are good too (12-14° strength).

The town itself is a pleasant place, as wine towns usually are, with a parish church of mixed ancestry, but having an old Romanesque thirteenth-century apse, and spacious naves (sixteenth century), as well as the Santuario de Angustias by the side of the Río Cua, with a splendid façade. In the middle is a very nice little plaza flanked by houses with arcades. Cacabelos was a Roman settlement and Pliny the Elder had a palace here for 18 years. Before going further north, visit an even older 'Cacabelos', which lies just off the road to Villafranca, near the village of Pieros. Here is the Castro de la Ventosa, which was the ancient hilltop Astur city of *Bergidum*, later conquered by the Romans, which was excavated in 1976. Finds included some ceramics of 1,500 years old, which suggests a return by a later people to this depopulated site.

Returning to modern Cacabelos, our route is the LE712 through meadows and vines to Arganza, another village with a wine co-operative. Here the lowland ends, and the road climbs through chestnut groves and pinewoods to Ocero. Then through more pine-woods with some oak to Vega de Espinareda, which will be de-scribed later. Here the valley of the Río Cua is rejoined, continue to Sésamo, and then take a winding road into the natural park of the Sierra de los Ancares, with its rugged, but varied scenery of lofty hills covered with thickets of broom, heather, cranberries and gentians. These are interspersed with woods that are sometimes a century old, of yews, oaks, chestnuts and the capudre, which is similar to the mountain ash with red berries, but indigenous here. In the deep green valleys are beech, hazel, birch, wild plane and holly, which here is a sizeable tree. The Sierra de los Ancares rise to nearly 2,000m (6,560ft) and extend into Galicia, and are a large, relatively unknown region, with great opportunities for exploring, and are really a world of their own, with distinctive villages and way of life. The landscape may remind visitors of certain similar regions in Europe and the temperate Americas, like Vermont in New England, but in some aspects it is quite different. Here only a small part can be described, which it is hoped will encourage the reader to penetrate along the many forest roads to see for him or herself.

The route climbs, and then descends into the valley of the Río Ancares to the village of **Candin**. The *pallozas* are typical of the Ancares region. These were the primitive houses of circular con-struction on a granite base, their walls not much over 1m (3$^{1}/_{4}$ft) high, with a conical roof of straw, a door and a small window high up to let out the smoke. Inside was divided into small rooms for sleeping, with straw beds; one for pigs or calves; then a larger living room, and at the end a stable for cattle. The room opposite the door contained a crude stone oven, and there were two posts a good way apart to support the roof. They varied in size, some being quite large, and grouped into villages. They were lived in until quite recently, but many are now used as store houses, and some are preserved, like the village of Piornedo in neighbouring Lugo province (Galicia), which is virtually a historic monument.

At a large farm in Candin, where they grow excellent wheat, there are some enormous chestnut trees, far larger than in the Cévennes, that land of chestnuts. The reserved areas of the Ancares are haven for wild life also, including wolves, wild boar, fallow deer, chamois, foxes, martens and the large bird, urogallo — the latter species in one

*A* palloza, *or primitive house at Candin, Los Ancares*

of its last habitats in Europe, and the rivers of Ancares are, of course, good for trout. On from Candin is Pereda de Ancares, where the paved road ends and a long forest road leads to Balouta and Suarbol, two remote villages of *palloza* houses.

From the Ancares the route returns to **Vega de Espinareda**, an attractive town with the substantial remains of a Benedictine monastery. The actual buildings seen here, with a splendid façade and twin towers, were built from 1768-80. The foundation, however, dates back to 940. The church has an elegant nave, and even the ruined cloisters have a sense of grandeur. From Espinareda, the route strikes due east to Berlanga del Bierzo. This is a very pretty road, with vines, meadows, hedged fields with dog roses in the hedges and many oak trees. The bird life seems very prolific also — altogether a picture of rural charm, not often seen in many parts of Spain. Then comes the village of Tombrio de Abajo, quite picturesque, and at length the Río Sil valley is reached, and the small industrial town of Toreno, which is quite pleasant, and belies the opencast coal mining nearby. The town has the only example in El Bierzo of a medieval stone pillory, set in the middle of a small plaza. The river valley here is very narrow, and the mineral railway runs quite close, but has quite a different route to Ponferrada from the road, as it keeps to the river, and runs by the side of the wide Embalse de Barcena. The route turns right onto the main road C631, and until near Fresnedo is winding, wooded and open. As it mounts to the summit of a steep hill there is a far-off glimpse of the Barcena HEP lake and, in an unusual combination, the steam can be seen rising from the tall cooling towers of a huge thermal power station at Compostilla, beside the lake. The road, after some bends, now becomes almost dead straight to the village of Cabañas de la Dornilla, and then under the NVI into Ponferrada.

## Carracedo, Corullón and Villafranca del Bierzo

From Ponferrada this route takes the main NVI, and then turns right to the Benedictine monastery of **Carracedo**, a short way off the main road. It is forlorn and ruinous, but still magnificent in its abandonment. It was originally founded in 990 by Bermudo II of León, but early in its life, suffered from attacks by the Moors, and was rebuilt, becoming the most important and powerful monastery in El Bierzo. Much of the present structure dates from the twelfth and thirteenth centuries. The chapter house is twelfth century, and contained in the building is a royal palace dating from the thirteenth century, the first work of the transition from the Romanesque style to the Gothic. This part is very interesting, especially a room known as 'Cocina de la Reina' (Queen's Kitchen) — ask the old lady who acts as a caretaker for the key. The outlook from here is very fine, and known as El Mirador de la Reina, (Queen's Balcony or Lookout). To see it from the outside, go down a lane past some market gardens or cultivated plots, to the rear of the monastery, and peer through the bushes at this singularly beautiful part of the building. The cloisters, now sadly decayed, were started in the sixteenth century along with the sacristy and the refectory. The imposing tower was built in 1602, and the church rebuilt in the eighteenth century, although much of the older, more primitive part is left. The mixture of architectural styles might be considered a hotchpotch by some, but the general effect, in spite of partial ruin is good, if a little uneven. It was not until 1929 that it was officially recognised as a monument. The visitor, after having seen some of the monasteries of El Bierzo, may care to reflect on the famous decree of Mendizábal in 1835, which dissolved the Spanish monasteries. It came much later than that of Henry VIII in England, and revolutionary France, but did as much if not more damage. The nineteenth century was very bad for Spanish buildings of all kinds.

From Carracedo it is only a short distance under the NVI bridge to the nearby village of **Carracedelo**, where the parish church is worth a look, with its fine Romanesque door, and also the unusual rector's house. The route now returns to the NVI and continues for some 10km (6 miles) along the main road westwards to the turn off for Villafranca, but this is not taken just yet. First, turn left onto a road that climbs up to the village of **Corullón**, where the two churches provide interest, as well as an immense view over nearly all El Bierzo. The parish church of San Miguel is restored Romanesque, whilst the older San Esteban (late eleventh century) is completely preserved, except for the underground vaults. The roof eaves are interesting with various sculptures on brackets. On the wall of the Casa Rectoral (Rector's House) is a relief showing the stoning of San Esteban (St Stephen). At Corullón there are also the ivy covered ruins of a fifteenth-century castle that belonged to the Marquis of Villafranca. Further along, just beyond the village, is the hamlet of San Fiz with the small rustic church of San Juan (eleventh century), and also the remains of a sixteenth-century fortified mansion, but only one of the great towers survives silhouetted against the sky. Then about 1km ($^1/_2$ mile) onwards, where the road bends, is the Mirador del Bierzo. This is probably the best of all the views in the region, giving an extraordinary wide panorama of above and beyond the Sil valley.

Now return to the main road where the route into **Villafranca del Bierzo** is taken, a town that had great importance in medieval times, being born out of the pilgrimage road to Santiago, and growing in turn as a monastic nucleus. It was the goal for the pilgrims who were sick, because there they could reach the longed for indulgences granted in front of the Romanesque *perdón* (mercy, pardon) doorway of the church dedicated to Santiago, where following tradition, those who were sick and infirm need not complete the journey to Santiago. These were granted by Pope Calixto II, who in the twelfth century formulated the *Codex Calixtinus*, which was in effect one of the earliest 'tourist guides' for pilgrims. Among the concessions were two mayors for the town: one for the Spanish, and one for the French or Franks, hence the name of the town. Villafranca lies at the confluence of the rivers Burbia and Valcarce in the midst of a fertile region of vines, orchards and cereals. It has a history of nobility and culture, a marquisate was created at the end of the fifteenth century, and the family did much to develop the town, with fine houses, and the influence of the court in the sixteenth and seventeenth centuries (Madrid was not so important in those days). The cultural element was strong, with poetry festivals, and the town remembers, when it was an actual capital of the province of Bierzo-Valdeorras from 1822-33, before the modern provinces were created. Today there is still a Philharmonic Society, with international soloists and performers.

It is an extremely pleasant place with some fine central gardens laid out along the Almeda Alta, at the eastern end of which is the church of San Nicolas, the seventeenth-century Jesuits College, now belonging to the Pauline Fathers, with exotic sculptures brought perhaps from Latin America. The fine façade dates from 1649. Further along is the Convento Divina Pastora, and then at the end is the Palacio de Arganza, the palace of the first marquis, built at the beginning of the sixteenth century. A great quadrilateral building, unfortunately sacked during the Peninsular War, but afterwards rebuilt. On the other side of the gardens in the Calle F. Quintano is the collegiate church of Santa Maria, a large building totally rebuilt by the marquis of the town over a long period between the sixteenth and eighteenth centuries. It is an imposing structure in the form of a cross, on the old site of the monastery hospital of Cluny, and the church is based on the design of the church of St John of Lateran in Rome.

From here the route enters the Calle Santa Catalina, then to the Calle Agua, a street of beautiful houses, recalling a former life style, which has been likened to the palaces of Genoa in the seventeenth century. The houses have magnificent doors, and are certainly evocative of great things in the past. In this street are also *bodegas* (wine cellars), for Villafranca is very much a wine town, and has a co-operative, which probably helps account for it being such a pleasant place. Over the centuries it has always been regarded as the 'Eden' or 'Promised Land' of El Bierzo.

From this street turn right into the Calle Rúa Nueva, where, going down on the right, is the convent and church of La Anunciada. Built by the fifth marquis, Don Pedro de Toledo y Osorio in the sixteenth century for the barefooted nuns of the Order of St Clare, the church has a single nave, with a square chapel at the head, and choir with the family mausoleum at the foot. The great door is distinctly Italian, with a wide arch on Tuscan pillars. From here, go back up the street, and pass through the side streets of either Campairo or Yedra to the Plaza Mayor, with its terraces, and in a turning on the right is the convent of San Francisco. This is perhaps the best, architecturally, of Villafranca's many ecclesiastical buildings, with a Romanesque outline, principal doorway of the thirteenth century, and a nave which is ornamental Moorish from the fifteenth century. Returning to the Plaza Mayor, go out of the town towards Cacabelos by the Calles Puentecillo and Libertad, opposite the castle of the Counts of Peñarrimo built in 1490. Turn left along Calle Santiago, and a short road on the right leads to the church of Santiago, the haven of the pilgrims. A large, though simple Romanesque building, it is dominated by its splendid door: La Puerta del Perdón. This is one of the best examples of Romanesque sculpture in the entire province of

León. Finally, a mention may be made of a modern building, that of the *parador* in the Avenida Calvo Sotelo. It is on a fine prominent site, on the edge of the town, and is a very pleasing structure set in attractive grounds. Villafranca is a very good base from which to explore the region round about, with its contrasts between fertile cultivated plain and mountain.

From here it is possible to penetrate into another part of the Sierra de los Ancares, although the roads are not paved for any great distance. Nevertheless a road runs up the Río Burbia valley to Paradaseca, where a prominent scarp of reddish rocks is called the Las Médulas de Paradaseca. The paved road ends at Paradaseca, but by using forest roads and paths, it is possible to penetrate right into the heart of the *sierras*. However, the going is quite tough.

Before leaving the town a very good view of it can be seen by crossing the bridge over the Río Burbia and turning sharp right on to a road that climbs up from the river past old houses, with wooden balconies in a district called Barrio Tejedores amidst terraced plots and vegetation.

From Villafranca the route continues from the bridge on to the old main road (NVI), and comes out westwards of the newer road tunnel. Keeping on the main road the route, now climbing into the hills, is followed through the villages of Pereje and Trabadelo, up the valley of the Río Valcarce until the turn on the left to Ambasmestas is reached. From this village the route now goes under the main road into the beautiful wooded valley of the upper Río Valcarce to the hamlet of Quintela, and beyond to the village of **Balboa**. The name is said to originate from the Latin *vallis bona* meaning 'good valley'. Balboa has a strange small church, and perched on a hill overlooking the valley is a ruined castle, whose history seems quite obscure. It is possible to go further from the hamlet of Quintela to El Portelo on the Lugo-León border, and into the Parque Natural de Ancares by a long forest road. Other excursions can be made by branching off from villages along the NVI between Vega de Valcarce and Villafranca.

## Along the Margins of Ponferrada — the Sil and Boeza Valleys

From Ponferrada many short or slightly longer excursions can be made along the valleys of the two rivers Sil and Boeza that meet in the city. The first is a short trip just outside the city, about 1km ($^1/_2$ mile) northwards to Santo Tomás de las Ollas. The church here reveals a most interesting mixture of styles: Mozarabic, Romanesque and baroque, but the tenth-century apse is simple and remarkably beautiful, with its horseshoe-shaped arches.

Also from Ponferrada, the *huerta* (orchards) of the Río Sil is worth a short visit for the sight of the vast spread of orchards and greenery along the river valley. One takes the old N120 (Avenida del Castillo leading into the Avenida de Portugal), and instead of continuing into the hills, go along the side road through the villages of Dehesas, Villaverde and Villadepalos, from there to Carracedelo, and then return via Dehesas. This route doesn't contain any old churches of great tourist interest, or castles, but is delightfully rural and tranquil.

Next take the main NVI eastwards out of Ponferrada, and turn right at **San Miguel de las Dueñas**, where there is a Cistercian monastery of 1152 foundation. It is in use but, as it is a strict closed order, only the church can be visited. However, one may get a glimpse of the great Romanesque door into the chapel. The church, one of the best in the Romanesque style in León, has an exceptional piece of sculpture, the *Virgin and Child*, considered unique, and also sculptured capitals. The route continues along the left bank of the Río Boeza, through a rural landscape to the village of **Castropodarme**. Here indeed is a village of the past, which in Roman times was one of the scenes of their goldmining operations. From here, go across country to the small industrial town of **Bembibre**. Its surroundings are quite green and pleasant, and give little hint of the extensive opencast anthracite mines nearby. This town is full of legends concerning the castle, which the author Enrique y Gil Carrasco, wrote about. The castle was demolished in the nineteenth century, and only a few ruins remain. However, on August evenings in Ponferrada, a stage version of *El Señor del Bembibre*, is acted in the floodlit castle of the Knights Templars. Bembibre also has a sanctuary, rebuilt in the nineteenth century, which celebrates a fiesta each year, accompanied by a noted dish of El Bierzo. This is *El Botillo*, which takes its name from the small leather wine bag, and consists of meat encased in a skin, sausages and potatoes.

From Bembibre one can take the LE461 and go over the bridge across the main road and up the Río Boeza valley through the villages of Albares, La Ribera, Folgoso de la Ribera, and to Boeza itself, and beyond to Igüeña where the paved road ends. Other valleys which can be explored from Bembibre are the Río Tremor, from Torre del Bierzo, and the one leading northwards from the town to the village of Noceda, which is interesting for archaeological operations, as there are about a dozen ancient camps nearby.

# Further Information
## — El Bierzo —

(☎ code León 987)

## Activities

**Bembibre**
Fiestas: Santo Ecce Homo, 28 July; Santo Criso, 15 September.

**Boeza**
Fiesta: San Antonio, 13 June.

**Cacabelos**
Fiesta: de la Vendimia (grape harvest) in August (variable).
Fiesta: Santisima Virgen de la Quinta Angustia, 7 April; San Roque, 16 August.

**Castropodarme**
Fiesta: Santa Colomba, 31 December.

**Folgoso de la Ribera**
Fiesta: San Juan Bautista, 24 June.

**Igüeña**
Fiestas: Santa Apolonia, 9 February and Santa Marina, 18 July.

**Noceda**
Fiesta: San Pedro Avincula, 1 August.

**Ponferrada**
Fiesta: Nuestra Señora de la Encina, 8 and 9 September.

**Pieros**
Fiesta: San Martin de Tours, 11 November.

**Quilós** (north of Cacabelos)
Fiesta: Santo Tirso, 28 January.

**San Miguel de la Dueñas**
Fiesta: San Miguel Arcángel, 29 September.

**Tombrio de Bajo**
Fiesta: Santa Isabel, 2 July.

**Toreno**
Fiestas: San Juan, 24 June and Santa Barbara, 4 December.

**Torre del Bierzo**
Fiesta: San Roque, 16 August.

**Villafranca del Bierzo**
Fiestas: Santo Tirso, 28 January and Santisimo Cristo de Esperanza, 15 September.

## Sports

### Swimming Pools

**Ponferrada**
Piscina Natación Club
Carretera Molina
☎ 411010

Piscina Club de Tenis
P-1 (Gericol),
☎ 410214

### Fishing

*Upper Río Sil*
Matarrosa to Palacios. Trout (iris arch and common).

*Lower Sil*
Matarrosa to confluence of Río Cabrera (including Embalse de Barcena). Carp and black bass, 'escallos and boga'.

*Sil Tributaries*
Ríos Burbia, Valdueza, Cabrera and Fiera. Trout (common, salmon and iris arch).

*Coto 16*
Río Valcarce between Trabadelo
and Pereje on NVI (Villafranca-
Galicia).

*Coto 15*
Río Cua
For permits etc, enquire Ayuntam-
iento, Ponferrada or Jefatura
Piscicola, León.

## Transport

### Rail
RENFE ticket office
Travesia Gómez Nuñez 2
☎ 41000

### Buses
Autos Arias
Gen Sanjurjo 45
☎ 410054 to Villadepalos.

Autos Pelines
Calle Ramón y Cajal 3
☎ 410359 to Toreno, Vega de
Espinareda, Fresnedo, San Clemente and Noceda.

Empresa Fernández
Avenida Maria
☎ 411537 to Bembibre, Torre del
Bierzo, Cacabelos and Villafranca
del Bierzo.

Auto-Estación Vázquez y Alonso
Camino de Santiago 13
☎ 410666 and García Morato 6
☎ 410609: buses to Fabero, Cacabelos, Pereda (Los Ancares).

Town Buses
Calle General Moscardó 9
☎ 410609

### Taxi Stands
Calle Cómez Nuñez
☎ 411148 and Calvo Sotelo
☎ 411055

## Places of Interest

**Ponferrado**
Castle
Open: 9am-1pm and 3-5pm (2-6pm
October-end March).

Meteorological Observatory
Calle Ancha
☎ 41 01 00

## Tourist Information Offices

**Bembibre**
Ayuntamiento
Plaza Generalisimo 1
☎ 51 00 01/12 13

Casa Cultura
☎ 51 05 54

**Cacabelos**
Ayuntamiento
Plaza Mayor
☎ 54 60 11/61 51

**Ponferrada**
Avenida de la Puebla 3
☎ 41 55 37

Ayuntamiento
Plaza del Ayuntamiento
☎ 41 22 50

**Toreno**
Ayuntamiento
1 Plaza Mayor
☎ 53 30 03

**Torre del Bierzo**
Ayuntamiento
Avenida de Santa Bárbara
☎ 53 62 31

**Villafranca del Bierzo**
Ayuntamiento
23 Plaza del Generalisimo
☎ 54 02 91

# 7 • The Rías Altas

This is a remote coastal region which is the Atlantic seaboard of the old province of Galicia, from Ribadeo on the border between Asturias and Lugo to south-westwards from La Coruña to Cabo Finisterre, a distance of nearly 400 km (248 miles).

The coastline is characterised by granite rocks of the ancient crystalline foundations of the north-western Iberian Peninsula, and cut into by long, wide inlets called *rías*. This Spanish word means estuaries, but the term has come to mean a river estuary or mouth that has been submerged or drowned by a rise in sea level. They are wide, funnel-shaped inlets, becoming narrower and shallower inland to where one or two quite small rivers enter the head of the estuary.

This part of Spain is rather different from the popular image of the country, in that the landscape, climate, and to a certain extent the people, have similar characteristics to the Atlantic coasts of Ireland, Cornwall and Brittany. The people themselves are of mixed origin, the few original Celtic inhabitants being subdued by the Romans, followed by barbarian invasions of the Suevi, the Visigoths, incursions by the Normans and Arabs with, afterwards, the great medieval pilgrimages to Santiago de Compostela. Some claim to be a Celtic people, but it is hardly justified. Nevertheless a Celtic strain persists in the more remote inland areas, and near the Portuguese frontier. But their language, a dialect of mixed Portuguese and Spanish, is from Rome; all traces of an original Celtic tongue have vanished in the 2,500 years which have elapsed since their arrival.

The landscape is rugged with ridges of folded hard rock, bare and used to build compact, thick-set houses roofed with heavy slabs to resist the wind. The coast varies with cliffs, many sandy beaches, creeks and dozens of small fishing ports — particularly in La Coruña — whilst part of the Lugo coast is often low lying. The vegetation is luxuriant owing to the mild humid climate, especially along sheltered valleys. Evergreens, like laurels and fuchsia, flourish and the slopes are well wooded with ilex, chestnut, eucalyptus and maritime

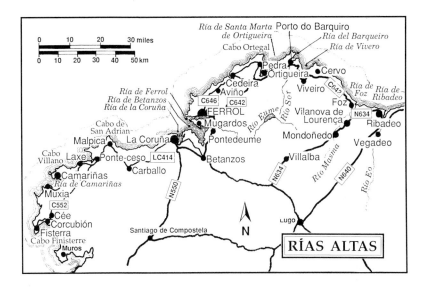

pine. This rich vegetation is often referred to as Lusitanian, from the Roman name for Portugal. Along the many rivers are meadows, and orchards of apples, pears and cherries; whilst pigs are seen everywhere in the scattered fields over hills and terraces.

The towns of this coastal region are numerous. The first one in Lugo, Ribadeo is on the Río Eo, then comes Mondoñedo, a cathedral city upstream on the Río Masma, then Burela, a busy fishing port next to Viveiro on a large and beautiful *ría*. Then into the province of La Coruña, where the first town is Ortigueira on a long and sinuous *ría*, then the west coast of Galicia is reached with the pretty town of Cedeira, and afterwards the large naval base of Ferrol, an old departure point for sailing ships to the Americas. Next the picturesque town of Pontedeume, reached by a long bridge across the Río Eume, followed by the long narrow *ría*, and town of Betanzos. Now comes the port and historic city of La Coruña and then then the western *rías*, and the inland town of Carballo, the fishing port of Malpica, the small port of Corcubión, and so to Cabo Finisterre, the edge of the ancient world.

Galicia is not exactly underpopulated, but there do exist many uncrowded beaches, bays and quiet corners, and long stretches of very green countryside. Of course, the better known beaches tend to be overcrowded in high summer, and with the increased mobility of the Spanish tourist from the big cities trying to escape the torrid heat of the interior, August may not be the best month. However, outside of the peak season there is plenty of opportunity for exploring the lesser visited *rías*, going upstream of the sheltered river valleys, and seeing some of the smaller unknown towns that are full of history, along with their buildings, and the many fishing ports which are always interesting places to wander about.

The climate of the region is definitely warm and damp, with an average rainfall of over 1,000mm (40in) a year. Summers are warm 21-2°C (70-2°F), and winters mild and rainy. Springs are slightly cooler than autumns: May about 17°C (62-3°F), while October is 18-19°C (64-6°F). In spite of the rain, sunshine hours are quite high, although better inland. There are drier stretches of coast. For example Cabo Finisterre is drier than the city of La Coruña, and surprisingly the coast west of Viveiro is drier than the eastern strip.

## Travelling to the Area

### By Road
Access to Ribadeo from Madrid airport via *autopista* A2 (Av de America) and C. Abascal to NVI road, then Lugo, and N640 to Ribadeo: 615km (381 miles).

From Santiago de Compostela airport to Ferrol *autopista* A9 and NVI 116km (72 miles), to La Coruña 87km (54 miles).

### By Rail
From Madrid (P. Pio) via Lugo to Ferrol.

## The Lugo Coast — Ribadeo to Ría del Barqueiro

The coastline of the province of Lugo is only 80 or 90km (50-5 miles) long, but it is full of variety from where it begins at the estuary of the Eo, which forms the boundary between Asturias and Galicia. The sides of the *ría* are verdant, with fine views, and the river, which is fast flowing in its upper reaches and good for salmon, flows into the sea past the port of **Ribadeo**.

The port was very active in the eighteenth and nineteenth centuries, when its coasting sailing vessels were in the Baltic wheat, hemp and flax trade, and went to ports like Memel (Prussia) and Riga in Latvia. This is reflected in the old streets full of fine houses which lead down to the harbour. In front of the Plaza España is the eighteenth-century palace of Ibañez, Marquis of Sargadelos, who built the first blast furnaces in Spain and created the famous ceramic works of Sargadelos, as well as trying to make Ribadeo the maritime capital of northern Galicia. He was assassinated in the street on 2 February 1809, the day the Spanish arose against the French occupation. Since

1944 it has been the municipal palace. Nearby is the imposing building of the eighteenth-century Custom House, another reminder of the port's past maritime prosperity. The lighthouse and the *paseo maritimo* are worth visiting, but before leaving, go up to the Cerro de Santa Cruz. From the summit there is a splendid panoramic view over the entire *ría*.

The coast westwards is low lying with some splendid sandy beaches, among which Reinante, Os Casros and Benquerencia are outstanding. The main coast road, N634 runs inland via the village of Reinante to Barreiros, where the Ría de Foz is reached. Before going to Foz, the route goes up the valley of the Río Masma to see two towns. The first, **Vilanova de Lourença** has the monastery of San Salvador, with a beautiful baroque façade. The high altar of the church is equally impressive, whilst the Romanesque chapel of Santa Maria de Valdeflores contains the tomb of the Conde Osorio, the monastery's founder. This is made of a rare stone brought from the east, which has a hole through which one can touch the Conde's bones!

From here there is an interesting hilly trip inland to the second town of **Mondoñedo** by the LU131 and LU124. The roads are empty, except for many small vans delivering fish. A shorter, but duller route to the town is via the N634 main road. It is a most interesting place, with a superb cathedral, which was on the coastal route to Santiago. The façade in golden stone is flanked by two eighteenth-century baroque towers, whilst the central rose window is thirteenth century. This presents a fine sight when the sunlight catches the stone. The interior is beautiful, but a little dark and sober. Amongst the many relics is the famous Tudor-Gothic sculptured 'English Virgin', brought from St Paul's cathedral, London, by the city burghers in the sixteenth century to escape the Reformation of Henry VIII. The old town is delightful to wander in. The façades of the white houses display coats of arms, while above are little wrought iron balconies, and nearby flagstone passages with arcades and also the 'Fuente Vieja', an old stone fountain with steps, to say nothing of the many baroque-style buildings like the hospital. Set back behind the cathedral is the seminary of Santa Catalina, an enormous building. Twenty years ago it was said Mondoñedo was a place of silence, broken only in the dawn by the nuns singing in the church of Las Madres Concepciónistas, and a solitary bell. The town is famous for its confectionery, *empanadas* (meat pasties), and bread, which apparently is even sent out as far as Asturias. The Hostal Montero in Avenida San Lázaro, can be recommended as a place to eat.

Returning to the Ría de Foz, the coast road, now the C642, is taken

*Haymaking in the traditional manner on the Lugo coast*

to a turn on the left, LU152, which leads to the monastery of San Martín de Mondoñedo, of ancient foundation, isolated in a rural setting. It is an impressive and massive building, with buttresses against the apse of the very early Romanesque church. Inside are sculptured chapels, part of the three apses. It was a bishopric until 1112, and a refuge for monks and the abbot of the monastery of Dumio in Braga, Portugal.

Returning to the main road **Foz** is reached. This is a lively and very attractive port, engaged in deep sea fishing, and in medieval times was a whaling port with famous shipyards. It has colourful public gardens, and nearby sandy beaches like Rapadoira, beyond the promontory. Further along at **Fazouro**, there is a Celtic *citania* (burial ground), and the whole region abounds in *castros* or hill forts. The valley here is full of apple and cherry orchards. Soon one comes to Burela, another busy fishing port, and on to **Cervo**, where one can make an excursion to the old ceramic factory of Sargadelos, where the manor house of the marquis, and most of the original works, are preserved. It started life as a foundry for making cannon, and Goya is thought to have painted his portrait of the marquis here. The ceramics fetch a high price because of their unusual design.

A few kilometres after Cervo there is a turn to the tiny fishing port of San Ciprián on its winding river and jutting out cape. From here there is a whole area of coast that can be explored between the main road and the sea. At length one approaches the fishing port of

Celeiro, renowned for shellfish, and soon the large and beautiful Ría de Viveiro comes into view. The town of **Viveiro** preserves part of its old walls with the gate of Charles V, which has the emperor's arms and carved watchtowers in the plateresque style. There is a park-like waterfront, and a fine medieval bridge, La Misericordia, which carries the main road over to the immense sandy stretch of the Covas beach. Viveiro has some good buildings: the Gothic church of the old convent of San Francisco, with its small cloisters, and fine lancet windows in the apse, and two Romanesque churches. Holy Week here is more solemn than anywhere else in Galicia, and around the Ría de Viveiro is a splendid landscape of sea, mountains, and wooded countryside like a huge garden with a lake.

The road goes on through agreeable surroundings to near the village of Vicedo on the side of the Ría de Barqueiro. Here the Río Sor flows from its pastoral interior into a picturesque *ría*, considered by many to be the most beautiful of all the Galician *rías*. To see it at its best, however, pass the small port of **Barqueiro**, with its white houses and slate roofs, and noted for crayfish, and turn right on to the LU100, the road to Bares. This road in itself is very fine, being almost a forested coastal corniche, and after a short while, a superb view of the *ría* appears. Go to the small town of Vila de Bares, and its tiny Porto de Bares down on the *ría* itself, with a prehistoric breakwater nearly 300m (186ft) long. Further on still is the Punta de la Estaca with its lighthouse, the most northerly point in Spain, traditionally used by transatlantic aircraft as a navigation point.

## La Coruña — Ría de Barqueiro to La Coruña City

The route has now crossed into the province of La Coruña, as the Río Sor is the boundary river. The main road leaves the coast, but still passes through wooded and pleasant countryside to reach the village of Espanante. From here one can go down to Porto de Espanante on a side road. This port used to be noted for its *bonito* fishing fleet; the *bonito* is a fish with a delicious taste, the small striped tunny, more common in the tropics than western Atlantic waters. There are good beaches on both sides of the promontory here, Espanante and San Antonio. Returning to and continuing along the main road, a view of another *ría* soon appears, and a very long (5km, 3 mile) beach, Mourouzos, of very fine-grained sand. The *ría* too, is very large, and has a very long name: Ría de Santa Marta de Ortigueira, or simply **Ortigueira**. The town seems quite big in spite of its small population, built out along the side of a peninsula, but seems to have been important in the past. There is an ancient camp, on which was a count's castle, an old walled town and a moat. Inside the town, the fourteenth-century convent of Santo Domingo, rebuilt in eighteenth-century baroque, is a pleasing building.

The road goes on past the head of the *ría*, which at low tide, has extensive mud flats and marsh, to **Mera**, on the river of the same name. Here the narrow gauge railway line (FEVE), which has hugged the coast from Ribadeo — sometimes much closer than the road — branches off into the interior, and our route turns sharp right along the side of the *ría*. The road here to the village of Feás gives a much better view of the *ría*, which is very large. The route onwards via the village of Pedra, to the port of Cariño is heavily forested with a luxuriant vegetation of eucalyptus, maritime pine, maple and chestnut right down to **Cariño** itself. The port is quite large and appears very busy and industrious, with canning factories, but there is a fine large beach, La Concha, and another much further along, called Fornos.

Return to Pedra from the port, and turn right, climbing up steeply through woods, and eventually to the high open moorland of the Sierra de la Capelada. This is probably the most remote section of the coast between Ribadeo and La Coruña. It is a high landscape of tufted grass, with cattle and wild horses grazing, and above the tree line. There are very good views of the sea, and huge cliffs. It would be possible to walk to Cabro Ortegal, but the way would be by tracks and paths for there are no roads. Out at sea ocean-going vessels can be seen, huge supertankers, coasting the northern extremities of Spain. The highest point here is the Garita de Herbeira (620m, 2,034ft), and the coast as a whole is considered to be the highest in Europe.

The road now descends to where there is a right turn to the sanctuary of San Andrés de Teixido (St Andrew). This is a little church with an elegant tower on a fine site overlooking the sea, cliffs, woods and meadows, and surrounded by the nucleus of a hamlet, 140m (459ft) above the sea. Inside the church there is a very fine altar, with a statue of the saint holding his cross. Outside a rocky route over cliff tops leads to the Mirador de Cima de Costa, again with superb views of coastal scenery, and the Punta Candelaria.

Back to the Sierra de Capelada road, which now descends through woods to the town, and the beautiful Ría de Cedeira. The *ría* is enchanting even at low tide, but is at its best when the tide is high. The town of **Cedeira** is extremely attractive, with well laid out streets, high white houses with elegant glassed-in upper storeys, and lower storeys with neat iron balconies. Some of these date from sixteenth and seventeenth centuries, and were from noble families

*Sanctuary of San Andrés
de Teixido*

with names like Andrade, Montenegro and Piñeiro. But those of the nineteenth and early twentieth century are equally dignified with glassed-in façades. The church of Santa Maria, in spite of the last two centuries' additions, keeps some of the original fourteenth-century Gothic, with a sixteenth-century main door. The waterfront down to the port leaves the old town with its gardens and goes to a modern, well equipped fishing port with a very lively fish market, where the variety of fish displayed is considerable. Cod, bream, hake, *rape* and shellfish, crayfish, sea-calf, spider crabs, prawns, shrimps and goosebarnacle or acorn shell (related, but not the same as the common species) — considered a delicacy here. On a hill near the port, are the walls of the Castillo de la Concepción, an eighteenth-century fort, built to defend the *ría*.

The road, C646, around the *ría* is wooded, giving fine views, but swings away from the coast now, which is lower-lying with sand dunes, and a dozen fine beaches between here and Ferrol. These have few roads leading to them, so many are isolated, being ideal for solitude, and exploration. But the more accessible beaches like Frouxeira, near Valdoviño, are very crowded in summer to offset this apparent paradise! The C646 road is through a pleasant countryside of woods, meadows and cultivated fields but there are many villages and hamlets, which shows how densely populated some of the rural areas of Galicia can be. The route now approaches **Ferrol** and its fine *ría*, and the city is dominated by its naval arsenal, the most important

*Cedeira*

in Spain. It used to be in three parts: Old Ferrol, New Ferrol and Esteiro. The old medieval town is west of New Ferrol, and built around the dock of Curuxeiras, but the new town was created in the eighteenth-century, with the building of the naval dockyards and arsenal, and has expanded since into a modern naval base, with ship-building yards. It was laid out into six long streets crossing two fine plazas, and intersected by nine shorter streets at right angles. It retains much of its eighteenth-century elegance, as does the arsenal with its impressive gate, which can be visited. Two contrasting buildings are the eighteenth-century cathedral in neo-classical style, and the older thirteenth-century church of San Francisco, originally a Franciscan convent. Esteiro is between the new city and the ship-yards.

The strategic position of Ferrol, not only commanding the narrow entrance to its own *ría*, but also that of the three *rías* converging, Ferrol, Betanzos and La Coruña, made it a world class naval base. Not surprisingly, William Pitt, the British Prime Minister, once remarked: 'If England had a port like this on its coastline, the Government would surround it with a wall of silver'.

From Ferrol the route takes the main NVI to Cabañas. The road is built up, and traffic is very dense, not with tourists, but the ordinary commerce between two large cities only 50 or 60km (30-40 miles) apart. To avoid this, take a right turn at Fene, and go to **Mugardos** on the southern shore of the Ría de Ferrol.

This is a pleasant town with a small fishing harbour, and a long waterfront leading to a beach. Octopus is cooked here in a local dish, *a la Mugadesa*, which is quite famous. The countryside of the peninsula is very pretty, especially the road across it to the Ría de Ares, and the village and beach of Chanteiro, where there is an extremely good view southwards to the Ría de Betanzos. An exploratory excursion can be made from here to the open sea at Punta Coitelada. Then to Ares, a fishing village, but really a resort, with a whole string of beaches of which Seselle is outstanding. Nearby is a curious fifteenth-century fortified church at Lubre, and so along the estuary of the Río Eume to Cabañas, with its beach surrounded by pinewoods near the railway bridge across the river. Crossing by the long medieval road bridge of the NVI, the town of **Pontedeume** is reached.

This is one of the most picturesque towns in Galicia, and was the seat of the very powerful family of the Counts of Andrade, two of whose members are notable: Fernando Pérez, a great builder in the fourteenth-century, and Fernando, a hero of the Italian wars in the sixteenth century. Reminders of their feudal power are a great square tower with a coat of arms carved in stone, the remains of a fourteenth-century palace, standing in the middle of the town, and the ruins of a thirteenth-century castle on a hill nearby. The other tower on the skyline of Pontedeume is the baroque one of the eighteenth-century church.

From here two excursions can be made inland. The first is to the monastery of Caaveiro. This route leaves the town by the main road, then turns left on to the LC152, and left again on to a minor road by the side of the *ría*, which has good views, then continues upstream of the Río Eume until a little bridge is reached.

Then one walks through a wood, and there, almost encased in thickets of vegetation on a spur of rock, stand the noble solitary ruins of Caaveiro, founded by San Rosendo. The Romanesque church of the twelfth century has a splendid semi-circular apse, and alongside is the great fortified gateway with its escutcheon, and bell tower. These surviving portions stand out against a background of steeply wooded slopes, and luxuriant encroaching greenery in impressive isolation.

Return to the LC152, and take this road south-eastwards to the village of **Monfero**, where off on a side road are the remains of the twelfth-century Cistercian monastery of Monfero. It is set in a fertile, but isolated valley in rustic surroundings, backed by rugged granite hills. It is of colossal proportions, rebuilt by Juan Herrera, the architect of Philip II, in 1575. The enormous baroque façade of the church, in chequerboard stone of slate and granite, flanked by huge tall pillars, is outstanding, whilst the cloisters have beautiful vaulting, with hanging keystones. It is being restored, as it surely deserves.

Returning to Pontedeume, the route now takes a right hand side road round the Ría de Betanzos, a most picturesque passage by the wooded beach of Ber, where the pines reach down to the sea. Then past the village of Perbes, to Miño on the right bank of the *ría*, in very leafy surroundings. Next, continue on the NVI to the town of **Betanzos** at the head of the *ría* and at the centre of a rich valley region, known as 'Las Mariñas', of hop bines, wheat, fruit and vineyards. An old city, the Roman *Brigantium*, and later famous for its fairs, is full of churches, old buildings and splendid houses arcaded and glassed in upper storeys. There are three Gothic churches in the centre, one being the convent church of San Francisco, founded by Conde Fernando Perézde Andrade in 1387, in the form of a Latin cross, with three apses. This contains his tomb under the pulpit, which is quite impressive, supported by a wild boar and a bear — his emblems. Amongst the many interesting buildings are the classical eighteenth-century Archives Palace, the complex of the parish church of Santiago, the sixteenth-century municipal tower, and the palace of Bendaña.

From Betanzos it is possible to get to La Coruña by a variety of routes, but take the side road on to the peninsula that separates the *rías* of Betanzos and La Coruña. The road reaches **Sada**, with a glimpse *en route* of the fine Pedrido bridge across the *ría*, which avoids Betanzos. This is a resort pure and simple, with a beach of fine sand, and calm waters. From Sada the route hugs the *ría* to the fishing village of Fontán, then goes through a pleasant landscape of pines and apple orchards to **Lorbé**, which has a beach, and famous mussels. Then across to the tiny fishing hamlet of **Mera** on the *ría* of La Coruña, where one can see the city, and its spectacular Tower of Hercules. Then along to **Santa Cruz**, with its islet in the bay, and fine green coastal scenery, and the city of La Coruña is approached.

**La Coruña** ('Corunna' to English speakers), is the largest, and perhaps, apart from Santiago, the most historic city in Galicia. It is of Roman origin, built out on a rocky peninsula, and connected by a narrow isthmus to the land. Witness to this is the Tower of Hercules, the only Roman lighthouse still functioning. Built originally in the second century AD, and restored in 1682, and again between 1788-90, it stands 104m (341ft) above the sea. The city later had walls, and saw two great incidents of history, both tragic: the departure and return of the invincible Armada of 1588, with the loss of 15,000 men and sixty-three ships; followed by the retreat and evacuation of the British army of 1809, with the loss of their general, Sir John Moore — called by a Spanish author 'The first Dunkirk'. There are many things to see here, and some of the best are: 'the Cristales', the great bank of glassed-in galleries built in the nineteenth century, along with the gardens bordering Los Cantones, in front of the port; next, in the old city: the Puertas del Mar, 'sea gates' in the ancient walls; Puertas San Miguel, del Clavo and de la Cruz in the Paseo del Parrote. There is also the pretty Plaza Azcárraga, and the old church of Santiago. Perhaps one of the most picturesque places is the Garden of San Carlos. This was laid out inside the ramparts and fortress of San Carlos in 1809, and there is a fine view over the old walls and bay. Here also is the tomb of Sir John Moore.

## La Coruña to Cabo Finisterre

From the city this route leaves on the C552, and takes the road to **Caión**, a small fishing village on a rocky peninsula, facing the open sea. This was an ancient whaling station, and has some interesting old houses, and a convent. The coast further west is low lying, with many sand dunes and beaches, but difficult of access by paved roads.

Returning to the C552, the route continues inland to the town of Carballo, and from there take the LC414 to the busy fishing port of **Malpica**. It is both sheltered, and dominated by the Monte de San Adrián and its jutting cape. The quays are piled with nets and the fishermen have a reputation for tales about gigantic waves. Perhaps they are not all fables, for the port is busy being rebuilt with massive new breakwaters. South-westwards from here, the coast is rockbound, subject in the winter to the full force of the Atlantic waves, and is known as the Costa del Muerte (Coast of Death). The route, however, takes a picturesque road, LC430 to Ponte-Ceso on an enclosed part of the Ría de Laxe, estuary of the Río Anllóns. The scenery along the *ría* is verdant with the road going to the fishing village of **Laxe** on the southern side of the outer *ría*. This has a pleasant central Plaza del Arco, with old balconied manorial houses of stone blocks, and two beaches northwards along the *ría*. From Laxe the road swings inland via the villages of Traba and Ponte do Porto, by Xaviña with its Romanesque church, to the large fishing village of **Camariñas**. This is at the end of a wooded inlet of maritime pines and a fine wide beach on the Ría de Camariñas. It is a centre for a long established cottage industry of lace-making.

From here one can go out to Cabo Vilán and its lighthouse, situated high above the sea, which in winter is sometimes forbidding. Then on to Muxia the other side of the *ría* at Punta de la Barca, where there is a church, N. Señora de la Barca, with a magnificent eighteenth-century retable. From here southwards is a maze of roads inland, but not along the coast, so there is scope for exploration, for example to the most westerly point of Spain, Cabo Touriñan, by devious indirect ways.

Now the route takes the C552 again to Cée, a small industrial town on the last of the superb Rías Altas, that of **Corcubión**. This is a pretty fishing village, with a busy commercial port and a summer resort with the fine beach of Quenje. It was also the scene of treasure trove in October 1986, for naval divers from the salvage vessel, *Poseidón*, recovered from a galleon sunk nearly 500 years ago: bronze cannon, gold coins, a bronze punch, lead and a crucifix belonging to the *tercios* (troops) in Flanders. The finds are all now in the naval museum in El Ferrol.

And from here to **Fisterra** (Galician for Finisterre), a fishing village with a Romanesque church, and old houses with escutcheons, and then to that place of legends both maritime and religious, a long cape stretching southwards into the sea — Finisterre. The road to the cape is a corniche with fine views over the wide bay, shut in by layers of mountains. This is the end of the ancient world, and this region as well.

# Further Information
## — The Rías Altas —

### Activities

**Barqueiro**
*Fiesta*: 8 September.

**Barreiros**
*Fiesta*: 24 August.

**Betanzos**
*Holy* Week: (Monday and Tuesday): Romería de la Magdalena, 'Breaking of pots', picnics and public dancing; 23 and 28 July: illuminated processions at night. *Fiesta: Patronales (San Roque)*: 14-25 August: various, including launching at night of huge paper balloon (*globo*). Fireworks on water. Decorated boats on Río Mandeo.

**Cariño**
*Fiesta*: 24 August.

**Cedeira**
*Fiestas*: 15 August, Nosa Señora do Mar, maritime procession; Sierra de Capelada, Montoxo, last Sunday in June: 'Rapa das Bestas'; *San* Andrés *de Teixido sanctuary*, *Romerías* second Monday in September until end of November.

**Chanteiro** (Ares)
*Romería*: 24 September.

**Corcubión**
*Fiestas:* April 25; *Romería*: 29 June.

**La Coruña**
*Fiestas:* Maria Pita. Throughout August. Bullfights. Regional dances.

**Fene**
*Fiestas:* 16 July; 5 August; *Romería*: 16 July.

**Ferrol**
*Fiestas:* Las Pepitas 18 March; Romería de Chamorro, Tuesday of Holy Week. Other processions during Holy Week; *Fiesta*: 16 July; Grana (Ferrol) 15 August.

**Finisterre** (Fisterra)
*Holy Week:* 'Desenclavo' Good Friday (strange religious festival with actors — 'un-nailing' of Christ). Resurrection acted on hill nearby on Easter Sunday; *Fiesta*: Easter Saturday and 7 September.

**Foz**
*Fiestas:* 16 May; 16-17 July and 8-12 August.

**Laxe**
*Fiesta*: 15 August; *Romería* 30 August.

**Malpica**
*Fiesta*: 4 August.

**Mugardos**
*Fiestas:* Las Pepitas 18 March; Saturday nearest 16 July.

**Ortigueira**
*Fiesta*: 28 July to 1 August.

**Pontedeume**
*Fiesta:* 10 July
*Romería*: 8 May and 11 September (decorated boats on Río Eume).

**Ribadeo**
*Fiestas:* 1st Sunday in August, *Romeria Campestre* to Santa Cruz; 8 September. Santa Maria del Campo. (Starts on 7th September until dawn 10 September.)

**Valdoviño**
*Fiestas:* 11, 17-19 and 25 July.

**Vicedo**
*Fiesta*: 1-6 August.

**Viveiro**
*Fiestas:* 24-29 June, San Juan/San Pedro (Covas); First Sunday of July 'La Rapa das Bestas' (gathering of wild cattle and horses at Boimente, 10km (6 miles) on LU161; 16 July N.S. del Carmen, at Viveiro, Magazos and Celeiro; 25 July Santiago Apostól (Celeiro), maritime procession and regattas; 26 July Santa Ana (Magazos); Patronales de Viveiro: 14-19 August to San Roque (viewpoint); fourth Sunday August: Romería de Naseiro in San Pedro (5km, 3 miles) famous 4 days; 8 September at beach of Area, Faro: Romería de Nuestra Señora; 16 September San Ciprián/ Viveiro Romería.

N.B. *Romerías* are usually pilgrimages, but can vary. Cabo Vilán is usually known to seafarers as Cape Villano.

## Places of Interest

**La Coruña**
San Carlos (fort)
Visits: 10am-1.30pm, 4-7pm (2-6pm in winter).
Gardens: open until dusk.

Castle of San Antón (Archaeological Museum)
Beyond San Carlos fort.

Torre de Hercules
Road to foot of tower.

**Ferrol**
The Arsenal
Visits: 4-6pm (enquire mornings on working days at Secretariat of the Arsenal).

**Mondoñedo**
Cathedral Museum
Open: beginning July-mid-September 11am-1pm, 4-7pm; rest of year 12noon-1pm.

## Tourist Information Offices

**Betanzos**
Casa Consistorial

**Cedeira**
Casa Consistorial
☎ 48 00 00/01

**La Coruña**
Tourist Office
Dársena de la Marina
On the waterfront, beyond gardens
☎ 22 19 56

**Ferrol**
Tourist Office
Palacio Municipal
Plaza de Armas
☎ 32 02 11

**Ribadeo**
Tourist Office
Oficina Municipal
Pl España
☎ 11 06 89

**Viveiro**
Tourist Office
Calle María Sarmiento 9
☎ 56 01 53

## Transport

**Ferrol**
FEVE station (Ferrocarril de Via Estrecha — narrow gauge)
Avenida Compostela
☎ 31 52 53

The Transcantábrico
Luxury 7-day train trip running between Ferrol and León via coast regions of Cantabria, Asturias and Galicia. 1,000km (625 miles), through 147 tunnels. Trains leave from Ferrol or León on alternate Saturdays between June and October. Sightseeing trips, and stops at night for sleeping.
For reservations:
Marsans International Travel
205 East 42nd St
New York
NY 10017
☎ 800-223-6114, or in New York State 212-661-6565

RENF station
☎ 31 46 55
Service to La Coruña via Pontedeume, Miño and Betanzos.

'Ideal Auto SA'
Plaza España 7
☎ 31 33 76
Buses to Ares, Betanzos, La Coruña, Mugardos and Viveiro.

'Riaisa'
Av da de Compostela
☎ 31 59 55
Buses to Cedeira and Valdoviño
Empresa.

Emp. 'El Rápido'/Cuntis (Bar
Gabeiras)
☎ 31 00 05
Bus to Monfero.

**Ribadeo**
FEVE (rail)
☎ 11 06 99

ERSA (buses)
Clemente M. Pasarón 2
☎ 11 00 42
To Viveiro, Foz, Mondoñedo.

Taxis
Parque Municipal.

**Viveiro**
FEVE (rail)
Trains to Ribadeo and Ferrol.

Frequent bus services to Ribadeo,
Mondoñedo and Foz. All start
from along waterfront (Plaza Lugo
to Avenidas José Antonio and
Onesimo Redondo.

# 8 • The Western Marches of Spain

This region consists of the Sierra de la Peña Francia, Ciudad Rodrigo and the Sierra de Béjar in the province of Salamanca in Old Castile, with Las Hurdes and the Sierra de Gata in the province of Cáceres in Extremadura.

None of these areas are very well known, and represent the Portuguese border marches. They have great variations of landscape, from the broad plains and rugged mountains of Extremadura with its base of old crystalline rocks of granite and schists, to the schistose mountains of the extreme south of Salamanca, and the plains of the south-west corner of the northern Meseta near Ciudad Rodrigo on the road to Portugal.

Traditionally Extremadura was the land of the *conquistadores* (conquerors), and Salamanca province one of wheat and sheep lands and academic brilliance, but this region is really on the fringe of both of these, and more remote. The attractions lie in just this remoteness — sparsely populated, rural landscapes and isolated villages, but the scenery at times is quite beautiful, and the mountain areas are always impressive. The wildlife is more easily seen here than in other regions, whilst in late spring the wild flowers are abundant, and some of the small towns are extremely interesting and picturesque. For those who like aquatic activities and expanses of water, there are two very large HEP and irrigation *pantanos* or artificial lakes near the region in isolated surroundings. There are a number of small towns and villages in the region, but the larger towns tend to be on the periphery.

The most attractive and historic city is Ciudad Rodrigo, 89km (55 miles) south-west of Salamanca, then in the heart of the Sierra de Francia is La Alberca, which has kept its character, then to the south-east is Béjar at the foot of the *sierra* of the same name. Then moving into Cáceres province of Extremadura, is Plasencia at the meeting point of the limestone *sierras*, and the ancient crystalline plateau of Extremadura, and a good place to begin an exploration of the region.

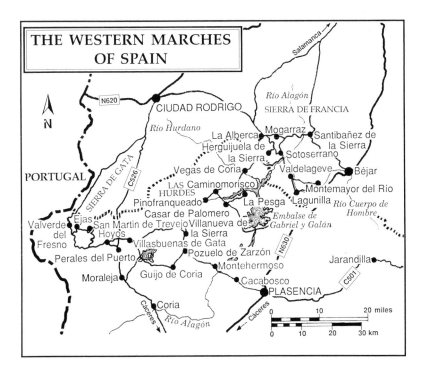

Then some way westwards is Moraleja, an old town that has expanded in recent years, and a good centre for various journeys. There is a great deal to explore in this region and now, with a larger number of paved roads than formerly, there is immense scope for penetrating into quite wild areas, especially in the Sierra de Gata, near the Portuguese border, and opportunities for some rock climbing, mountain walking and even skiing in the Salamanca *sierras*. For people with time to spare, there are many excursions to be made to villages and little towns still redolent of old Spain, in spite of the upsurge of regional activity brought about by the creation of the autonomous areas. The climate varies according to the relief of the land, but in general it is continental, dry and sunny. The two areas of Salamanca and Cáceres have differences chiefly in winter and summer.

Ciudad Rodrigo, and the lower parts of the Sierra de Francia are slightly less hot than Cáceres (further south) in the summer: Salamanca July 29.6°C (85°F); Cáceres July 33.5°C (92°F). Winters in Salamanca are colder than Cáceres. Salamanca January 8°C (46°F); Cáceres January 11.3°C (52°F). Both are cold at night, however, and in the Sierra de Béjar (Salamanca) at 900-1,200m (3,000-4,000ft) snow begins in autumn, and can last until early spring. Rainfall is low, 420-80mm (16$^1/_2$-19in), and except for the dry summer months is well distributed in Salamanca, with December the wettest month (53mm, 2in). Cáceres is generally similar, but March and the spring season are prone to wet weather (71mm/2.8in). Sunshine hours are long, Salamanca having as much as 12$^1/_2$ hours daily in July, and 8 hours in April and September; Cáceres is similar, but there are no figures available. A word concerning winds. Both areas have a temperate humid wind called the *Abrego*, which blows from the south-west. Extremadura suffers from a hot land breeze in the summer, caused by the sun, which lasts from early on until past midday, known as a *Solano*.

## Travelling to the Area

### By Car
From Madrid (Barajas) airport to Plasencia. *Autopista* A2 to ring road, then NV to Navalmoral de la Mata. Turn right to Jarandilla, then left on to C501 direct to Plasencia (257km, 159 miles).
Return from Salamanca: N620 to Tordesillas, NVI to Adanero, then A6 *autopista* to NVI outside Madrid, then Calle Abascall and *autopista* A2 (Av de America) to airport (about 300-10km, 186-92 miles).
From Salamanca to Madrid (P. Pio).

### By Rail
From Madrid (Atocha) to Cáceres. Then Cáceres to Plasencia.

## Extremadura — Northern Cáceres

### Plasencia
This city is situated on the banks of the Río Jerte, a river which seems to attract storks, for there are many here from February to July. A very picturesque medieval bridge, incorrectly called 'Roman', crosses the river, with six arches, cutwaters and abutments. In the old quarter, the first building to see is the cathedral. Started in the thirteenth century, it was completely reconstructed in the sixteenth century, separating the nave and the apse, so it is part Romanesque and part Gothic. Entering the newer part by the north door, one sees slender pillars and vaulting, built by master architects of the Renaissance: Juan de Alava, Covarrubias and Diego de Siloé. Access to the old part is by a door, and then the finely sculptured cloisters are seen, with the nave of the earlier church.
The old quarter is worth walking round: Calles Quesos and

Arenillas, with the Plazas Santo Domingo and San Nicolás. The Mirabel Palace, houses with coats of arms, alleys with steps, hidden nooks, all present an atmosphere already different from the towns and cities further north and east. Finally, one comes to the fine irregular shaped central square, the Plaza de España, with many white arcaded buildings, except at the end where there is one in golden stone, with an arcaded first storey, with a clock and bell tower.

## Las Hurdes

From Plasencia this route goes north-westwards by the C501, through the village of Carcabosco to **Montehermoso**, a village which is famous for its plaited straw hats, sometimes decorated with coloured yarn, and even mirrors, which can be seen on market days. On to **Pozuelo de Zarzón**, with its tree-lined streets, a slightly run-down town, that seems to have been re-juvenated recently. The route now strikes northwards on the C512 road to the well named Villanueva de la Sierra, for this is the beginning of the hills. The road is also much better as one moves into the Sierra de Los Angeles, but looking upwards from the pleasant pastoral scenery below, a sad sight is met — extensive areas of burnt conifer forest, some of which was due to severe storms, but most deliberate and intentional. Apparently, a few disgruntled shepherds wanted more pasture, and others with political motives, burnt the woodland, with grave danger to humans and wildlife, quite apart from destroying years of work and growth, and thus endangered the landscape with soil erosion.

The route now enters what was a very isolated region for a long time, that of Las Hurdes. Soon the pleasant little town of **Pinofran-queado** is reached, in the valley of the Río de Los Angeles, with eucalyptus, and, in late May, spring flowers of ox-eye daisy, or the moon daisy — the 'alpine' version. Then the town of **Caminomorisco** is seen, set in a deep verdant valley, with vegetable plots, and fruit trees, and signs of new development in the form of schools and colleges, both commercial and residential.

Here, for those in need of sustenance, the *mesón* (inn) El Abuelo, (The Grandfather), can be thoroughly recommended for a very good and cheap lunch. From here, the route turns right to Casar de Palomero along a winding road bordered with many flowers, and groups of bee-hives.

After crossing the Río de Los Angeles, which here is beginning to widen out before flowing into the large Embalse de Gabriel y Galán, the road climbs up through schistose rocks to the surprisingly large

village of Casarde Palmero. Our route then turns left through terraced olive groves, with many sheep along the road, often climbing
up the banks and foraging amongst orchards. The fruit trees increase
as one approaches Ribera Oveja, which means 'sheep-bank' — an
extraordinarily appropriate name!

After this village, the road follows the contours above the *embalse*,
(dam) which has much mud-coloured water. Between here and the
next village of La Pesga the road in the afternoon seems full of
livestock: goats being led by women, sheep walking alongside men
on horseback, mules, donkeys and a horse being led with the goats.
The village of **La Pesga** has much livestock also, a scene of the once
traditional Spanish village, with the basic way of life unchanged for
centuries, in spite of irrigation lakes, electricity, and paved roads. It
appears that the *embalse* has virtually cut Las Hurdes in half, but one
can cross by turning left in La Pesga, and down a road that bridges
the waters, and then through a very pleasant wooded landscape,
where it climbs back to the C512 at a col, the Portilla Alta (560m,
1,837ft).

Now the route goes down a winding road bordered with eucalyptus to **Vegas de Coria**. This is set in the pretty valley of the Río
Hurdano, an area ideal for exploration. The beauty is somewhat
offset by more burnt woodland, and a new concrete bridge, but no
doubt the wounds will heal. Then the road goes on, bends right at a
T-junction, and follows the densely wooded river valley of the Arroyo de Batuecas, going past the abandoned hamlet of Riomalo on
the right, and crosses over the confluence with the wider Río Alagón
into the province of Salamanca, on the road to Sotoserrano.

## The Sierra de Béjar

**Sotoserrano** is a delightful small town at the south-eastern extremity
of the Sierra de Francia. It has narrow streets, and an attractive
central plaza, with balconied houses of wood and stone, sometimes
arcaded and sometimes on pillars. From here the route leaves the
C512, and turns right to Corrales de Soto, and the confluence of the
Ríos Alagón and Cuerpo de Hombre. This is a very pleasant spot,
with the wide valley of the Alagón bordered by meadows, holm oaks
and mountain scrub and bushes. At the confluence the route turns
right again, and follows the valley of the Arroyo Servón, similar to
the Alagón, but narrower and more isolated. At length it climbs to
Valdelageve, where the landscape suddenly becomes covered with
olive groves, and on mounting higher the countryside is more rocky,
but still very green. The route is now fairly high up in the granite hill

country of the Sierra de Lagunilla, over 1,000m (3,280ft) and part of the Sierra de Béjar. The views are widespead and panoramic, covering the *sierras* of Salamanca, and the Meseta of Extremadura. The vegetation is surprisingly green and leafy for granite terrain. The road now climbs higher gradually in a plateau landscape to El Cerro at nearly 1,200m (3,936ft), with wide views all the way on the northern side over the valley of the Río Cuerpo de Hombre. At El Cerro the descent begins through cultivated fields to Peñacaballera.

Here a road leads off on the left to **Montemayor del Río** set on a hill, and full of interesting buildings. There is an old castle with very thick walls, and with trees growing on and all around them, but only the towers and turrets remain. Nevertheless it is an impressive ruin. The thirteenth-century church is a mixture of Romanesque and Gothic styles with narrow windows, and great stone buttresses flanking the bell tower. The Plaza Mayor is large, and typical of the province. From the town there is a fine view over the valley of the Río Cuerpo de Hombre. This area has much scope for exploration, being quite wild but not too far from villages.

Returning to Peñacaballera, the road descends down to the N630. At this point an excursion can be made to the town of **Béjar** 10km (6 miles) northwards. The town is on a fine site, high up (959m, 3,146ft), and is famous for wool and cloth textiles. There are several interesting buildings, including the old walls, built during the time of the Moors, which now have gardens within them. The best building is the Ducal Palace, with a double arcaded patio built in 1568, and the façade has two solid towers, called the 'Mirador' and 'Las Cadenas', which were part of the old Moorish keep. There is a sculpture museum of the works of Mateo Hernández (1884-1949), in the old restored church of San Gil. Also a wide Plaza Mayor and several churches and a private 'artistic garden' called El Bosque, built by the Duke of Béjar in 1567 as a summer residence, with fountains and a large pond.

The route from here goes southwards down the N630 to a right turn on to the C513 road, which passes via the southern end of the Embalse de Gabriel y Galán, and to Villanueva de la Sierra on the C512 (on our original route), and so to Pozuelo de Zarzón. Now continue to Guijo de Coria, turning right, where it passes the Embalse de Borbollón, where there is a good camp site at Santibañez el Alto, or continue to the town of Moraleja, via La Moheda. This is well off the beaten track for tourists outside Spain, but it is quite well provided with hotels and hostels. One, the Hotel Delphos, can be warmly recommended for food, comfort and hospitality.

## Moraleja

This is an interesting town for showing the contrast between the two different parts of a municipality: the old quarter, and a relatively new modern area. Yet they blend harmoniously. The old quarter has the usual narrow interesting streets and houses, with central plaza and church, whilst the new is more or less based on the main road from Coria (15km, 9 miles), the regional capital, northwards to Ciudad Rodrigo (69km, 43 miles), forming a modern main street. But it is wide, and well laid out with trees, and gardens, plus parallel service roads, giving plenty of parking space, and lined with reasonable looking buildings.

The town was, and still is an important centre for breeding Miura bulls, but it is also at the nucleus of a network of irrigation canals from the Embalse de Borbollón, which was constructed more than thirty years ago, in 1954, following on the general improvements in Extremadura, which began with the famous Badajoz plan for peasant colonies and vastly improved agriculture. Of the large area comprising the municipality (14,000ha, 34,580 acres), nearly half are irrigated, and the local agriculture has greatly expanded over the years, so that they produce maize, tobacco (an old crop), cucumbers, tomatoes, irrigated meadows for dairy and beef cattle, and fodder crops — hay and silage.

## The Sierra de Gata

The route chosen for this can start from Moraleja, but goes to the camp site at the Embalse de Borbollón, as this is a more interesting way, and hardly less direct. From the crossroads outside the camp site entrance, the route is taken northwards to Villasbuenas de Gata. This road can prove unexpectedly interesting, and rural, as it begins with olive groves and mountain scrub, followed by woods and many wild flowers. One meets donkeys loaded with fodder, and horses and carts loaded with brushwood. All around are hawks circling, and the lapwings seem very tame. Nearing Villasbuenas de Gata there are pinewoods, just outside the village are enormous eucalyptus, and visitors then enter a forgotten corner of Extremadura: the Sierra de Gata.

**Villasbuenas de Gata** is on the C513 road, from Villanueva de la Sierra (beginning of Las Hurdes), and has some interesting alleyways and a church, N.S. de la Concepción, the area appearing to have a kind of rural prosperity based on forestry and olive oil. Also nearby is a sort of thermal establishment, called 'Baños de la Cochina' ('Baths of the Sow'), whose waters apparently cure rheumatism.

*Hoyos, Sierra de Gata*

From here the route goes westwards to the crossroads of the C526 (Ciudad Rodrigo road) and the C513. Continue westwards for 5km (3 miles) to the very small town of **Hoyos** — it is bigger than a village, but not much! This is a pleasant, quiet and tranquil place surrounded by hills, with solid narrow streets and houses largely of granite, having iron balconies and grilles. Some have heraldic shields on their façades, and in the main plaza are old buildings with pillars, presided over by the *ayuntamiento* with a certain air of solidity. Also in the square is the parish church, an unusual building for Spain. With its square tower and broached spire, it seems to belong more to northern Europe, Normandy or Kent, yet again there is something Portuguese about it, which would not be surprising, as the frontier is only 25-30km (15-18 miles) distant. However, it was built at the end of the fifteenth century, with its main door in the Romanesque style, and inside are three naves with a vaulted transept, sanctuary and choir. The retable panel — described as *barroca de columnas Salomónicos* (baroque Salamanca columns) — are certainly Spanish. But the dedication is unusual too: *Nuestra Señora del Buen Varón*, meaning: 'Our Lady of the Wise or Prudent Man'.

Before leaving Hoyos, perhaps a little history of the region might be apposite. It was settled early by a tribe called the Vettones in 600BC, who cultivated the land in fragments communally, and had sheep, pigs, ewe's milk, honey and brewed beer. Later the Romans arrived and built a road, the Calzada de Dalmacia, part of which connected *Caurium* (Coria) with *Miróbriga* (Ciudad Rodrigo), and exploited gold and minerals in the granitic rocks near Valverde del Fresno. Then came Barbarians, Visigoths and the Moors, who were ousted by the military-religious Order of Alcántara (like the Templars). Later came the War of Portuguese Independence (1640-88), invasions by the Portuguese, and finally the Peninsular campaign of 1808-14, when it was said: 'from the first moments the inhabitants of the Sierra de Gata were on the side of the Duke of Wellington'.

From Hoyos the C513 road leaves behind the orange groves and vines of the *huerta* around the town, and climbs gradually through scented pinewoods to the granite scenery of the hills. The granite landscape is far from bare, indeed it is covered with a relatively dense vegetation of bushes like *carquexias* (Spanish medicinal broom), rockroses with white and yellow flowers, heather, and occasional pines and chestnuts, with a prolific bird life, and, in late May, spring flowers. Soon the road opens out above a wide valley basin, with softer clay rocks, and cultivation of olive groves and vines, with views of distant villages clustered on the hills. Amongst the vegetation there are sometimes bee-hives — relics of an older honey producing industry, now rather decayed. The road winds on, and eventually climbs up to the town of **Valverde de Fresno**, which has lost population heavily since 1950, when it had 4,450 people, two cinemas, a theatre, a casino and a rug and blanket factory. It may recover now that the road goes through to Portugal, and there is a route north over the hills, with cols along the Portuguese border to Ciudad Rodrigo, so it has become a crossroads town. The town itself is not over interesting, perhaps due to its run-down condition. It is, however, surrounded by hills and very pleasant scenery.

It is worth taking the road to Portugal for some way, as this passes through a very attractive rural and rustic landscape of cultivated land, meadows and woods, with an astonishing bird life. Buzzards perch on the road, and kestrels fly low over the countryside, and it is very tempting to continue right into Portugal, but the nearest town, Penamacor is some way off. Returning to Valverde, and going past it for some distance, an excursion can be made to some hill villages, by taking the first left turn on a winding road to **Eljas**. This was a Roman settlement called *Ergastulum*, and has some interesting architecture, and it seems much more lively than Valverde. It has a remarkable castle dating from 890, built by the Moors, and rebuilt later by Alfonso IX of León, which was captured by the Portuguese in 1641. After this it decayed, but there are some interesting towers left. Then on to San Martin de Trevejo, another old place with a curious plaza, the houses having porches, and heraldic shields on their granite façades. There is an old Franciscan convent, solitary and abandoned, but perhaps the most interesting things here are the huge olive trees, over 100 years old amid the verdant vegetation.

Our route returns to the C513 via the village of **Villamiel**, a place completely redolent of past glories and archaic houses of former *hidalgos* (noblemen), but peaceful with its chestnut woods and pines. The name Villamiel, means 'honey town', but its origin is obscure. On the C513 our route is direct to Moraleja via the C526, cutting a corner from Hoyos to Perales del Puerto. This town has a discotheque, 'El Paso', which seems a little incongruous here.

## Southern Salamanca

### The Sierra de Peña de Francia — Las Batuecas Route

There are several ways of entering this chain of crystalline mountains, which separates the north and south Mesetas, but the most spectacular is by way of Las Hurdes from the south. Therefore, the route takes the C512 from Guijo de Coria (after arriving from either Moraleja or Borbollón). After passing Vegas de Coria the route arrives at a T-junction, where the left turn is taken on to the SA201 road. This follows the Arroyo de Las Batuecas upstream to Las Mestas, the last village in Cáceres province and our route crosses into Salamanca. From now onwards the road climbs through astonishing greenery, and a truly verdant landscape of oaks, pines, cork oaks and *madroñas* (species of strawberry tree).

The rocky scenery of schists is impressive, and this part of the route is called 'El Valle de Catedrales'. After climbing some way, on a bend, a path leads up by a stream, the Arroyo de Las Batuecas, to the Santuario del Santo Desierto de San José de Batuecas (a ruined monastery). There are also some Neolithic rock paintings of hunting scenes, goats, fish, lines and points nearby. After this the road mounts higher and higher, with, eventually, a magnificent view on the left over the *sierras*, before a series of incredible tight hairpin bends (at least six), brings travellers to the Col de Portillo (1,240m, 4,067ft). From here the route leads on to a veritable jewel of Salamanca — La Alberca.

## La Alberca

This village is in the heart of the Sierra de Francia, and has retained the character of its ancient way of life, which has a strong religious tradition, especially in the great celebrations of 15 August (The Assumption), followed on 16 August by the ancient mystery of the 'Loa' (praise), for the triumph of the Virgin over the demons of evil. On these occasions special costume is worn, with singing and dancing.

The old houses of the village, with their overhanging upper storeys of balconies, built above the ground floor of stone construction, are set in winding stone streets and alleyways. The main plaza is irregular in shape, and partly lined with porches. It is obviously a very old settlement, and the inhabitants are of mixed descent from their long past isolation over the centuries from Neolithic, Celto-Iberians, Romans and Visigothic ancestors. The church, rebuilt in the eighteenth century, contains a twelfth-century sculptured granite pulpit. Not least is a tradition of good eating here. There are many meat dishes and sausages of various meats, along with the domestic sweets of butter cake, almond cakes and fritters, wafers and dishes made with pollen and honey. La Alberca tends to become crowded with visitors from Salamanca during August.

## The Sierras

There is a great deal to explore in these ranges, with many walks, but a basic circuit starts with the route to **Mogarraz**, a village which is high up and surrounded by very dense vegetation of many wild species. Then down to **Miranda del Castañar**, just off the C512, a most attractive village, a place of great dignity, with very narrow streets and overhanging houses, and flowery balconies. There are 300-year-old noble houses, with armorial bearings, a Plaza de Toros, and an old castle, but the most fascinating thing here is the 'Ronda de la Muralla' — a walk literally through the walls, with four gates of access.

From Miranda, return to the C512 road, and continue southwards to **Cepeda**, which has some interesting houses, but is more modern than the others. Beyond is a fine viewpoint over the Alagón valley, and it is possible to re-visit Sotoserrano, if it was missed before (Sierra de Béjar). Now the route turns right, and one can return to La Alberca via the village of **Herguijuela de la Sierra**, off on the left with its steep streets, fountain in the plaza, plus cherry orchards round about. Next off on the right is **Madroñal**, with many streams and which is a great place for fruit: cherries in summer, grapes in Septem-

*The plaza at La Alberca*

ber, with a cherry fiesta in July. The name, perhaps, is a somewhat apposite one, with a reference to the many strawberry trees (*madroñas*) in the region.

From La Alberca, once more on the route of Las Batuecas, one goes northwards on the SA202, a picturesque road, to a junction, and camp site (Nava de Francia). Here the left fork is taken, and a very spectacular, and winding road leads to the summit of the Peña de Francia (1,723m, 5,651ft), a peak of schist, and geologically an example of inverted relief—an eroded syncline. From the top, amid the foliated green schists, one has a tremendous panorama: westwards the mountains of Portugal, northwards the Meseta up to Salamanca, southwards the hills of Las Hurdes, and to the east the snowy summits of the Sierra de Gredos. At the summit there is a Dominican monastery, Monasterio de la Peña, with a *mirador* by the gates: 'Balcón del Fraile'. It is occupied in the summer, and has a hostelry.

*Plaza Mayor, Ciudad Rodrigo*

There is also a path, which leads to the summit from El Caserito (between the camp site and the SA202), with waymarking by orange flashes, which goes on via a high firebreak and some fountains, and then by a path marked with crosses ('Camino del Viacrucis') to the top. On a floral note, in some of the villages, and Santibañez de la Sierra in particular, there are massed banks of wood anemones — white petals, purple splash and yellow centres, making for a very colourful backdrop.

## Ciudad Rodrigo

After descending Peña de Francia, the road continues to El Millo, on the C515 road, where the route turns left through a pleasant rural landscape with cattle and sheep to the beautiful walled town of Ciudad Rodrigo perched on its hill, with a Roman bridge across the Río Agueda. Named after Don Rodrigo González Girón, who conquered and resettled it in the twelfth century, it was later (during the

Peninsular campaign of 1812) occupied by the French, and freed by a brilliant night action of Wellington, who was presented with a silver key to the city, which had an engraved plate and chain, and was made the Duke of Ciudad Rodrigo. There is so much to see here that really the city is one vast monument, and from the *mirador* over the river there is a panoramic view. The walls are 2km ($^1/_2$ mile) long, and were completed in 1712. The cathedral, started in 1170, is a blend of Romanesque, Gothic and plateresque, and has a splendid façade with statues of the twelve apostles above the thirteenth-century Puerta de la Virgen (west door). Not far away is the Cerralbo Chapel (1588-1685), noted for its severe, but pure lines. The Plaza Mayor is superb, wide and spacious with two beautiful Renaissance palaces: the *ayuntamiento*, having two storied arcades with basket-handle arches forming a gallery, and porch; and Los Cueto, where a frieze separates the two storeys. Near the north wall in the Plaza Conde is another fifteenth-century palace, the Conde Montarco, with a beautiful door. Just to walk around is a joy, especially in the spring sunshine which shines on the golden stone with a clear blue sky overhead, whether in the market place or in the Plaza San Salvador with its row of noble escutcheoned houses. To complete the picture, there is a splendid *parador* here, converted from the medieval *alcázar* (built by Enrique II of Trastamara), and finally there is a very interesting Spring Cattle Fair.

# Further Information
## — The Western Marches of Spain —

(☎ codes Cácares 927, Salamanca 923)

### Activities

**La Alberca**
*Fiestas* : 15 August, Corpus Christi.

**Béjar**
*Fiestas*: Patronales 8 September; San Miguel 29 September.

**Cepeda**
*Fiestas*: 25 April San Marcos; 24 August San Bartolomé (bullfights and 'Capea' — amateur bullfight, bull not killed.

**Herguijuela de la Sierra**
*Fiesta*: 16 July, Patronal.

**Madroñal**
*Fiestas*: 26 July, Santa Ana; 27 July, Fiesta de la Cereza (cherry).

**Miranda del Castañar**
*Fiestas*: 2 February, Las Candelas (Candelmas); 15 August, Corrida de Toros; 7-10 September Santiago and San Ginés.

**Mogarraz**
*Fiestas*: 25 July, Santiago (Corrida);
3-5 August, Virgen de la Nieve.
(Corrida—bullfights.)

**Montemayor del Río**
*Fiesta*: 14 September, Santo Cristo
de las Batallas.

**Sotoserrano**
*Fiesta*: 30 August, San Ramón.

## Tourist Information Offices

**La Alberca**
Ayuntamiento
Plaza Mayor
☎ 43 70 05

**Béjar**
4 Paseo Cervantes
☎ 40 30 05

Ayuntamiento
☎ 40 01 15

**Caminomorisco**
Ayuntamiento
Plaza de Don Francisco Martin
☎ 43 60 85

**Cepeda**
Ayuntamiento
☎ 43 21 01

**Ciudad Rodrigo**
Plaza Amayvetos
☎ 46 05 61

Ayuntamiento
11 Avenida de Conde de Foxa
☎ 46 24 95

**Herguijuela de la Sierra**
Ayuntamiento
☎ 43 21 66

**Hoyos**
Ayuntamiento
3 Plaza Mayor
☎ 51 40 02

**Madroñal**
Ayuntamiento
☎ 43 21 55

**Miranda del Castañas**
Ayuntamiento
☎ 43 20 01

**Mogarraz**
Ayuntamiento
☎ 43 70 15

**Moraleja**
Ayuntamiento
Plaza España
☎ (927) 51 55 82

**Plascencia**
Plaza Mayor
☎ 41 27 66

**Sotoserrano**
Ayuntamiento
☎ 43 23 28

**Valverde del Fresno**
Ayuntamiento
Plaza de la Constitución
☎ 51 00 13

# 9 • Extremadura and Huelva

Extremadura and Huelva lie, one above the other, along the border with Portugal and have a certain amount in common. Neither is very densely populated and both are much given to growing olives, producing wine and planning for an influx of tourists in the future. There are a considerable number of small rivers, a large percentage of which dry out in the hot weather. A rugged, mountainous region to the north gives way to extensive, fertile plains followed by delightfully hilly country with plenty of trees about and, eventually, flat sandy beaches and marshland washed by the Atlantic.

Major roads link all the main centres and a great deal of time and effort is being put into bringing the surface of the secondary variety up to an acceptable standard. Towns like Cáceres, Mérida, and Huelva are on the national railway system that links them with each other and with places further afield such as Madrid and nearby provincial capitals. Most towns of any size have at least one bus service and an odd taxi or two, cars and bicycles can be hired in the majority of tourist areas but there are few paths designed for hikers, and people trying to hitch a lift will usually be disappointed. Hotels are moderately easy to come by and quite a few of the large and medium sized ones will accept credit cards of one kind or another although most filling stations expect to be paid in cash. There are tourist offices in the larger towns and hotel keepers are often a fund of information once they understand what you are talking about.

The two provinces also share a long and varied history going back to prehistoric times. Megalithic monuments are to be found in several fairly restricted areas whereas the Romans constructed roads and bridges all over the place and surpassed themselves in Mérida, a city of tremendous importance in the great days of the Empire. The Moors who followed them left even more evidence of their occupation, not only in the way of fortifications but also in the style of architecture, which suited local requirements and has remained popular ever since.

With the discovery of America and the exploitation of the New World by explorers who came, for the most part, from Extremadura, greater wealth led to the building of large, if severe, mansions and palaces, generally constructed round inner courtyards in the Moorish tradition and seen to good effect in Cáceres. These were followed in their turn by a fever of reconstruction and decoration, particularly where churches were concerned, and later by a determination to preserve as many relics of the past as possible, which led to even quite small villages opening their own museums. Huelva has been less diligent than Extremadura in preserving its old buildings, perhaps the earthquake of 1755 discouraged the local authorities of the time, but the province is certainly rushing to catch up with modern developments before the twentieth century runs out. High-rise buildings are appearing in suburbs and coastal resorts and a determined effort is being made to provide all the amenities and attractions that will lure future tourists away from the overcrowded holiday playgrounds along the Mediterranean.

## Extremadura

Beauty is said to lie in the eye of the beholder although, somewhat less romantically, it often boils down to little more than comparison between things that are strange and others which are familiar. For instance, anyone besotted with the delicacy and fragrance of an English spring would undoubtedly find Extremadura austere and occasionally desolate whereas somebody popping over from North Africa for a short holiday would get a different impression altogether.

The name means the land 'beyond the Duero river' and, because it is the birthplace of the *conquistadores* who divided their time between fighting at home and sailing the Atlantic to open up the New World, it has gained the reputation for being as hard as the granite that predominates on the plateau. But this is by no means an accurate description of Extremadura as a whole. It takes no account of the vast fields of wheat and olive groves that blanket the hills and lowlands as far as the horizon and beyond, cork oaks neatly stripped of their bark and then treated to give the trunks a modicum of protection or the vineyards that keep the inhabitants liberally supplied with wine, adding a surplus that goes for export. Sheep, accompanied by a shepherd, and sometimes by as many goats, graze on the plateau during the winter despite the bitter winds but are driven up into the hills for the summer months when the plains shimmer with a heat

The Monastery of Guadalupe, Extremadura

*Brightly painted local pottery, Cordoba*

Sign outside the inn
of Don Quixote,
Puerto Lapice,
Ciudad Real

La del alba seria cuarndo
Don Quijote salio de la a venta,
tan contento, tan gallardo, tan
alborozado por verse ya ar-
mado caballero que el gozo
le reventaba por las cinchas
del caballo.

(Don Quijote de la Mancha, cap IV)

The palace and church of Viso del Marqués, Ciudad Real

EXTREMADURA
AND HUELVA

that can become almost intolerable. Pigs are raised in large numbers, there are some cattle but very few of the famous black bulls, while mules are used extensively for transport as well as being harnessed to dust carts and suchlike in the smaller towns and villages. Everywhere dogs can be seen taking themselves for walks and, generally speaking, keeping a weather eye open for passing traffic: far fewer seem to die on the roads of Extremadura and Huelva than in the regions further east.

Wide open country, extensive national parks and game reserves, as well as smaller private preserves, make the region a hunter's paradise with everything from stags and wild boar to quail, partridge, hare and wild turkeys, but it is necessary to get permission, and a licence from the authorities, before going out in search of any of them. Lynx are a protected species and may not be killed, captured or exported but there is no objection to photographing them. Some hunts are organised, with or without the help of beaters or dogs, but an individual who prefers to do things on his own usually picks a small area where he can stalk his prey or simply lie in wait for it. Pheasant, said to have been introduced by the Romans, can be found in small preserves along the Tajo river. Fishermen also need a licence whether they are after trout in the swiftly-flowing streams, where there is a limit to the number that can be caught in any one day, or black bass, carp and so on in the less turbulent waters of the rivers and reservoirs.

Generally speaking the people of Extremadura tend to congregate in towns and villages along the river courses where they grow cotton, vegetables and tobacco, the last of which can often be seen hanging up to dry through an open window. The houses, frequently stark and almost invariably in need of a fresh coat of paint, huddle together for company along cobbled streets memorable mainly for the size, variety and frequency of their potholes. When enough inhabitants are gathered together they treat themselves to a bullring or a football ground, sometimes even both, built on the outskirts and publicised with as much enthusiasm as the swimming pool and the local disco. The larger hamlets usually run to a fuel pump, although motorists would be wise not to rely too heavily on this, as well as a basic inn and a small tavern with nothing much on the menu but a friendly atmosphere once initial contact has been made.

Roads throughout the region vary considerably. The main highways linking Extremadura with France and Portugal as well as with Madrid and other major cities in Spain are generally good, although they can deteriorate quite suddenly and without any warning into half-repaired surfaces where the going is rough. This is especially true where villages are being bypassed. It is not unknown for a workman to hold up the traffic during what seems like an eternity, particularly when there is nothing in sight and no small turnings that might provide a deviation. Just as all hope has been abandoned he has a casual word with a cyclist or an approaching donkey cart and raises a green handkerchief or a more up-market sign that says 'go'. The last car through is presented with a piece of wood to be handed to his companion at the far end, an outward and visible sign that he is now officially in control of the one-way system. Some minor roads are surprisingly good in parts and unexpectedly nasty in others but there is no difficulty in getting through provided one takes things slowly and carefully. Nor are you ever very far from human habitation, even in the more sparsely populated areas, be it no more than substantial gates at the end of a farm lane, a modest villa beside a swimming pool of comparable size or a minute home belonging to someone working on the land. Deep ditches along the roadsides make it almost impossible to pull off for a picnic under the olive trees. These, like both large fields and small paddocks in predominantly hilly country, are surrounded by dry-stone walls and, with the possibility of a bull turning up to investigate at any moment, the idea of an *al fresco* meal has little to recommend it.

Hotels in Extremadura range from the definitely up-market to the frankly basic with plenty of others to choose from in between. There are four national *paradores*, all in historic settings, well over two dozen comfortable and well equipped establishments where the rooms have private bathrooms and the water is piping hot and some small inns that are usually acceptable if you are stuck for the night. However, the Spanish like the French prefer bolsters to pillows, but do not keep any of the latter in reserve for foreign visitors, so anybody who needs one in order to get a good night's rest would be well advised to take their own. Nor do all hotels have restaurants, and here and there a *Hotel Residencia*, as they are called, will send its guests out to a nearby café for breakfast which can be a trifle disconcerting the first time it happens. Very few people in Extremadura appear to speak any English, although some have a smattering of French, but this hardly matters to the traveller armed with a small dictionary and a lot of determination. Sign language works wonders and provided the newcomer attempts an occasional 'good morning' and 'thank you' the local people will fall over themselves to be both helpful and hospitable.

Probably the most memorable area of Extremadura lies roughly in the centre of the province between the Tajo and Guadiana rivers, containing as it does places like Cáceres, Trujillo, Mérida and Guadalupe. Driving down from the north, past the rugged stone crags that contrast sharply with the Embalse de Alcántara, the first logical port of call is **Cáceres**, capital of its own province and a treasure house of ancient buildings. Most, but not all of these, are conveniently encircled by medieval walls and towers to one side of the modern town. The city was founded by the Romans in 28BC but the name only goes back to the Moorish occupation when it was known as *Cazies*. An hour or so should be enough to wander round the narrow streets of the old quarter, inspecting the golden-brown walls and secluded courtyards of mansions built by the warrior families of the fifteenth and sixteenth centuries. They are fashioned mainly from rough stone with very little in the way of decoration apart from the coats-of-arms of their various owners emblazoned over the doors. All but one of these stately homes have lost their fortified towers. Isabel the Catholic got so fed up with the constant feuding and fighting that she ordered the occupants to pull them down in 1477, so reducing the outward signs of their power and prestige by a considerable footage.

Apart from the churches — San Mateo which is rather bare except for the family chapels and their individual tombs and Santa Maria where it is almost too dark to see the intricately carved figures properly — very few buildings are open to the public. Notable exceptions are the House of the Weathervanes which incorporates an eleventh-century Arab cistern and a small archaeological museum and the Casa del Mono, so called because of the monkey-like gargoyles on the façade, which devotes itself to the fine arts. It is possible to see the patio of the Golfines de Abajo palace if the caretaker happens to be about and catch a glimpse of the pillars and arches at the Storks' House which retained its tower complete with battlements and is now occupied by the army. Some distance away, on the far side of the Plaza Santa Maria, is the Toledo-Montezuma mansion which has a domed tower built after the others were destroyed. It was the home of Juan Cano de Saavedra and his wife, an Aztec princess whose father, Montezuma, lost his kingdom to the *conquistadores*.

Cáceres itself has one very comfortable hotel complete with a swimming pool, a restaurant and space to leave the car. Most of the other establishments send you out to eat at any of a reasonable selection of small restaurants, the only trouble being to find somewhere to park nearby, especially when the entire population appears

*Trujillo*

to have the same idea in mind. The city celebrates the festival of Candelaria at the beginning of February with a pilgrimage to the hermitage of San Blas during which it is customary to eat a special type of honey cake baked for the occasion. Towards the end of April they honour St George with a bonfire in the main square and a Parade of Christians and Moors, recalling the liberation of the town, attended by participants in national dress. A week or so later there is a pilgrimage to the sanctuary of the Virgen de la Montaña, built in the seventeenth century on a hill a few kilometres to the south-east. The chapel of this Mountain Virgin shares an excellent vantage point with an enormous statue of Christ which keeps watch over the city and the plains beyond.

Due east of Cáceres and about 50km (31 miles) away along a good, straight road through flat country punctuated by little hills and covered with olive trees, is the smaller and much quieter city of **Trujillo**. The main square is said to be one of the most interesting in Spain and, apart from anything else, it certainly is an unusual shape, not quite triangular and built on different levels connected by wide flights of steps. To one side is an enormous equestrian statue of Francisco Pizarro dating from 1927 and the work of two American sculptors, Charles Runse and Mary Harriman. The *conquistador* is in full war regalia and his horse has thoughtfully been provided with a helmet to match. Francisco, the son of a local swineherd and one of five brothers who carved out names for themselves in the New World, is dubbed the Conqueror of Peru. After a rewarding but decidedly bloodthirsty career he was eventually murdered in 1541. His brother Hernando managed things much better than the rest of the family. He married his half-Inca niece, arrived home safely with an enviable fortune and built the palace on the other side of the square from his brother-cum-father-in-law. The large family crest was added after he had received the title of Marqués de la Conquista in recognition of services rendered.

Other buildings thereabouts include the House of Chains, presumably because shackles forced on so many Christians captured by the Moors were left there as offerings after the prisoners were released, the church of San Martin liberally paved with gravestones and the San Carlos Palace, now a convent, whose nuns will show visitors round the inner courtyard in answer to a ring on the bell. Sundry shops and restaurants share the view over the car park in the middle of the square. The old town, reached through one of its seven original gates, climbs up the hill behind with narrow streets leading past the church of Santa Maria, which if closed will be opened on request, to the ancient castle made of granite taken from the ledge on which it stands. All in all, Trujillo is a delightful town, well worth wandering about, with its own *parador* housed in the ancient convent of Santa Clara and a tranquil atmosphere that belies its title of Nursery of the Conquistadores.

Just as impressive, some people say even more so, is the Monastery of Guadalupe set majestically on a mountaintop a couple of hours' drive away. As there is no main road it is necessary to opt for one of the minor ones. The route through Zorita has a surface that could do with some professional attention although it improves after the turn-off to Logrosán, a nice little place with some quite attractive gardens. As the countryside becomes progressively more hilly, vines appear between the olive trees, pigs snuffle around under the prickly pears that grow along the dry-stone walls and an occasional stream, rare enough to catch the eye, trickles down between the rocks. The views become more and more dramatic as the road twists its way up through wooded hills falling back in folds from the sides of deep ravines until, from the top of the final ridge, you look across at **Guadalupe**.

The monastery is a huge fortified complex of battlements and turrets, slate roofs and belfrys and a small grey dome or two rising above the encircling ramparts which in turn give way to a cluster of whitish houses littered about the hillside below. Distance lends enchantment to the little medieval village which fades a trifle on closer inspection. It is moving resolutely into the twentieth century with all the attendant demands of tourism such as restaurants and cafés, shops full of souvenirs, postcards and items of religious significance while the traditional art of the local coppersmiths is being adapted to suit present-day requirements. To balance all this a fountain plays happily in the main square. Cobbled streets, where you are quite likely to meet an over-loaded donkey plodding patiently along, are fringed with houses whose balconies are covered with flowers in the spring. The local *parador* is worth seeing even if you do not intend to stay. It is a converted sixteenth-century castle with a restaurant, some mosaics, appropriate furniture and courtyards scented by strategically-placed orange trees. There is also a beautiful garden with a tennis court and a swimming pool and space to park the car. Another hotel of roughly the same size, also with a restaurant, has taken over a small section of the monastery. For tourists who have neither brought nor wish to hire a car there is a daily bus service to and from Cáceres as well as some organised tours.

If it is mildly disappointing to discover that Guadalupe is not as inaccessible as a half-forgotten temple in the wilds of Outer Mongolia at least the monastery itself lives up to all one's expectations. It was founded during the fourteenth century to house the Virgin of Guadalupe, a little statue carved in oak — some people attribute her to St Luke — which was discovered by a local cowherd around the year 1300. The church, one of the earliest buildings in the complex, is reached up a flight of steps from the village square and through either of two massive pairs of doors decorated with bronze reliefs. Beyond is a wealth of treasures recalling the great days when it was a centre of learning with its own medical school, a printing press and an embroidery section which was justly famous for the volume and quality of its work. As so often happened the whole set-up went into a decline and in 1835 the monastery was abandoned altogether. All credit then, to the Franciscans who took it over in 1908 and restored it to much of its former glory.

During long conducted tours any morning or afternoon visitors are shown the most historic rooms and courtyards. Foremost amongst them is the mudéjar cloister with its two tiers of horseshoe arches and a profusion of flowers and shrubs surrounding a Moorish fountain surmounted by a small, elaborate pavilion. Next door, in the former refectory, are any number of intricately embroidered vestments and altar fronts while the chapter house is filled with ancient illuminated manuscripts and small paintings by Zurbarán, one of the most talented artists of the Seville school during the Golden Age. Some of his larger works adorn the extremely ornate sacristy where every available inch of space is highly decorated. The same concentration of richness is to be found in the *camarin*, a small, round, chapel-like area set aside for the Virgin. Not that one can see very much of her under the voluminous scarlet and gold robes and equally sumptuous head-dress over which, on important occasions, she wears a heavy, jewelled crown. The Child is dressed in exactly the same fashion and together they occupy a modern but not too obtrusive enamel-encrusted throne. Amongst the many other things to be seen and admired are the beautifully carved choir stalls and the Gothic cloister which is light, airy and surprisingly restrained by comparison, probably because it was once part of the pharmacy supplying a group of hospitals maintained by the monks. These days it is filled with chairs and tables where guests staying in the hotel can drink their coffee in the sun.

Two scenic roads lead north from Guadalupe but for anyone travelling south it is necessary to retrace one's steps to Zorita and then branch off in the direction of **Villanueva de la Serena**, a neat small town with fairly broad streets and a bronze statue of its most famous son, Pedro de Valdivia, lauded as the Conqueror of Chile. Its attractions include a baroque church, two convents and several hermitages, one of which is reached down a basic road to the south but has the ruins of a castle close by and some attractive views. The local hotel is small but adequate with a restaurant of its own. From here it is a short drive to Don Benito on the way to Medellín.

On the face of it **Medellín** is a typical little hamlet totally dominated by a large fortified castle overlooking the Guadiana river. Its main claim to fame lies in the fact that it was the birthplace of Hernán Cortés who wanted not so much to exploit the New World as to colonise it. When he landed there in 1519 he literally burned his boats and within two years was firmly installed in the Aztec capital, now Mexico City. A statue of him, planting the flag of Castile in his newly conquered territory, with his sword sheathed and his helmet shading his eyes, stands on a pedestal surrounded by modest gardens and two-storey terraced houses in the town square. Apart from the castle there is a clutch of churches and a seventeenth-century bridge in a good state of repair over the wide, but frequently rather dry, Guadiana river.

The minor route connecting Medellín with the somewhat busier road from Trujillo to Badajoz is less daunting than one is led to believe and provides an easy and quite varied drive to **Mérida**, one of the gems of Extremadura. It started life as a Roman township on the banks of the Guadiana in 25BC, guarding the intersection of two important highways linking Toledo with Lisbon and Salamanca with Seville. The settlement grew steadily in importance, collecting temples, a theatre, an arena and a racecourse on the way, and was soon recognised as the capital of Lusitania. The poets of the day compared it more than just favourably with Athens although the Greeks, then as now, insisted that their city was infinitely superior. Two bridges built by the Romans, one on the Path of Silver to the north and the other giving access to the southern highway to Seville, are amongst the many ancient landmarks along with the remains of two aqueducts that fed their own artificial lakes on the outskirts of the town. The theatre and the arena are now totally enclosed and the hedge is too thick for even the most enterprising schoolboy to find a peephole large enough to see through. As a result it is worth parking outside and waiting for the gates to open — officially from 8am to 8pm or 9am to 6.30pm depending on the time of year but like everything else they are almost certain to close for lunch.

The theatre, built by Agrippa in 24BC, is definitely a site to see. It still has its stage with most of the colonnade, added some 25 years later, virtually intact and in a reasonably good state of repair although the statues disappeared a long time ago. The passageways, covered with large blocks of granite, have stood the test of time remarkably well but the semi-circle of stone tiers, designed to accommodate about 6,000 people, are definitely showing their age. However, with the help of a cushion or two, today's audiences make themselves quite comfortable for the classical dramas that are presented there during the summer months. The arena next door, which is slightly younger, could hold well over twice as many spectators without turning a hair and specialised in popular entertainments such as contests between gladiators and wild animals, feats of strength and daring, and was even flooded occasionally for the reinactment of various naval battles. Part of it has been repaired but a great deal is missing, probably carted off by subsequent administrators who no doubt looked on it as nothing more than a convenient source of building materials. Across the car park is all that remains of a Roman villa dating from about the same period and worth seeing for its mosaic floors and pavements. The National Museum of Roman Art is claimed to be the best in Spain with its ever-growing collection of bits and pieces found in the vicinity and augmented by discoveries from other parts of the country. There are busts and statues, coins and glass, pottery and religious relics, pillars, mosaics and other fragments housed in a building specially designed to show them off to the best advantage.

A certain amount of imagination is necessary to visualise the chariot races that once drew Roman spectators in their thousands to the now almost non-existent circus just off the main road to Madrid. Less is required for a visit to the little temples of Mars and Diana although the former is also known as the Oven of Santa Eulalia, a child martyr who is enshrined in the church next door. Additional places to explore are the church of Santa Maria, the Mithraeum and the *alcazaba* where enough remains to interest its visitors inspite of all the debris lying about. It is especially proud of the cistern, dug to the level of the river bed and kept topped up with filtered water for Romans, Moors and Templars in turn.

Mérida has two comfortable hotels, one of them a delightful *parador* which has served as both a convent and a prison and has managed to hang on to its monastery garden all the time. Some of the small restaurants make a feature of local dishes like *frite*, which is made of lamb, partridge cooked in the Alcántara style, stewed kid and smoked ham thinly sliced from large joints, complete with trotters, which can be seen hanging by the dozen in shops, bars and restaurants everywhere. The town's main celebrations take place in June with the emphasis on traditional music, dancing, national costumes and bullfights held in the ring about half way between the Roman theatre and the river. They feature again in September when the fair lasts without interruption for most of the first week.

A major road connects Mérida with **Badajoz** which lies due west on the border with Portugal and is the capital of the largest province in Spain. It was a fairly unimportant centre in Roman days but rose to quite giddy heights under the Moors. From then onwards its history was turbulent to say the least of it. Alfonso IX recaptured the town in 1229 after which it made a point of getting involved in all the Wars of Succession. Wellington lost a large proportion of his army there when he besieged the stronghold in 1812 and after its capture during the Civil War 124 years later many of the defenders and some refugees were mowed down in the bullring by machine-gun fire. Understandably the townspeople are putting the more unsavoury aspects of its past firmly behind them but have retained one or two tangible memories of the Romans and the Moors. The most atmospheric section is to be found in the vicinity of the old *alcazaba* with its octagonal tower and archaeological museum. There is a certain elegance about the perfectly restored monumental gateway, once the entrance to the walled town, which now leads to the Bridge of Palms.

*A roadside farmhouse*

Other tourist attractions include the cathedral which started life in the thirteenth century and has some fairly ancient tapestries and the more or less central Museum of Fine Arts. There are several hotels, restaurants and shops in this essentially modern town, covered markets which are functional rather than picturesque and some attractive gardens. One of these borders on the river and continues round on either side of the main road behind the *alcazaba*. St John the Baptist, the patron saint of Badajoz, is honoured during a week of traditional festivities at the end of June.

Anyone with a day to spare could do worse than head south-west to **Olivenza**, which was part of Portugal until 1801. It boasts a castle built in the early fourteenth century, a library with a doorway in the Manueline style that incorporates nautical symbols with Moorish designs and the extremely viewable church of Santa Maria Magdalena. Its main features are the spiralling pillars which support the arches on either side of the nave and an ornate, though rather dark, altar complimented by several small chapels.

If the idea of Badajoz does not appeal to you it takes roughly the same length of time to drive due south along a very scenic road from Mérida to Zafra, passing through **Almendralejo** on the way. The latter is the capital of the Tierra de Barros, a fertile region which produces both olives and grapes in profusion, as well as melons that should definitely not be overlooked. Because of the clay soil it is also well known for its pottery. There are three castles, a brace of stately homes, a medieval church, a selection of little hotels and restaurants and an extremely small zoo.

The focal point of **Zafra**, reputed to be one of the oldest towns in Extremadura, is undoubtedly its medieval castle conveniently situated in the town rather than perched up on the top of a hill. It was originally a Moorish *alcázar* (castle), was adapted by the Dukes of Feria in the fifteenth and sixteenth centuries as a highly desirable palatial residence and eventually re-equipped with all the aids to gracious modern living and converted into a *parador*. Hidden away amongst its nine solid round towers is a small chapel and a splendid marble patio thought to have been designed by Juan de Herrera, Philip II's favourite architect who was responsible, amongst other things, for the *escorial* and the cathedral at Valladolid. It has some two dozen very comfortable rooms, an excellent dining room and an outdoor swimming pool. Nearby is the Plaza Mayor surrounded by eighteenth-century arcades and the smaller Plaza Vieja which dates from the sixteenth century. The Candelaria church, of comparable age, is open every morning and afternoon and is especially proud of its altarpiece painted by Zurbarán in 1644.

Zafra is known for its cattle fairs and particularly for the one held as part of the celebrations in honour of St Michael during the first week in October. Incidentally, it is useless to ask for stamps at the local post office in order to send letters home. They do not exactly fall about laughing but indicate, with something akin to pity, that only a foreigner would come up with such an odd request. Everybody knows that you buy stamps from the tobacconist down the road. If, after such an experience, one looks at the postbox-like slit in the wall with a doubtful expression the local policeman will nod reassuringly — it is quite safe to pop them in there but he is not prepared to say how long their journey will take, be it overseas or to the next town just a few kilometres away.

Motorists heading for Cordoba could usefully pause at **Llerena**, 42km (26 miles) down the road. It has an especially attractive main square facing the church of Our Lady of Granada, referring it seems to the pomegranate over the entrance and not the famous city further to the east. It is an imposing building for such a modest little town with a long white façade incorporating two tiers of arcades and a balustrade. The way in is through a heavy, decorative doorway flanked by four workmanlike pillars and blind windows outlined in the same dark stone. Above all this rises a huge baroque tower, totally different in both colour and design, which looks as though it was added as an afterthought or, better still, belongs to a more conventional church immediately behind. Unfortunately this choice of route leads away from the southernmost part of Extremadura which is a pity if one has enough time to continue the journey to the coast.

A visit to **Jerez de los Caballeros** means deviating slightly from the main road to Huelva but is well worth it for a number of different reasons. In the first place it is a delightful town all set about with cork oaks and olive trees and secondly it is another of the fortified centres closely connected with the *conquistadores*. Balboa, who discovered the Pacific, was born there in 1475. His statue, poised on a pedestal and shading his eyes with one hand in order to get a better view of nothing in particular, is one of the first things to be seen on entering the town. The gesture is, of course, symbolic. Although poetic licence attributed the discovery to 'stout Cortés' it was in fact Vasco Núñez de Balboa who 'stood silent on a peak in Darien'.

Important as all that may be to purists and local inhabitants alike the history of Jerez de los Caballeros goes back very much further. Less than 5km (3 miles) away is the Dolmen del Toriñuelo, sacred to the sun-worshiping inhabitants of prehistoric times, and the most outstanding of several megalithic monuments to be found in the immediate vicinity. Coming much more up to date in a single stride, there are traces of a Moorish *alcazaba* round the Castle of the Templars which has been thoughtfully restored. The whole place was given to the knights, known as the *caballeros*, by Alfonso IX in 1230 after it had been recaptured from the Moors. They held on to it for more than 70 years and some local people will tell you that the last and most defiant of them died fighting for their rights in the Bloody Tower. Others maintain that the Order was being disbanded anyway and resistance would have been both futile and illogical. Whatever the truth of the matter they lost control in the early fourteenth century and nobody bothered very much about buildings of architectural interest for the next four hundred years. After this there was a burst of feverish activity with towers shooting up everywhere. San Miguel appeared in the mid-eighteenth century closely followed by the much decorated tower of San Bartolomé with its liberal sprinkling of blue to match the blue and gold façade of the church. The distinctive church of Santa Catalina added its version before the century was out, giving the town a distinctive skyline that can be easily identified from a long way off. Jerez also lays claim to Hernando de Sota, described variously as the 'Hero of Florida' and the 'Explorer of the Mississippi', although he was actually born in Barcarrota, a bare 10km (6 miles) further to the north.

A good, attractive minor road cuts across country to join the main route from Zafra at Fregenal de la Sierra, a small picturesque mountain village known principally for its nearby hermitages and its proximity to at least two ruined castles just across the border in Huelva.

# Huelva

It is not in the least surprising that the far north of Huelva is indistinguishable from the deep south of Extremadura since the border was defined by man and not by nature. However, subtle differences do start to appear quite rapidly. The interminable olive groves give way in places to forests of chestnuts which are a blaze of colour in the autumn and provide a bountiful harvest at the same time. The ground on either side of the roads is littered with empty husks where the local people have been filling sacks and baskets with ripe fruit to be loaded on to mules and driven slowly home at the end of the day. Eucalyptus trees introduce a different shade of green, alongside oak and pines which increase in number as one approaches the coast, intermingled with cork and oranges.

The foothills of the Sierra Morena level out gradually towards the sandy beaches of the Costa de la Luz and the marshlands at the mouth of the Guadalquivir. Much of this low lying area to the east, for centuries a hunter's stamping ground, is now a national park, providing Europe with one of its biggest nature reserves as well as a haven for birds and animals. The population includes deer, badgers, otters and lynx along with wild cats, weasels and foxes and the always-present rabbits and wild boar. Foremost amongst the birds are golden eagles, buzzards and kestrels in addition to flamingo, heron and a dozen other familiar species. Carp and eel share their part of the marshes with fresh-water tortoises and there is no shortage of reptiles, nor unfortunately of mosquitos.

Hunting, except for things like hares, partridge and pigeons is not one of the major sports in Huelva but fishermen have a wide choice all along the coast and in some rivers, particularly the Piedras which joins the sea near El Rompido, roughly mid-way between the capital and the Portuguese border. Boats put out to sea every day in search of deep water varieties that give visitors an excellent day's sport and local fishermen a reasonable living. Windsurfing and sailing are both extremely popular, riding stables in the Matalascañas area are open throughout the year and there are frequent bicycle races and motocross events during the Fiestas Columbinas at the beginning of August. Golf enthusiasts can take advantage of the facilities at the nine-hole Bellavista club at Aljaraque on the outskirts of the capital while football, said to have been introduced into Spain by British mining personnel during the nineteenth century, is played extensively. There are some tennis courts, mainly in the holiday resorts, as well as swimming pools and a sprinkling of other sporting activities. The weather throughout the region is more kindly than it is further north, hovering round the 25 °C (77 °F) mark at the height of summer and seldom dropping below about 9 °C (48 °F) in the depths of winter.

Roads throughout the region vary as much as they do in Extremadura. A splendid highway is being constructed from the north down through the Sierra de Aracena and is due to be completed by 1991. In the meantime there are a few rough patches which nobody seems to bother about because they are due to be bypassed at any moment. Two very respectable main roads link Huelva with Seville to the east and another, just as good, connects the capital with Ayamonte where there is a ferry across the Guadiana river to Portugal. Plenty of smaller roads thread their way between the various towns of special interest or importance, and these can produce an occasional surprise but no serious problems. In addition there are just as many of the minor variety with surfaces alternating between good, fair and the kind that are better forgotten. Speed limits apply in all built-up areas and some communities even reinforce them with several pairs of 'sleeping policemen' just on the outskirts. Once a car has bounced cheerfully over the first couple the average motorist is usually only too willing to observe the official regulations.

When it comes to accommodation *paradores* are decidedly thin on the ground. The two at present in existence, one at Ayamonte and the other on the coast road near Mazagón, are both comfortable but of no historic interest whatsoever. In addition there are a few up-market hotels and many more smaller ones which have all 'mod cons', perfectly adequate public rooms and occasionally restaurants but do not go in for any additional frills and flounces. Some little villages produce an inn or a tavern which can be either a delight or a near-disaster so it is as well to inspect the premises before coming to a decision. Another thing to bear in mind is that, although a selection of hotels in the coastal resorts stay open out of season, their standards may occasionally slip a little. The food is usually quite good and the bed linen is spotless but it is frustrating to find yourself with a decent-sized bath and a total absence of hot water, especially when this state of affairs may last for days, weeks or, at the very worst, until the first holiday crowds are scheduled to put in an appearance. A few apartments are available, mainly in Almonte and Punta Umbria, and there are some excellent camp sites in the coastal area, the officially recognised ones having a wide range of facilities.

The people of Huelva celebrate at fairly frequent intervals throughout the year, particularly around Easter, at Whitsun and in September which seems to be the most favoured month for honouring patron saints in the traditional manner. This usually involves a solemn pilgrimage to a special hermitage or outlying sanctuary when the procession can be very colourful. In addition there are fairs and carnivals with music, dancing, traditional costumes and much feasting and general jubilation. The Fiestas del Carmen in mid-July are a case in point and in August everyone gathers to pay tribute to Columbus and the men who accompanied him on his voyage of discovery across the Atlantic. But there is no need to wait for a feast day to sample the local specialities. Pork, lamb and rabbit stews are served everywhere, venison is likely to be on the menu in Almonte but the greatest variety is undoubtedly to be found amongst the fish and seafood. One can become almost addicted to swordfish, served either hot or cold, not to mention large prawns, crayfish and lobster. Sole and fresh anchovy appear as frequently as tunny but the chef may need an hour's notice to produce a *paella* and may even refuse to make it if the restaurant is too crowded. *Gazpacho*, the delicious cold soup based on tomato and sometimes cucumber, may be the staple diet in the mind of a visitor but it is almost unobtainable during the winter. A typical dinner ends with pastries, which can be a little on the dry side for some people, or delicious strawberries, peaches, melons, grapes or quinces depending on the season. Local wines go well with the traditional dishes and the coffee is invariably good, whether or not accompanied by a glass of eau-de-vie such as *hierro* produced in Zalamea la Real. Souvenirs to look for include rugs and embroidery as well as copper, leather and pottery.

Just south of the border with Extremadura a thoroughly pleasant small road through wooded country leads to **Aracena**, an attractive little town built on a hillside and watched over by the ruins of a castle once occupied by the Templars. However, its main attraction lies in the series of caves hollowed out by underground rivers as they forced their way through faults in the rock. Apart from all the strange and sometimes colourful formations there are pools of clear water, narrow sections that are little more than passages and a Snow Well, so called because of its sparkling white crystals, which was the first of the complex to be discovered. Incidentally, for people who enjoy pottering about below ground level, there are some other caves at Alájar, a short distance away. Aracena also has its fair share of churches, a hermitage and an aged synagogue and goes in for

*Windmills at Campo de Criptana, Ciudad Real*

*Plaza de Espana, Cádiz*

*The church of Santa Maria de la Anunción, Arcos, Cádiz*

*The view from the parador at Arcos, Cádiz*

*The huge open-cast workings of the Río Tinto mines*

embroidery and pottery, the latter in quite a big way. Visitors can choose between a hotel and a hostel as well as two or three small restaurants in the vicinity of the caves.

To the south, and well worth seeing if you have the time to drive there and back, are the gigantic open-cast Río Tinto mines. The area provides more than half the copper and all the pyrites mined in Spain and was already hard at work in Roman days. The British moved in during the nineteenth century, extending the operations, increasing the population and bringing fresh prosperity to the area. However, they unsettled a lot of small farmers in the process, some of whose families have never quite forgiven them. The mines are remarkably colourful and exceedingly strange to the untutored eye, not at all what one would expect to find on the banks of a river in Europe.

West of Aracena, on the far side of the new southbound highway, **Cortegana** introduces a note of prehistory with a megalithic burial ground, preserves a section of Roman road and a medieval castle, throws in two small churches as a bonus and then points the way to **Aroche**. This somewhat smaller village tends to do things in style. It has turned its castle into a bullring, opened a little archaeological museum and attracts ever-growing crowds to its annual carnival when merrymaking is the order of the day. An equally popular event is the Whitsun pilgrimage during which the atmosphere is somewhat more restrained. The majority of other small hamlets in the area also have similar attractions of interest to the visitor but it takes a good deal of time and a certain dedication to discover them all. Most people are inclined to return to the main road and head south past Valverde del Camino, where it is an idea to inspect the local crafts on offer. However the musically minded would probably find Alosno more to their liking. It specialises in folklore and tradition, presents songs and dances which are often accompanied by the sound of little bells and puts on its most imaginative performances during the Crosses of May celebrations and at Christmas time.

Whichever route one takes it leads eventually to the town of **Huelva** a short distance inland on the banks of the Odiel river. Even the most enthusiastic sightseer would have to search quite diligently to find something to get really excited about. Practically all the tangible evidence of its long and chequered history was destroyed in the earthquake that devastated Lisbon in 1755, since when it has turned itself into a typical industrial city and a busy port. But it would be much too easy to dismiss it altogether. The Plaza de las Monjas, filled with palms, is a good place to start exploring and is not all that far from the church of San Pedro which occupies the site of an ancient mosque. The cathedral, which was once the convent of La Merced, is a good brisk walk away. There is one first rate hotel standing in the shadow of the Law Courts that provides all creature comforts and will arrange for its guests to play golf or tennis, go swimming, change money and park the car but oddly enough has no restaurant of its own. There is another hotel which is not quite so up-market in spite of having a dining room, and a dozen or so in the lower price brackets where the facilities are basic or, in some cases, practically non-existent. This probably explains why most visitors, apart from people who are there on business, prefer to stay out of town. Huelva celebrates Christmas with carols and the Cavalcade of the Three Kings who arrive bearing sweets for the children, holds traditional festivities during Holy Week, has its own version of the widely-popular annual carnival and pulls out all the stops early in August when it recalls the departure of Christopher Columbus a little more than 500 years ago.

The nearest coastal resort to the capital is **Punta Umbria**, some 20km (12 miles) distant on the far side of the river, across a long bridge which spans both the water and the marshes alongside. It is a typical fishing village turned holiday playground with a clutch of not-very-memorable hotels, although most of them do have restaurants and reasonable food. The beach is long and sandy and is reached by way of gaps between the villas that stand cheek by jowl along the shore. One can swim, waterski, sail, go fishing, visit the local discos or watch flamenco dancing during the season. The marina, like most others in this part of the world, is really only a collection of buoys in the river, designed to take small craft and with nothing in the way of pontoons or other such facilities for visiting yachts. A coast road runs along the dunes to **El Rompido**, a cheerful little place with a pleasant, well-equipped camp site beyond which yet more marshes at the mouth of the Piedras river force the road inland to Lepe, an excellent place to buy strawberries, melons and figs. The area round about is good for fishing and there is some shooting in the vicinity.

The last town on the route to the west is **Ayamonte** with its permanent ferry to Portugal and a customs post that operates all through the year. It is a nice little fishing village which is building furiously in an effort to become a thriving coastal resort. Apart from a couple of beaches nearby it has two elderly churches, a *parador*, one or two small hotels and the Casa Barberi, a restaurant which guarantees that its *paella* and other local dishes are as good today as they were when it first opened in 1917. To the north is **Villablanca** with a church dedicated to the patron saint of the village and the remains of some windmills, which all goes to prove that Don Quixote did not have a monopoly, although La Mancha has a great many more of them. **San Bartolomé de la Torre** looks even further back over its shoulder with some sparse remains of a Punic tower. There is also some slight evidence that the Romans once occupied the site in the wake of even earlier inhabitants who left one of their dolmens behind. **Gibraleón**, on the road back to the capital, was obviously once a walled town and still has two convents and three churches, one of which started out as a temple and then became a mosque before being converted to Christianity.

Driving south-eastwards from the town of Huelva, through an area occupied almost exclusively by petroleum companies, the first impressive sight is an enormous statue of Columbus, the work of Gertrude Vanderbilt Whitney, which dominates the Punta del Sebo. It completely dwarfs the palm trees growing in the little square at its feet and a collection of small boats at their moorings in the river beyond. A dozen or so kilometres (about 7 miles) away is the Franciscan monastery of La Rábida, an attractive and very restrained white building standing in colourful gardens with a modest hostel and restaurant attached. At the entrance is a monument to Columbus and the men who sailed with him, most of whom came from the surrounding area and had very little choice in the matter after a royal proclamation made it an offence not to sign on. Part of the monastery has been turned into a museum almost entirely devoted to Columbus who arrived on the doorstep with his son Diego in 1485. He lived there for the next seven years while enough money was collected to enable him to discover America, or at any rate San Salvador, in 1492.

Tours conducted by the monks every morning and afternoon include the small room where the explorer first put his theory that the world was round to the far-sighted prior of the time, and the refectory where he lived and worked while Isabel and Ferdinand were being persuaded that the venture was worthy of royal support. There are paintings of his arrival and of the crowd who gathered to wish him Godspeed and who, judging by their expressions, apparently never expected to see him again. Portraits of all the main characters involved in the project hang round the walls — the king and queen, Columbus and his captains and the two monks without whose efforts the expedition would probably never have got off the ground. Scale models of the three ships stand in glass cases in the corridors, there are charts, documents and old books and a room given over to the flags of the various American countries emphasised by caskets of soil from each one. Everything has its own label in four different languages, including English, so it is not necessary to understand Spanish in order to appreciate the items on display. The tour also includes the church, which dates from the early fourteenth century, a mudéjar cloister of comparable age and a statue of the Virgin looking rather doubtful but surrounded by the appropriate emblems with models of the three ships — the Santa Maria, the Niña and the Pinta — in full sail at her feet.

**Palos de la Frontera** is now silted up but still retains the well from which Columbus is reputed to have taken on water for the voyage. The law forcing local seamen to join his expedition was read out in the church of San Jorge where, incidentally, Hernán Cortés is also thought to have asked for divine assistance before sailing off to conquer Mexico some thirty-five years later. **Moguer**, another one-time port that has been left high and dry, does just as well with a fourteenth-century convent of Santa Clara and two museums. One is devoted to religious art and the other to the works of Juan Ramón Jiménez who won a Nobel Prize in 1956. Personal possessions, books and tributes from an enthusiastic press are all on show in the house where he lived, open each morning and afternoon throughout the year. Further north still is **Niebla**, steeped in history, which was fortified by the Romans, had its walls reinforced by the Moorish invaders but managed to retain its original bridge. Also on view is a church that served first as a temple and then as a mosque, the fifteenth-century Santa Maria hospital and some very elderly houses which provide additional atmosphere.

Along the seafront to the west development is rapidly becoming the order of the day. At the moment there are wide sandy beaches, forests of pine trees looking for all the world like large green powder puffs on stalks, citrus trees and, here and there, brilliantly coloured flowering shrubs, but this may not last for very long. **Mazagón**, which does nothing much except cater for tourists and holiday crowds, is setting a pattern for the future in bricks and concrete but still has quite a way to go. The only hotel of any note is the *parador*, so far isolated about 6km (4 miles) along the coast. It overlooks the beach, provides tennis and a swimming pool, has a restaurant and will change money to save its guests driving into town. Much the same can be said of **Matalascañas** which is larger and somewhat noisier than Mazagón with facilities for riding and a whole range of water sports. Its main hotel has all the same advantages as the *parador*, adding a hairdresser, a nursery, a doctor and a night club for good measure. There are up-market camp sites along the coast with everything from swimming pools to shops as well as tennis, riding and fishing, restaurants and bars, somewhere to post letters, make a phone call or find someone to wash the car.

From Matalascañas there is literally nowhere to go but north, the coast road ends abruptly on the outskirts, giving way to the marshy delta of the Guadalquivir and the Doñana National Park. However this does not mean that there is nothing further to see or do. Some 16km (10 miles) away is **El Rocio** which really only comes to life at Whitsun during a pilgrimage which is said to be one of the biggest and probably the oldest in Spain. Anything up to a million people converge on this tiny backwater hamlet, arriving in flower-decorated carts, on horseback, in cars and coaches and even on foot. The main religious celebrations take place at night with the processions of the Rosary and the Virgen del Rocio, but between times the crowds concentrate on less serious matters with each and every one determined to enjoy their outing to the full. Visitors are accepted but no special attempt is made to attract them to what is, after all, a highly emotive occasion.

In complete contrast to the noise and bustle of the El Rocio festivities a tour of the Doñana National Park is a joy for anyone who is anxious to get away from it all. Special conducted tours are available using Land Rovers to cross the dunes, skirt round the marshes and bounce across the scrubland as guides point out the different species common to each area. Of course it is quite possible for a motorist to drive through a large section of these lowlands bordering on the park by simply following any of a number of very minor roads. However they can be in a sad state of repair and keeping one's eyes glued to the way ahead is hardly the best method of seeing the wild life on either hand. Bird watchers, amateur naturalists, hikers and anyone preferring two wheels to four should be especially careful not to wander off into a patch of quicksand or a bog as there is unlikely to be someone else about to lend a helping hand.

There is very little to see in Almonte or Bollullos par del Condado, the last small towns to be encountered before joining either of the two major roads to Seville. The former is an administrative centre dating, to a large extent, from the eighteenth century while the latter is in much the same style with a fairly run-of-the-mill church and a small hermitage. The countryside thereabouts is given over to olives, oranges and vines and is pleasant without being in any way spectacular. There are entrances onto the main highway while the upper road is joined at La Palma del Condado with its two convents, a fifteenth-century hermitage and a parish church that is a typical example of Andalusian baroque and may or may not be open if you want to look inside. If time is pressing it is much better to cut your losses and join the traffic to Seville.

# Further Information
## — Extremadura and Huelva —

### Places of Interest

**Aracena**
Caves
Guided tours: 10am-6pm.

Río Tinto Mines
34km (21 miles) due south of Aracena.

**Badajoz**
Alcazaba
Open: 9am-1pm and 3-6pm.

Archaeology Museum
Open: 10am-2pm. Closed Sunday.

Fine Arts Museum
Open: 10am-2pm. Closed Sunday.

**Cáceres**
Casa de las Veletas
Open: 10am-2pm and 5-8pm.
Winter 4-6pm. Closed Sundays
and holidays.

Palacio de los Golfines
Patio open: apply to caretaker.

Archaeology Museum
Open: 9am-1pm and 4-7pm.
Closed Mondays.

Sanctuary of the Virgen de la
Montaña.

## Guadalupe
Monastery
Guided tours: 9.30am-1pm and
3.30-7pm.

## Huelva
La Rábida
Monastery
Guided tours: 10am-1.30pm and 4-
8pm. Closed Monday in winter.

## Mazagón
Doñana National Park
Details of conducted tours from
tourist office in Huelva.

## Mérida
Alcazaba
Open: June to August 8am-1pm
and 4-7pm. Otherwise 9am-1pm
and 3-6pm. Closed Sunday and
holiday afternoons.

Arena and Theatre
Open: June-August 8am-8pm.
Otherwise 9am-6.30pm. Sometimes
closes for lunch.

Archaeology Museum
Open: 10am-2pm and 4-6pm.
Closed Sunday and holiday after-
noons, and Mondays.

## Moguer
Museum
Religious Art
Open: 11am-1pm and 4-6pm.

Zenobia-Juan Ramón Museum
Open: July and August 10am-2pm
and 4.30-8.30pm. Otherwise 10am-
2pm and 4-8pm.

## Trujillo
Church of Santa Maria
If closed enquire at Tourist Office.

## Zafra
Candelaria Church
Open: 10.30am-1pm and 7-8.30pm.
Sunday and holidays 11am-
12.30pm.

## Tourist Information Offices

### Badajoz
Pasaje de San Juan 2
☎ 22 27 63

### Cáceres
Plaza General Mola
☎ 24 63 47

### Huelva
Plus Ultra 10
☎ 24 50 92

### Mérida
Del Puente 9
☎ 31 53 53 or 30 21 61

### Trujillo
Plaza Mayor
☎ 32 06 53

### Zafra
Plaza de España
☎ 55 10 36

# 10 • Seville and Córdoba

Although Seville (the English version of Sevilla) and Córdoba are completely independent of each other they are very much alike in many different ways. Both capitals are high up on the list of places nearly every tourist wants to visit and yet comparatively few people get to know either of them thoroughly. Each one has its own province, sharing a common border and neither has any coastline at all. When it comes to olives and orange trees the average person would be hard put to tell them apart. They are linked by road, by rail and by the Guadalquivir river, have mountains to the north which are largely under-populated and open country to the south with any number of little villages and hamlets but fewer interesting small towns than one would expect.

When it comes to history their stories also run very much in parallel, having been shaped by events which were alternately beneficial and ruthless, but not in the way a superficial knowledge of those far off times would suggest. To all intents and purposes it began with the Romans who were building away furiously before the birth of Christ and gave the towns almost equal status in their province of *Baetica*, although Córdoba was officially the capital. The next momentous event was the arrival of the Moors in 711. Their occupation was to last for some 500 years although Granada was only recaptured in 1492, the same year that Columbus discovered America. The Moors seldom get anything like the amount of credit that is due to them. Under their administration everything flourished, merchants prospered, once arid lands were irrigated and produced large crops, a totally new conception of art and architecture was introduced and learning was encouraged, all in an atmosphere of tolerance that was preached as well as practised nearly everywhere.

Throughout this time the forces of Christendom were fighting the infidel with every means at their disposal, from conventional weapons to some far less admirable methods similar to those employed

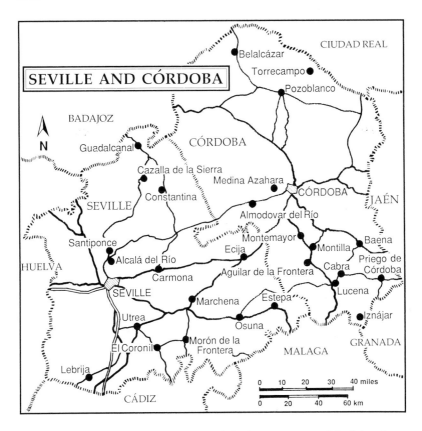

later by the Inquisition. In 1070 Córdoba became part of the kingdom of Seville, was liberated in 1236 and almost at once went into a decline from which it has never completely recovered. Seville was recaptured by Ferdinand of Castile twelve years later but was much more fortunate. After the discovery of America and the New World exploits of the *conquistadores* it monopolised the lucrative trade routes across the Atlantic until the Guadalquivir silted up in the eighteenth century and Cádiz took over its role as the busiest port in southern Spain.

The two provinces are well supplied with lakes and rivers, have several highways, a comprehensive network of secondary roads and a quantity of the small, if sometimes questionable, variety which are conspicuous by their absence in the mountains to the north. These areas produce more in the way of paths and cart tracks although nothing of outstanding interest when it comes to nature parks and wildlife reserves. There are plenty of places where one can stop for the night but not many very comfortable hotels outside the two provincial capitals. As elsewhere one can catch a bus, call a taxi or hire a car, join an organised excursion and, in both Seville and Córdoba, ride round in a horse-drawn buggy whose driver promises to show his passengers all the sights but nevertheless keeps very much to the well worn tourist route. Seville undoubtedly has the best known, most spectacular and most overcrowded festival in Spain but there are many other colourful fairs and fiestas for people who prefer taking their traditional celebrations in slightly smaller doses. Souvenirs tend to be both flamboyant and predictable, the local dishes are not particularly exciting, and when it comes to weather, you can freeze or fry quite easily, depending on the time of year.

## Seville

It would be complicated, although not impossible, to travel eastwards from Huelva without driving through **Seville**, and once in so captivating a city, few visitors could pass by without a second glance, even though it is very much on the beaten track. There are two major roads linking the city with the town of Huelva, which run due west and are almost parallel with each other. Another, not in such good condition, divides just short of the border, with one fork heading for Aracena in the north of Huelva province while the other continues up past Zafra, in Extremadura, to Cáceres. To the south there is a choice between a main road and an *autopista* to Cadiz while two or three alternative routes give easy access to Córdoba, Málaga and Granada. A number of secondary roads twist their way up into the Sierra Morena, take the line of least resistance along the Guadalquivir and across the plains nearby or make brief sorties into the marshlands bordering on the Atlantic. Minor roads in varying states of repair can be found everywhere but, with only a few exceptions, they are not particularly scenic or interesting and do not make ideal shortcuts between towns and villages. For anyone in a hurry Seville has air links with Madrid and a handful of other Spanish cities, regular train services run to and from most of the surrounding provincial capitals and quantities of buses operate on schedule throughout Andalusia and even further afield.

The number and variety of hotels and restaurants on offer will hardly come as a surprise to anyone. The biggest, most luxurious and consequently the most expensive hotel in Seville, although not in the whole of southern Spain, stands alone in its own gardens quite close to the *alcázar*. Others, only slightly less aware of their own importance, are scattered like confetti all over the town, interspersed with

*Giralda Tower and part of the cathedral, Seville*

smaller places that frequently have all the aids to comfortable living and rather more atmosphere. Restaurants are just as plentiful and most of them can be relied upon to turn out something in the way of a local speciality which, more often than not, will be fish.

When it comes to feasts and festivals Seville is almost unbeatable, especially during Holy Week. From Palm Sunday onwards processions converge on the cathedral carrying statues of Christ or the Virgin Mary, often bedecked with jewels, garlanded with flowers, sometimes candlelit and weighing anything up to half a ton. Although theatrical in the extreme, this is essentially a religious festival, whereas the April Fair that follows it is given over to songs and dances, bullfights, parades, fireworks and any other forms of entertainment that come to mind.

The city is rather less congested at other times of the year and especially so in summer when it can be unbearably hot. The best time for a visit is during the spring or the autumn when moving about can really be a pleasure. It is a good idea to take a cruise up the Guadalquivir, select a horse-drawn vehicle from the tree-lined square in the shadow of the cathedral and trot round the narrow streets filled with the scent of orange blossom or find a tiled seat in the gardens of the *alcázar* beside a small fountain where jasmine grows in profusion.

The first place to visit is the cathedral. It is the third largest in Europe, after St Peter's in Rome and St Paul's in London, but is rather dark and gloomy with massive pillars, some impressive art work and a lot of carving and gold leaf. Two kings, St Ferdinand and Alfonso X, are buried in the Chapel Royal watched over by Our Lady of Monarchs who is patron saint of the city. She is said to have been given to Ferdinand by his cousin and fellow saint, Louis of France. The so-called tomb of Christopher Columbus, who is actually buried elsewhere, was added less than a hundred years ago. Adjoining the cathedral is the massive Giralda Tower which was once a minaret. Inside there are a series of ramps linked by steps which make it comparatively easy for anyone with enough time and energy to climb to the top where the view is magnificent.

Sharing the tree-filled square beside the cathedral is a sixteenth-century building housing the archives of the Indies. It is quite literally overflowing with documents, maps, charts, detailed reports and a host of other items collected during the discovery and conquest of Central and South America. Whatever you want to know about those historic events will be there somewhere, although even the people who are responsible for this unique and priceless collection do not pretend to have been through the whole thing thoroughly. However they are making good headway, taking time out to change the items on display at regular intervals so that anyone who is seriously interested will always find something new and unexpected to examine.

The *alcázar* next door is a fourteenth-century building occupying the site of a Moorish palace of which only a very small part remains. However, it is no less interesting for that. Pedro the Cruel started it off along the lines of the Alhambra with some arresting halls and courtyards, Ferdinand and Isabel could not resist changing it and substituting their own favourite decorations but these obviously did not appeal to Charles V who insisted on adding a palace of his own. Since then various apartments have been further changed and updated and even Franco is said to have enjoyed spending an odd holiday there in the spring. The Admiral's Apartments, where many plans were laid for exploiting and colonising the New World, has, appropriately, the famous sixteenth-century *Virgin of the Navigators* altarpiece and a model of the *Santa Maria*, the ship used by Columbus on his voyage of discovery. A grand staircase leads up to the royal apartments on the first floor which are decorated in a number of different styles, have some delicately carved stone archways and a large wrought iron screen doused in gold. The Court of Maidens is surrounded by several attractive little rooms, amongst them the Ambassadors' Hall with its cedarwood dome, beyond which is the delightful Court of Dolls, but the best place for tapestries is in the section added by Charles V.

The gardens, which cover a larger area than the buildings themselves, are exceptionally attractive with pools and fountains, trees, shrubs and brilliantly coloured flowers. A small covered passageway leads from the Flag Court to the old Jewish quarter of Santa Cruz. This is a little gem of a place, full of narrow streets, tiny squares, wrought iron grilles, flowers, palms and orange trees. Parts of it have become very fashionable but others, sadly, are in urgent need of a fresh coat of paint.

The San Telmo Palace, which was once a naval school, lost its extensive grounds to the Maria Luisa Park in the nineteenth century. They are now vast pleasure gardens full of plants and promenades, pools, pigeons and exhibition halls. Part of the university nearby is housed in the eighteenth-century tobacco factory where Bizet put Carmen to work, thereby making it more famous than it might otherwise have been. At the opposite end of the gardens is the city's archaeological museum, whose Roman section full of mosaics and statues from *Itálica* is a pleasant place to visit when it gets too hot outside. The Museum of Popular Art and Customs concerns itself with all things traditional while, much further afield, there are works by Zurbarán, Murillo and El Greco, amongst others, in the Fine Arts Museum.

Visitors in search of yet more places to inspect would probably enjoy seeing Pilate's House, said to have been inspired by the original in Jerusalem over 400 years ago. Then there is the Basilica of La Macarena with a much-loved Virgin who weeps crystal tears, the highly ornate chapel of San José and the Torre del Oro on the river bank that guarded the busy quays in Moorish times and now plays host to a small maritime museum.

Armed with a map and wearing a comfortable pair of shoes it is a rewarding experience to explore all the other nooks and crannies of this fascinating old town. It is a jumble of tiled roofs which look as if they have been put together from thousands of broken flower pots, blank white walls with an occasional outburst of decoration to break the monotony, shuttered windows behind heavy iron grilles, balconies festooned with flowers and equally colourful laundry hanging out to dry and an odd donkey or mule running a delivery service. Near the Alameda de Hércules which, with its weatherbeaten statues was once a fashionable meeting place, is the ancient convent of Santa Clara complete with a medieval tower.

The main shopping area is to be found round the Calle Sierpes, a 'pedestrians only' thoroughfare bristling with antiquated shops that have been attending to the needs of their customers for many hundreds of years. Most of the tiles, whether they are colourful, amusing or simply functional, are made in Triana, an ancient suburb on the far side of the river from the bullring and the Torre del Oro. Quite a few factories will look favourably on visitors, especially if they are planning to buy something on the way out. The area is also known as the 'Cradle of Flamenco', although several other places in Andalusia would question this, and a sprinkling of cafés and bars provide music along with refreshments and may charge accordingly.

Anyone who is looking for a change from sightseeing can play golf, go boating on the placid waters of the Plaza de España, which may not cover any great distance but does provide a new angle on the splendid Palacio Centrale with its ornamental bridges, or watch a bullfight provided the tickets have been obtained well in advance. There are also concerts and exhibitions as well as a racecourse and excursions in and around the area. All the necessary details are available from the information office just round the corner from the *alcázar*.

Approximately 8km (5 miles) to the north of Seville are the village of **Santiponce** and the ruins of *Itálica*. The former is known chiefly for the monastery church of San Isidoro del Campo with its far from attractive figure of St Jerome in the centre of the altarpiece. Guzmán the Good, who founded the monastery at the beginning of the fourteenth century, is buried there with his wife and son. *Itálica*, on the other hand, was a large Roman town in the third century BC which fell into ruins when the empire started to crumble and, for some reason, the Moors never bothered to do anything about it. In its heyday the town was the birthplace of three emperors, Trajan, Hadrian and Theodosius, had an amphitheatre which could seat 40,000 people as well as a theatre, several temples and all the other refinements that were part and parcel of an important city closely linked with Rome. A good deal of excavation work is going on but the site is open every day, winter and summer. It is possible to make out the lines of streets along the hillside and the foundations of some villas as well as seeing the ruins of the amphitheatre, selected mosaics and something of the theatre on the other side of the main road. The splendid view over to the Guadalquivir must have made it almost impossible for a potential enemy to launch a surprise attack from the north.

There are other traces of Roman occupation in **Carmona**, 33km (20 miles) to the east. Something like a quarter of the 800 tombs in the necropolis there have been excavated, many of them turning out to be little more than funeral chambers with niches for urns in the rock walls. However, two have come to light which are quite spectacular by comparison. The Elephant Tomb, so called because of the elephant at the entrance, has three large chambers, presumed to be dining halls, a kitchen and running water. It is thought that the priests used this area for some kind of ritual banquet in honour of the dead. The Servilia Tomb is even larger with pillars, a vaulted ceiling and arches that would not look out of place in a wealthy home.

Carmona's other tourist attractions include a large Roman mosaic in the town hall patio, a Moorish gateway on the road to the capital, two elderly churches and the convent of Santa Clara with portraits of women from the seventeenth century. It is an atmospheric town with the remains of its ancient walls, some very desirable old residences opening off its little alleyways and others from the seventeenth and eighteenth centuries surrounding the main square. It also has a splendid *parador*, built inside the remains of a Moorish *alcázar* on the top of a hill, which was opened by the king and queen a decade or so ago. Although the building itself is new it was designed to blend in with its surroundings and has attractive little touches like a fountain in the patio, arcades to protect guests from the sun, appropriate furniture and a most inviting swimming pool.

There are no places of any great moment in the south of the province but some minor roads find their way down into the marshlands that Seville shares with Huelva and Cádiz towards the mouth of the Guadalquivir. It is a good place for birdwatching provided one does not wander off into a bog or a patch of quicksand and has possibilities for hunting and fishing on a small scale nearby. How-

ever it is essential to contact the ICONA headquarters in Seville
before setting out on any such expedition.

**Lebrija**, on somewhat firmer ground near the *autopista*, has a
twelfth-century mosque complete with domes and a matching tower
which was built later to give it added status after its transformation
into the church of Santa Maria de la Oliva. A few ruins are dotted
about on the eastern side of the *autopista*, some of them with no names
and no approach roads which makes inspection a trifle difficult for
anyone who is driving. Nor are things that much easier for travellers
on foot because many of the best fighting bulls are raised on the local
ranches and they are allowed to wander about very much at will. On
the whole it is probably easier to stick to the main road, which runs
through fields of sunflowers and an astonishingly large number of
wayside bars, or branch off to **El Palmar de Troya**. This is a small
hamlet which is convinced that the Virgin Mary paid it a visit in the
late 1960s, an event that has kept the resident clergy fully occupied
ever since. The road carries on to **Utrera**, with its small and entirely
forgettable sanctuary, before leaving motorists free to decide
whether to make for Écija or Osuna.

There is no particular reason why one should not visit both places.
**Osuna**, away to the east, has delusions of grandeur measured in
centuries rather than decades. To start with it was a military centre
under the Romans who departed without leaving many traces behind, then it marked time under the Moors before leaping to promi-
nence when the Dukedom of Osuna was created in 1558. It already
had a university and in no time at all added palatial town houses with
elegant courtyards behind great wooden doors and a modest church
or two. Foremost amongst the religious buildings is the collegiate
church with paintings by Ribera, who was in the service of the Duke
of Osuna when the latter was Viceroy of Naples in the early seventeenth century. Its double crypt is open every day except Mondays
for specially conducted tours. A patio with decorated marble arcades
leads to the ducal sepulchre consisting of a miniature church and an
upstairs vault filled with the coffins of bygone dukes. The town's
other tourist attractions include the chapter house, the old law
courts, and a small archaeological museum in the Torre del Agua
which was once part of the surrounding walls.

**Écija**, a trifle over 30km (19 miles) due north of Osuna, was
founded by the Greeks, built over by the Romans and has a few rather
fine medieval mansions which are not open to view. However it is
impossible to miss all its distinctive belfries, decorated with colourful ceramic tiles, which stand out against the rather drab country-

side. For obvious reasons it is known to some people as the City of Towers but others insist on describing it as the Furnace of Andalusia because of the oppressive heat during the summer months. Several of the churches are now in ruins but the church of St James was largely rebuilt after the ground underneath shifted alarmingly in the early seventeenth century. Parts of the original structure survived and make a good foil for the decorative high altar. The town has nothing very exciting in the way of hotels and restaurants but motorists can stop off at a predictably noisy motel on the road to Córdoba.

Most of the villages hereabouts have something to offer in the way of an ancient ruin, a restored church, medieval houses and, perhaps, a hermitage or two but only the dedicated sightseer would attempt to visit all of them. However, a tour of inspection would reveal some attractive buildings and a delightful garden in **Morón de la Frontera**, the remains of an antiquated castle near the Moorish quarter in **Constantina**, a fifteenth-century Carthusian monastery and some original walls at **Cazalla de la Sierra** and the caves of Santiago and San Francisco near **Guadalcanal** which were occupied in prehistoric times. For anyone who would prefer to spend the day hunting or fishing the hills are full of deer and wild boar, not to mention lesser game such as partridge, duck, hares and rabbits. Those who like fishing will find black bass in the El Pintado dam, barbel round Écija or shad and dace in the Guadalquivir.

## Córdoba

Like Seville, Córdoba (both the city and the province) is in constant touch with the rest of Spain both by road and by rail. There are highways linking the provincial capital with Madrid, Cádiz, Seville, Granada and Jaén as well as less direct but nevertheless major routes to Málaga and Badajoz. Plenty of trains run to Madrid and Seville while regular services maintain contact with Barcelona, Valencia, Granada, Málaga and Algeciras. Buses operate round the province itself and to other more distant places, amongst them Cádiz, Jerez, Ubeda and Barcelona. As elsewhere there are cars for hire as well as taxis.

The province of Córdoba has plenty of hotels including a *parador* just outside the capital but nothing with any pretensions in the villages round about. Its restaurants range from those in the city, some of which are excellent, through the usual country taverns with their fairly predictable homemade dishes to an occasional café that makes you wish you had brought along your own sandwich and a flask of

*The bridge and mosque, Córdoba*

coffee instead. The southern half of the province is mainly interested in wine and there are several places where visitors are welcome to inspect the presses and the cellars before trying any of the samples on display. Quite a few of these wine centres have other tourist attractions as well. At **Montemayor** there is an unusual fortified castle dating from the fourteenth century while **Montilla** and **Aguilar** have a dozen or more interesting old buildings between them. Although **Monturque** has preserved one or two bits and pieces from Roman times pride of place must go to **Lucena** where Boabdil, the last of the Moorish kings of Granada, was imprisoned for a while in the Moral Tower. The most memorable of its many churches is the San Mateo because of the ornate Sacrarium Chapel, thought to be an original shrine. The town is well known for its brass, bronze and copper crafts and many of the articles made there, including oil lamps, are sold throughout Spain and exported overseas. Holy Week is marked by extremely colourful celebrations, there are fiestas in May and the whole area is out and about for the grape harvest festivals in September.

There are half a dozen or so delightfully scenic drives in the vicinity, the shorter ones leading to small, isolated sanctuaries with doors that are firmly locked and barred, windows that look as if they would only open under protest and no-one about to produce a key or distract one's attention from the view. The longer routes take in an attractive lake at **Iznájar**, stocked with trout, where one is tempted to park the car and wander about on foot, or a short, sharp dash to **Priego de Córdoba** with its medieval castle, a nice line in squares and fountains, and two or three small churches which will appeal to anyone more impressed by the baroque style than by interiors which are understated. A reasonable road cuts across country to **Cabra** and then heads north for **Baena** with a short detour to **Zuheros** to inspect the ruins of a fortified palace and the Neolithic Cave of the Bats which sounds better if you call it Los Murciélagos. Both Cabra and Baena put a lot of thought into their preparations for Holy Week and the former's fiesta at the beginning of September has been officially described as a tourist attraction.

Baena is just over 60km (37 miles) south-east of the city of **Córdoba**, one of the oldest and most famous cities of southern Spain and the best possible reason for visiting this part of the country. It was an Iberian settlement before the Romans arrived and in the years that followed increased both its status and its reputation to become the provincial capital and an important centre in the realms of both art and science. In view of this one would expect to find the remains of temples and baths, a theatre, an arena and a circus at the very least, together with the foundations of impressive villas and an original road or two. However, were it not for the foundations of one bridge over the Guadalquivir, a sadly-ruined temple and a few mosaics in the archaeological museum, visitors could be forgiven for assuming that the legions had never passed that way at all.

Christianity moved in at roughly the same time as the Romans started to pull out but left little more tangible evidence of its presence than the Visigoths who were ousted in their turn by the Moors at the beginning of the eighth century. This occupation marked the emergence of Córdoba as a city of unparalleled influence and importance, a vast conglomeration of palaces and public buildings, mosques, markets and bazaars, schools and a university, all illuminated by the first street lights to be installed in Europe. People of every creed and colour lived peacefully together, contributing their share to what was described at the time as 'the ornament of the world'. But all good things come to an end and after Ferdinand liberated the city in 1236 things changed drastically until eventually it was famous for its superb leatherwork and very little else. Today silver and leather goods from Córdoba are still highly prized, but the boundaries are being pushed out again to make room for factories which, together with tourists, are helping to restore at least part of its earlier pride and prosperity.

Córdoba, like Seville, is a much-visited city and strictly speaking has no place in this particular guide. However, as the provincial capital it merits at least a mention, especially in view of all its lesser known attractions that tend to be overlooked by a large percentage of tourists.

Mention Córdoba to any casual visitor and the first, and probably only thing they think of is the mosque with its forest of pillars, red and white arches and the sixteenth-century cathedral plonked down in the middle. Even Charles V, who was not exactly famous for preserving beautiful Moorish structures, accused the churchmen responsible of having 'destroyed something unique in order to build something commonplace'. Originally the mosque was open on every side with a tree-filled courtyard and plenty of room to expand by simply adding more columns from the ruins of other old temples and churches. This habit was practised over the years and accounts for the fact that by no means all the arches look exactly like the others. There is a great deal to admire in this strange building from the bronze-covered Door of Forgiveness to the sacred niche at the end of the main aisle, with its domed enclosure decorated with mosaics and gold, which was reserved for the caliphs.

The Villaviciosa Chapel and the Chapel Royal blend in quite well, which is more than one can say for the cathedral. It includes a little bit of everything, ostentatiously designed to out-do the Moors, with eye-catching pulpits and impressive choir stalls. However, it only succeeds in being thoroughly indigestible when compared with the simple grandeur all around. Most people come away feeling a trifle disorientated but considerably impressed.

Anyone who wonders what Córdoba was like in its greatest days should pop in to the fourteenth-century Calahorra Tower on the far side of the Roman bridge. It is somewhat heavy, not exactly squat and is vaguely forbidding inside its low, surrounding walls. The tower houses a little museum, tracing the history of the capital with items like suits of armour, reproductions and illustrations of the city including one with lighting that changes to show how it looked from before dawn until after sunset, and sections devoted to music and philosophy.

The Calahorra Tower also has a good view across the river to the *alcázar* of the Christian Kings. It was rebuilt in the fourteenth century, used by the Catholic Monarchs and the Inquisition and is now open to everybody each morning and afternoon. It is floodlit on summer

*Calahorra Tower, Córdoba*

evenings. There are some delightful patios, pools and fountains as well as shady terraces and a well kept area that is said to have produced fresh vegetables for more than 1,000 years. Amongst the exhibits in the very substantial Hall of the Mosaics overlooking the gardens is a splendid and much decorated Roman sarcophagus and a highly imaginative mosaic of Adam and Eve. Neither of them look very pleased with life in the Garden of Eden and they are accompanied by a strangely fascinating and extremely cheerful serpent with an ornamental tail and two large ears.

The Municipal Museum, a few minutes walk from either the mosque or the *alcázar*, is housed in a typical old mansion and will tell you a little about local leather and silver, all you want to know about bullfighting but precious little else. An enthusiastic student of the art can discover how fashions in bulls have changed, find out who does what with which piece of equipment and why, inspect the heavily-embroidered costumes worn in the ring and admire the old posters that were not so much advertisements as works of art. Famous local bullfighters like Manolete and El Cordobés are practically enshrined in the building with mementoes of both triumphs and disasters such as the hide of the bull that put paid to Manolete's spectacular career.

If you prefer art in some of its less aggressive forms there is a Fine Arts Museum on the far side of the Plaza del Potro which has some good paintings but somehow does not quite come up to expectations.

Adjoining it is an extremely popular collection of the works of Julio Romero de Torres, presented by his family following his death in 1930 and housed in a building that has been named after him. Also overlooking the square with its famous sixteenth-century Colt Fountain, topped by the little animal in a prancing mood, is the inn of the same name immortalised by Cervantes in *Don Quixote*. It has not changed very much over the years, apart from the fact that instead of providing accommodation for visitors it is occupied by a great deal of silver and leatherwork. The Plaza del Potro is not all that far from the Archaeological Museum, housed in a medieval palace and reputed to be one of the most comprehensive of its kind in Spain. It has some rather endearing stone lions guarding the patios, items from every period of Córdoba's history, colourful Roman mosaics and an informed review of Moorish art along with early Christian relics.

The old Jewish quarter has become quite fashionable of late — another facet which Córdoba has in common with Seville — but upstages its rival by preserving one of the very few ancient synagogues still to be found in Spain. The square room with its balcony set aside for women has survived more than 500 years without too much trouble, and the caretaker will show visitors round any morning or afternoon on request. It is about a block away from the Almodóvar Gate, is within sight of the Municipal Museum and is all of a piece with the Zoco with its flamenco displays and craftsmen turning out the sort of things that make tourists wish they had not left all their surplus cash at the hotel.

It is impossible to make a bee-line through Juderia. The streets and alleys curve away in all directions in search of tiny squares, past houses painted white with protective grilles over the windows and balconies smothered in flowers. Most of these are built round enchanting little patios which are cool and shaded in contrast to the heat outside. If you have to get lost anywhere this is undoubtedly one of the most picturesque places to choose.

Once you have got your bearings, and a reliable map, however, it is worth while venturing further afield because there are literally dozens of places waiting to be discovered inside the old city. There are something like twenty different churches, each with its own particular claim to fame, from the church of San Pablo with its Virgin of Anguish to the understated church of Santa Victoria that borrowed a few ideas from the Pantheon. Everyone has a special favourite from amongst the innumerable squares which may be small and secretive or famous because of some statue or monument. The Corredera Square is unique with its seventeenth-century arcades that made it a perfect venue for bullfights in the good old days, the unusual Christ of the Lanterns is to be found in Capuchinos Square while San Raphael keeps popping up all over the place. It would be very hard to miss the opulent statue of Manolete in full fighting gear, flanked by riderless horses attended by grooms with the head of a bull facing in the opposite direction, that fronts the church of Santa Maria de las Aguas Santas. Other places of interest include the Royal Stables near the *alcázar* with their magnificent horses and a good half dozen palatial mansions, the most outstanding of which is the former home of the Marqués del Viana with no less than fourteen patios and rooms filled with pictures and tapestries, books and furniture, porcelain and a valuable collection of embossed leather. If an undiluted diet of history and architecture becomes too much of a good thing there are plenty of attractive gardens, a small zoo in the Parque Jose Cruz Conde which is open all day, an eighteen-hole golf course, a sports stadium and, of course, the bullring.

Córdoba city is definitely a place to pause for a while and fortunately there is no shortage of accommodation in any price bracket. If it is comfort you are after this is to be found in a modern hotel in the Victoria Gardens which has the advantage of being quite central and possesses a good restaurant and a swimming pool. The *parador*, some 3-4km (2-2$^1/_2$ miles) away and a good choice for people who want to get out of town, is also a modern building surrounded by oleanders and orange trees with a tennis court, a large swimming pool in landscaped gardens and all the attendant facilities. Surprisingly there are four hotels only the width of the street away from the mosque, one of them large and comfortable with no restaurant but the indescribable blessing of a garage for the car. The others are smaller and one of them offers its guests both a menu and a parking space. Restaurants are no more difficult to find than hotels and range from good through unpretentious to very forgettable little bars. Anyone who wants to try the local specialities should keep an eye open for *rabo de toro*, a decided improvement on oxtail, *churrasco* which is pork smothered in a peppery sauce, lamb cooked with honey in the Moorish style and seafood in all its different forms. Local wines are served everywhere and one or two *bodegas* (wine cellars) in the city are only too happy if you can find the time to call in and choose your own.

In spite of decorated floats and the parade of horses taking part in the pilgrimage of Santo Domingo during Lent and all the religious fervour of Holy Week, May is definitely the month for festivals in

Córdoba. It starts with local competitions to see who can dream up the best floral decorations. These range from strictly personal arrangements that fill the patios and little balconies, to community efforts covering whole streets and squares. The celebrations reach their peak at the end of the month when everyone goes to the fair. It is a lighthearted mixture of all the usual entertainments with special emphasis on traditional costumes, flamenco songs and dances and bands determined to make themselves heard above everybody else. A national flamenco contest is held every 3 years and the Virgen de la Fuensanta is honoured in September to the tinkling of hundreds of tiny bells.

It is a little over a thousand years since building started at **Medina Azahara**, 10km (6 miles) or so due west of the capital. Originally it was intended as a country residence for the caliphs but one thing led to another, each more exotic and costly than the last. By the time the Berbers sacked it in 1013 the palace had grown into a small township which caused a great deal of comment, even in those extravagant days. Excavations have been going on there since World War II and the small part which has so far been restored is open for inspection every day except Tuesdays but closes for a long lunch at noon. You can see the salons of the kings and the viziers, get an idea of the mosque which is being recreated with infinite care and tour the small museum that has been opened on the site.

With the exception of Las Ermidas, a favourite location for hermitages as long ago as the sixth century, this more or less rounds off the list of tourist attractions in Córdoba province. However, open-air enthusiasts will find plenty of mini roads and footpaths through the hilly country to the north. Sited on the so-called Route of Holm Oaks and Granite is **Pozoblanco**, a fairly modern village with one or two humble hotels, a golf course and a reputation for staging a particularly lively pilgrimage to the sanctuary of the Virgen de Luna in the spring. It is only one of many in this part of the country where all the fairs and fiestas are designed as local celebrations rather than as entertainments for tourists who, quite frankly, are few and far between. A wanderer might well call in at **Belalcázar** which has the remains of an old castle or **Torrecampo**, whose antiquated El Moro Inn takes an informed interest in private art collections. Sportsmen are more likely to congregate along the northern border where there is plenty of game and the various hunting organisations make up parties that visiting guns are welcome to join on payment of an entrance fee. Fishermen will have greater success further south where carp and black bass can be found almost everywhere and an occasional dam is stocked with trout. For drivers the choice is more limited — negotiate a hairy stretch of road to reach a village of no great consequence or keep to the highway for a quick and easy drive from Córdoba to Jaén.

# Further Information
## — Seville and Córdoba —

### Places of Interest

**Carmona**
Roman Necropolis
Guided tours: 9am-2pm and 4-6pm. Closed Monday.

**Córdoba**
Alcázar
Open: May to September 9.30am-1.30pm and 5-8pm. Otherwise 4-7pm.
The gardens are floodlit on summer evenings.

Cathedral and Mosque
Open: April to September 10.30am-1.30pm and 3.30-7pm. Otherwise 3-6pm. Closed 25 December afternoon.

Archaeology Museum
Open: 10am-2pm and 4-8pm. Closed Sunday pm.

History Museum
Open: mornings and afternoons.

Municipal Museum
Open: 9.30am-1.30pm and 5-7.30pm. Closed Monday.

Synagogue
Open: 9.30am-1.30pm and 4.30-7.30pm. Apply to caretaker.

Viana Palace
Open: mornings and afternoons. Closed Wednesday.

Medina Azahara
Open: 10.30am-12noon and 4.30-7.30pm (3.30-5pm in winter). Closed Tuesdays.

**Osuna**
Collegiate Church
Guided tours of vaults: June to September 10am-1.30pm and 4-7.30pm. Otherwise 3-6.30pm. Closed Monday.

**Seville**
Alcázar
Open: 9am-12.45pm and 4.30-7pm (3-5.30pm in winter) Saturday and Sunday 9am-12.45pm. Closed 1 January, Good Friday, Corpus Christi and 25 December.

Casa Lonja
Archives of the Indies
Guided tours: 10am-1pm. Closed Sunday and holidays.

Cathedral, Treasury and Giralda Tower
Open: 10.30am-1pm and 4-6pm (3.30-5.30pm in winter).

Museum of Archaeology
Open: 10am-2pm. Closed Sunday and Monday.

Museum of Fine Arts
Open: 10am-2pm. Closed Monday.

Museum of Popular Arts and Customs
Open: 10am-2pm. Closed Monday.

Maritime Museum
Open: 10am-2pm. Sunday 10am-1pm. Closed Monday.

Pilate's House
Open: 10am-1pm and 3-7pm. Partly closed Saturday afternoon, Sunday and holidays.

*Itálica*
Open: April to September 9am-7.30pm. Otherwise closes 5.30pm.

**Tourist Information Offices**

**Córdoba**
González Murga 13
☎ 47 12 35

**Écija**
Av de Andalucia

**Osuna**
Sepulcro Ducal
☎ 81 04 44

**Seville**
Av de la Constitución
☎ 22 14 04

# 11 • Jaén

Jaén is an attractive province, roughly the same size as its immediate neighbours, with something of interest for everyone. The scenery is extremely varied, there are towns where even the most world-weary traveller would feel the need to explore and others which invite their visitors to relax and do nothing except, perhaps, take the waters or amble gently round a small and not very demanding museum.

To the north, where Jaén borders on Ciudad Real, there are the mountains of the Sierra Morena, well supplied with lakes and rivers plus an occasional wildlife reserve and scenic drives over minor roads, the smallest of which are either unsurfaced or are in need of a good deal of repair. It is possible to walk for hours on end without coming across any villages at all and only a very occasional isolated sanctuary. This state of affairs is ideal for the experienced hiker but rather daunting for anyone whose idea of strenuous exercise is a short stroll along a forest path with frequent stops at attractive little country inns.

To the north-east, in the direction of Albacete, it is much the same story although there are quite a few small hamlets dotted about amongst the olive groves before you get to the Sierra de Segura where, once again, animals are almost the only inhabitants and there is hardly a car to be seen. Just as many tracks but rather more roads are to be found in the hilly country along the border with Granada. The villages become more numerous, as do the olive trees, and there is even the odd place to park a caravan. Extensive plains cover the region to the west with a network of small roads, all of them going to or through rural communities which are kept fully occupied growing wheat and other cereals, tending vines or keeping an eye on the olives. The area is rich in minerals, particularly along the Guadalquivir, with the mines and their attendant industries concentrated round Linares and La Carolina. The country here is rather arid scrubland and looks its best towards the end of the year when the large tracts of sunflowers are spectacular before they give up their seed for cooking oil and margarine.

Sportsmen you meet insist that the Sierra de Cazorla is one of the finest hunting grounds in Europe, rich in ibex, buck of various descriptions and, of course, wild boar which do a lot of damage and are consequently regarded as fair game for approximately two months from the beginning of September. The ram, introduced from Corsica in 1953, has increased in numbers very considerably and is to be found in the national park where it can be hunted under licence during the autumn and early winter. Fishermen are equally enthusiastic about the area, boring their friends with stories of the large trout they almost, but not quite, landed from one of the two well-stocked rivers — the Borosa and the Guadalentin. Pike, bream and barbel swim about in the Guadalquivir almost asking to be caught. The rules and regulations governing the different types of fish and the size, the seasons and the number which may be taken over a specified period apply fairly generally throughout the country and details are available from the ICONA headquarters in the different provinces.

When it comes to moving about in Jaén the options are many and various. You can choose a major road from Córdoba that divides before it gets to the border, the left-hand fork heading for Bailén and the highway to Madrid while the right-hand fork runs straight to the provincial capital. The city of Jaén has a direct road to Granada, a slightly more roundabout route to Málaga and two other good roads to Almería and Murcia respectively. There are plenty of secondary roads across the plains, some of which are quite attractive and are usually in good condition. For anyone with an adventurous streak there is frequently the option of a side turning which may save mileage but often takes a good deal longer. For this type of inspection a good map is essential if you do not want to arrive at some vantage point, miniscule village or farming community where the road ends abruptly and the only way out is also the only way in. Trains, of course, are more predictable but they are not exactly numerous and unless you are on the way from the city of Jaén to Madrid or Córdoba it is usually better to catch a bus. Towns like Ubeda have their own bus stations with services around the province and links with cities like Valencia, Seville and Granada — or, of course, it is possible to hire a car in the provincial capital.

There is no shortage of hotels in Jaén, starting at the top of the list with four *paradores*, one each in Jaén and Ubeda, the third at Bailén on the Madrid-Cádiz highway and the fourth very much out on a

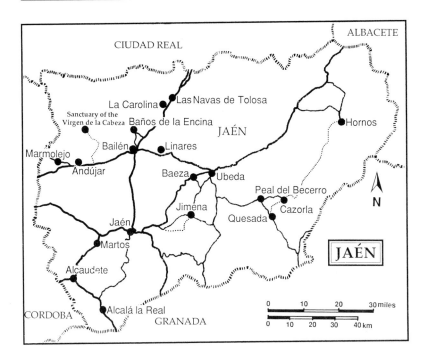

limb in the hills near Cazorla. Other options include four or five comfortable hotels and hostels, more than twice as many places with fewer facilities and a crop of little inns situated in out-of-the-way villages and hamlets. Do not expect too much from local restaurants even if the height of your ambition is to sample only local dishes. For anyone who dislikes roast kid, peppers and spices the choice is somewhat limited although one can always fall back on soup, smoked ham, fish or an omelette. Snack bars and cafeterias are no more enterprising but do offer things like prawns, olives and a selection of other bits and pieces to go with the drinks, followed by sandwiches which are usually either cheese or ham and may occasionally be toasted.

Festivals in Jaén are roughly akin to the celebrations held elsewhere in southern Spain. Bonfires are lit in honour of San Anton on 17 January followed by a traditional supper. On the last Sunday in April there is a pilgrimage to the shrine of Neustra Señora de la Cabeza in the hills above Andújar. Holy Week is marked by processions that are both solemn and colourful whereas June is given over to fairs of one kind or another. The province holds its main fiestas in the middle of October, concentrating very largely on bullfights and fitting in as many as possible before the end of the season, after which there is the festival in honour of Santa Catalina to look forward to in late November. Souvenir hunters should allow plenty of space for their bargains which are liable to take the form of wrought iron ware, especially lanterns, wickerwork, guitars, almost anything made from straw including carpets and glazed pottery of every shape and colour.

Jaén shares a common heritage with all its neighbours. There is practically nothing to link it with prehistoric times and, when it came to establishing large settlements, the Romans appear to have been fully occupied elsewhere. However the Moors descended on it in considerable numbers, calling it *Geen* to indicate that it was on the caravan route, and fought long and hard to retain it in the face of repeated attacks until they were driven out altogether in the thirteenth century. After that everyone started building, restoring, refurbishing and redecorating, creating some little architectural gems in the process which somehow managed to survive the wars that followed. The British and French came to blows near Bailén in the run up to Waterloo when General Castaños, commanding a combined Anglo-Spanish force, won the first victory over Napoleon in the Peninsular War. Foremost amongst the small historic towns are Baeza and Ubeda, which should definitely not be missed, while other places contribute a handsome church or two. There are castles with entire hills all to themselves, a good sprinkling of ruins and even little spas, which is not something you come across every day in this part of the world.

Approaching Jaén from Córdoba the direction you take at the fork in the road depends very largely on what you want to see and how much time you have available. With a little forward planning it is quite possible to have the best of both worlds, a brief spell in the mountains and a tour of the main towns, without having to retrace your steps too often or too far. Travelling along the upper route, the first town to be encountered is **Andújar** which is worth more than a passing glance in spite of the fact that it is industrial. Amongst its many old houses and chapels, built during the fifteenth and sixteenth centuries, the ones that stand out are the church of San Miguel in the Plaza de España and the Santa Maria church which, for some reason best known to itself, is closed from the beginning of November until the middle of April. The former has a most impressive wooden door and ceiling, both beautifully carved and watched over by the figures of the prophets, while the latter uses a wrought iron grille to protect the El Greco painting *Christ in the Garden of Olives* which hangs in one of the chapels. The town offers an interesting little motor museum, a couple of small hotels and several hostels, none of them particularly memorable, and an odd café or two plus a well equipped camp site with a swimming pool and somewhere for the children to paddle. Anyone on the lookout for something a trifle more up-market in the way of accommodation will find it at **Marmolejo**, not more than 10km (6 miles) away. It is a small spa town that keeps itself occupied making guitars and has a hotel with a garden, a swimming pool and a restaurant which spills out onto the terrace when the weather is good.

A minor road runs north from Andújar, through a small game reserve, to the sanctuary of the Virgen de la Cabeza which, quite apart from anything else, has an exceptionally good view. A chapel was built out on the top of a lonely rock shortly after the Virgin had appeared to a local shepherd there in the thirteenth century. Some three hundred years later it was replaced by a monastery which had very few problems until the Civil War broke out. A large number of nationalists, civil guards and townspeople took refuge there in September 1936 and when they surrendered eight months later the whole place was in ruins. On the last Saturday in April members of the various brotherhoods take part in a procession of decorated carts up to the sanctuary followed by festivities which last well into the next day.

A couple of minor roads thread their way north through the hills to join up eventually with the highway to Madrid while similar ones find their way south to **Martos**. This is generally described as the largest olive growing area in Spain but to the inexperienced eye the trees do not seem to be planted any more densely or cover a lot more territory than they do in other parts of the country. Martos has its obligatory hilltop castle, a small church and some Roman relics like coins and tombstones which it preserves with tremendous care. A major road carries on southwards past **Alcaudete** where anyone who is determined not to miss a single castle will find a Moorish example and a small cathedral. Then it is on to **Alcalá la Real** which certainly has a ruin to boast about. The village is completely overshadowed by the castle of La Mota which looks like a rather delapidated tiara pulled down over the brow of the hill. Other attractions include the remains of a homage tower, some modest churches and a passable fountain in the main square. There are opportunities for shooting in the area round about and some very gentle climbing in the hills to the north but no hotels or cafés worth mentioning. However this does not really matter as there are a couple of scenic options open which provide an alternative route back to the capital.

*Jaén from the* parador *of Santa Catalina*

Although it is not very large as provincial capitals go there is a great deal to recommend **Jaén** to the casual visitor or to someone looking for a comfortable place to stay for a day or two. The *parador* of Santa Catalina inhabits an enormous castle perched on a long, narrow mountain-top with breathtaking views all round. It has been very tastefully restored so as not to damage either the original fabric or the atmosphere created by priceless tapestries, beautiful furniture and vaulting that would do credit to a cathedral. It has even managed to set aside ample areas for parking and space for a swimming pool. People with no head for heights might prefer a comfortable hotel overlooking a small garden in the centre of the town where you can book a suite and have an entertaining evening. Anyone who is unimpressed by castles or hates dancing can choose from a number of smaller places and some quite acceptable restaurants within easy reach. The town has both a bullring and a racecourse, some stately homes and enough churches to keep the average sightseer busy for quite a while.

The cathedral, which completely dwarfs all the surrounding buildings, was started in about the year 1500 on the site of an ancient mosque and took some two hundred years to build. Its façade is, if anything, a trifle over decorated with columns supporting a balustrade, statues, coats-of-arms and other art work all sandwiched between tall square towers, each topped by a matching dome. It was designed by Vandelvira and the theory is that he rather over-reached himself because there was not enough space for his typically grand ideas and no-one either would, or perhaps could, scale them down to fit in with their surroundings. The result is an impressive cathedral but unless you get a pilot's eye view it is very difficult to see more than a small part of it. Inside there are three matching naves, heavy pillars and choir stalls carved in the fifteenth and sixteenth centuries. Its prize possession is a gold casket encrusted with jewels holding the Sudarium, variously described as part of a veil or a handkerchief which St Veronica is said to have used to wipe the face of Christ on the road to Calvary. Nobody seems to know quite how San Euphrasjus, the first Bishop of Andújar, got hold of it but he is credited with transporting it to Spain. Close by is the Virgen de la Antigua who is believed to have gone to war with St Ferdinand.

The oldest church in Jaén is La Magdalena while the Capilla San Andrés is the most decorative with a delicate wrought iron screen covered in gold leaf which was the work of Master Bartolomé, undoubtedly the town's most famous son. The convent of the Barefoot Carmelites is extremely proud of its St John of the Cross manuscript *Cántico Espiritual*, leaving the monasteries of Santo Domingo and Santa Clara to rely on their cloisters for publicity. The cathedral has its own museum tucked away in the basement filled with all sorts of treasures. The Sudarium is in a class of its own and is shown to the faithful after mass on Fridays. The Provincial Museum is near the Parque de la Victoria. It has a number of interesting archaeological exhibits on the ground floor including a fine Roman mosaic and makes much of its Iberian Bull of Porcuna. The art gallery is upstairs on the first floor and has nothing of really outstanding interest to write home about.

There is no very simple or straightforward way of driving across country from Jaén to Cazorla but it is more fun sorting out the back roads than traipsing from one highway to another even if the initial outlook is olives, olives and yet more olives. Of the two or three alternative routes none has any particular advantage over the others from the point of view of scenery or places to stop. **Jimena** with its caves is one possibility, **Peal del Becerro** for the nearby Iberian sepulchre of Toya is another or the choice might be **Quesada** with an eye to the Zabaleta Gallery and the Sanctuary of Tiscar. Like other eagle's nest type villages in the area Quesada clings precariously to its own patch of ground, huddled between a deep gorge, stark dragon's tooth crags and rocks worn into strange shapes by wind and weather.

When it comes to ease of living the town of **Cazorla** is much better placed, having room to expand along the valley, plant its crops and entertain its visitors. The ruins of the Arab castle of La Yedra are close enough to explore without taking along anything except perhaps a packed lunch. However, most people heading for the Sierra de Cazorla are much more interested in nature than in anything the previous occupants left to posterity, no matter how spectacular. It is a wild, mountainous region with magnificent views, densely wooded slopes, crystal clear streams, lakes and waterfalls. Flowers grow in profusion, the air is heavily scented with thyme and lavender, butterflies of every colour bask in the sun while bees are hard at work all round them. Eagles and osprey share their environment with many other kinds of more familiar birds while buck, wild boar and ibex are thick on the ground. It is the largest area of protected woodland in Andalusia and people are encouraged to explore, particularly along trails which are clearly marked and for which maps are available from the National Tourist Offices. Anyone who fails to identify every flower, shrub and butterfly they see has no need to be downhearted, it is said that there are some examples which cannot be found anywhere else in the world.

The Guadalquivir rises in the Cañada de las Fuentes, not far from Quesada, and then runs northwards to the Tranco dam which is one of the biggest in the country. Apart from irrigating the farmlands to the west it is being developed as a holiday resort with all the usual water sports and other tourist attractions. From **Hornos**, at the northern tip of the dam, small scenic roads and cart tracks make off in all directions, calling at old ruins like the ones at Segura de la Sierra, nodding at little communities hardly big enough to be called hamlets, tracing the course of a river, discovering an odd cave or picnic site and running out of steam before they reach the Guadalmena dam. This is another large expanse of water which is taking itself so seriously as a potential holiday playground that it has already founded the first nautical club in the province.

The highway to Albacete passes nearby, on its way from **Villacarrillo**, known mainly for its Church of the Assumption and its proximity to several local beauty spots and other assorted places of interest. In spite of the fact that it has a modest inn with a dining room, the average motorist prefers to press on to Cazorla where the comparable hostels are less bothered by traffic. They generally run to a private bathroom and, in some cases, will rustle up something to eat if necessary. The *parador* stands all by itself an appreciable distance away, along a road that twists in a most uninhibited fashion

*St James' Hospital, Ubeda*

through the pine forests. It is a rather ordinary looking white building with quite pleasant gardens but nothing fancy like tennis courts or a swimming pool and is favoured mainly by people who are there for the hunting, fishing or walking. Self-catering enthusiasts can find some basic apartments at Santiago de la Espada, a mere stone's throw from the border. The Guadalentin river is said to provide the best trout fishing in the area and permits are obtainable from the ICONA headquarters in the capital.

Less than 50km (31 miles) from Cazorla is **Ubeda**, without any doubt one of the loveliest towns in Jaén. It owes a certain amount to the Moors who were thrown out in the mid-thirteenth century but an even greater debt to Andrés de Vandelvira, the architect who was responsible for the majority of its most distinguished buildings. With so many of them to see it is fortunate that they are mostly grouped together in a fairly small area, with the exception of St James' Hospital on the far side of the town near the bullring. The high relief of St James Matamore in militant mood over the entrance is enough to tempt one off the road for a closer look at the attractive patio and the grand staircase, but beware of children bearing footballs in the courtyard. When they really get going a Cup Final fades into insignificance.

The ideal place to start exploring is in the Plaza Vázquez de Molina with the splendid church of El Salvador standing at right angles to a sixteenth-century palace which is now a *parador*. If the church is locked it is a simple matter to knock on the first door in the Calle Francisco de los Cobos and the sacristan will be only too pleased to show you round. The interior of El Salvador is incredibly ornate with a monumental wrought iron screen, a massive altar piece and a beautiful sacristy that has more than a touch of Italy about it. In keeping with the overall atmosphere of the square is the Casa de las Cadenas, designed by Vandelvira in 1562, which takes its name from the chains round the forecourt and is now the town hall. Having admired the façade, the small garden and the very restrained fountain outside it is an idea to slip round the corner to the patio and ask to see the mural paintings on the first floor, which come from the former chapter house. The church of Santa Maria, with its old cloister and little chapels, for which Master Bartolomé supplied most of the grilles, is the last building to see before setting out for the highly decorated Casa de las Torres a few minutes' walk away.

In whichever direction you turn there is something to catch your attention and persuade you to linger a while. It may be the stone roses on St Dominic's church, the palace of El Marqués de Mancera, one time Viceroy of Peru, which does not really look like a palace at all, or the impressive doorway of the church of San Pablo. It is worth going inside here to see the rich carvings and especially Vandelvira's Heads of the Dead Chapel before moving on to inspect the twisted columns of the Montiel Palace round the corner.

If all this history becomes a little overpowering anyone with a nice sense of the ridiculous should make a point of spending a few minutes in the Plaza de Andalusia. Its centrepiece is a statue of General Sero whose fascist ideas did not go down too well with the townspeople. At the first opportunity they peppered it with bullets and left the now extremely draughty general up on his pedestal for all the world to see. Even if you are not heading for anywhere in particular Ubeda is a delightful place to wander about, investigating picturesque little alleys and tiny squares and, perhaps, making a special trip to the gipsy quarter which does a roaring trade in souvenirs.

The most atmospheric hotel in Ubeda is, without question, the Parador Condestable Davalos which would be one of the tourist attractions even if it was not functional as well. It has a charming inner courtyard and lovely original fireplaces, an old wine cellar, a good restaurant and a forecourt where a willing attendant helped by posts and chains keeps an eye on the cars. Few of the other hotels and hostels are quite so well placed for sightseeing but then most of them are considerably less expensive and have fewer amenities. On the

*Church of El Salvador and the* parador, *Ubeda*

other hand, wherever you start from it is quite a walk to the Hospital de Santiago, the large and vaguely modern-looking construction that dates back to the mid-sixteenth century and is known as the Andalusian Escorial.

A bare 10km (6 miles) from Ubeda on the main road to Jaén is the equally fascinating town of **Baeza**, the first place in southern Spain to be recaptured from the Moors. After its liberation in 1227 the Christians set about adding a few churches of their own but the only one that has survived, possibly because of constant attention down the years, is the otherwise unremarkable church of Santa Cruz. Opposite it is the Jabalquinto Palace, built some four hundred years later, with a large empty courtyard behind heavy, studded doors. Two stone lions guard the staircase inside, that sweeps up to the first floor, making promises which are never kept. At the moment the rooms resemble nothing so much as a school for DIY enthusiasts, their every corner filled with all the tools and materials necessary for repairing the ravages of time.

A little street running down beside the palace leads past the old university which was founded towards the end of the sixteenth century and was fully operational until about a hundred years ago. It does not seem to keep any particular hours but when the large main doors are open people wander in and out of the courtyard over-looked by the first-floor corridors which have been filled in with glass. There is not a great deal to see apart from a very viewable ceiling in the large amphitheatre.

Above and beyond this historic little complex is the Plaza Santa Maria, overlooked by the cathedral from the top of a wide flight of steps. Parts of the original mosque can be seen in the cloister but the interior is pure sixteenth century with protective grilles and an interesting metal pulpit. The whole place is definitely on the dark side but lights can be turned on by employing the well known coin-in-the-slot method. In return for spending a little time and money the chapels turn out to be both ornate and colourful with quite a lot of gold and silver about.

Adjoining the cathedral is the Casas Consistoriales Altas deco-rated with coats-of-arms inherited by Charles V from his parents, Juana the Mad and Philip the Fair. On the third side of the square is the seminary which was home to students from the mid-seventeenth century onwards and where it was customary for them to write their names and the dates on which they graduated in bull's blood on the outside of the front wall. The centrepiece of this sloping cobbled square is the Santa Maria Fountain which is better described as a decorated triumphal arch standing in a shallow basin without a drop of water and no obvious means of filling it, let alone making it flow. A narrow pathway leads through to a small square and on to the Plaza de los Leones which takes its name from the four much-mutilated lions which support the little fountain.

The buildings surrounding the plaza are mostly antiques adapted to modern needs. The early law courts with their decorative win-dows, curious little balcony and six doors behind which the notaries conducted the business of the day, are now home to the Tourist Office. On one side is the Jaén Gate, an impressive archway built in honour of Charles V who passed that way in 1526 en route for Seville to marry Isabel of Portugal. Opposite is the former abattoir which looks more like a private mansion with heavy grilles over the windows, a covered balcony and an extremely large imperial coat-of-arms. Like Ubeda, Baeza is a good place to wander about discovering other attractions such as the old market square, the town hall which was once a prison and the original Corn Exchange, although there is no sign of the printing press established in the town in 1551. The sixteenth-century church of St Francis must have been extremely impressive in its heyday but unfortunately the greater part of it has now fallen down. All that remains are part of the transept and the apse and some stone altarpieces standing back from the pavement and not protected in any way.

With practically no hotels or restaurants Baeza is a better place to spend the day than to arrive at dusk in search of dinner and a room for the night. Although there are places to see in Ibros, Rus and Canena, which incidentally is also a spa, the wise traveller with comfort in mind will probably make straight for **Bailén** on the highway from Córdoba to Madrid. It boasts a *parador* with a garden and a swimming pool, a handful of other hotels and a motel where every room has its own private entrance shaded by wisteria with roses and strawberries in the front garden and covered parking for the car. There is also a site nearby for anyone who is carrying a tent or towing a caravan. A few kilometres to the north of Bailén and slightly off the main road is **Baños de la Encina**, a growing village with a large church and an even larger castle in an excellent state of repair. It is surrounded by farmlands and is conveniently close to the river and its somewhat erratic dam. Bailén is also only a short run from Linares, the largest town in Jaén apart from the capital, but it is not at all inviting unless you have a mind to examine the items on display in its archaeological museum.

There is not much to choose between **Linares** and **La Carolina**, a comparable mining and industrial centre on the road to Madrid. However this is an excellent route to take if you are still short of souvenirs: the roadsides break out into a rash of low buildings crouching behind wire screens covered with decorative plates, mounds of pots and other articles which might be quite useful when you get them home. Gradually the olive groves give way to pines and eucalyptus trees, there are wayside hotels and cafés, with a very comfortable establishment just south of La Carolina which has a restaurant and a swimming pool as well.

At **Las Navas de Tolosa**, on the far side of the town, there is a small hostel where one can swim and play tennis or set up a base from which to explore the **Desfiladero de Despeñaperros,** a region with an impressive gorge adjacent to a small game reserve. The scenery in the area is greener and more mountainous, with hardly an olive to be seen, and a fairly run-of-the-mill camp site at Santa Elena for anyone who wants a break on the journey home. Quite unexpectedly the road turns itself into a dual carriageway with each half taking off in a different direction, disappearing from view almost immediately behind a hill, on the other side of a valley or into the mouth of a tunnel. By the time they decide to get together again Jaén has been left behind and the northbound traffic is heading into La Mancha.

# Further Information
## — Jaén —

**Places of Interest**

**Andújar**
Santa Maria Church
Open: 11am-1pm and 6-9pm.
Closed November to April.

**Baeza**
Cathedral
If closed enquire at the Tourist Office.

Palace and University
Open: mornings and afternoons. If closed enquire at the Tourist Office.

**Cazorla**
Ruined castle of La Yedra and Museum
Open: morning and afternoon.

**Jaén**
Cathedral and Museum
Open: June to September 10am-1pm and 4-7.30pm. Otherwise 11am-2pm.

Museum of Archaeology and Fine Arts
Open: 10am-2pm. Closed Monday and some holidays.

**Quesada**
Zabaleta Gallery
Open: 12noon-2pm.

**Ubeda**
El Salvador Church
If closed apply to sacristan, first door on the right in the Calle Francisco de los Cobos.

Museum
Open: mornings and afternoons. For precise times apply to the Tourist Office.

**Tourist Information Offices**

**Baeza**
Plaza del Populo
☎ 74 04 44

**Jaén**
Arquitecto Bergés 1
☎ 22 27 37

**Ubeda**
Bajos del Ayuntamiento
☎ 75 08 97

# 12 • Ciudad Real and Albacete

Ciudad Real and Albacete together form part of La Mancha, a vast tableland south of Madrid which visitors either find extremely fascinating or detest on sight. It takes its name from the Arab word *manxa* meaning parched earth and for most of the year has no difficulty whatsoever in living up to it. On the other hand it is not quite so arid as one might think. Wheat is grown extensively on the seemingly never-ending plains, turning them from green to gold and finally to brown when the harvest has been gathered and the land prepared for the coming year. It also has something like a million acres of vineyards as befits the largest wine-producing area in Spain and these are a blaze of colour in the autumn. Large tracts of land are given over to maize which is left to dry before being cut down and, of course, there is no getting away from the interminable olive trees for long. In addition, it also produces the biggest crop of saffron in the world and takes on the appearance of a gigantic collection of purple lakes when the crocus plants are all in full bloom.

Apart from one comparatively small area to the south, hills can usually be seen along the horizon and the landscape is dotted about with little igloo-like constructions made from hundreds of separate stones cemented together, tiny wells, workers' cottages that would fit into a medium sized room and are all painted white, and an odd flock of sheep or goats. Here and there the hazy outline of a faraway village shimmers in the intense summer heat like a desert mirage, usually disappearing altogether after the sun goes down. The winter is correspondingly cold with snow and biting winds of the kind most people would associate with Siberia. However, in the spring and autumn the temperatures are perfectly acceptable with warm sun and a slight nip in the wind which enables travellers to move about in comfort. The landscape has often been described as lonely but it has the same strange attraction that one finds in similar wide open spaces in other parts of the world.

Both hunting and fishing are available, the former consisting mainly of partridge, hare and rabbits with wild fowl concentrated in the area round Daimiel. The same region does a nice line in crayfish as do several towns along the Segura river in Albacete. However there are probably more carp than anything else and the best place to find them is in and around the lakes and lagoons at Ruidera which have been compared, rather too enthusiastically one feels, with their counterparts in Switzerland. Nevertheless the region has some pretty little waterfalls, an appreciable amount of greenery and the makings of a popular holiday resort on Lake Colgada which is the biggest of them all.

Although southern La Mancha is not exactly over-blessed with roads, the main highways and most of the secondary routes are kept in a remarkably good state of repair. Occasionally a minor one may give the motorist some cause for concern, especially in bad weather and, as elsewhere, the village cobblestones can shake both a car and its occupants until their doors and teeth rattle. When it comes to stopping for the night there are three *paradores*, one at Manzanares north of the town of Ciudad Real, another at Almagro and the third a kilometre or two from the capital of Albacete. The area boasts a sprinkling of other very comfortable hotels and a large number of the smaller type which offer facilities according to their official status. *Hotel Residencias* and *Hostel Residencias* do not usually have a restaurant although they may run to a cafeteria and a few tables where one can get rolls and coffee for breakfast. Even the most humble inns are generally clean and hospitable but they do have their limits. With very few exceptions the service is excellent, no-one has yet told the local innkeepers that the customer is not invariably right. Restaurants follow much the same pattern and anyone who wants to sample the local dishes should order partridge cooked in any of a dozen different ways, rabbit in Almagro, mountain stew in Albacete and cheese almost anywhere. There are some delightfully drinkable local wines and something called *zurra* or *cueva*, depending on who is providing it, made from wine, fizzy water, sugar, sliced lemons and bananas which, ideally, should be served in special cups that are said to date from prehistoric times.

Getting about in southern La Mancha is perfectly simple. There are trains from Ciudad Real to Madrid and Badajoz on the Portuguese border some of which stop at Almagro. Valdepeñas, Manzanares and Alcázar de San Juan all have regular services to the nation's capital as well as being linked to Andalusia while Albacete is on the main route from Madrid to Murcia and Alicante. Many of the smaller towns have buses and taxis, cars can be hired in the main centres but

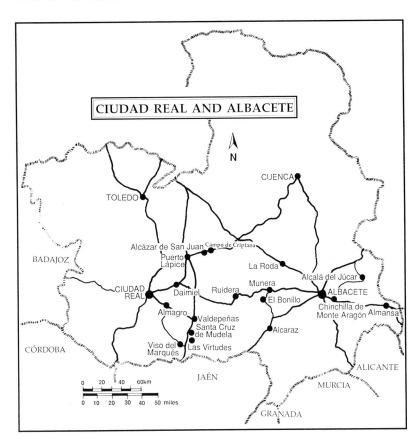

there does not seem to be much demand for bicycles which, considering the climate, is hardly surprising. Fuel is available for cash at reasonably frequent intervals but very few garages have heard of credit cards. There are hardly any camp sites, but one just outside Valdepeñas is well equipped and offers a shop and a swimming pool as well as all the usual facilities.

Local celebrations, often with a high religious content, are usually very colourful affairs with singing and dancing to the music of guitars, lutes and tamborines. There are solemn processions, floral events, competitions of various descriptions, a 'Song of Spring' and harvest festivals, theatrical performances and, of course, bullfights which invariably draw capacity crowds. Handmade lace from Almagro is a good choice if you are looking for souvenirs along with various fabrics from El Bonillo, steel items like scissors and razors manufactured in Albacete and a whole range of ceramics that can be picked up practically anywhere.

On the whole history has left fewer traces in southern La Mancha than it has to the north in Cuenca and Toledo, not to mention Madrid. Since the very early days the area has been marched through and fought over by successive armies including the Romans, the Moors, the French and the British, but few of them stayed long enough to put down roots and build towns of any great importance. However Miguel de Cervantes redressed the balance somewhat when he sent Don Quixote and Sancho Panza trotting through in search of windmills. Many of these can still be seen, the majority consisting of nothing more than a round, mouldering, tower-like structure punctuating the skyline without roof or sails to identify it. Others, practically always on the outskirts of small towns or villages, have been restored down to the last detail. The area leans heavily on Don Quixote and it is quite usual to come across a silhouette of him on horseback, cut from a sheet of iron and attached to a stone wall on the road into a hamlet. Every centre worthy of the name claims to have been the setting for one of the famous knight's more extraordinary adventures and scholars have been known to argue endlessly without coming to any satisfactory conclusion.

Visitors who stick firmly to the main highways in order to get through the region as rapidly as possible miss any number of outstanding attractions, often only a few kilometres away. For example, the first deviation when driving up from Jaén might well be to **Viso del Marqués**, one of those places where you need to keep a sharp lookout for the turning off to the left. The palace built by the first Marqués de Santa Cruz in the late sixteenth century is really a splendid place, highly decorated without being overpowering, with statues and suits of armour, lofty rooms and uninterrupted views across beautiful formal gardens. Although well away from the sea it is now a museum devoted to the history and archives of the Spanish navy, a point brought home in no small measure by the ancient cannons standing guard outside.

Next door to the palace is an equally memorable church founded by Alfonso VII and apparently consecrated on 21 August 1157. This information appears below a very small and incredibly white statue of the king which stands on its pedestal outside, so out of proportion with its surroundings that it looks as if it was left behind by mistake when the owners were moving house. The church itself is fairly bare but with plenty of light and has a much-decorated altar on which stands a statue of the Virgin, extravagantly dressed in white and gold, wearing a crown and surrounded by gilt and marble. There is no sign of a Child or a crucifix and the only cross of any size hangs,

*Interior of the church at El Viso del Marqués*

a trifle incongruously, behind the main door. Beyond it is an elaborate casket, occupying a niche in the wall, which holds all that is left
of the marqués, while high above the nave on the opposite side is a
decidedly moth-eaten crocodile that is said to have been shot in

Africa four hundred years ago. The caretaker is also the resident organist and, without any warning, he will launch into some intricate variations on *God Save the Queen* for the benefit of British visitors.

Not far away, and equally well worth seeing, is the hamlet of Las Virtudes which claims that its modest bullring is the oldest in Spain. Admittedly it looks like it, being square instead of round with elderly seats and woodwork that would appear to give disturbingly flimsy protection to all the participants in the face of an irate bull. The arcade along one side shares the heavy stone wall belonging to the fourteenth-century sanctuary of Our Lady of Holy Virtue with its interesting ceiling and altar piece. The turning to **Las Virtudes**, another of those easy-to-miss examples if one is driving fairly fast, is off the main Madrid highway beside the Pensione El Puente. The hamlet, at the end of its own private road, has charmingly put up two signs on the outskirts, one of which says 'Welcome' when you arrive and, on the reverse side, thanks you for your visit as you drive away. Mind you, this enterprising little community does not have things all its own way. **Santa Cruz de Mudela**, slightly further along the main road, not only insists that its rectangular bullring is the oldest in the country, but also sites it alongside a fourteenth-century shrine whose decorations were added a good three hundred years later. The town was founded by Spanish crusaders in the year 1200 or thereabouts, pays tribute to the Virgen de Las Virtudes as its patron saint and celebrates in the traditional manner at the end of July, coinciding with the festivities at Viso del Marqués.

Roughly 15km (9 miles) to the north is **Valdepeñas**, which gets just as excited about its grape harvest as it does about Don Quixote. It is a nice open town with an attractive main square, a small medieval church which has been designated a national monument and a large windmill that has been turned into a museum. It houses the works of one Gregorio Prieto who apparently had little time for people and places outside La Mancha. Tourists are invited to inspect the wine vaults, described as cathedrals because of their size, where production is said to exceed 22,500,000l (5,000,000gal) a year. Anyone sampling more than the legal limit would be well advised to stop at a comfortable motel in the vicinity which has a restaurant and a swimming pool which is useful when it comes to cooling down and sobering up. The inhabitants of Valdepeñas believe in doing things in style and celebrate on and off for almost a month starting with bullfights, processions and all the fun of the fair at the beginning of August. They take a short breather during the last week of the month and return to the fray with added vigour for the harvest festivals and poetry competitions in early September.

From Valdepeñas the road to Ciudad Real runs through vineyards where, in the autumn, the tops are lopped off the vines to approximately a foot from the ground and burnt *in situ*, resulting in clouds of pleasantly fragrant smoke. At this time of year it is quite easy to see the small water wheels, festooned with buckets, which operate on a principle similar to the one introduced by the Moors over a thousand years ago. Then it is back amongst the olives again, planted in soil which is anything from deep red to rust with craggy grey hills for a backdrop. Occasionally a shepherd, assisted by dogs, can be seen leading or driving his flock across the mildly undulating countryside in the vicinity of a small pond. Further on a group of children may come rushing out of an isolated schoolhouse to work off their surplus energy on a well-maintained tennis court or football pitch nearby.

**Ciudad Real**, in spite of being the capital of the province, is a town which once seen can easily be forgotten. Its overall atmosphere is not aggressively Spanish although the traffic dashes about in the usual do-or-die manner and motor cyclists are a positive menace. The buildings vary from comparatively modern six-storey affairs to semi-derelict sites which are obviously being prepared for reconstruction, while one or two half-completed examples promise to be almost futuristic. There are some quite nice shops, a few not very remarkable hotels and taverns and a handful of restaurants that fall into the same category. The town was founded by Alfonso X in 1255 and achieved its royal status approximately two hundred years later. However, it is singularly lacking in places of historic interest, about the only things to see being an old Moorish gateway that was once part of the fourteenth-century walls and two rather bare churches with statues scattered about. Having once landed up in the centre it is quite a business finding the road out again because there are very few signs and all the streets look exactly the same. However it does possess a bullring which, like the rest of the town, explodes into life on 15 August when there are carriage competitions, floral games and various other activities in honour of the Virgen del Prado who has taken the inhabitants under her wing.

Nothing could provide a greater contrast than **Almagro**, which lost its position as capital of the province to Ciudad Real well over a hundred years ago. It is an enchanting town with a main square that is as unusual as it is colourful. In the first place it is a great deal longer than it is wide with ornamental paving in the middle, gardens at each end and a road down either side bordering on unbroken colonnades.

Behind the pillars are all sorts of little shops and cafés that spill out over the pavements, above which uniform two-storey houses form continuous lines, painted green with bands of white masonry and spotless curtains draped across small, identical window panes. Midway down the south side is the Corral des Comedias, reputed to be the oldest theatre of its kind in existence anywhere. It is a fascinating place consisting of an open courtyard with two tiers of covered balconies on three sides for the audience, oil lamps, heavy wooden doors, a pit and a little stage. It has been extremely well preserved and classical plays are performed there during the San Bartolomé Festival at the end of August and for 2 weeks in late September. It is also open to visitors each morning and afternoon throughout the year but in the off-season may need a little prodding from the town hall at the end of the square.

Almagro was once the stronghold of the Knights of Calatrava and their former monastery with its original cloister is another of the main sights in the town. Others include a quantity of elderly houses and some more imposing mansions which turn a blind eye, but very decorative doorways, to the narrow, cobbled alleys outside. The town has a bullring with a good reputation and a delightful *parador* installed in the fifteenth-century convent of Santa Catalina. Small church enthusiasts will find plenty to occupy them while the ancient university, founded in the sixteenth century, is only a block or two from the main square. Anyone who decides to spend a few days in the town can swim, enjoy traditional dishes, catch a bus or hire a taxi, buy handmade lace and baskets, study folklore or join an excursion to places of interest in the surrounding area. These include Calatrava la Nueva with its ruins of a monastery which was once the headquarters of the local knights and the Campo del Calatrava where they battled long and hard against the Moors.

A good secondary road leads north to Daimiel, known chiefly as a wine centre and for the national park nearby. The area has more than its fair share of marshland with large expanses of water covered with little islands that seem to float on the surface like so many giant water lily leaves. Understandably it is full of birds, some of them local residents while others are just passing through. Shooting is allowed there under licence from approximately the middle of September to the beginning of March and all the necessary details are available from the authorities in Ciudad Real. Permits are also required by fishermen and will not usually be issued more than three days in advance. The National Institute for the Conservation of Nature, ICONA for short, is in overall charge and has provincial

*The New Bridge, Ronda, Málaga*

*A typical modern suburb, Málaga*

*The harbour at Puerto Banús, Málaga*

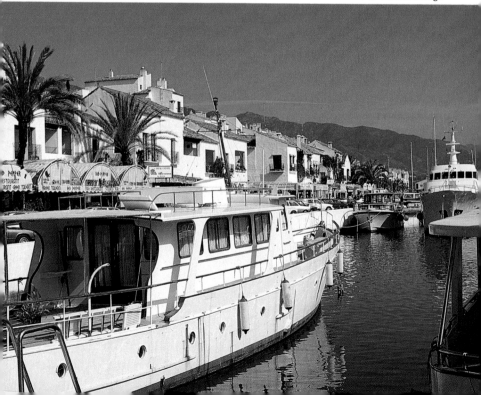

*The inn of Don Quixote, Puerto Lápice*

headquarters in nearly all the big towns in Spain but the local information offices can usually supply the initial details and tell visitors where to write or what number to telephone.

Anyone who is interested in neither fish nor fowl would probably head for the main road at Manzanares where the *parador* lays on hot and cold buffets for breakfast as well as lunch and dinner, charges a set price and invites you to eat as much or as little as you feel inclined. Visitors who prefer to be waited on, or who shudder at the idea of dashing up and down trying to put a name to the dishes on display, would doubtless do better at another comfortable hotel a short distance away which also has the advantage of a garden and a swimming pool.

There is not much of interest at Tomelloso, to the east, if one discounts the stories about a wine cellar built over an enormous vat, so you can save time and fuel by following the main road to **Puerto Lápice**. The only reason for stopping off in this quite ordinary little village would be to inspect the inn of Don Quixote which, quite frankly, sets itself out to attract tourists with a liberal coating of blue and white paint and a shop bursting at the seams with appropriate souvenirs. It has an attractive courtyard, a statue of its namesake without his horse for once, various bits and pieces of armour propped up beside something that looks like an old well and a restaurant with red and white table cloths and outdated farm implements hanging from every nail. Anyone planning to spend the night will find a bed and bath at a small hotel on the outskirts of the village. Local residents maintain that Cervantes was a frequent visitor to Puerto Lápice, was no stranger to the inn and used it as a pattern for the one where Don Quixote was dubbed by the innkeeper of the day, but whether this belief has any basis in fact is anybody's guess.

**Alcázar de San Juan** has much more tangible evidence of an historic past. Some Roman mosaics have been discovered near the castle keep, which itself knew both the Moors and the Knights of St John, and can be explored by simply calling in at the town hall. It is an attractive small town that bustles about, especially on Saturday mornings when every man, woman and child appears to have something important to do and is at least half an hour late. In spite of this everyone, including the police standing in pairs at the street corners, finds time to be both helpful and courteous and has an understanding smile for visitors who stop to admire the life-like statues of Don Quixote and Sancho Panza, both mounted and surrounded by greenery, in the main square. The town's most important festival is called 'The Song of Spring' and is reputed to attract more sightseers than many others twice its size. Accommodation for this event causes a certain amount of problems because there are few hotels and restaurants, none of them in the top-flight bracket.

**Campo de Criptana**, a short drive away, was apparently described by Walter Starkie as the most charming town in all La Mancha, although not everyone would agree. The distant view from the road linking it with Alcázar de San Juan is decidedly encouraging — a cluster of white houses and, above and behind them, a line of windmills, their sails wide open to the sky and any winds that happen to be passing. There are some nice little streets with predictably introspective houses, which have iron grilles protecting every lower window, and most unfriendly holes among the cobblestones.

The unusual red cross on the town's coat-of-arms is the only evidence you will find that it once belonged to the Order of Santiago and even the most determined search will not turn up anything except a small church and a library named after Alonso Quijano. The windmills, in both fact and publicity value, overshadow everything else. Pictorial signs point the way up fairly steep inclines and round corners towards the flat windswept hilltop where you are suddenly surrounded by these tall white towers with their pointed roofs. All round the top are disproportionately small square openings, for all the world like empty eyes keeping a look-out for a present day Don Quixote. Long poles standing at an angle from the roof to the ground add to the fantasy of inanimate giants ready and willing to do battle. Some of the windmills will accept visitors, inviting their paying guests in to a ground floor room filled with appropriately rustic furniture, followed by an inspection of the machinery and a long climb up to the attic. The view across the plains to the mountains may well be outstanding but, everything considered, it is only marginally better than the one you get with far less effort by keeping both feet firmly on the ground.

There is not a great deal to see along the road from Campo de Criptana to Albacete apart from **La Roda** which is visible from a long way off across the plains. It has a castle and a high tower attached to the large church of El Salvador, some quite attractive little streets and houses and the Antonio Martinez Museum. There are a couple of modest inns where you can find a bed and a bath for the night, though Albacete, as the capital of the province, is naturally much better equipped, with one first-class hotel and another comfortable one (although neither has its own restaurant) and a handful of smaller places a few blocks from each other and all within easy reach of the main square. Roughly 5km (3 miles) away is a *parador* that has everything on the premises including tennis and swimming at a very competitive price.

**Albacete** is a prosperous looking place with high-rise buildings, wide, straight streets and a cathedral that was set on fire during the fighting in 1936. The siege in July of that year left a lot of scars behind but they have nearly all healed now and the town prefers to forget the Civil War as far as possible and the fact that it was closely connected with the International Brigades. It is an industrial centre fully involved with artichokes, saffron and steel, turning the latter into a variety of useful articles which are exported and show a handsome profit for the manufacturers. Amongst Albacete's somewhat meagre attractions is the Archaeological Museum, generally thought to be one of the most important in Spain. It stands in a large park, is open every morning and afternoon except on Mondays and has an extensive collection of antiques including tiny amber and ivory dolls left behind at Ontur by the Romans. The quite ordinary bullring on the other side of the town has a full programme of events during the fair, held in the first half of September. It is an occasion when religion and business interests both get an equal crack of the whip — the former being concentrated on the festivities in honour of the Virgen de los Llanos while commerce puts on a show at the National Cutlery Exposition which is attended by buyers from all over the country.

With a few days to spare, and a feeling that you would like to get to know the area a little better, there are a number of places still waiting to be seen. The nearest to Albacete itself is **Chinchilla de Monte Aragón** which climbs up an incline below the castle walls and has mansions left over from the days when it was a stronghold of considerable wealth and importance. In fact, it was the provincial capital for a time in the nineteenth century but lost its title to Albacete, since when it has settled back to rest comfortably and peacefully on its laurels. **Munera**, away to the west, is known chiefly for its weaving but also has an attractive little church and a windmill that has been extensively restored by the author García Solana. **El Bonillo**, practically next door, is a place which mixes fact and fantasy in almost equal proportions. The tourist with a no-nonsense attitude to local attractions will appreciate the main square, the town's old weaving looms and some pictures, one by El Greco, in the small museum. Others in search of a legend or two are more likely to gravitate towards the figure of Christ which, it is said, ran with perspiration to enable impoverished workmen to knead the dough for their bread. Believers maintain that it was a sign of the help available from on high for anyone striving to make a living by the sweat of their brow, particularly when everything dries up and the temperatures soar to near boiling point.

In modern times the population of southern La Mancha relies less on miracles than on machinery to make ends meet and when they want to cool off many of them just get out the car and head for the lakes and lagoons of **Ruidera**. There are about twelve in all, surrounded by trees and shrubs with a number of little waterfalls, several streams and plenty of opportunities for shooting and fishing in and around the national park. Lake Colgada is being developed into a holiday resort where one can swim, waterski, windsurf or take out a boat while other less energetic members of the party ask for nothing better than a cold drink and somewhere to sit in the shade. Opportunities to explore are provided by the ruins of an old castle, the Cave of Montesinos which claims a close association with Don Quixote and the town of **Alcáraz** whose main square has been declared a national monument. It boasts a collection of old buildings including a sixteenth-century town hall and the church of the Holy Trinity, built a hundred years earlier, up-dated at intervals and now the possessor of a small museum of sacred art. The little alleys run hither and thither, most of the steeper ones being more like staircases which come in useful for visitors puffing their way to the top. The sanctuary of the Virgen de Cortes is famous for the number of pilgrims who arrive week after week to pay their respects and ask for help in dealing with their problems. The numbers increase considerably in early September, particularly on the 8th which is the date of the traditional procession to the shrine. Some stay on in the area for other religious events, sporting fixtures and bullfights which go to make up Munera's annual festival at the end of the month.

Once back in the town of Albacete it would be a pity to miss **Alcalá del Júcar**, one of the most fascinating little hamlets that you are likely to come across anywhere. It is literally built into the face of a cliff with a castle tower on one side and a church on the other. No cars are allowed inside even if they could get there. Instead visitors have to do their sightseeing on foot up steep alleys between houses carved out of the rock with a through-draught finding its way into long passages from a balcony at the other end. One of the houses, the Masagó, holds an open day on Sundays and public holidays but is not at home to visitors on winter afternoons.

The most scenic approach to Alcalá del Júcar is by means of a minor road that twists and turns along beside the river past half a dozen or more little villages which are marginally pleasant to look at but have absolutely nothing in the way of tourist attractions. Another not so obviously minor route almost, but not quite, connects it with **Almansa** on the main Albacete-Valencia road. This was once a Moorish town and huddles in the time-honoured fashion round a limestone hill capped by a medieval castle whose ramparts appear to grow up out of the rock. It was the scene of a battle in the early eighteenth century when the Duke of Berwick defeated the British forces in one of many similar confrontations during the Spanish War of Succession. The Duke was an illegitimate son of James II who took a dim view of both his father and his fellow countrymen, became a Marshal of France and worked off his resentment by attacking British troops whenever he could find them. Almansa has a mildly interesting church and a medieval mansion as well as some prehistoric caves not far away. They have suffered from the effects of time and exposure but it is possible to see the figures of hunters armed with bows and arrows, deer attempting to avoid them and sundry other characters dressed in long robes and taking very little interest in the proceedings. Orders to view are obtainable from the town hall in Alpera provided you call there in the morning.

At this point on the journey one is faced with the all-too-frequent problem of where to go next. The main options are, of course, the major roads that run north-east to Valencia, south-east to Alicante or back to Albacete where the choice is even more varied. For southbound holidaymakers anxious to avoid highways whenever possible a secondary road crosses somewhat sparsely populated country to Hellin. There is really no good reason for going there apart from the fact that it is probably the quickest and easiest way of getting to Murcia.

# Further Information

## — Ciudad Real and Albacete —

### Places of Interest

**Albacete**
Museum
Open: 10am-2pm and 5-7pm (4-6pm in winter). Closed Sunday and holiday afternoons, and Mondays.

**Alcalá del Júcar**
One house open: 9am-2pm and 4-9pm on Sundays and holidays in summer. Otherwise closed and also on winter afternoons.

**Alcázar de San Juan**
Castle tower and mosaics
Open: apply to the town hall.

**Almagro**
Corral de Comedias
Open: 9am-2pm and 4-9pm.

**Almansa**
La Vieja Cave
Apply in the morning to the Alpera town hall.

**Campo de Criptana**
Windmills
If one is open ask to look inside.

**Valdepeñas**
Windmill with museum
Open: enquire at town hall.

Wine vault
Open: during working hours.

**Viso del Marqués**
Palace with naval museum
Open: mornings and afternoons.

### Tourist Information Offices

**Albacete**
Av Rodrigues Acosta 3
☎ 22 33 80

**Almagro**
Carniceria 11
☎ 86 07 17

**Ciudad Real**
Av Alarcos 31
☎ 21 29 25

# 13 • Cádiz

Cádiz is the most southerly of all the Andalusian provinces and therefore of Spain itself with a coastline bordering on both the Atlantic and the Mediterranean. It consists of three quite different types of country — a mountainous region in the north-east which it shares with Málaga, an agricultural belt which is fairly industrial at the eastern end but gives way gradually to grazing lands and vineyards in the west, and a mixture of sand dunes, salt flats and golden beaches by the sea. In due course the shoreline will probably become one long, built-up holiday playground but so far it is only punctuated here and there with quite small resorts. The province has less than a dozen cities and towns of any consequence, most of them either on the sea or within easy reach of it, but a great many smaller places scattered about along the coast and up into the mountains. Temperatures do not fluctuate very much and official figures indicate that the area only has 30 days of rain a year. However, the confirmed cynic will usually insist that they all bunch together for the express purpose of ruining his or her holiday.

Although it is somewhat out on its own the province has three main highways. One runs due north to Seville, more or less parallel with the *autopista*, the second heads east from Jerez de la Frontera through the northern section of the region to join up with Granada while the third hugs the coast, bypasses Gibraltar and finds itself in Málaga. Secondary roads radiate out from Medina Sidonia across grazing lands populated by the famous black fighting bulls, in addition to which there are some scenic routes that wriggle their way through hilly country past forests of oak, pines and Spanish firs with clumps of walnut trees, quince and cherry orchards, oranges, wild olives and prickly pears. Minor roads are comparatively scarce and those that do exist are often better ignored, especially as they seldom end up anywhere in particular. There is absolutely no way of driving from Huelva to Cádiz without popping in and out of Seville because there are no roads across the Doñana National Park and its attendant marshlands at the mouth of the Guadalquivir.

The airport at Jerez has regular flights to Madrid, Barcelona and Valencia as well as Mallorca and Tenerife; trains connect Cádiz with Seville and buses run to places of interest like Arcos de la Frontera and Ronda, across the border in Málaga. In addition to all this, ferries operate out of Cádiz to Genoa, in northern Italy, Mallorca and the Canary Islands as well as calling at selected Spanish ports, while Algeciras offers a choice of ferries to North Africa, trains to Madrid and buses along the Costa del Sol.

Finding an hotel is fairly simple as they come in all shapes and sizes although few of them are actually luxurious. First class establishments with all the trimmings can be tracked down in Algeciras, Sotogrande and Jerez de la Frontera as well as in the capital, with a splendidly situated *parador* in Arcos de la Frontera. Most towns of any interest, including the newer coastal resorts, have at least one reasonable hotel apiece, a choice of smaller ones and sometimes a camp site nearby. The restaurants are entirely predictable and it is as well not to expect too much of little out-of-the-way places where the best bet is to stick to fish along the coast and meat up in the mountains. No matter how limited the menu, it is always possible to start off with a glass of wine from Jerez, known to all the rest of the world as sherry.

Quite naturally Jerez's wine festival in September is an extremely exuberant and colourful affair but it is by no means the only event worth mentioning in Cádiz. The year gets off to a good start with a carnival in February, said to be amongst the best in the country, followed by all the elaborate celebrations marking Holy Week. May is the month for spring fairs with traditional singing and dancing, bullfights, plenty of horses and general merrymaking in towns and villages throughout the province. June, July and August all have their special fêtes and fiestas, September pays homage to the grapes and Jerez rounds off the whole programme very neatly with a flamenco competition in December. When it comes to collecting souvenirs the best buys are usually to be found in the villages where they originate. For example, amongst the places known for their particular crafts are Grazalema which specialises in capes and ponchos, Ubrique concentrates on leather, Arcos de la Frontera is more interested in carpets, Olvera is the place to find saddles and Chiclana breaks new ground with all kinds of dolls.

Cádiz, along with the rest of Andalusia, has had a turbulent existence stretching back into the mists of time. Ignoring prehistory for the moment, the capital maintains that it is the oldest city in Europe with documents to prove that it has kept going without a

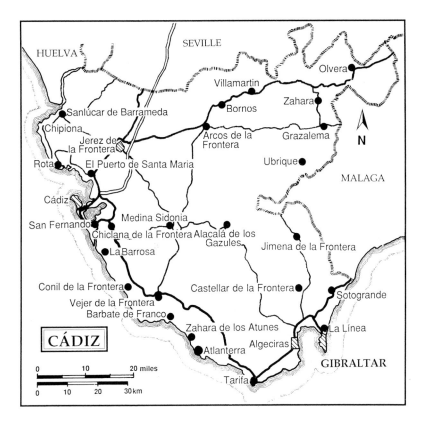

HUELVA
SEVILLE
Olvera
Villamartin
Zahara
Sanlúcar de Barrameda
Bornos
Chipiona
Jerez de la Frontera
Arcos de la Frontera
Grazalema
N
Rota
El Puerto de Santa Maria
Ubrique
MALAGA
Cádiz
San Fernando
Medina Sidonia
Chiclana de la Frontera
Alacalá de los Gazules
Jimena de la Frontera
La Barrosa
Conil de la Frontera
Castellar de la Frontera
Sotogrande
Vejer de la Frontera
Barbate de Franco
Zahara de los Atunes
La Línea
Algeciras
CÁDIZ
Atlanterra
GIBRALTAR
0   10   20 miles
0   10   20   30 km
Tarifa

break, although with constant rebuilding and up-dating, for at least 3,000 years.

According to legend and also, incidentally, to the city's coat-of-arms, the first primitive settlement was established after Hercules pushed Africa and Europe apart, creating the Straits of Gibraltar and a sea lane through to the Atlantic Ocean. The Phoenicians arrived in search of tin and copper, found the arrangements very much to their liking and, on the advice of an oracle, built their own city in 1100BC, calling it after Gadir, the son of Neptune. The Carthaginians muscled in later, Hannibal set up home there, Julius Caesar looked in for a while and the Visigoths, who took over from the Romans, were defeated by the Moors near Barbate in the early eighth century. Alfonso the Wise recovered much of the area in plenty of time for it to play a part in the discovery of America, Francis Drake singed the King of Spain's beard at Cádiz and Nelson won his last and greatest battle off Cape Trafalgar. Things began to settle down after that and today the capital is an active port and a delightful city which deserves a much higher spot in the pecking order of well known and popular centres in southern Spain.

Because of the lie of the land and the way the towns and villages are distributed it is difficult, if not downright impossible, to plan an itinerary that will include all the places of note, linked by a single route. A more satisfactory plan is to divide the province up into areas and then explore any or all of them in turn. For beach-orientated visitors travelling east from Huelva via Seville, and then turning south towards the coast, the first place to be encountered is **Sanlúcar de Barrameda**. It is an historic town which saw Columbus off on his third trip to America and Magellan on his much longer voyage round the world, and now occupies itself fishing and making a particularly delectable sherry called *manzanilla*. The large cellars, some of which are open to visitors, are concentrated in the old quarter, which has the ancient castle of San Marcos as its focal point. Other buildings worthy of note include the palace of the Dukes of Medina Sidonia which houses the family archives, the sixteenth-century church of Nuestra Señora de la O with its beautifully decorated doorway and the elderly stone convent of Santo Domingo. However it is the beach which draws the largest crowds, with its golden sand, all the usual water sports and the added attraction of horse racing in August along the water's edge. The river plays a major part in the life of the community, which explains why the townspeople hold a special Festival of the Exaltation of the Guadalquivir every summer.

Next comes **Jerez de la Frontera**, known the world over as the home of sherry, although it makes quite a feature of its brandy as well. The town began life as *Ceret* under the Romans, the Arabs renamed it *Scherish*, which accounts for the word 'sherry', after which it progressed to *Xérès* and finally settled for Jerez. Most people make straight for one of the famous *bodegas* where arrangements are made to show them round any weekday morning except during August. It is fascinating to see the process in action, tour the various rooms and cellars and inspect the casks set aside for famous visitors, each one bearing its owner's signature. Anyone planning to spend the night in Jerez is bound to find a suitable hotel, be it first class accommodation or something fairly modest.

Most of the historic attractions are conveniently grouped together near the *alcázar*, now less of a Moorish fortress than an ancient wall surrounded by gardens with the remains of some fifteenth-century baths. The impressive collegiate church of Santa Maria with its free-standing tower, where the grape harvest is proclaimed every year, is only about a block away. Equally worth seeing is the old town hall

*Display of old bottles of sherry, Jerez*

facing an attractive little square and containing a small archaeological museum. There is a clock museum in the Palacio de la Atalaya, another devoted to all things flamenco in the Calle Quintos and, somewhat further afield, the comprehensive Museum of the Horse and the Wine. Its home is in the nineteenth-century Recreo de las Cadenas Palace which is also the headquarters of the famous Andalusian School of Equestrian Art with some of the most superb horses to be seen anywhere. Displays are staged there at various times and, if possible, should definitely not be missed. Another outstanding attraction is the fifteenth-century monastery of Cartuja de la Defensión, slightly to the south of the town. It once provided stables for breeding the Carthusian horses which kept the name even after they moved to new quarters. The monastery is memorable chiefly for its magnificent façade and the dignified cloister with a fountain in the middle and contrasting pillars supporting the arcades all round.

Horses and wine are of equal importance in Jerez and the May Horse Fair along with the Harvest Festival in September, are two of the most outstanding celebrations in the town's colourful and varied

*The main square, Jerez*

calendar. Where spectator sports are concerned the most popular events include polo and football matches, bullfights, motor racing and riding displays or one can simply wander round the Tempul Park and spend some time at the zoo.

Motorists leaving Jerez can easily become a trifle schizophrenic, torn between the Route of the White Towns leading eastwards to Arcos de la Frontera and the main road south to the capital. Assuming that the coast wins by a short head, at any rate for the time being, the run to **El Puerto de Santa Maria** is quick, easy and not particularly attractive. It is a busy port much involved with the sherry trade, has wine cellars of its own and boasts a reasonable share of holiday attractions. Places of historic interest in the town range from the much restored thirteenth-century castle of San Marcos and the slightly older monastery of Nuestra Señora de la Victoria, through a handful of small churches to the stately homes built with fortunes amassed by families who owned vineyards in the area. In addition to its large, white and Moorish-looking casino, the only one so far in western Andalusia, El Puerto has a nine-hole golf course, a sailing club, the occasional hotel and some very pleasant beaches strung out along the bay. **Rota**, on the northern tip of the Bay of Cádiz facing the capital, possesses a number of typical seaside hotels and taverns, beaches fringed with pine trees and all the entertainments one would expect to find so close to an American naval base.

From this point onwards the road south could hardly be described as inviting, especially after it crosses the *autopista* near Puerto Real, providing an alternative but equally dreary approach to the city of **Cádiz** across salt flats and industrial sites of no interest whatsoever. Eventually the two meet up again, cutting through modern suburbs to the Puerta de Tierra which marks the entrance to the old city. It would be quite impossible to miss this one-time obstruction with its massive stone walls, sturdy tower supporting little look-out posts that resemble nothing so much as pepper pots and fronted by a fountain and a couple of decorative columns. Behind it lies a spider's web of tall, narrow streets which all know exactly where they are going and head straight for their destinations, pausing briefly at an odd square on the way. The most demanding structure in the immediate vicinity is the eighteenth-century cathedral with its domes and towers dwarfing the low buildings that separate it from the sea. There is nothing very remarkable about the interior, although anyone with a soft spot for things like silver tabernacles would probably appreciate the collection of treasures, the most valuable of which is the 'Custodia del Millón', so called, they say, because it is encrusted with a million jewels. Music lovers might well prefer to pay their respects to Manuel de Falla who is buried in the crypt. Just around the corner is the old cathedral known these days as the church of Santa Cruz.

It really does not matter which way you go from here because

*Entrance to the old city of Cádiz*

there is something to be seen in almost every direction. On the far side of the atmospheric Plaza Topete is the Municipal Museum with a very splendid wood and ivory model of the city as it was in 1779. As nothing has changed appreciably in the last 200 years it is possible to admire the detailed workmanship and get one's bearings at the same time. A near neighbour is the somewhat unusual church of San Felipe Neri where the people of the city tried to establish home rule during the Peninsular War. If it is closed, and it often is between services, the key is available from the house on the right. Somewhat further away collectors of small churches will find the Oratorio de Santo Cueva which inspired Haydn to compose his *Oratory of the Seven Words of the Holy Grotto of Cádiz* and which is justifiably proud of its Goyas.

Overlooking the delightful Plaza de Mina there are two museums for the price of one, namely the Archaeological Museum and the Museum of Fine Arts, which overlap a bit when it comes to exhibits and have plenty to occupy the visitor. The Phoenicians are well represented with such things as jewellery and sculptures and especially by a sarcophagus from the fifth century BC, discovered in 1980. Foremost amongst the pictures are paintings by Rubens, Murillo and other such masters as well as a fine collection of the works of Zurbarán. To round off the visit on a less usual note there is a selection of traditional and engaging marionettes and the scenery involved in their performances.

A block or two further on, in the direction of the port, is the Plaza de España, the centre of it almost completely taken up with a large monument covered in statues and reliefs which commemorates the Parliament of Cádiz. Alternatively, it is no distance at all down the Calle Zorrita to the Alameda de Apodaca, frequently described as a balcony, with its stone balustrade and ornate lamp standards overlooking the bay and facing into the sunset. Further round the perimeter the Parque Genovés, full of palms and cypress trees, makes an ideal setting for the José Maria Pemán theatre which stages open-air performances during the season. After this it is no great distance to the sheltered and frequently crowded beach at La Caleta with alternative places to swim at La Victoria and Cortadura. Cádiz caters for all tastes with enchanting old quarters like the flower-filled Barrio de la Viña, El Populo and Santa Maria; you can take your pick of pavement cafés in the Plaza de San Juan de Dios, find whatever you are looking for in shops that range from the sophisticated to the small and curious and tie up your boat in the yacht harbour. Hotels of all kinds are quite easy to come by. However it would be as well to book

*Parque Genovés, Cádiz*

for a visit that coincides with the February Carnival, the Holy Week celebrations or any of the main attractions at the height of the season.

Just as there are only two ways into the city of Cádiz, so there are only two ways out, but only one across the salt flats for anybody carrying on round the coast through **San Fernando**. It may not be the most attractive place along the route but it was an important sea port in its time, watched over by the castle of San Romualdo, built by Alfonso the Wise to discourage pirates and other potential enemies. It has a Pantheon of Illustrious Mariners, a Carmelite convent and the Teatro de las Cortes where the short-lived Free Spanish Parliament met in 1810 and 1813. The next place to stop might well be the wine town of **Chiclana de la Frontera**, full of elderly houses with a couple of small churches and the spa of Fuente Amarga quite close by. Almost within nodding distance is the Sancti-Petri lighthouse which, according to legend, was built on the mythological ruins of the Temple of Hercules but more realistically has a thirteenth-century castle and a small beach. However **La Barrosa**, further down the coast, is a better bet for anyone planning a day beside the sea.

From this point onwards you cannot fault the beaches, but then nor can you find a coast road or anything much in the way of resorts, so it is back to the highway with the option of a turn-off to **Conil de la Frontera** after 30km (19 miles) or so. This is a fishing village on the river Salado with a ruined castle, superb golden sands and a camp site but not anything to get excited about when it comes to restaurants and hotels. A minor road manages to locate Cape Trafalgar but finds little there except a lighthouse and the view, and so moves gently on to **Barbate de Franco**. This typical fishing village is a good deal busier than most because it has its own canning industry, auctions off the catch at its local fish market with the maximum amount of fuss and, in August, holds a Sardine Fair on the beach.

**Vejer de la Frontera**, slightly inland, is a most enchanting Moorish town, complete with the remains of an Arab castle and a particular attraction for storks. Anyone climbing up the narrow winding streets to inspect either the thirteenth-century church or the view might possibly meet a woman wearing a long dark cloak that covers her from head to foot. Until quite recently the *cobija*, as it is called, was an essential part of any female wardrobe but these days the younger members of the community infinitely prefer T-shirts and jeans. Although Vejer celebrates at regular intervals just like everywhere else, it also holds a Cut-Horn Bull Fair in April. The proceedings include the running of bulls through the streets, when the less agile inhabitants watch from doors and windows or from a respectable distance to the rear.

The well maintained highway through pleasant, undulating country is amply supplied at intervals with small hotels, restaurants and camp sites on its way to Tarifa, the most southerly point on the mainland of Europe. The visiting motorist in search of solitude combined with comfort will find it at **Atlanterra** which consists simply of a brace of hotels, some up-market villas and a superb beach at the end of a small road through **Zahara de los Atunes**. Zahara itself is mainly interested in tunny fishing and does not even have a connecting link with some quite recently discovered Roman ruins of *Baelo Claudia*. They include the remains of a theatre and a burial ground, have a short road to themselves and are close to another secluded beach.

**Tarifa**, less than 14km (9 miles) across the Straits of Gibraltar from the mountainous coast of Morocco, is an old town with cobbled streets, the remains of some ramparts and an ancient gateway. Its well preserved Arab castle was overrun by the Christians in 1292, only to be besieged by the Moors a short time afterwards. They captured the son of the fortress commander, one Alonso de Guzmán, threatening to kill him unless the garrison surrendered. Guzmán's reply was to throw down his dagger 'in case you need a knife for the murder', with the result that he lost his son but kept the castle. There are guided tours every Friday and Saturday morning that include

*Pottery and craft shops at Purullena, Granada*

*A view of Sorbas, Almería*

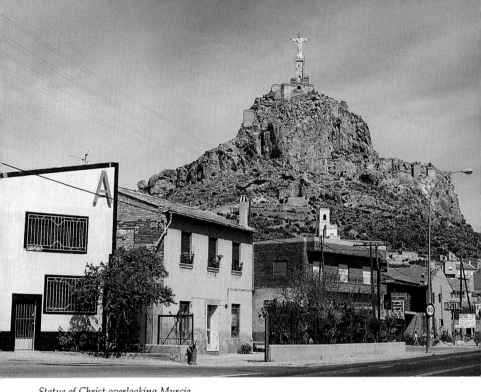

*Statue of Christ overlooking Murcia*

*Wickerwork shops, Gata, Alicanté*

the tower which was the scene of this barbaric encounter. Amongst the town's other attractions are a brace of small churches, a windsurfing club, a choice of camp sites and a handful of modest hotels, at least two of them with tennis courts and swimming pools.

Although there are some little roads amongst the sand dunes to the east they are not open to the public so the only approach to Algeciras is along the highway, a pleasant enough route but not a particularly memorable one. **Algeciras** is, first and foremost, an extremely active port and few people bother to call in unless they are catching a ferry to either Cueta or Tangier. It has one or two small gardens and some good restaurants and hotels but nothing else to attract the traveller or the tourist who can get a fairly accurate impression by simply driving through.

The highway carries on round the bay and anyone with a passport to hand can turn sharp right at San Roque for a visit to **Gibraltar**. Although geographically part of Spain, the Rock is British in every other respect and has been so officially since the Treaty of Utrecht in 1713. It manages to squeeze a busy airport, where traffic is held up beside the runway for planes landing and taking off, a dock area, a network of tunnels, a Moorish castle and a museum, a cave of stalactites, several hotels and restaurants as well as shops and offices into a remarkably small space. There is still room left over for a couple of spectacular drives, one at sea level that utilizes a long tunnel through the rock and another which winds its way up to the top with an occasional place to pull off to admire the breathtaking views or meet the famous Barbary apes.

**La Línea**, an unexceptional town with a museum full of paintings which draw their inspiration from the African continent, faces Gibraltar across the border, but has little else to attract the visitor. On the other hand there are some quite good reasons, most of them energetic ones, for calling in at **Sotogrande**, just short of the border with Málaga. It has two golf courses, plays polo, is interested in riding and water sports and provides its guests with a comfortable hotel in which to relax, play tennis and swim in the heated pool.

Having exhausted all the possibilities along the coast it is time to turn one's attention to the mountains, which means a certain amount of 'to-ing and fro-ing' no matter which area you choose as a starting point. Anyone who is walking or riding should not have any problems but for drivers the first respectable road back from Sotogrande along the coastal route is slightly west of San Roque and heads due north to Jimena de la Frontera.

Although the country round about is fairly mountainous the

route itself does not do a great deal of climbing, except if you decide to deviate slightly to visit **Castellar de la Frontera**. Serious attempts have been made to turn it into a holiday centre, which has not exactly improved the old quarter. Nevertheless there are some ancient ramparts, a lake and a splendid view to counteract the somewhat unfortunate type of modern atmosphere. **Jimena**, on the other hand, has a good deal more in its favour, including a Moorish castle that was restored in the fifteenth century and has received a certain amount of attention since then, a Franciscan convent built at about the same time and two small churches.

At this point one is faced with a choice of roads, both scenic and both much given to twisting and turning. One crosses the border into Málaga, calling at **Gaucin** with its ruined Eagle's Castle, on the way to Ronda. The other cuts through a nature reserve before splitting itself into three at Puerto de Galiz. The only attraction straight ahead is a large lake, to the right lies **Ubrique** which is famous for its leather work while the left-hand fork pitches up in **Alcalá de los Gazules**, an ordinary sort of village that spreads itself all over the hillside and has roads connecting it with the coastal highway not far from Tarifa and also with Medina Sidonia.

The determined sightseer will find something of interest in nearly all the different villages, even if it is only an historical association, but to the casual observer there is a certain uniformity about them. The streets are invariably narrow, the only colour contrasts depend on how recently the owners have got to work with a paint brush dipped in white and the roofs are a mass of rounded tiles weathered into varying shades of gold and reddish brown. There is no denying that they are attractive but it is possible to have too much of a good thing — just as lovers of the English countryside might get a little tired of thatched cottages lying wall to wall all the way from the Scottish border to Land's End.

**Medina Sidonia** is no exception to the rule although its history is better documented than some of the others. The town was established in the fifteenth century with a freshly created line of dukes whose job it was to defend the whole area against attack and help with the colonisation of America in their spare time. The church of Santa Maria la Coronada dates back to the reconquest of Granada and has the remains of some ancient ramparts to keep it company. The church of Santiago was built a little later and, with the ducal palace, the eighteenth-century town hall and a few old mansions, more or less completes the list of places to be seen. Added to this there are secondary roads linking it with the coast, with Vejer de la Fron-

*The main square and palace, Arcos*

tera, Jerez de la Frontera and the spectacular town of Arcos de la Frontera to the north.

**Arcos** is, without doubt, one of the most fascinating and atmospheric of all the White Towns with its old quarter balanced precariously on the top of a rocky spur surrounded by perpendicular cliffs that separate it from the Guadalete river far below. The approach road climbs up through a comparatively modern suburb, squeezes itself into a small opening between the elderly houses and loses itself in a maze of tiny streets, many of them hardly wide enough for one car, let alone two. Facing on to the Plaza de España with its limited amount of parking space is the sixteenth-century church of Santa Maria de la Asunción, the home of the Virgin of the Snows who is patron saint of the town. The high altar and choir stalls are worth seeing once you get inside, along with several paintings and one or two items that are kept in the sacristy. It is a little disconcerting to discover a family living up in the tower when, at the insistence of the locals, you climb a steep and rather narrow staircase leading from a small door on the square.

On the right looking out from the church is the town hall and, behind it, the extremely well preserved ducal castle, while to the left is the long white Casa del Corregidor, a comfortable *parador* with a paved patio and a superb view across seemingly endless vineyards, orchards and olive groves. A short walk from the Plaza de España,

*Zahara*

where the local museum and the treasury are housed in the Casa
Rectoral, and past a sixteenth-century convent, one can visit an art
gallery, discover yet another convent of slightly later vintage and
inspect the carpet factory to see the looms in action. Roads with
names like the Alley of the Clock Weights and Paradise Street, edged
with anything from an antiquated chapel to a pottery shop, arrive
eventually at the ruins of an old market and beyond it the church of
San Pedro. It completely dominates its own end of the spur and has
a collection of religious art including a sad little child Jesus, dressed
as a shepherd and trying hard not to cry. Arcos is definitely a place
to explore, full of old houses, an occasional small square and a
sprinkling of cafés and restaurants as well as a strategically placed
photographic shop for anyone who runs out of film. It provides a
perfect setting for the Holy Week celebrations that are officially
recognised as some of the most memorable to be held anywhere in
the country.

   For the visitor in a hurry, or for people who feel that any further
White Towns would come as an anti-climax, the highway runs
straight from Arcos, through Bornos on the edge of a substantial lake,
and on to Olvera, the last town of any size before Málaga. However,
there are quite a few places to inspect along the route which runs
through fields of wheat and cotton, past large ranches and tiny
hamlets clinging like lumps of snow to their respective hilltops,

relieved here and there by brilliant patches of bougainvillaea and hibiscus and scented with herbs and oranges.

**Bornos**, which was built by the Arabs, boasts a palace that has definitely seen better days as well as a small church and the Roman ruins of *Carixa*, 5km (3 miles) away. **Villamartin**, on the other hand, only goes back to 1503 and has unusually wide streets for this part of the world, along with the church of Las Virtudes which makes much of its sculptures. At Algodonales, 25km (15$^1/_2$ miles) further on, the road divides, presenting the driver with a choice between **Olvera** with its distinctive silhouette and **Zahara**, dominated by a medieval castle which was a bone of contention between Alfonso the Wise and the Sultan of Morocco. The Moors held on to it until the early fifteenth century, after which it became the property of the Marqués de Cádiz. It is reached by way of a rather nasty little road that bumps about all over the place but is worth negotiating for the sake of the watch tower, the church of Santa Maria de Mesa and the view. Another possible deviation is to **Grazalema**, full of flowers and modest houses and the best place to go for anyone in search of a poncho or a distinctive cape which are the hallmarks of the village. An attractive minor road rejoins the main route just over the border in Málaga with nothing much to offer before it gets to Ronda, an unforgettable place, rivalled only by Arcos for pole position along the famous Route of the White Towns.

# Further Information
## — Cádiz —

### Places of Interest

**Arcos de la Frontera**
Santa Maria church
If closed enquire from sacristan.

Museum and Treasury
Open: Sundays and holidays 1-3pm and 4-6pm, otherwise on request.

Carpet Factory
Open: during working hours.

*Baelo Claudia*
Roman ruins, near Bolonia beach west of Tarifa.

Cádiz
Cathedral and Museum
Open: 10am-1pm and 5-7pm; November to February 4-6pm. Closed Saturday afternoon, Sunday and holidays.

San Felipe Neri Church
Visit during services, also on request.

Museum of Archaeology
Open: 9.30am-1.30pm. Closed Mondays and holidays.

History Museum
Open: June to September 9am-

3pm. Otherwise 9am-1pm and 4-
6pm. Saturday and Sunday 10am-
2pm. Closed Mondays and holidays.

**Jerez de la Frontera**
Bodegas
Open: weekday mornings except
in August. Enquire at reception
offices.

Archaeology Museum
Clocks Museum
Flamenco Museum
Horse and Wine Museum

Open: most mornings and afternoons. For specific times enquire
at the town hall.

**Tarifa**
Castle
Guided tours: Friday and Saturday
9.30am-1pm.

## Tourist Information Office

**Cádiz**
Calderón de la Barca
☎ 21 13 13 or 22 48 00

# 14 • Málaga

Málaga is the smallest province in Andalusia, bordered by Cádiz to the west, Seville and a few kilometres of Córdoba to the north and Granada to the east, and while the Costa del Sol may not have all the traditional atmosphere of Spain, there are enough out-of-the-way places to satisfy anyone who is prepared to search for them. Málaga has mountain ranges, forest areas, natural lakes and spectacular views, not a lot in the way of agricultural land but three nature reserves full of deer and mountain goats where hunting is allowed at certain times of the year. Fishing, either from the land, underwater or by boat, is available all along the coast and there are bridle paths and mountain trails for people who want a change from golf, tennis and all the various water sports. Sophisticated marinas, some of them home to extremely luxurious craft, have ample space for visiting yachtsmen while the historically minded can inspect old buildings and wander round the local museums. Shops are many and various with a lot of decidedly run-of-the-mill souvenirs, although anyone anxious to take home a more lasting memento of their holiday would be wise to think in terms of leather, wood, copper, traditional pottery and possibly even musical instruments, not forgetting castanets.

Festivals, carnivals, processions and pilgrimages are held regularly throughout the year beginning with the Cavalcade of the Three Kings in January. Mardi Gras precedes the celebrations marking Holy Week, setting the tone for festivals of every description in both towns and villages during the summer months. Mijas has bull running in the streets, Paloma style, in September, Torrox follows with festivals of both rock and flamenco in early October and December ends with a massive folk singing and dancing competition in the mountains all round. Amongst the many local dishes are *ajoblanco*, a cold soup made from almonds with the addition of peeled grapes, and a salad called *salmorejo* consisting of tuna fish and hard boiled eggs with things like onions and peppers lightly dressed. There are

247

all sorts of fish, fried, grilled in the open air or made into stews as well as veal with garlic and almonds, fried kid, partridge stew and smoked pork sausages. If none of this appeals to you the holiday resorts can provide restaurants of every nationality, all of them busy turning out their own specialities.

The history of the province is very much akin to the rest of Andalusia, beginning with the earliest inhabitants who lived in caves up in the mountains. When the Phoenicians looked in they founded *Malaka* and *Sexi*, the second of which is in Granada and changed its name later to Almuñécar. The Greeks were hot on their heels, followed by such well known owner occupiers as the Romans, the Visigoths and the Moors, each of whom added their own particular characteristics before they were sent packing by somebody else. The Catholic Monarchs, Ferdinand and Isabel, recovered all Spain's lost property, including Málaga, in the fifteenth century but in spite of a fairly intensive building programme the whole area went rapidly to seed, partly due to neglect and partly to plagues, droughts and other such disasters. Commerce and industry flourished in the mid-nineteenth century but were badly hit by revolts and disturbances that culminated in civil war in the 1930s. It was only quite recently, when tourists gave the Costa del Sol their unqualified seal of approval, that prosperity returned to Málaga. With it came luxurious hotels and excellent restaurants, backed up by a vast number of others offering less and charging accordingly, all the way down to basic inns and little pavement cafés. Casinos opened and supermarkets appeared, although where visitors are concerned the latter description can be a trifle misleading. It could apply to a large complex, all marble paving stones, fountains and shops with names as familiar as your own, although more often it turns out to be a barn of a place with masses of shelves and a roof that may leak when it rains or a small room whose owners could not make up their minds whether to opt for groceries or fresh vegetables and so decided to stock a few of each.

Málaga keeps in touch with the rest of the country through an extremely busy airport which divides its attention between internal services and charter flights. It is connected by train with Madrid, Valencia, Barcelona, Seville and Córdoba and has buses that dash about in every direction. They operate in a steady stream between the various coastal resorts, slightly less frequently to inland towns and villages and keep to an undemanding schedule where other provinces like Almería and Alicante are concerned. Motorists will find three major roads into the capital, one of which runs along the

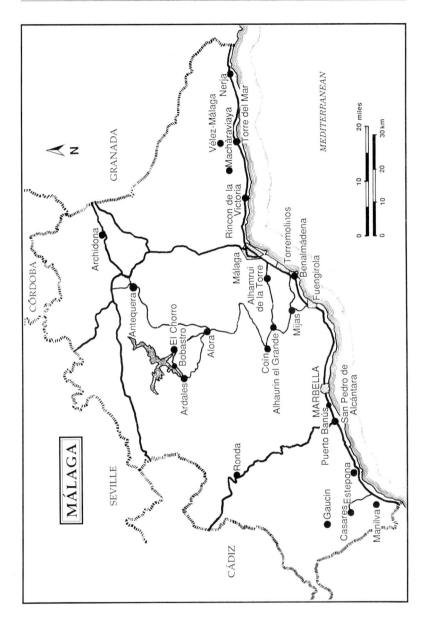

coast, the second recently built and almost parallel to it, while the third is a scenic winding road to the north of the province where it joins the existing highways leading to Seville, Córdoba and Granada.

Another very good but amazingly serpentine route, chiselled out of the mountainsides, climbs resolutely up from the corniche west of

Marbella to Ronda, on its own small plateau, and then carries on until it meets the highway to Cadiz. There are any number of secondary roads, mostly scenic but by no means all in good condition, that wander about and arrive at their destinations without giving drivers too many unhappy moments. The minor roads are less predictable and need to be treated with due care and attention. Even a small turning off the corniche to a new development a few kilometres up the hill may well present the odd difficulty, especially if there are deep holes along the edge just at the point where a bus or an over-loaded lorry appears round the bend. Most local people admit that the majority of their roads are badly in need of repair but provided one allows plenty of time and keeps an eye open for the odd speed merchant there is really nothing the average driver cannot handle quite easily.

Anyone visiting Málaga from the west has three main options open to them, as well as a few less obvious ones. The coast road from Gibraltar is fast and sometimes furious and makes straight for Este-pona, the Cádiz highway sidles along the northern border past An-tequera while the Route of the White Towns leads eventually to **Ronda**, one of the most popular and therefore most tourist-conscious hilltowns in this part of Spain. Its main feature is a narrow gorge with perpendicular walls up to 100m (328ft) high in places dividing the old quarter from a slightly more recent one and spanned at the top by its famous New Bridge. This was built in the eighteenth century, about a hundred years after a less ambitious one was completed a good deal closer to the water and not far from the extremely well preserved Arab baths. High above them, reached by more than 350 steps, is the palace of the Marquess of Salvatierra which is privately owned and sometimes allows small groups inside although, judging by the very ordinary patio, this might well prove to be a disappoint-ment. The House of the Giants, on the other hand, contains some fourteenth-century plasterwork reminiscent of the Alhambra. Some-what surprisingly the House of the Moorish King, which can also be visited on request, takes its name from the tiled portrait of a Moor on the wall outside but is, in fact, only about two hundred years old.

A short walk away, down a series of little cobbled streets, is the collegiate church of Santa Maria la Mayor. It has an arch that was once part of the original mosque, a minaret up-dated in the sixteenth century, some beautifully carved choir stalls and two large altars, one of which is drenched in gold. The sacristan lives in far less palatial quarters on the premises above an arcade. The town hall occupies some elderly barracks facing the same square, directly

*Ronda, the old entrance to the town*

opposite the convent of St Clare.

On the far side of the New Bridge are several places of interest including the Posada de las Animas, an inn where Cervantes is said to have stayed, and the comfortable and well equipped Reina Victoria Hotel which played host to the German poet, Rainer Maria Rillke, and has turned his room into a little museum. However the main attraction is the bull-ring, built in 1785 on the site of an older one, and the birthplace of bullfighting in the classic style. The rules were laid down by Francisco Romero in the seventeenth century, elaborated by his son Juan and perfected in practice by his grandson Pedro, who became one of the great bullfighters of Spain. There is a small but fascinating museum inside, some souvenir shops housed in the walls outside and a modest park nearby.

Driving back through the Plaza de España, across the New Bridge and down to the ancient convent of San Francisco outside the walls, it is worth making a sharp turn to the left. On the far side of an ancient gateway are the Moorish baths and the old bridge which can be inspected without having to negotiate all those steps. Alternatively the road on the right, the Camino de los Molinos, commands a spectacular view up the gorge to the New Bridge before carrying on to the power station.

About 30km (19 miles) from Ronda, surrounded by mountains which were riddled with highwaymen barely a century ago, are the

*Bullring Museum, Ronda*

Pileta Caves. They are reached along a very questionable road and are full of prehistoric drawings, including enormous fish, which are thought to be more than 25,000 years old. They were inhabited at a much later date by Bronze Age families and, apart from bones and weapons found inside, there were pieces of pottery said to be the earliest ever discovered in Europe. The caves should be seen in the company of a guide who lives in a small farmhouse close by. Other ancient attractions in the area include the dolmen of El Chopo at the turning off to Grazalema and the ruins of *Acinipo*, a Roman city which has largely disappeared, although work is going on to preserve the remains of its original theatre.

The highwayman, or *bandolero*, is as romantic a figure in Spain as he is in Britain and appears regularly at the local festivals, often accompanied by traditional songs and dances, colourful processions and firework displays. Each of the White Towns celebrates in its own way, and Ronda uses the bullring for a tribute to Pedro Romero in

September, recreating the scene that would have been familiar to the painter Francisco de Goya nearly two hundred years ago.

Two routes lead south from Ronda and one heads eastwards into the mountains, through somewhat barren countryside where the rare *pinsapos*, or Spanish firs, can be seen growing wild, interspersed with odd corners full of tiny flowers and inhabited by Hispanic goats that share their territory with smaller animals and birds. The best road is undoubtedly the one to San Pedro de Alcántara which is extremely well maintained. However, it makes so many turns around the mountainsides to avoid the deep valleys between, that motorists should allow anything from 45 minutes to an hour for the 49km (30 miles) involved.

The second, more inferior road to the coast heads for **Gaucin**, the scene of several battles between the Christians and the Moors, with its ruined castle, sixteenth-century church and somewhat younger convent. The same route continues across the border to Jimena de la Frontera in Cádiz but stout-hearted visitors can take a calculated chance on a very rustic shortcut to **Casares**. It is an attractive village of jumbled up houses, built one above the other in the shadow of a ruined Arab castle on a site previously occupied by the Romans. In addition there are two unremarkable churches dating from the seventeenth century and just the hint of an Iberian village at Alesipe near the town. The area round about is well blessed with wild life in spite of being only 14km (9 miles) or so from the coast.

Having explored the immediate countryside, which is decidedly lacking in both roads and villages, the motorist has only two options open: return by the same route, or carry on to the coastal highway. This entails a visit to **Estepona**, so far a bit more restrained than the other seaside resorts in Málaga, but still a popular holiday area. Until fairly recently it was concerned mainly with agriculture and fishing and still delivers sardines and anchovies along with the rest of the catch for sale at the local fish market. The town was started by the Romans and enlarged by the Moors and still has the Aqueduct of Salduba (but only those involved in research can now visit it), the remains of an Arab fortress and some old walls to prove it. The modern attractions which have been added include two eighteen-hole golf courses, a sailing club and a yacht marina with space for approximately 900 boats, some of which can be hired. Alternatively, visitors can water ski, go fishing or shooting and spread themselves along the beaches including the Costa Natura which was the first place in Spain where people could take all their clothes off without attracting the attention of the police. There are quite a few hotels and restaurants, especially along the coastal highway where two large establishments add tennis courts as well as outdoor and indoor swimming pools to their other amenities. The town celebrates in style with a procession in honour of San Isidro in mid-May, fairs in June and the Feast of the Virgen del Carmen in July marked by regattas, other water born events and illuminated by fireworks.

San Pedro de Alcántara, a few kilometres down the road, answers to much the same description. It provides the first opportunity for turning inland again, but only for anyone wishing to visit Ronda. There are no side roads leading across the nature reserve in the Serranía de Ronda to the east. However, the Romans, who made their home in the vicinity, have left behind a collection of ruins, among them the baths of Las Bóvedas and the basilica of Vega del Mar, used later by the Visigoths as a burial ground. To all intents and purposes San Pedro is all of a piece with Puerto Banús, a rather up-market version of a popular seaside resort full of restaurants and expensive villas but decidedly lacking in hotels. This hardly matters because it is virtually a suburb of Marbella which is positively bursting out in all directions with first class establishments providing every luxury at prices not everybody can afford. Some people are under the impression that the town was born in the 1950s, but they are sadly mistaken. Marbella entertained the Iberians, Phoenicians, Romans, Visigoths and Moors to mention only about half of them; and all that was after the ancient cave dwellers had vacated their home at Pecho Redondo, discarding all manner of things like axes, bead necklaces and pottery. Admittedly it is a little difficult to find any relics of the past in the midst of all the frantic modern development but parts of Marbella *are* off the beaten track, and the old quarter has a couple of antique towers still standing, along with a handful of antiquated buildings. These include a hermitage, a hospital and the Casa del Corregidor, built and decorated in the sixteenth century. The town entertains its guests one way or another all through the year, with the addition of some traditional celebrations such as pilgrimages in early May and the first half of June, the latter staging a cavalcade, bull-fights and regattas in honour of San Bernabé.

There are only three roads out of Marbella: a small scenic route to the north, the new highway and the long established coastal road which hugs the shoreline without interruption to Fuengirola where there is an open-air art gallery, zoo with a children's playground, a ruined Arab castle, built in the tenth century and much restored by Charles V, and some old Roman baths at Torreblanca del Sol. Four white marble columns from a local quarry, dating from about the

*The harbour at Puerto Banús*

same time, adorn a square in Los Boliches, apparently because no-one could think of anywhere else to put them. Holidaymakers can indulge in all the usual water sports, have tennis coaching, learn to fence, play football, basketball and such, ride and even take lessons in Spanish. There is an open-air market each Tuesday and festivals every month from June through to October, one of the most famous of which is the Feast of the Virgen del Carmen in Los Boliches, the area named after street traders from Genoa who settled there in the fifteenth century.

Some 8km (5 miles) away, up a well maintained road into the mountains, is **Mijas** which was comparatively unknown two or three decades ago but is becoming more popular with each year that passes. It is a delightful little town connected in the minds of most people with its donkey taxis. They stand about in groups, saddled for anyone who wants to ride or pulling little carriages for less energetic visitors who would like to be shown round. The average tour lasts about half an hour and takes in all the main attractions such as the square bullring, built in 1900, which made its film debut with Brigitte Bardot. Immediately opposite is the old parish church complete with a bell tower left over from a Moorish castle that once occupied the site. The Virgen de la Peña, discovered in the castle tower in 1586, stands surrounded by votive offerings in a small hermitage carved out of a rock and protected by the remains of an ancient wall. The village bristles with shops, restaurants and bars and is home to craftsmen of various nationalities who earn their living making things like carpets and pottery as well as beautifully inlaid wooden articles of every description from chess boards to chairs and tables. The main hotel provides both tennis and a heated swimming pool in addition to a magnificent view. There is an eighteen-hole golf course within easy reach, a mini museum and any number of traditional celebrations, foremost amongst them the week-long festival of the Virgen de la Peña in early September when the bulls due to appear later in the ring run free through some streets in the town.

From Mijas a small but quite acceptable road carries on northwards in search of other villages like **Alhaurín el Grande** and Cartama, complete with the ruins of an Arab fortress in the Monte de la Ermita and the shrine of the patron saint, Nuestra Señora de los Remedias. **Coín**, slightly to the west, is an agricultural centre in the Valley of Orange Blossom with a large fruit and vegetable market which is open to visitors. The Arab quarters have not changed much down the years and there are one or two old buildings to inspect before joining a donkey safari into the mountains. The town celebrates at regular intervals starting at Easter, decorates all its streets and courtyards for the festivals of the Vera Cruz in early May and mounts an extremely long and colourful procession to the shrine of its patron saint at the end of the month. August is the time for flamenco while December is given over to folklore and to the traditional songs and dances performed by groups from all over the area.

**Alora**, a bit further up the road, has its own Roman and Moorish memories just like all the other villages thereabouts, with the added advantage of the gorge of Los Gaitanes a short drive away. It is a canyon eaten away by the river Guadalhorce with deep, perpendicular-sided ravines and a narrow, frequently dangerous footpath half way down known as the King's Way. The whole area is sometimes described as the Caminito del Rey, which means the same thing, and is definitely worth visiting, especially as a road circles round it so one can go up one side and return along the other.

Taking the right hand fork outside Alora, the route leads through some spectacular mountain scenery to **El Chorro** which consists of a hydro-electric power station, a house or two, a railway line, a reservoir and a small but cheerful tavern. A narrow concrete water chute clings to the bare mountainside opposite, connected to a tower-like structure that seems to have its head in the stars and enjoys the company of birds like falcons, eagles and vultures. Further along the road is a nature reserve, all set about with man-made lakes, and a

*Mijas*

well signposted turning off to **Bobastro**. It was known as 'The Impregnable' at the time of the Caliphate of Córdoba, although it has now almost entirely disappeared except for a ninth-century basilica. This was carved out of solid rock, along with its naves and arches, on the orders of Omar ben Hafsun, an Arab ruler who may or may not be buried there. By the time you have climbed up even higher to the Río Verde reservoir the tower and the power station look like toys on the mountain tops below and the stars are just as far away as ever.

**Ardales**, where the road starts its journey back, is a village with interesting prehistoric connections although no-one seems to have known much about them before an earthquake opened up the Cave of Doña Trinidad Grund in 1821. It is a great place for people who like pottering about under the ground, inspecting one hall after another filled with stalactites and stalagmites and looking at wall paintings in the cavern known as El Calvario. There is nothing much of note except for the scenery between this point and Alora, after which it is simply a case of retracing one's steps to Mijas and then heading east for **Benalmádena**, another pleasant little hilltown with a large and somewhat over-populated coastal section almost, but not quite, attached. The village, known to the locals as Pueblo to distinguish it from its overgrown offspring, has a small archaeological museum, a delightful little square with an attractive fountain and a bullring a kilometre or so away. Benalmádena Costa, on the other hand, wallows in all the fun of the fair, and can in no way be described as off the beaten track.

Alternatively, there is an equally acceptable road linking Coín with **Alhaurín el Grande**, which was in turn an Iberian colony, a Roman town and an Arab stronghold. It boasts a sixteenth-century church built on the ruins of an ancient castle, a few reminders of its past occupants and a reserve for birds of prey in the pine forests nearby. During Easter week the Brotherhood of the 'Greens' and 'Purples' re-enact the events surrounding the Crucifixion — a much more solemn festival than the traditional Fair which is held in May. A short distance away is **Alhaurín de la Torre** where Pompey lost his head but it is more newsworthy these days for its citrus fruit and avocado pears and the Torre del Cante celebrations, described as the most important flamenco festival in Andalusia, although this might be challenged elsewhere. **Churriana**, a few minutes' drive from both Alhaurín de la Torre and the capital, has never quite got over the fact that Ernest Hemingway made his home there. It lists 'La Cónsula', the house where he lived, along with the gardens at El Retiro and the botanical park as its most worthwhile attractions.

**Málaga** itself is one of those unfortunate places which has grown older without mellowing and although it can meet all the needs of the average visitor it is a long way from being most people's favourite holiday playground. As a result it only has one hotel of any standing in the town, augmented by a small *parador* occupying a superb site on the top of a tree-covered rock overlooking the sea. Nor are the restaurants anything to write home about and the port area, in spite of all the gardens thereabouts, is the sort of place one only visits in order to catch a ferry. However it would be a mistake to write off the capital as a disaster area because there is plenty to see if one takes the trouble to look for it.

The old sector, or what remains of it, covers a smallish area in the shadow of the ruined Gibralfaro castle, built by the Moors in the fourteenth century on a site originally chosen by the Phoenicians. It is linked by an ancient wall to the *alcazaba*, which must have been a magnificent fortress in the tenth century when it was the home of the Arab kings of Málaga but is now really only a shell filled with delightful little gardens. It also houses the archaeological museum with rooms devoted to the Romans and the Moors as well as much earlier relics found in the area. The Museum of Fine Arts is only a short walk away, occupying a medieval palace that once belonged to the Counts of Buenavista. Apart from Roman mosaics and a Moorish cross there are paintings and sculptures by many famous artists

*Ploughing by mule*

including Picasso who was born in Málaga and has a special library dedicated to him. Other collections can be seen in the Museo de Semana Santa full of statues, thrones and typical arts and crafts associated with Easter, the Museo de Artes Populares accommodated in an old inn with a domestic flavour personified by implements used for farming and making wine, and the Cathedral Museum full of paintings, tapestries and manuscripts.

The cathedral itself was started in 1528 on the site of an ancient mosque and was not completely finished when work stopped more than 250 years later, by which time it had been equipped with an organ and some rather extrovert statues of the Catholic monarchs. Other places of interest in the town include the remains of a Roman theatre near the *alcazaba* and some small churches like the Shrine of Nuestra Señora de la Victoria with its special room where the statues are dressed, the family vault of the Counts of Buenavista and the much publicised Dolorosa de Meña. The bullring is open for inspection every day, there are horse-drawn vehicles for leisurely trips round the town and all the usual sporting facilities. The city takes its traditional celebrations very seriously from the Cavalcade of the Three Kings in January, the events of Holy Week and Corpus Christi, the summer festivals and the Verdiales, concerned almost exclusively with folk music and timed for late December. Carnival, which marks the beginning of Lent, dates back to pagan times and was banned by the Inquisition and later by Franco but has made a determined comeback in recent years. Málaga has even revived the Sardine Funeral which brings the festivities to a close when a minute coffin accompanied by mourners dressed in black, muffled drums and dirges is carried through the streets to the harbour and consigned to a watery grave.

Málaga is justly famous for its plants and flowers, including a garden with a few Roman remains at Finca de la Concepción, 7km (4 miles) along the highway to the north. This joins the road to Granada on the far side of **Antequera**, an old town with plenty to recommend it. Not least amongst its attractions are the dolmens of Menga, Viera and Romeral. The first is both the oldest and the largest with an oval chamber supported by three pillars and including a stone said to weigh 180 tons. It dates from 2500BC whereas Viera is younger by about a hundred years, although it had been in existence for some time when Romeral joined the party with its double false dome and a reputation for being the first example of true architecture in Europe. A clutch of churches in the shadow of the *alcazabar* includes the basilica of Santa Maria la Mayor, with more than a passing look of Rome about it, and the church of Los Remedios, home of the town's patron saint. It has a high altar framed by slightly overbearing columns and walls decorated with scenes from the life of the Virgin Mary and the role of Franciscans through the years. The museum, complete with a watch tower and an attractive courtyard, has a wide range of exhibits and makes much of the Efebo de Antequera, a Roman bronze from the first century. There are some old palaces and mansions dotted about and, for people in need of a bed for the night, a comfortable modern *parador* has all the necessary facilities plus a swimming pool.

From Antequera one can drive east to **Archidona**, another centre with ancient connections which boasts a most attractive square and a mountaintop mosque built by the Moors and said to be the only one of its kind in Málaga and possibly the oldest in Europe. It is the shrine of the Virgen de Gracia, the patron saint of the town, and is the focal point for a pilgrimage on the night of the 14 August. Alternatively one can head south again from Antequera through El Torcal, a mountain area worn into weird and wonderful shapes by the elements and criss-crossed by rough tracks and paths. The most interesting routes have been marked with arrows and anyone who needs additional information can get it from the local hunters' lodge. Less energetic travellers would no doubt prefer to follow one of the scenic routes that wander about a trifle but arrive eventually at the coast.

*Mimosa in flower*

**Rincón de la Victoria**, east of Málaga, was, according to Pliny, the site of the ancient Temple of the Moon. It has the remains of an old castle and a sandbank just off the shore where one can fish for *coquina*, a delicious kind of clam, or hire a fishing boat in the hope of catching a few anchovies to grill on the beach afterwards. Guides are available each morning and afternoon for anybody who would like to inspect an underground cave called the Cueva del Tesoro which was believed in medieval times to be the treasure storehouse of the five Mohammedan kings.

**Torre del Mar**, further along the coast, could easily have been part of the Greek town of *Mainake* which was destroyed by the Carthaginians, although they overlooked some bits and pieces of Phoenician architecture described as the oldest so far discovered anywhere in Spain. It has a long, somewhat greyish beach, a spa and a sailing club, boats for hire and a reputation for serving particularly good grilled lemon fish. There are a couple of camp sites and a modest hotel or two, as one would expect because it is the seaside resort for **Vélez-Málaga**, sitting surrounded by vineyards and olive groves a few kilometres inland. Vélez-Málaga, founded by the Phoenicians in the sixth century BC, is the capital of the Axarquia region, has its obligatory little churches and Arab remains and celebrates with great gusto from July to November.

The whole region is peppered with small villages like the brooding hamlet of Iznate, each with its own individual history. A perfect example is **Machàraviaya**, once known as Little Madrid, which now consists of a few houses and a disproportionately large church built in 1785 by José Gálvez, the Marqués de Sonora who was minister for the Indies at the time. The family played a leading role in the history of America and achieved immortality across the Atlantic when the Texans named Galveston after them.

The last town of any note before the border with Granada is **Nerja** which has gone all out in an effort to rival the other leading coastal resorts of the Costa del Sol. It has a tendency to sprawl and put up new villas wherever it can find an empty space, at the same time adding more shops, discos, clubs, cafés and restaurants to keep them company. However, because most people go there for the sea and the sun, the old quarter with its narrow streets and little church is largely unspoiled. The town's major claim to fame lies in the Nerja Caves, a couple of miles away, discovered in 1959 and christened 'The Cathedral of Prehistory'. There is plenty of proof that they were occupied 3,000 years ago, evidence of which can be found in the small museum which is open every day from the beginning of May to the middle of September. The pathways leading through the various underground halls are well signposted so there is no need to wait for a guided tour, although it is as well to book for the festivals of music and ballet which are held in August against the background of floodlit stalactites. There are one or two small hotels and a *parador* on the top of the cliffs with an attractive garden, tennis, swimming pool and a lift that saves its guests walking down to the beach. The Balcony of Europe on a rocky headland complete with an esplanade lined with palms and chestnut trees commands a magnificent view of the Mediterranean and over the rooftops of Maro to Granada.

# Further Information

## — Málaga —

**Places of Interest**

**Antequera**
Castle and churches
Open: enquire at the tourist office.

Museum
Open: 10am-1.30pm. Saturday 10am-1pm. Sunday 11am-1pm. Closed Monday.

The Dolmens
Guided tours of Menga and Viera 10am-1pm and 3-6pm (winter 2-5pm), closed Wednesdays.

The Romeral Dolmen
Collect key from sugar refinery.

**Benalmádena**
Archaeological Museum

Open: 10am-2pm and 6-9pm.
Closed Monday.

**Casares**
Remains of Iberian village nearby.

**Fuengirola**
Sohail Castle

Zoo
Open: 10am-2pm and 5-9pm.
Winter 9am-1pm and 3-7pm.
Saturday, Sunday and holidays
10am-9pm.

**Málaga**
Alcazaba with Archaeological
Museum
Open: summer 10am-1pm and 5-
8pm. Winter 4-7pm.

Diocesan Museum
Open: 10am-1pm and 4-7pm.
Closed Saturday and Sunday
afternoons and holidays.

Easter Museum
Open: 10am-1pm. In winter also 6-
8pm.

Fine Arts Museum
Open: 10am-1.30pm and 5-8pm.
Saturday and Sunday 10am-1pm.
Closed Mondays.

Popular Arts Museum
Open: 10am-1.30pm and 4-7pm.
Summer 5-8pm, Sunday 10am-
1pm.

Municipal Museum
Open: 11am-1pm and 5-8pm.
Closed Saturday and Sunday.

Roman Theatre
Open: all day.

**Marbella**
Archaeological Museum

Open: 11am-1pm and 5-8pm.
Closed Saturday and Sunday.

**Mijas**
Museum of Miniatures
Due to open again shortly.

**Nerja**
Prehistoric caves
Open: May to September 9am-
9pm. Otherwise 10am-1.30pm and
4-7pm.

**Ronda**
Arab Baths
Open: apply to caretaker.

Bullring and Museum
Open: 10am-2pm and 4-7pm.

Santa Maria Church
If closed apply to sacristan.

Salvatierra Palace
Open: 11am-6pm by appointment.

**Ronda (near)**
Pileta Caves
Contact guide who lives nearby.

**Torre del Mar**
Remains of Phoenician village.

## Tourist Information Offices

**Antequera**
Coso Viejo
☎ 84 21 80
Information also available at the
airport.

**Benalmádena**
Castillo de Bil-Bil
☎ 44 13 63

**Estepona**
Paseo Maritimo Pedro Manrique
☎ 80 09 13

**Fuengirola**
Plaza de España
☎ 47 61 66

**Málaga**
Larios 5
☎ 21 34 45

**Marbella**
Miguel Cano 1
☎ 77 14 42

**Nerja**
Puerta del Mar 4
☎ 52 15 31

**Ronda**
Plaza de España
☎ 87 12 72

**Torre del Mar**
Av de Andalusia
☎ 54 11 04

# 15 • Granada and Almería

Granada and Almería, fitted together like pieces of a jigsaw puzzle, complete the picture of Andalusia, the composite name given to the eight most southerly provinces in Spain. Geographically they are at the eastern end adjoining Murcia with no more than a hint of a common border with La Mancha to the north. Scenically they have something of everything except marshes, including mountain peaks covered in perpetual snow and areas which, although not actually desert, are the next best thing to it. Their Mediterranean coastline is made up of a string of bays and headlands which, given time, will lose their attractive air of isolation to become popular holiday playgrounds. Parts of Almería could almost be described as the vegetable garden of Europe while Granada concentrates its agricultural and farming interests along the Genil river valley in the north-west of the province.

Historically the two regions are very much bound up with each other. They were inhabited by prehistoric tribes, gave refuge to the Phoenician traders, played host to the Romans and, with Málaga, were the last part of Spain to be governed by the Moors.

There are no problems in either Granada or Almería when it comes to travelling about. Almería is connected by air with both Madrid and Barcelona and by ferry with Melilla on the North African coast, while trains keep the provinces in touch with each other as well as with cities like Barcelona and Valencia in addition to Madrid. There is no shortage of buses and, apart from the highways converging on the region from every direction, a network of secondary roads in a very reasonable state of repair keeps the traffic moving between smaller towns and villages. Outlying hamlets are served by minor roads that usually come as a surprise, sometimes pleasant and sometimes not.

Accommodation varies considerably from comfortable hotels in both provincial capitals, a sprinkling of slightly less up-market examples in the more important towns and holiday resorts to small and sometimes extremely basic hostels with very little to recommend them. Anyone thinking of patronising the last category would be wise to look round before checking in, especially as the innkeeper will usually offer the best room first and is seldom offended if it is turned down, although he may counter a refusal by dropping the price. Apartments are quite easy to come by and there is a good selection of camp sites.

The number of different entertainments available ensures that everyone will find at least one of their favourite sports or pastimes close to hand. Fresh air enthusiasts can shoot, fish, play golf or tennis, swim, walk or ride. There are boats and bicycles for hire, opportunities for snorkelling and windsurfing as well as skiing in the winter and bingo all the year round. Nightclubs are scarce but this is balanced by the number of discos and even more small bars, especially in Granada, that put on special flamenco shows. Traditional celebrations are held nearly everywhere, from the sophisticated International Music and Dance Festival to fiestas and village fairs where it is possible to see dances which originated with the Phoenicians. Souvenir hunters are faced with a wide choice including blankets and baskets, copper and carpets, embroidery, guitars, leather, silver and wrought iron. When it comes to food some local dishes to try are sardines grilled in the open air, white garlic and almond soup, clam stew, kid cooked with garlic and *trigo*, which is a mixture of wheat, pork and beans flavoured with herbs.

## Granada

It is practically impossible to mention Granada without thinking of the Alhambra, one of the world's great masterpieces as far as buildings are concerned. It has inspired musicians like Manuel de Falla who paid his tribute with *Nights in the Gardens of Spain*. The Spanish poet and dramatist Federico García Lorca drew on it repeatedly and nostalgically, Washington Irving is remembered chiefly for his *Tales of the Alhambra* and Frank Sinatra sang about Granada with so much feeling that one was almost tempted to go there straight away. The great rust-coloured castle attracts so many visitors that the queues are sometimes allowed in 'only a few hundred at a time' whereas on rare occasions it is possible to have the whole fortress almost to yourself. Although Granada is one of the last places that could possibly be described as off the beaten track, there are out-of-the-way corners in the province, in the city and even in the Alhambra itself that seldom receive a visitor and escape the average tourist altogether.

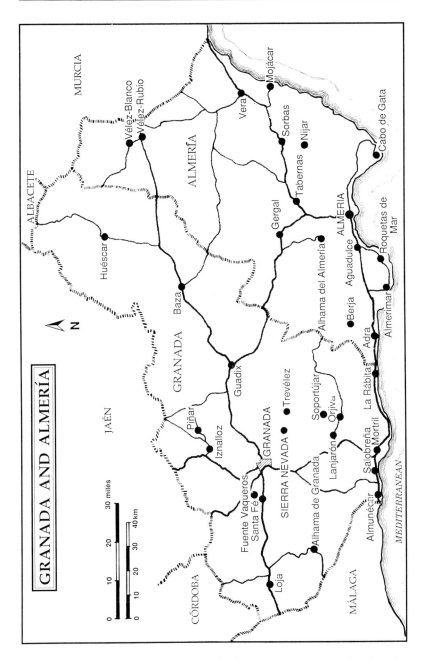

Scenically Granada is a region of infinite variety with refreshingly few areas devoted to olives. Wheat and other cereals are grown on the plains while farmers in the foothills of the Sierra Nevada concentrate on citrus fruits, grapes and almonds, the last of which cover everything in a delicate pink haze when the trees are in full bloom. Higher up the slopes are forests of oaks, chestnuts and pines above which tower the lofty peaks which are covered in snow from one year's end to the next. The whole province is etched with small rivers and streams, and although these dry out in hot weather, it does not appear to have much effect on the larger dams or the modest spas dotted about, which earn their living from a continuous flow of clients in search of cures for their rheumatism. The coastline is short and pleasantly scenic, backed by fertile areas producing avocado pears, bananas, pomegranates and custard apples, and fronted by beaches where the sand is somewhat grey but the water is warm and inviting. All the little holiday resorts are expanding as fast as possible and some are busy blowing large holes in the hillsides to make room for additional hotels, apartment blocks, restaurants and places of entertainment.

Granada, like all the other provinces bordering on the Mediterranean, was no stranger to the Phoenicians or to the Greeks who founded trading posts wherever they came across a reasonably protected anchorage. They were followed by the Carthaginians, the Romans and the Visigoths who all tramped about creating little of any lasting value. This was left to the Moors who made up for their predecessors' lack of enterprise by building forts, encouraging trade and industry, designing palaces, laying out gardens and beautifying their towns and cities.

After playing second or even third fiddle to Córdoba at the time of the caliphate, Granada reached its full potential in the thirteenth century and continued to increase its power and prosperity for the next two hundred years. Eventually trouble broke out in the royal harem, the king was deposed and his son installed in his place, the court divided its allegiance between the two monarchs and the climate was ripe for a takeover. The Christians were far too clever to miss an opportunity like this. They fuelled every fire as it started and were so successful that Ferdinand was able to walk into the city, keys in hand, in 1492, thereby ending nearly eight hundred years of Moorish rule.

For a while Granada was able to hold its own, producing artists of the calibre of Alonso Cano, but the church took a dim view of Muslim tolerance while the Spanish rulers had no doubt that they could improve on Moorish artistry. The result was that, between them, they managed to ruin both the atmosphere and most of the architecture. However there is a saying that 'Allah watches over the

Alhambra' and this must have been particularly true during the Peninsular Wars. When Napoleon's forces under Count Sebastiani were forced to retreat in 1812 a decision was taken to blow up the entire fortress. Fortunately a Spanish soldier decided otherwise and secretly cut the fuse, thereby earning himself a commemorative plaque and the heartfelt thanks of every succeeding generation.

In spite of the fact that there is a small airport a few kilometres from the city all the main flights touch down at Málaga, about 130km (80 miles) away. Here cars can be hired for an attractive drive through the mountains or along the impressive corniche beside the Mediterranean with a sharp turn-off to the north near Motril. Either way it is a good idea to allow plenty of time for the journey which will take longer than you expect. Other highways converge on the city from Jaén to the north and Murcia and Almería to the east, augmented by a few secondary roads whose main function is to explore the nearby mountains and, in particular, the Sierra Nevada. There are all the usual minor roads, half-made tracks and footpaths which are fairly numerous to the north-west but tend to be quite widely spaced elsewhere.

For people who prefer to catch a train, daily services run to Madrid, Almería, Seville, Córdoba and Algeciras, stopping at intervals along the way. Buses cover just as wide an area, adding centres like Alicante, Valencia and Barcelona to the long list of stopping places in Andalusia. Excursions by coach up into the Sierra Nevada are usually fully booked during the season but are worth waiting for if your nerves get the better of you when driving along spectacular mountain roads, looking forward to seeing another human being but dreading the sight of a car approaching from the opposite direction.

As with Seville and Córdoba, there are ample hotels to choose from in Granada itself but relatively few elsewhere in the province if you discount a *parador* and three quite up-market establishments — two of them in the mountains some 30km (19 miles) away. Nor are things much better when it comes to restaurants. The most acceptable ones are scattered about the city at quite infrequent intervals and become even more difficult to track down the further afield you travel. Things start looking up again in the coastal area where the standards generally are not exceptionally high but the number of options is increasing every season. It is possible to rent apartments, some of which are well equipped and not particularly expensive, although they do vary so it is as well to inspect both the premises and the small print carefully to find out exactly what is included in the price. For people who arrive with tents and caravans there are camp sites with all the usual facilities and at least some of them can be relied upon to stay open twelve months of the year.

From whichever direction you approach the province the highway is bound to wind up in the capital because they all take a roundabout route towards it like animal tracks leading to a water hole. This makes it difficult to visit all the more distant minor sights without dithering about quite considerably. The best way to save both time and fuel is to work out a rough plan and, within reason, stick to it. For example, one might start off from Málaga but, instead of crossing the border at Salinas, follow a minor road for a few kilometres northwards to Finca la Bobadilla, book in at a comfortable and very secluded hotel and play tennis, swim and patronise the restaurant while deciding where to go next.

One option might be south to **Alhama de Granada** which is a spa with an average sort of hotel in attractive gardens and a thermal pool that functions in the ancient Moorish baths, glorying in the official title of a monument. **Loja** is somewhat larger and answers to much the same description although it has no thermal baths. However there is an *alcázar* built in 895 and two or three historic buildings of much more recent vintage. From the town a well surfaced major road passes the local airport, opposite which a small turning runs straight up to the village of **Fuente Vaqueros**, the birthplace of García Lorca. Sadly he was shot in 1936, and officially ignored until after Franco's death thirty-nine years later. Now he is generally acknowledged to be Spain's greatest modern poet and his old home has been turned into a small museum which is open, with guided tours, every morning and afternoon except on Mondays.

Still skirting the capital, and using very minor roads to find the way across from one highway to another, the next place to visit might well be the **Parque del Cubillas** where an artificial dam is being developed into a holiday resort. There is a camp site and facilities for sailing and speedboating along with other water sports as well as space to park the car for anyone with an urge to explore the surrounding countryside on foot. To extend this excursion even further, follow a roundabout route through **Iznalloz**, with its wayside inn and Moorish castle, to **Piñar** where it is possible to get permission to visit the ancient cave of Carihuela on the outskirts of the village. The spa hamlet of **Zujar** has little of interest in its own right but it does give the energetic sightseer an opportunity to climb laboriously up to the pilgrim sanctuary of the Virgen de la Cabeza to admire the view. It is also on a minor route to **Huéscar** which boasts a couple of churches, an old burial ground, some cave paintings and a Roman mosaic or two. **Baza**, on the way back, has its own national monuments. Apart from the recently restored Moorish baths in the old Jewish quarter there are the remains of an Arab fortress, a sixteenth-century cathedral and the rather pleasing Fountain of the Golden Pipes. However if time is short it would be wiser to skip this area altogether in favour of a visit to **Gaudix.**

The hills around Guadix are decidedly intriguing, resembling nothing so much as a kindergarten drawing of a landscape on the moon. They are relatively small and very bare, somewhat pointed and all jumbled up together as though they were pushed to one side at the time of the creation, then overlooked because they did not quite fit in anywhere else. It is no surprise to find that the area has its roots in prehistoric times although the inhabitants do not appear to have occupied themselves painting the walls of their caves. Both the Romans and the Visigoths chose the spot for staging posts to guard the road to Murcia before the Moors moved in. They, rather belatedly, built a typical fortress which was immediately refurbished by the Christians after they captured the town at the end of the fifteenth century. The cathedral dates from approximately the same time and together they completely overshadow the buildings all around.

Perhaps more than anything else Guadix is famous for its hill houses. For centuries some of the inhabitants have made their homes in caves, hollowing out rooms of quite reasonable size from the soft tufa stone and shutting them off from the outside world with white-washed doors and shutters over the windowpanes. Until quite recently one could see goats munching away happily at the grass a few feet above, being careful to avoid the chimneys emerging like mushrooms and sending up little puffs of smoke reminiscent of the Home for Lost Boys in Peter Pan's Never Never Land. Time has brought some changes which do nothing from the picturesque point of view but make life a good deal better for the people living there. Covered porches have been added, there are roads lined with very ordinary little houses and the chimneys are more likely to be accompanied by television aerials than by any livestock other than an occasional dog or cat. The hill houses are strung out along the road as far as Purullena where everybody seems to be involved in making pottery. There are dozens of shops cluttering up the roadsides filled to capacity with ceramics of every description as well as copper and anything else which is likely to catch the eye of holidaymakers passing through.

It is worth making a detour of 18km (11 miles) or so to **Lacalahorra**, on the road to Almería. It is close to the iron mines at Alquife, there are some quite inviting footpaths through the hills and an

*Craft shops alongside the road at Purullena*

unidentified ruin north of Jerez del Marquesado. Lacalahorra itself is a typical village topped by a rather splendid domed castle with a delightful patio surrounded by arcades, some decorative windows and a well designed staircase leading up to the balustrade. This more or less exhausts the local sightseeing possibilities and as the only alternative roads lead through the Sierra Nevada and into Almería it is a case of returning to the main highway and revisiting Guadix. A modest hotel in the town will provide a room and bath if necessary and something to eat in the cafeteria but there is usually enough time left for the short drive to **Granada**.

The first view you get of the capital from this direction is slightly disappointing, especially if it is partly obscured by a smokey haze. The impression is one of comparatively modern buildings intermingled with small tiled roofs instead of the expected magnificence of the Alhambra, surrounded by spectacular gardens, dwarfing everything for miles around.

The city has some extremely good hotels, a vast number of smaller establishments, several interesting places to eat and plenty of shops in addition to the ones trading exclusively in souvenirs. The Parador of San Francisco is probably the most famous in Spain, largely because it occupies the site of an ancient Franciscan monastery on the hill beside the Alhambra. Only a fraction of the original building has been preserved, namely the main entrance, the tower and the temporary sepulchre where Ferdinand and Isabel were buried before they were moved to the Capilla Real next to the cathedral. However, the rest of the *parador* is very much in harmony with its surroundings and has beautiful formal gardens of its own with a terrace overlooking the Generalife. It is fairly small, usually fully booked and reasonably expensive but if you arrive too late, or short of cash, it is often possible to find accommodation at half the price in a modest little hotel, also inside the walls, which is open from March until early November.

A tour of the Alhambra begins at the Gate of Pomegranates, built by Charles V, which guards a small forest of poplars and English elms that the Duke of Wellington planted before dashing off in the direction of Waterloo. There is a road through the trees and a steep footpath both of which lead to the Justice Gate with the *alcazaba* to the left, the Palace of Charles V somewhat closer to hand and the best known and most frequently visited rooms and courtyards of the Alhambra immediately behind it. The *alcazaba* is far and away the oldest section of the fortress, dating back to the ninth century, with part of the walls and three towers still intact and a few foundations where the buildings used to be. If you have enough energy to climb the old watch tower, from which the Moors kept in touch with their outposts in the mountains, the view over the city and the surrounding country is magnificent.

The way in to the palace is through the Mexuar which was originally an audience chamber but served later as a chapel with an oratory added at the far end. Luckily no significant changes were made to its adjoining courtyard where a small fountain and intricately carved and decorated walls set the scene for things to come. The first of these is the famous Court of Myrtles, more than 42m (138ft) long with a mirror-like pool down the centre flanked by beautifully manicured myrtle hedges and white marble paving stones with colonnades at either end. Immediately to the left, through a small gallery, is the Hall of the Ambassadors where, with the addition of a throne, the kings would receive important guests and hand out their orders for the day. It has a domed ceiling inlaid with stars and other geometric patterns denoting the seven heavens of Islam, sets of horseshoe windows on three sides to let in the light and delicately carved and coloured stone walls with Arab poetry and excerpts from the Koran woven in to the overall design.

On the opposite side of the Court of Myrtles, through yet another small gallery, is the equally famous Court of Lions. It was built by Mohamed V in the fourteenth century and is the private patio attached to the royal apartments. The centrepiece is an alabaster fountain surrounded by twelve grey marble lions that might just be described as precocious cubs but otherwise bear no resemblance whatever to the animals in question. On every side are beautifully carved stone porticoes supported by a hundred or more slender marble columns which separate it from the rooms all round. The Abencerrajes Gallery on the right with its impressive ceiling is reputed to have been the scene of a particularly nasty family massacre, but quite who murdered whom depends on which legend you believe and if you are willing to accept that the stains on the marble floor are blood. The decorations in the King's Chamber, straight ahead, are rather out of character but things revert to normal in the harem, beyond which are the royal baths. Having soaked themselves thoroughly the various members of the family would recline on a much-decorated alcove seat in the dressing room, watching the water splashing in the fountain, eating sweetmeats and listening to music played by the court musicians in the gallery above their heads.

Terraces connect the enclosed and blissfully tranquil Daraxa Gardens with the outer walls and their small but superbly decorated towers. The Lady Tower, dating from the early fourteenth century, looks down on the Darro river, hardly more than a stream, which runs far below while the Mihrab Tower and those of the Captives and the Infantas have an uninterrupted view of the Generalife.

This was the summer palace of the kings of Granada, built on the Mountain of the Sun and reached along avenues of oleanders and lofty cypress trees around which are some of the most idyllic gardens to be found anywhere in Spain. A narrow pool between beds of roses, water jets and assorted shrubs and flowers has a pavilion at each end, forming a fairly restrained complex with the royal apartments and the adjoining gallery. All round are terraces filled with flowers, hedges fashioned into walls and archways and even a stairway with water running down the rails on either side. The air is heavy with the scent of jasmine and orange blossom and there is seldom anyone around to break the silence because the coachloads of tourists invariably head in the opposite direction to inspect the palace built by Charles V.

A lot of people shudder at the mere mention of this palace, probably because a large section of the Alhambra was destroyed to make way for it. But this was only doing exactly the same as the Moors had always done. They built for the moment on a basis of old stones and rubble, each ruler tearing a bit down and starting again, usually on a larger scale. It says much for the successive Spanish guardians that the Alhambra is still standing and in an excellent state of preservation. The Renaissance Palace got off to a flying start but, for various reasons, it was never completed. The initial work was in the hands of Pedro Machuca, who was trained by Michelangelo, and he created a heavy square building with a large circular courtyard in the middle, used in its time as both a bullring and an arena. Apart from some reliefs showing highlights from the Emperor's military exploits there is very little to see outside the two museums. The Museum of Fine Arts is largely given over to religious paintings and sculptures and has nothing of outstanding merit, but the Hispano-Moorish Museum is certainly worth visiting. There is a whole host of items removed for safekeeping from their appointed places in the original courtyards and apartments such as braziers and small pans that were used for burning perfume. Other items include aids to astrology, bits and pieces of sculpture, paintings, wall panels and screens.

Even people who have the time and inclination to visit the Alhambra more than once should make a point of seeing at least a few of Granada city's other attractions as well. They are scattered about as widely as little silver charms in an outsize Christmas pudding so the simplest way is to divide the whole place into sections and tackle them one at a time. At the top of the list might well be the Albaicín, an ancient and somewhat impoverished area on the hillside opposite the Alhambra. It was the site chosen by the Moors for their first city before Mohamed ibn Alhamar decided to start afresh on the Red Hill across the Darro river.

Apart from the general atmosphere, and the certain knowledge that nothing has changed very much in the past five hundred years, there are several individual buildings that add to the pleasure of looking round. The Moorish Baths are a case in point. They date from the eleventh century, were restored in 1928 and are now regarded as the finest example to be found anywhere in Spain. The baths are open all day but if the door does happen to be locked you only have to ring the bell. Further along the river, past the remains of a Moorish bridge, is the sixteenth-century church of St Peter and St Paul which holds a flamenco mass on the third Sunday of every month. A stone's throw away is the richly decorated Casa de Castil, considered by many to be the most beautiful mansion in Granada, which is the home of the city's archaeological museum. Built in the reign of Ferdinand and Isabel it contains a number of relics from prehistoric times, coins and suchlike, recalling the Greek and Roman occupations and, of course, several objects that originated with the Moors. The Convent of Santa

Catalina de Zafra goes one better by giving house room to a little Arab home built in the eleventh century. A labyrinth of narrow cobbled streets climbs up the hill between white-walled houses whose patios are filled with flowers. They call at a handful of small churches which took the place of earlier mosques, sneak round the church of San Nicolás where there is an ancient fountain and a superb view of the Alhambra, and stop just short of a section of the antiquated Moorish walls.

There are almost as many atmospheric streets in the Alcaiceria, hard by the cathedral. It was once the silk market, but after a fire that raged through the area something over a hundred years ago the original buildings were replaced with replicas which are now occupied with selling handicrafts. The cathedral itself is large, dark and not as interesting as its impressive façade leads one to expect but the Capilla Real next door makes up for it. The chapel was built in the early sixteenth century as a resting place for Ferdinand and Isabel who, with their daughter and son-in-law, are buried in the crypt. The chancel, protected by Master Bartolomé's superb wrought iron screen full of crowns and coats of arms, cherubs, lions, dolphins and two cheerful-looking saints, contains the royal mausoleums. The whole interior is decorated in a similar manner while the sacristy is hung with the queen's favourite pictures by leading artists of the day and also contains her crown and sceptre as well as one of Ferdinand's swords. Across the street is the Palace of the Madraza which started life as the Moorish university, was transformed into a town hall by the Christians and latterly reverted to its university status for use as an exhibition centre and conference hall. It is said to be open during office hours but there are times when no-one is about to open the door. On the other hand the old University of Granada, founded by Charles V in 1526 with its headquarters on the opposite side of the square, moved out after some 250 years and the building was taken over by the church. Also in the vicinity is the Corral del Carbón, a unique example of a Moorish inn where merchants could spend the night, having left their goods in a warehouse thoughtfully provided for the purpose. The Christians used it as a theatre and it is now a centre for national crafts and keeps the same hours as shops and offices.

A straight road runs up from the side of the cathedral towards the sixteenth-century monastery church of San Jerónimo which is one of the oldest in the city. It was very badly treated by French troops during the Peninsular Wars but has now been restored and is open every morning and afternoon. A block or two away is the somewhat younger but far more lavishly decorated church of San Juan de Dios, with a tiled dome and an enormous gilt altarpiece. Behind the gold and silver door in the middle is the tomb of St John of God who founded the order of the Knights Hospitallers and the ancient hospital up the road, taken over in more recent times by the university.

Provided you have a map and either a car or a bus timetable, other places worthy of note are the Royal Hospital, built by the Catholic Monarchs and now part of the university, and the Carthusian monastery still further away whose chapel and sacristy almost defy description. There are twisted columns like sticks of barley sugar, marble of every shade and colour, gold, silver, extravagantly framed pictures, carved cedarwood and an overpowering amount of decorative stone. Fortunately it does not restrict visiting times to the hours when mass is held but allows people in every morning and afternoon. On the opposite side of town the Villa of Martyrs with its gardens, trees and artificial lake can be found in the shadow of the Alhambra and is open every Sunday. A close neighbour was Manuel de Falla whose home has been turned into a small museum filled with memories of the composer. The same compliment has been paid to García Lorca in the house where he lived on Arabial Street in the more modern part of the city. About half way between the two lies the elderly Hermitage of San Sebastian, a thirteenth-century mosque which was transformed into a Christian chapel shortly after Ferdinand and Isabel met Boabdil there to arrange for the handing over of Granada.

Sacromonte, on the hill opposite the Generalife, is, and has been for centuries, the main gipsy quarter. A percentage of the population still lives in surprisingly comfortable caves, spending the time thinking up new ways of parting sightseers from their money. They will invite the casual visitor inside for a session of flamenco music and dancing, fetch bottles of wine at their guests' expense at very inflated prices, tell fortunes and then speed the tourists on their way, poorer if not wiser for the experience. The standards reached by these entertainments is not usually very high but provided one is aware of the object behind them and acts accordingly there is no reason why everyone should not enjoy themselves enormously.

There is usually something going on in Granada, starting with the celebrations at the beginning of January to mark the entry of the Catholic Monarchs and the end of Moorish rule. A pilgrimage through Sacromonte in honour of St Cecil, the patron saint of the city, follows in February, giving way later to all the colour and excitement of Holy Week. May sees the festival of the Holy Cross with its 'Day of the Carnation' and for a fortnight from the last week in June the city is crowded for the International Festival of Music and Dancing which centres mainly on the Alhambra. Whitsun and the Day of Our Lady of Sorrows are both marked by all sorts of entertainments including bullfights and there are special events in the winter for people attracted by the snow on the mountains. Details of these and other events are available from the Information Office in the Casa de los Tiros, an impressive mansion overlooking a square on the Calla Pavaneras which also houses a museum of history and handicrafts.

No matter where you go in the capital it is usually possible to catch a glimpse of snow on the Sierra Nevada and the more you see of it the more tempting it becomes. However there are really only a couple of ways of getting up to it, one straightforward and comparatively easy and the other even more scenic but certainly not recommended in the later stages for people of a nervous disposition. Almost from the moment it shakes itself clear of the suburbs the road begins to twist and turn as though in two minds about the advisability of going on any further. Occasionally it sends out a feeler track which takes a quick look round and returns defeated after a few kilometres.

The first stopping place is the Prado Llano complex of Sierra Nevada which in many ways is a rather good place to stop. It is at the centre of a large nature reserve and also of the Solynieve ski area which explains why the larger hotels with their indoor swimming pools close firmly in the spring and do not open again until December. Fortunately there is also a modern *parador* which welcomes summer guests as well as winter ones. All the usual facilities for winter sports are provided such as cable cars, ski-lifts, lessons at the official ski school, shops specialising in all the necessary equipment and apartments for people who prefer to do their own catering.

The two highest peaks, Veleta and Mulhacén, both in excess of 11,000ft, have splendid views over much of Andalusia and across the Mediterranean to Morocco. During the summer one can either take a cable car or drive up to the Pico de Veleta using a section of the route widely publicised as the highest in Europe. From here onwards it is a fairly lonely drive down to the Alpujarras with its choice of mountain roads linking several small, and so far unspoiled, villages where the Moors held out until the beginning of the seventeenth century. For anyone who enjoys walking it is an ideal spot with plenty of wild country on either side of the Guadalfeo river and some delightful stopping places, the least accessible of which are almost primitive. Foremost amongst the better known hamlets are **Soportújar** surrounded by oaks and chestnuts, **Bérchules** where carpet weaving has been a major industry for about five hundred years and **Trevélez**, described as the highest village in Europe and known for its snow-cured hams. The easier route from Granada runs due south, crossing a ridge known as the Suspiro del Moro, or the Sigh of the Moor. The story goes that the last king, Boabdil, paused here on his way into exile for a backward glance at the Alhambra, thereby earning himself a caustic comment from his mother. She remarked that he wept like a woman for something he had failed to fight for like a man, but who overheard and recorded this vindictive observation is less well documented. Some 40km (25 miles) down the road there is a turn-off to **Lanjarón**, the quickest and easiest way to the Alpujarras. It is an attractive hill village and a well known spa, popular with people who have liver or digestive problems or who simply want to relax at one of the modest hotels. Villagers who are not kept fully occupied attending to their guests spend the time making baskets or producing vast quantities of mineral water that are sold all over Spain.

At this point one is faced by three alternative routes leading down to the sea. The first and longest wends its way through the mountains to join the coastal highway at La Rábita, just inside the border with Almería. The second, also excellent from a scenic point of view, blazes a slightly erratic trail to Motril while the main road cuts through equally majestic country to Salobreña. Although there are plenty of likely picnic spots along the way the innumerable small inns and restaurants at frequent intervals, offering a variety of refreshments at extremely reasonable prices, make the whole business of shopping, cutting bread and butter and filling vacuum flasks seem quite unnecessary. A word of appreciation is due to the drivers of heavy vehicles on these serpentine roads. They are extremely helpful, giving signals to warn of approaching traffic or indicating that it is safe to pass. In spite of this it is as well to be a little cautious before overtaking in case they have credited you with the speed of a greyhound when the best you can manage is a rather sluggish tortoise.

Heading south from the capital an attractive little road branches off at the Suspiro del Moro for a jaunt through the Cazulas range to **Almuñécar**. This is the last resort of any size before the border with Málaga, with small but adequate hotels, a considerable number of cafés and restaurants and a great many apartments in highrise blocks overlooking the sea. The town dates from the Phoenicians and a collection of ruins enclosed in gardens behind the headland are said to be the remains of cellars where they stored their salt. Plans are afoot to restore the old medieval fortress at the top of the hill and tidy up the ancient burial ground beside it. A large collection of alabaster urns, filled with the ashes of ancient Egyptians and appropriately inscribed, were discovered in the necropolis and handed over for safekeeping to the archaeological museum in Granada. Other things surviving from these bygone days are the Roman aqueduct, the Monk's Tower and an extremely large and antique water storage tank known as the Cave of the Seven Palaces.

Almuñécar goes to a lot of trouble to keep its visitors happy. Cars can be hired in addition to motor cycles of various descriptions, including the kind that operate on water. The sand is greyish looking and a bit rock-strewn in places but this is no problem for anyone armed with a beach bed and a sun umbrella, both of which are immediately available. There are some pleasing small gardens, an attractive promenade along the front with palm trees and plenty of space for parking and enough shops and markets to meet everyday requirements. The usual discos are augmented by a Saturday night barbecue combined with a flamenco show at Venta Luciano where, for an all-in price, customers are encouraged to eat and drink as much as they like. It is three or four kilometres inland on the mountain road to the capital.

The entire length of coastline in this part of the country is guarded by dozens of ancient watch towers, approximately one to each headland and rocky promontory, most of them isolated and in various stages of decomposition. Occasionally one is accompanied by a little fort of comparable vintage or by a collection of small white houses in the Moorish style that have grown up quite recently after apparently making sure that it would not collapse on top of them. The views from the road as it slices its way round the hillsides high above the water is magnificent and there are occasional places to visit en route. To the west, only a few kilometres from Almuñécar, is the fishing village of **La Herradura** which has the only skin diving and underwater fishing school yet established on the Costa del Sol.

Leaving Almuñécar and heading east it is only a short drive to **Salobreña**, a village built on the cliffside below a fortress that originated with the Phoenicians, was rebuilt by the Arabs, ignored during the Middle Ages but completely restored comparatively recently. A comfortable hotel with tennis and a swimming pool, sited on a hilltop near the corniche, is ideally placed to take advantage of the golf course which Salobreña shares with Motril, 4km ($2^1/_2$ miles) away. Although it is essentially a busy port, exporting sugar from the extensive cane fields behind, along with the output from sundry other refineries, **Motril** finds time to enjoy itself. It has a nautical club and facilities for visiting yachts in the port area, where you can also hire a boat and learn to sail. There is windsurfing during the season, squash and tennis at the Torrenueva Club and an Olympic sized pool at the sports centre but nothing very memorable in the way of restaurants or hotels. From here the road hugs the shoreline, passing through several little resorts of no particular moment, skirting rocky inlets and inspecting the view from assorted headlands until it reaches La Rábita and the border with Almería.

## Almería

Almería has fewer historic towns and scenic attractions than the other provinces of Andalusia, thus creating something of a backwater where tourists are concerned. However, the traveller will find an unexpected variety of places to visit and things to do, some of them unique in southern Spain and others entirely predictable. Much of the area is sparsely populated without a great many roads, hardly any olives, some citrus farms and a reasonable selection of hills and mountains. There is an arid, semi-desert area used by American filmmakers to recreate the Wild West, a fertile stretch along the coast where tomatoes and other vegetables are grown in their millions, mostly under thin sheets of plastic, a sprinkling of caves, old forts and antiquated houses and quite a few modern attractions, particularly where recreation is concerned.

Plenty of evidence is available to show that people have been living in Almería without a break since approximately 4,000BC. Like the rest of Andalusia it was constantly bothered by invaders in the early days, most of whom settled in nearby provinces such as Granada, pausing only to build an odd fortress here and there to protect themselves from surprise attack, especially by sea. Almería itself had a brief moment of glory in the eleventh century, but after Boabdil, the last Moorish king, sailed for Africa from Adra the province relapsed into a pleasant state of obscurity. It was only shaken out of its stupor in fairly recent times with the building of a solar energy platform and an important observatory followed by the realisation that a little attention paid to the tourist industry would be no bad thing. Today the province boasts an airport, trains to Madrid, Valencia and Barcelona as well as Seville and Córdoba, bus services linking the capital with all the larger towns and villages in addition to cities like Madrid, Alicante and Algeciras and a car ferry to North Africa. For motorists there are three major roads into Almería, one from Murcia, the second from Granada and the third along the coast from the Costa del Sol. Half a dozen or so quite scenic routes lead across country and also follow the coastline round Mojácar, in addition to which the usual hotch-potch of minor roads are available to anyone walking or driving a jeep.

Where accommodation is concerned the outlook is encouraging with a *parador* and several comfortable hotels, a number of smaller and often rather basic ones, plenty of apartments and just short of a dozen camp sites. The restaurants tend to be down-market but if you do find a good one in the capital or any of the larger coastal resorts, local dishes to look for include clam stew, fresh sardines and *cuevas del Almanzora*, a sort of biscuit that can be a little too dry if the cook has been stingy with the liqueur. Traditional crafts include ceramics, blankets and basketwork, not forgetting items made from very high quality white marble found at Macael. Folklore plays a large part in Almería's fêtes and festivals, beginning in January with a procession of decorated carts and horses, singers and dancers and enthusiastic crowds who gather for the Virgin of the Sea pilgrimage to Torre García. Holy Week is marked by as much devotion and colour as it is in other parts of Spain but August is the time for fairs and carnivals with all manner of different events including bullfights. Amongst the various dances to be seen is a *fandango*, a kind of flamenco that was popular with fishermen, Adra's *El Cortijero Robao*, said to have been introduced by the Phoenicians and *Las Seguidillas* which may well be the oldest of the lot.

The area that you choose for your holiday depends very largely on what you plan to do. For sports enthusiasts there is no doubt that the coast provides the greatest number of possibilities with tennis and golf, under-water fishing, sailing, swimming and, for sun worshippers, special camps and beaches run by the Naturist Association of Andalusia. The first town on the coastal route is **Adra**, once a Phoenician port of call, later a Roman harbour and now a very ordinary little place that divides its attention between fishing, sugar cane and vegetables with nothing worth mentioning in the way of hotels and restaurants, but several camp sites. Beyond it a small road breaks away and heads north towards the mountains, calling at **Berja** with its vineyards and elderly houses, while the main highway continues on its journey towards the capital. Two of the province's most up and coming seaside resorts have their own turnings off this stretch of road.

The first is **Almerimar** whose only reason for being there at all is to keep holidaymakers fully occupied, but they tend to be Spanish

*A Wild West film set near Tabernas*

holidaymakers rather than foreign ones. It has a comfortable hotel in pleasant surroundings where guests can play tennis or spend their time on the golf course, villas and apartments for the self-catering fraternity and an unpretentious camp site. There is also a small marina along with all the usual water sports. **Roquetas de Mar,** slightly further up the coast, is well into its stride with an old village whose primary interest is in agriculture and a modern development which includes several unexceptional hotels, typical seaside restaurants, apartments, shops, discos and a yacht club. There is an eighteen-hole golf course, closed on Mondays, which like its counterpart at Almerimar is open throughout the year and has equipment that can be hired by anyone who has left the necessary gear at home. **Aguadulce,** where all this modernisation started, has much the same in the way of holiday attractions, makes room for a street market twice a month and holds its annual fiesta in July.

**Almería** itself, only 10km (6 miles) away, is a pleasant, atmospheric if rather hot and dusty sort of place which is at its best during the winter months. It has been around since Phoenician times, was nodded at by the Romans and adopted by the Moors who built the *alcazaba*, reputed to be the most powerful Arab fortress anywhere in Spain, soon after they arrived in the eighth century. Unfortunately it was badly damaged by an earthquake in 1522 and the palace on the nearby hill of San Cristóbal has completely disappeared. However, a large section of the walls is still standing, along with an occasional tower, and a certain amount of work has been done on the site of the royal apartments and the mosque next door. As well as some pleasant gardens there is a small experimental ranch in the valley below where animals and birds, brought over from the Sahara where they were in danger of extinction, are given a permanent home. There are no visiting hours as such but it is possible to get permission from the main office in the city to look around.

The old quarter with its narrow streets and typical little houses climbs the hillside to the ramparts with the Chanca, inhabited mainly by fishermen, on one side and the cathedral on the other. It is a very businesslike construction dating from the early sixteenth century, when it had to withstand repeated attacks by the Barbary pirates. Still in place are the original choir stalls, although the high altar, the statues and the paintings were added later. Amongst the city's other churches are those of San Pedro, Santiago El Viejo and the sanctuary of Santo Domingo which houses the Virgin of the Sea. The archaeological museum, a fair walk away unless you happen to be starting from the station, has sections devoted to discoveries made in various prehistoric caves, the early days of the port and items recovered from the *alcazaba* and the area surrounding it. The Street of the Linen Drapers is the oldest in town but the Avenida de Almería is better equipped for a shopping expedition or a gentle stroll down to the port where there is a yacht club, a good deal of commercial activity and a departure point for ferries to North Africa. The capital has two or three comfortable hotels complete with swimming pools, several more in the slightly lower categories, some very acceptable restaurants, apartments to let and a nearby camp site.

Local excursions might well include a visit to **Alhama de Almería**, whose warm thermal springs were as popular with the Romans as they are now, followed by Gérgal's ancient castle and modern observatory, considered to be one of the most important in Europe, and the solar platform slightly to the east. On the other hand, most people make for **Tabernas** in order to immerse themselves in the atmosphere of America's Wild West. Mini Hollywood is close to the main road, well preserved and ready to lay on a gun fight, hold up a stage coach or wipe out a few cowboys and Indians when enough sightseers are gathered round the 'frontier town' to make it practical. However, if one is prepared to negotiate an extremely hairy road, part of which runs along a dry river bed, the Decorados Cinematograficas set on the opposite side of the road is probably more authentic. The main street is rather delapidated, strictly uncovered wagons stand about and the Indian wigwams, although not made from animal skins, have the desolate air of a village long deserted by the tribe. It is quite fascinating to come across genuine hoofmarks in the sandy soil between low, dry patches of scrub, look closely at the little bare hills all round and realise that there is not a single horse in sight. The area is widely publicised as the place where part of *Lawrence of Arabia* was filmed but anyone expecting to find gently undulating sand stretching as far as the horizon in all directions, with perhaps a camel to break the monotony, will be sadly disappointed. It takes all sorts to make a desert and that particular sort is left to the Sahara, just across the Mediterranean.

Some of the hamlets in this part of Almería are well worth visiting. **Sorbas,** for example, is memorable for its tenacious white houses clinging to the face of a cliff. **Níjar** is a less spectacular but nevertheless charming little village where everyone not involved in making pottery will probably earn a living weaving a heavy and distinctive type of material, using methods which have been employed successfully for many hundreds of years.

To the south there are yet more sand dunes and a scenic road along the cliffs to Cabo de Gata with its lighthouse, small beach and sea conditions which are ideal for underwater fishing. Other small seaside resorts, interspersed with private nudist beaches, are beginning to appear all along the coast as it swings northwards towards the Costa Blanca, each one hoping one day to rival **Mojácar.** This is an extremely picturesque old town, perched above the sea with a background of mountains away across the plains. The original part, all flat roofs and white walls crowding in on each other, has a particularly timeless atmosphere with more than a passing belief in the supernatural. A 5,000-year-old symbol, consisting of a stick figure with its arms stretched out on either side to support a semi-circle over its head, is still secretly thought to have the power to ward off evil and, appropriately enough in view of its umbrella-like arc, give protection during thunder storms. It is a fascinating place to wander about, discovering an ancient cave, an Arab fountain or a flower-filled square overlooked by a fortified tower, neatly tucked away in a maze of little winding streets. Strangely enough the old quarter is frequently ignored by holidaymakers who head straight for the modern developments along the seafront, which include several hotels, amongst them a modern *parador* a few yards from the beach. The larger establishments provide heated swimming pools and tennis courts, serve meals out on the terraces when the weather is kind, which it usually is, and are within easy reach of the golf course and a riding club. There are plenty of shops, a street market each Wednesday, discos and buses into the capital every day except Sunday.

It would be a great pity to leave Almería without seeing at least some of the prehistoric caves, especially the Cuevas de los Letreros with their Neolithic wall paintings, particularly as they are to be found just north of Vélez Rubio on the upper road to Murcia. It is an easy run from Mojácar through Vera, where the Royal Hospital of St Augustine was founded by Charles V in 1521. From Huércal Overa, 17km ($10^1/_2$ miles) to the north, a secondary road cuts across country, almost but not quite ending up in Vélez Rubio with its eighteenth-century church and a small hostel where travellers can get something to eat and a bed plus bath for the night. Vélez Blanco is no distance away and has a castle built by the local marquis in the sixteenth century and a small church that is said to have replaced an earlier mosque. It more or less keeps an official eye on the famous caves which are sited close to the road linking the two villages. From here it is only necessary to rejoin the main road at Vélez Rubio and head west for Puerto Lumbreras, over the border in Murcia.

# Further Information
## — Granada and Almería —

**Museums and Places of Interest**

**Alhama de Granada**
Church of the Incarnation
Open: hours of masses.

Moorish Baths
In operation during the summer.

**Almería**
Alcazaba
Open: 10am-2pm and 4-9pm. In winter 9am-1pm and 3-6.30pm.

Cathedral
Open: 8.30am-12noon and 5.30-8pm.

Refuge for Sahara animals

Open: by permission. Enquire at the tourist office.

**Almuñécar**
Castle
Open: all day.

**Baza**
Alcazaba
Open: all day.

Arab baths
Open: private property so enquire.

Cathedral
Open: hours of masses.

**Granada**
Alhambra
Open: 9.30am-6.30pm.

Arab Baths
Open: all day.

Carthusian Monastery
Open: 10am-1pm and 3-6pm.

Casa de los Tiros
Open: 10am-2pm.

Cathedral and Museum
Open: 11am-1pm and 4-6pm.

Chapel Royal
Open: 11am-1.30pm and 4-7pm.

San Jerónimo Church
Open: 10-1.30pm and 3-6pm.

San Juan de Dios
Church and Museum
Open: 10am-1pm and 4-6pm.

Corral del Carbón
Open: during business hours.

Archaeology Museum
Open: 10am-2pm and 6-10pm.

García Lorca Museum
Open: on request. Closed Mondays.

Manuel de Falla Museum
Open: on request. Closed Mondays.

Villa of Martyrs
Open: Sundays only.

**Guadix**
Alcazaba
Open: all day.

Cathedral
Open: all day.

**Huéscar**
Cave paintings

**Iznalloz**
Cave of the Water
Open: by special permission.

**Lanjarón**
Ruined Arab castle
Open: all day.

**Motril**
Sanctuary of Our Lady of the Head
Open: hours of masses but 'look-out' at any time.

**Piñar**
Castle
Open: all day.

Cave of Carihuela
Open: by special permission.

**Purullena**
Hill houses.

**Salobrena**
Palace-fortress
Open: enquire at the town hall.

**Vélez-Rubio**
Prehistoric caves.

## Tourist Information Offices

**Granada**
Casa de los Tiros
Calle Pavaneras 19
☎ 22 10 11 or 22 10 22

**Almería**
Hermanos Machado
☎ 23 47 05

# 16 • Murcia and Alicante

Murcia and Alicante together account for approximately half the Levante region of south-eastern Spain, sharing the stretch of Mediterranean known as the Costa Blanca. It consists basically of two enormous bays with extensive rocky headlands and far reaching sandy beaches, edged in many places with pines and interrupted by salt water pools and lagoons. Beyond the shoreline is a fertile area, once farmed by the Moors, producing everything from citrus fruits to dates and rice, giving way eventually to stark grey hills and open plains which persist into the interior.

Like all the other provinces bordering on the Mediterranean, Murcia and Alicante have their roots firmly embedded in prehistory. Caves full of rock paintings and other relics bear witness to the palaeolithic communities who spent their lives there. The Phoenicians did a bit of prospecting in Murcia, the Carthaginians, the Romans and the Visigoths all moved in, settled down for a while and then moved out again to be followed by the Moors who liked it so much that the majority made it their home for the best part of five hundred years. The most persistent of them were only thrown out in 1609, a good century after Granada had been returned to the Spanish fold. Each subsequent period had its own individual problems which, these days, are comparatively minor ones as local interests are centred mainly on agriculture, a certain amount of industry and, in the case of Alicante, a well established tourist trade. Both provinces are helped considerably by the weather, which is hot in summer and mild in winter although it can sometimes be unpleasantly wet with flash floods in the autumn.

No-one should have any difficulty in getting either to or from the Costa Blanca. Both capitals have their own airports, but whereas Murcia is simply connected to Madrid and Barcelona, Alicante also has regular services to the Canary Islands, Mallorca and Seville and a large number of charter flights as well. There are trains linking the two cities with each other and with most of the large centres in the

surrounding area, augmented by buses that shuttle backwards and forwards inside the region and to more distant places like Barcelona, Granada and Málaga. Motorists are well served by a coastal highway that runs from the northern border of Alicante to Cartagena, another heads inland from the port through Murcia to Albacete while a third links Alicante with Murcia before pressing on through Lorca to Almeria. In addition to all this an *autopista* connects Alicante with Valencia and then continues without interruption to the French border. A network of secondary roads, usually in good condition, maintains contact between the larger towns and villages with the addition of several minor turn-offs for anyone who wants to break fresh ground and avoid the heavy traffic.

Both provinces observe all the national festivals with several places adding original events of their own. The processions marking Holy Week, some of them unusually spectacular, are followed by a Spring Festival in Murcia, Alcoy remembers St George with gratitude in April and Alicante pays tribute to St John in June. Elche puts on a mystery play in August, Petrel turns out in October to recreate a fiesta dating back to the sixteenth century and Christmas is welcomed with carols in Alicante and to the sound of bells in Murcia. At the same time Campo de Mirra holds a Festival of Fools that closely resembles one which was familiar to the citizens of ancient Rome. Anyone in search of souvenirs would be well advised to take home sugared almonds from Alcoy, toys from Ibi, hand-embroidered dresses and items made from grass in Murcia, not forgetting *turrón* from Jijona. This sweetmeat, generally thought to have been introduced by the Arabs, was mentioned in the *Thousand and One Nights* although both France and Italy also claim to have invented it. The original consists mainly of almonds, toasted and mixed with honey, but some modern manufacturers add other ingredients such as chocolate. *Turrón* in its various forms is eaten almost exclusively at Christmas and can be either delicious, a touch on the sweet side or positively sickly, depending largely on where it was made. Alicante has few of its own traditional dishes, borrowing *paella* from Valencia without the sea food, but items to watch for are *cocido de pelotas* consisting of minced meat wrapped in cabbage leaves and stewed with chicken or turkey, bacon, chickpeas, potatoes and spices and *arroz con costra* which contains a great many ingredients including pork meatballs, the whole lot covered with beaten egg and browned in the oven. Murcia has an individual way with vegetables, served on their own, in omelettes or in stews, and specialises in small, tasty prawns, fish like sea bass coated with salt and baked in the oven and the roe of the mujol. *Chorizo* is a traditional dish made largely from veal and minced meat wrapped in pastry, with a modern version known as *Pastel de Cierva*.

## Murcia

Even Murcia's most ardent champions have to admit that the province is more often overlooked by visitors than overrun by them. The average motorist is inclined to stop for a coffee, study the map, glance at his watch and decide to press on towards his destination. The reason may be that there are few large towns and much of the area is short on villages as well. Generally speaking the coast has still to be developed and the areas to the north and the north-west are arid and sometimes frankly uninviting. In spite of these apparent drawbacks Murcia is well worth exploring, even though its attractions tend to appear singly rather than in convenient batches.

Driving south along a most satisfactory road from Albacete the countryside is flat and strewn with rocks and stones. These persist even when it reaches a line of odd-looking hills, rather like a procession of giant dinosaurs with their heads and tails buried in the scrub. At the first crossroads searchers after old ruins can turn off to the east to Jumilla and Yecla. **Jumilla** is a sizable town surrounded by vineyards and overlooked by the somewhat isolated remains of its ancient castle perched on the top of the hill. Its other attractions include the church of Santiago which has been declared a national monument, cave paintings from various prehistoric settlements discovered in the vicinity, the town hall known to all and sundry as The Prison, and the local museums. The official one has rooms devoted to archaeology, natural sciences and traditional crafts but anyone interested in wine-making should make a point of seeing the privately owned collection of wine-cellar equipment, some of it dating back to the fourteenth century, which is open during office hours.

**Yecla** is slightly larger and more industrial, has its own ruined castle but lost its archives when Austrian troops launched an attack during the War of Succession. Its two main churches date from the sixteenth and seventeenth centuries but the Casa de la Cultura has several hundred exhibits covering a whole range of ancient cultures. An unexpected discovery is the museum of El Greco reproductions, some seventy-five in all, which are the work of a local artist, Juan Albert Roses, and have been on tour to places as far apart as Athens, Havana, Santo Domingo and Panama. Neither Yecla nor Jumilla has much to offer in the way of hotels but both have a sprinkling of typical restaurants with interesting local dishes.

By turning right instead of left at the crossroads the way is open to **Caravaca de la Cruz** which traces its history back to the Bronze Age but is better known as a stronghold of the Knights Templars. The town is dominated by a medieval fortress enclosing the impressive Sanctuary of Santa Cruz. Visitors are not allowed to look round the church during services but the sacristan will open the door at almost any other time. In May each year the village celebrates its own personal miracle, said to have occurred in 1232. Apparently a priest who had been taken prisoner by the Moors was about to demonstrate a mass for his captors when the cross which had been missing for some time suddenly reappeared. Unfortunately it was stolen again during the Civil War and when it failed to turn up for the second time the Vatican sympathetically provided a substitute.

Another most acceptable road leads on to **Lorca**, a large agricultural centre in the unexpectedly fertile and well populated valley of the Guadalentin with the remains of an ancient fortress and some attractive old buildings round the Plaza de España. Very little has changed in the original quarter since the days of the Moors and there is a pleasant climb up to the castle which played an important part in the reconquest of Granada. One reward is a splendid view over the heads of three elderly churches to the more modern town and the countryside beyond. Lorca is famous for its Holy Week festivities with ancient Romans and biblical characters taking part in the processions and the White and Blue Brotherhoods keeping alive a centuries-old rivalry which was not always so friendly or so colourful. The town is well placed on the highway from Almería to Murcia with a game reserve to the north balanced by Aguilas on the coast less than 50km (31 miles) away in the opposite direction.

Both Lorca and Aguilas have their own modest hotels and taverns for anyone who feels inclined to spend a night in the area. The road that connects them twists and turns through volcanic-looking hills which give the impression of having been tossed up by a subterranean disturbance rather than worn down by centuries of storm water forcing a way through to the sea. The landscape would be extremely arid if it were not for the seemingly endless terraces planted with tomato plants, often the height of a man and frequently covered with enormous sheets of white plastic. Many of the little houses and cafés along the route add splashes of colour with clumps of roses and hibiscus alongside orange trees, cacti and prickly pears.

Sadly, the Spanish have nothing to learn from us when it comes to litter: cans, plastic bags, bottles and paper are all left to lie where they fall, or have been dumped deliberately, joined on occasions by discarded furniture or the rusty remains of a car. Murcia makes a greater attempt than some of its neighbours to tidy up the mess and quite a few villages have their own scrapyards on the outskirts piled high with defunct vehicles and unwanted parts. Houses are treated very casually — it would seem that when the roof falls in the occupants simply move out, leaving the walls to crumble bit by bit like so many of the ancient watch towers mouldering on their rocky headlands all along the coast. The ruins are not particularly unsightly but the rubbish is a constant eyesore nearly everywhere you go in southern Spain.

**Aguilas** is, by Spanish standards, a comparatively new town although it was the site of an ancient city sacked by Barbary pirates and then more or less abandoned until mid-way through the eighteenth century. A lot of work has gone into restoring the original castle and just as much into building highrise blocks, establishing camp sites and providing a small marina inside the harbour walls. It is mainly a fishing port with every intention of becoming a popular holiday resort and is, in fact, the only place of any consequence along the shoreline between Cartagena and the border with Almería.

There are some pleasant beaches along this stretch of coast but the roads, if and when they do exist, are very minor indeed. As a result a large percentage of drivers return to Lorca the way they came and take the highway to the capital, a predictably busy road, more or less solid with little hotels, restaurants, cafés, bars and filling stations. However it is possible, with a bit of time and effort, to plot a course to **Mazarrón**. At one stage this was an important mining town but these days it relies almost entirely on tomatoes and tourists for a living. It offers its visitors the usual ruined castle, the sixteenth-century church of San Andrés, an area of weird rock formations known as the Enchanted City of Bolnuevo and some, as yet quite secluded, beaches a few kilometres away. At this point the road heads slightly inland in the direction of **Cartagena**.

As its name suggests this ancient port was established by the Carthaginians who captured a small settlement there in 223BC and proceeded to turn it into a town. The Romans expanded it still further but neither the Moors nor the Catholics showed very much interest in it until the sixteenth century when Philip II decided to protect the area with a number of small forts on the surrounding hilltops. Their sudden appearance did nothing to stop Francis Drake sailing in and spiking its guns in 1585 as a prelude to the defeat of the Spanish Armada about three years later.

Today Cartagena is both an important naval base and a busy commercial port without much to show for its Roman occupation, nothing to recall Drake's visit and only the ruins of a thirteenth-century cathedral, destroyed during the Civil War. Apart from the view from the Castillo de la Concepción, with its wide flights of steps leading up to a businesslike tower surrounded by a park, the port's main attractions are the arsenal, built in 1782, and an antiquated submarine. This was designed by a local inhabitant, Lieutenant Isaac Peral, in 1888 and was powered by two electric engines of 30hp each. It stands, a little self-consciously, surrounded by trees, fountains and souvenir stalls in a square a short walk from the well guarded gates of the arsenal. Cartagena also boasts an archaeological museum with Roman associations and a naval museum with everything from the remains of a Roman galley and items dredged up from the bottom of the harbour to a library specialising in marine archaeology. There is a much-restored Roman arena and various other bits and pieces, most of them below ground level, plenty of trees, wide streets which are extremely well maintained and some attractive beaches within easy reach. The selection of hotels is surprisingly limited, particularly in view of the large number of restaurants and the variety of apartments available. The town is famous for its Holy Week celebrations that are said to be amongst the most memorable in Spain.

Cartagena marks the beginning of the coastal highway that cuts across a large peninsula to the north with roads branching off to various unspoiled beaches and a scenic route running due east to the Cabo de Palos. The headland, complete with lighthouse, is steep and rocky to the south, contrasting sharply with the Mar Menor, a vast salt water lagoon on the opposite side. It is almost completely cut off from the sea by a natural sandspit called La Manga, or The Sleeve, which has already built itself into a popular holiday resort. There is a casino, half a dozen hotels, countless restaurants to choose from, quantities of apartments and a well equipped camping site as well as moorings for the boats. Tennis and golf are both available in the area and, with the Mediterranean on one side and the lagoon on the other, the opportunities for water sports are many and varied. Everything is on offer, from sailing and water-skiing to windsurfing, diving and underwater fishing. At the same time anglers maintain that the Mar Menor provides them with some of the most interesting fishing to be found anywhere in the country.

While all this is going on the highway from Cartagena carries on single-mindedly round the other side of the Mar Menor with small roads that dodge in and out to visit waterside hamlets shaded by almond blossom in the spring. It calls at **Los Alcázares**, an elderly spa set about with palms and lemon trees where the traditional game is bowls. It also has a few windmills which look very different from their famous cousins in La Mancha. The Murcian variety are smaller, and are fitted with a contraption resembling the frame of an umbrella which is equipped with a series of individual sails and twirls round over the shoulder of the mill in the manner of a parasol. As one approaches Santiago de la Ribera, crowded with servicemen from the Air Academy, there are signs inviting holidaymakers to play mini-golf or bingo, visit a disco, stop off at a motel, swim in the pool or tie up a boat in the small marina. By way of a change visitors can pop over to **San Pedro del Pinatar**, once a favourite watering hole for local Moorish kings which still uses some of the pools they splashed about in to treat people suffering from rheumatism. It also has a museum of the sea which can be visited. From San Pedro it is only a step to the border with Alicante, but more like 50km (31 miles) to **Murcia**.

The capital is an attractive town with wide streets, fairly modern buildings, plenty of palms and other trees and a river running through the middle. Its hotels range from first-class, through comfortable, to modest and small, the shops are inviting and there is at least one excellent restaurant and a reasonable number of less ambitious but nevertheless very acceptable ones. It also has an extremely elegant casino dating back to the nineteenth century with an Arab patio, a ballroom that calls to mind the Palace of Versailles and an old-world atmosphere said to be unrivalled anywhere in Spain.

*Mursiya*, as it was originally called, was founded by the Moors early in the ninth century only to be captured by the Catholics in 1266. For something like five hundred years it continued to earn a living from farming and weaving silk but in more recent times it turned its attention to light industry and is now very much involved in canning such things as fruit and vegetables and training students at the local university. Quite a few medieval streets can be found tucked away behind the modern avenues with a sprinkling of elderly buildings and some attractive gardens laid out along the river banks. Its most obvious attraction is the cathedral, built in part during the fourteenth century although much of it was added at intervals over the next four hundred years. It is highly decorative both inside and out with some intricate carving and a few unexpected additions such as a skeleton and an urn reputed to contain the internal organs of Alfonso the Wise. Its museum, occupying the Chapter House and part of the cloister, draws particular attention to the earliest exhibit, the Sarcophagus of the Muses dating back to the third century. Amongst the many items of sacred art is a statue of St Jerome with a lion at his feet which is generally regarded as one of Francisco Salzillo's greatest masterpieces. A splendid panorama can be seen from the belfry provided one is willing to trudge up a series of inclines and then tackle a slightly claustrophobic spiral staircase in order to get a bird's eye view.

The archaeological museum concerns itself with everything from 4,000-year-old funeral decorations, Roman relics and Moorish pottery to coins minted in the New World, nineteenth-century glass and reminders of World Cup football matches. The fine arts museum is largely devoted to paintings and sculptures but the works of Francisco Salzillo, the eighteenth-century local sculptor, have a home of their own in the church of Jesus. He was responsible for several of the magnificent floats that are carried through the streets during Holy Week. Particularly memorable are the enchanting nativity scene and the facial expressions in groups depicting the Last Supper and the betrayal in the Garden of Gethsemane. Other things to look for are his little figures of contemporary peasants going about their daily tasks.

*Moorish waterwheel at
Alcantarilla*

A museum of traditional costumes, which is being rehoused at the moment, will be worth seeing for its interest in foreign fashions as well as clothes associated with the various regions of Spain.

Although Murcia is justly famous for its solemn processions during Holy Week it is also known for the Spring Fair held just afterwards. It is a time for lighthearted merrymaking with a battle of flowers, fancy dress parades, music and dancing and a mock funeral service for the Burial of the Sardine.

Anyone with a day to spare in Murcia can arrange an interesting but not very demanding round trip, starting with a short drive to **Alcantarilla**. Originally an Iberian settlement, it passed into the hands of the Arab queen Al-Horra, then became the property of the Queens of Castilla, was destroyed by a flood in 1545 and later completely rebuilt just next door before being passed on to the church of Cartagena. It has an interesting ecology museum consisting of typical thatched farmhouses surrounded by trees and flowers with a modern building devoted to various crafts and a restaurant in the grounds. In spite of the displays of furniture, costumes, household goods, musical instruments, farm implements and the like its most outstanding attraction is the giant water wheel. It was built by the Moors and still scoops up water from the canal and deposits it into the irrigation ditches high above.

A minor road skirts round the south of the capital and squirms its way up to the Sanctuary of the Virgen de la Fuensanta, or Sacred Fountain, which is the focal point of an important pilgrimage early in September. The church was built in the seventeenth century, close to a cave where an actress known as La Cómica retired to do penance at the shrine of the patron saint of Murcia. The Virgin is an attractive figure some four hundred years old, dressed in elaborate silken robes embroidered with silver and gold and decked out with jewels. The site has a commanding view over the farmlands while nearby is the Cresta del Gallo, aptly named for the cock's comb of jagged red rocks that form the crest, beyond which are the bare peaks of the Sierra de Columbares, pitted with small craters. From this vantage point one is faced with a choice of routes, all of them small and rather winding. One finds its way to the capital, another wanders off towards the coast, a couple make for the highway just short of the border with Alicante while yet another keeps company with the river all the way to Orihuela.

## Alicante

The most obvious difference between Murcia and Alicante is the abundance of tourists in the latter. The province numbers its annual visitors by the million, many of them making straight for the beaches and spending their entire holidays toasting in the sun, patronising the restaurants, strolling along the promenades and occasionally visiting one of the local sights. Only a few venture off the beaten track and even then the majority opt for a conducted tour that gets them back in time for dinner. But there is a great deal more to Alicante than that. Admittedly its golden sands, rocky outcrops and attractive little coves are its greatest holiday asset but they do tend to become both over-built and over-crowded whereas the interior is just the reverse. There are mountains to the north-west with only an occasional village reached by way of a small, winding road, hillsides terraced in the Moorish style and planted with orchards and olive groves, farmlands with room to breathe along the valleys as well as the date palms and salt deposits of the area bordering on the Segura river.

**Orihuela** is the first large town to be encountered on the highway from Murcia and was, in fact, the capital of that province under both the Romans and Visigoths, losing out to Murcia itself in the eighteenth century. It has an oasis quality about it, enhanced by palm groves beyond which an intricate system of trenches and canals provides the necessary irrigation for oranges and lemons interspersed with mulberries. The town's main income comes from agriculture but there are enough reminders of its long history to make it worth a visit although it suffers from a shortage of hotels and, to a certain extent, of restaurants as well. The cathedral dates back to the fourteenth century and has a number of interesting features apart from a museum full of memorable paintings, including The Temptation of St Thomas Aquinas by Velázquez. The church of Santiago owes its existence to the Catholic Monarchs and is especially proud of its statues of the Holy Family attributed to Salzillo. The College of Santo Domingo, home of the university until it was closed down two hundred years ago, is only one of the many other religious buildings that contribute to the town's reputation for Gregorian music and the sound of church bells. The most unusual of its annual celebrations takes place in July when, apart from the parades of Moors and Christians, a couple of lights are placed in the castle ruins as a tribute to the two saints who ensured a Christian victory by guiding their forces into the Arab headquarters.

A few secondary roads and an even greater number of minor ones link Orihuela with the coast. The most southerly of them passes through **San Miguel de Salinas**, a delightful little town which can spring a few surprises on the unsuspecting traveller. It is quite capable of shutting off the main route so that everyone can go to a funeral and drivers forced to negotiate the narrow streets should keep an eye open in case a heavy door swings open suddenly to allow a small herd of goats to mingle with the traffic. The main coastal resort hereabouts is **Torrevieja** which has been producing rice since the Middle Ages and whose marshes and lagoons provide something like a million tons of salt a year. Some of it is piled into large white hillocks along the water's edge and anyone who is interested can call in to see exactly how it is produced. However, the more conventional attractions include an aquapark where cans, bottles and dogs are strictly forbidden, an eighteen-hole golf course, tennis courts, a football ground, a bullring and an aero-club. There are some most attractive beaches, a lot of villas in the Moorish style and a sprinkling of little inns and taverns as well as three comfortable seaside hotels anything from 4km to 11km (2-7 miles) away.

The coastal highway carries on northwards to **Santa Pola** which has spent the last two hundred years catering for holidaymakers. Originally they were mainly families from Madrid, Albacete and even Murcia but today the resort has gained a foothold on the international stage. Highrise buildings have appeared all along the front backed by shops and interspersed with restaurants specialising in fish landed daily from the fleet which operates out of the harbour. Part of the catch is offered for sale at the quayside market that has become almost as much of a tourist attraction as the sixteenth century fortress, the generous beaches and the offshire island of **Tabarca**. This was once home to several hundred Italians from Genoa who had been taken prisoner by the Berbers and held as hostages on the Tunisian island of the same name. Later Tabarca became a popular jumping off point for pirates, then a convenient anchorage for fishermen and is now known for its Roman associations, its under water fishing and a local dish called *arroz negro* from the ink of the squid which is its main ingredient. There are no hotels on the island, a minor consideration in view of all the ferry services, and not a great many in Santa Pola itself, although there are compensating apartments and camp sites.

The resort is only 18km (11 miles) from the capital, **Alicante**, which, in spite of its status as a tourist centre, has managed to retain a good deal of its original atmosphere. The Explanada de España with its red, cream and black marble paving and impressive palm trees, skirts round the port and the pleasure harbour in the shadow of the impressive but somewhat severe castle of Santa Barbara. The original fortress is said to have been built by the Carthaginians in the third century BC. Thereafter it was improved upon by successive occupiers, garrisoned at one time or another by everyone from the Greeks to the British, blown up by Philip V and eventually expertly restored. More recently it has been equipped with an access road complete with parking space for cars, a footpath and a lift for sightseers whose energy fails to match their enthusiasm for ancient buildings and exceptional views.

The cathedral of San Nicolas de Bari, on the site of an ancient mosque, shows little sign of the damage it suffered during the Civil War and competes for attention with the rather more elaborate church of Santa Maria, also in the old suburb of Santa Cruz. The archaeological museum is crammed with exhibits going back to the Stone Age, offset by some modern and almost-modern pottery. There is also a museum of twentieth-century art and a fair amount to see at the town hall including a mark on the steps outside which is used to calculate the height above sea level of any other place in

Spain. The Monastery of Santa Faz, just out of town, has another piece of the veil of Santa Veronica which it keeps in a silver casket. Alicante celebrates with enormous enthusiasm, lighting bonfires in honour of St John in the middle of June, letting off fireworks during the Feast of St Peter shortly afterwards and holding mock battles between Christians and Moors at the beginning of December. One of its more unusual events takes place on Easter Sunday when people go out for a picnic taking a *mona* which is a kind of roll with a hard-boiled egg in the middle to be broken over the head of anyone the owner finds attractive. It is more fun than sending a Valentine and some enthusiasts get so carried away that they stage a replay on Easter Monday.

Alicante is well blessed with hotels and restaurants, both in the city itself and along the coast at San Juan where the beach is superb, although invariably crowded, and everything is laid on to keep the holidaymaker happy. There are shops of every description, cafés, bars and an open-air cinema in addition to things like windsurfing boards and paddle boats for hire and a station for the narrow-gauge railway that runs between the capital and Denia, close to the border with Valencia.

There are any number of other places within easy reach of the city, the largest and best-known being **Elche** with its 200,000 date palms standing in groves that were designed by the Phoenicians. At one time the crop, the only one in Europe, was harvested to good advantage but this has become less and less of a viable proposition, making it rather unusual these days to see anyone shinning up to the top in search of a sackful of ripe fruit. The fronds are quite a different matter and thousands are gathered annually to reappear at the celebrations marking Palm Sunday. The centrepiece of the main grove is the Huerto del Cura, a delightful park full of cacti and other kinds of vegetation, shady walks and limpid pools one of which is presided over by a facsimile of the famous Dame of Elche. This rather petulant Iberian beauty with her unusual headdress and ostentatious jewellery was discovered at Alcudia, a few kilometres away, in 1897. The original stone bust has pride of place in Madrid's archaeological museum but many other relics discovered in the same ruins are housed in a museum on the site alongside some ancient foundations, a large well and a few pillars which were once part of a temple. Less well publicised are Elche's other attractions including a twelfth-century tower, the convent of La Merced, the church of Santa Maria famous for its centuries-old mystery play, and an elderly town hall in the Moorish quarter housing a museum of contemporary art.

*Grove of date palms, Elche*

From Elche a secondary road of no outstanding interest connects with the main route to Albacete which calls at **Sax** and Villena on the way. The former has one of the best preserved castles in the district, rising out of a large, jagged and isolated rock surrounded by fields and farmlands. **Villena's** fortress castle of La Atalaya is more accessible and more sophisticated with a fifteenth-century keep crowned with a series of sentry boxes. It once belonged to Henry of Aragon who is remembered as a poet but preferred to be known as a magician. The town that grew up round it has a brace of old churches, the most viewable being the church of Santiago, and an archaeological museum with a collection of gold and silver ornaments that were fashioned during the Bronze Age and discovered in 1963. The Festero museum with its collection of costumes is only open during the September celebrations in honour of the local patron saint but the unlikely-sounding Water Jug Museum will admit any visitor who is interested enough to telephone. Some 10km (6 miles) away to the east is the village of **Biar**, clustered at the foot of a steep hill crowned with a restored Arab fortress. One unusual aspect of the village is the system of arches that were used to close off the streets during the Middle Ages, both at nightfall and in the face of an enemy attack.

Armed with a good map it is quite easy to find a back-way through to **Jijona** with its *turrón* factories. One of them, the Turrónes el Loboy 1880, has an interesting little museum with figures dressed

*Biar*

in traditional costumes and all the hardware that was employed in making this age-old delicacy. Apart from seeing how it is manufactured visitors are invited to try a sample before they leave. The Caves of Canalobre are only a few kilometres away in the Cabesó d'Or mountains, near the village of Busot. A confirmed pot-holer would undoubtedly find them disappointing with their stalactites emphasised by concealed lighting and steps leading up through the giant cavern, but for anyone else they are certainly worth visiting. The caves are reached by a well surfaced road, are open all year round and, apart from a concert hall, there is a pleasant bar and a view across to the Mediterranean.

Anyone who is on a diet or has absolutely no interest in stalactites should follow the road from Biar through Ibi, known for its dolls and other toys, to join the scenic highway just south of **Alcoy**. The town is the third largest in Alicante without a great deal to show for its long history, due partly to the local habit of setting fire to elderly buildings or pulling them down at intervals to make way for something larger and more modern. It is an industrial centre involved with paper, textiles and canning olives stuffed with anchovies. On the credit side, where tourists are concerned, is the archaeological museum containing, amongst many other things, a lead tablet written on both sides in ancient Greek and called the Plom d'Alcoi. The Museo de Fiestas, housed in the only remaining medieval mansion, contains everything relating to the Festival of St George who is credited with personally outsmarting a Moorish attack in 1276. Three days of celebrations in late April include a gunpowder battle and end with a young boy appearing on the battlements of a cardboard castle in the Plaza de España in the absence of both the saint and the fortress. Of the half dozen bridges the most spectacular is the Pont de Sant Jordi, built in the 1920s to span a deep chasm in the town centre, rather on the lines of the New Bridge at Ronda, in Málaga. A comfortable hotel can be found close by but the most up-market and atmospheric restaurant is sited on the road to Valencia a short drive away.

The countryside to the south-west of Alcoy is a perfect place to wander, scented with herbs like thyme, mint and rosemary, full of little springs and shaded by ancient Mediterranean woods of oak and ash, yews, pines and other evergreens. A good place to start is at the Santuario de la Font Roja with its fountain of ice-cold water and panoramic views. Alternatively, an attractive and at times very winding road climbs up into the eastern Sierra de Aitana, looks down from a dizzy height on the Guadalest reservoir and pauses at the extraordinary little village of the same name. **Guadalest** was destroyed by an earthquake more than two hundred years ago, and the only way in is through an arch cut out of the rock beyond which is a ruined fortress. Predictably it has been turned into a popular tourist haunt, though it is no wonder that it has been primped and painted for the benefit of tourists when one realises that it is only a shortish drive from **Benidorm**.

There is really very little to pinpoint in this frankly tourist-infested but highly successful seaside metropolis, jam-packed with glass and concrete tower blocks, full of hotels, apartment buildings, shops, restaurants and camp sites, where the sun shines practically all the year round. It is amazing to think that its massive development programme is a bare half-century old, starting out from a small fishing village, a hint of which can still be found in the old quarter round a blue-domed church.

**Villajoyosa**, although not exactly charismatic, is colourful and very popular. It has a comfortable and secluded hotel built in the Spanish style, offering its guests every facility as well as an outstanding view, two swimming pools, a tennis court and steps down to an attractive beach club with opportunities for wind-surfing, water-skiing, sailing and deep sea fishing. The local inhabitants are kept busy making chocolate and fishing nets and many of them take part in a reconstructed Moorish landing, followed by a battle between Moors and Christians, during the last week of July. A whole variety of sports are available and there are some most acceptable beaches that can be reached by road or on foot.

**Altea**, roughly the same distance from Benidorm on the opposite side, is a picturesque fishing port famous for its lobsters, with a nine-hole golf course, some typical seaside hotels and a selection of coves as well as sandy beaches. Beyond it is **Calpe**, known principally for the Ifach Rock, linked to the mainland by a built-up sandspit and looking for all the world like Gibraltar's little brother. Anyone who resists an urge to scramble up to the top can get there by way of a tunnel carved out of the middle to make things easier. From Calpe a small road follows the coast through Buena Vista, which also has a golf course, to **Moraira**, a delightful resort with a most acceptable hotel, an extremely good restaurant, other establishments on a more modest scale, several shops and a great many private villas. It also boasts an ancient castle, a watch tower, a few sandy creeks and, ideal for the off the beaten track visitor, nothing much in the way of organised entertainments.

The same road wanders off across country to the outskirts of **Jávea** which makes no bones about its advantages as a holiday playground, although there is an attractive old quarter grouped round an elderly fortified church, in sharp contrast to the highrise developments which began in the harbour area and threaten to extend most of the way to Cap de la Nao. Modern villas, some forming their own tight-knit communities while others remain aloof in colourful gardens, can be seen everywhere and are dotted amongst the pine trees and along the hillsides overlooking the sea. The coast is one mass of little coves and grottos, floored with shingle, that make it particularly attractive for boating and under-water fishing. Apart from a *parador* of no historic interest there is an occasional modest hotel and a positive rash of cafés and restaurants, a nine-hole golf course and a general air of wellbeing.

A short, fairly ordinary road links Jávea with **Denia**, the last town of any size before the border with Valencia. It is an ancient port, supposedly founded by Greeks from Asia Minor and later occupied by the Romans who called it after the goddess Diana. Amongst its many attractions are the remains of a temple dedicated to her, the church of Santa Maria, part of the antiquated walls and a very businesslike castle built into the hill rather than on top of it. Also on the list, but slightly further afield, are the convent of San Jerónimo and the Torre del Gerro, a seventeenth-century watch tower standing guard on the cliffs. Visitors can choose between sandy beaches to the north and rocky ones to the south, inspect the Cova Tallada

*Elephants at the safari park, Vergel*

where the sea water is dark and deep or climb up to the Cova del Argua, half way to the top of Montgó, which collects fresh water filtered through the mountain. Facilities exist for all the usual sports except, so far, for golf, in addition to the yacht harbour, a daily ferry to the island of Ibiza, the small-gauge railway that makes frequent stops on the journey to the capital and an archaeological museum housed in the castle. The town's outstanding fiestas are held in March, early July and mid-August. The Fallas, accompanied by music and fireworks, mark the beginning of spring; the Santisima Sangre, dating back to 1624, has everything from boat races and a battle of flowers to bullfighting in the sea while the Moors and Christians recall the encounters of long ago in their August tribute to San Roque, the patron saint who watches over them.

Short, well maintained roads connect both Jávea and Denia with the main highway to the north, joining it close to the point where it runs through the village of **Gata** along a street lined with small shops and festooned with wickerwork and souvenirs. In the main they are useful as well as decorative and it is a good place to buy anything from bags to hats, not to mention such cumbersome articles as chairs and tables.

Alicante has one last surprise to offer. At Vergel, just inside the border, lions and tigers are to be found wandering about in the well protected Safari Park. Motorists are instructed to keep their car windows closed as they drive through the different enclosures and past the strong gates operated by rangers. Once clear of danger visitors can park their cars and share the open grassland with buck, a herd of zebra, some little ponies and a llama family, one of whom appears to have a soft spot for children's books and hair ribbons. Amongst the other residents are giraffe, elephants, camels and monkeys as well as dolphins performing, apparently quite happily, in their large pool. Feeding time for visitors lasts all day and it is pleasant to sit out on the terrace in front of the restaurant before rejoining the traffic heading for the north of Spain.

# Further Information
## — Murcia and Alicante —

### Places of Interest

**Alcantarilla**
Huerta Museum
Open: daily 10.30am-2pm and 4-9pm. Winter 4-8pm.

**Alcoy**
Museum of Archaeology
Open: weekdays 8am-8pm. Closed on holidays.

Museo de Fiestas del Casal de Sant Jordi
Open: weekdays 10am-1.30pm and 5.30-8pm. Holidays 10am-1.30pm. Closed Saturday afternoon.

**La Alcudia**
Museum and Excavations
Open: 9am-8pm. Closes 5pm in winter, Mondays and sometimes for lunch.

**Alicante**
Castillo de Santa Barbara
Open: 9am-9pm. April and May: closes at 8pm; October-March: closes at 7pm. Also closed Saturday afternoon.

Cathedral of San Nicolás
Open: weekdays 10am-12.30pm and 6-8.30pm. Holidays 9am-1.45pm.

Church of Santa Maria
Open: during services.

Museum of Archaeology
Open: weekdays 9am-1.30pm.

Museum of Twentieth-Century Art
Open: May to September 10am-1.30pm and 6-9pm; October to April 10am-1pm and 5-8pm. Closed Monday and Sunday afternoons.

**Bocairent**
Museum
Open: Sunday 12.30-1.30pm. Otherwise enquire at 14 Calle Cantereria.

**Canalobre Caves**
Open: April to September 10.30am-8.30pm; October to March 11am-6.30pm. Closed 25 December and 1 January.

**Caravaca de la Cruz**
Museum of Ethnology
Open: during school hours only.

Museum of Religious Art and
 History
Open: daily 10am-1pm and 4-7pm.

Soledad Museum
Open: daily 10am-2pm and 6-8pm.

Sanctuary of Santa Cruz
Visit on request.

**Cartagena**
Angosto Garcia Vaso Collection
Open: weekdays 4-6pm by appointment.

Museum of Archaeology
Open: 10am-1pm and 4-6pm.
Weekends 10am-1pm. Closed
Monday and holidays.

Naval Museum
Open: 10am-2pm and 5-7pm.
Closed Monday and holiday
afternoons.

**Denia**
Castle with museum
Open: 10am-2pm and 5-8pm.

**Elche**
Huerto del Cura
Open: 9am-8pm. Closes 6pm in
winter.

Museum of Archaeology
Open: 11am-1pm and 4-7pm.
Closed Saturday and Sunday.

**Guadalest**
Ruined village
For specific times enquire from
tourist office.

**Jávea**
Museum of History and Ethnology

Open: Saturday afternoon and
Sunday morning.

**Jijona**
Turrón Museum
Open: daily 9.30am-1pm and 4-8pm.

**Jumilla**
Museum of Archaeology
Open: 11am-1pm and 5-7pm, by
appointment only.

Museum of Wine Cellar Equipment
Open: during business hours.

**Murcia**
Cathedral and Museum
Open: 10am-12noon and 5-7.30pm.

Museum of Archaeology
Open: July and August 9am-2pm.
Closed Sunday and public holidays. Otherwise 10am-2pm and 6-8pm weekdays, 11am-2pm Saturday and Sunday. Closed Monday.

Fine Arts Museum
Open: July and August 9am-2pm.
Closed Sunday and holidays. Otherwise 10am-2pm and 5-7pm
weekdays, 11am-2pm Saturday
and Sunday. Closed Monday.

Salzillo Museum
Open: weekdays 9.30am-1pm and
4-7pm. Winter 3-6pm. Holidays
10am-1pm.

**Monastery of Santa Faz**
Open: weekdays 10am-1pm and 5-8pm.

**Orihuela**
Cathedral with Museum of Sacred
 Arts
Open: 10.30am-12.30pm. Closed
Sunday and holidays.

Church of Santiago
Open: 9am-1pm and 4-6pm.

Museum of the Reconquest
Open: 11am-1pm and 4-7pm.

Palace of La Granja
Open: 11am-1pm and 4-7pm.
Closed Sunday and holidays.

Santo Domingo College
Open: 9am-1pm and 4-6pm.
Closed Saturday, Sunday, and
holidays.

**San Pedro del Pinatar**
Maritime Museum
☎ 57 19 20

**Sax**
Castle, including museum
Open: weekdays on request.
Saturday 5-7pm. Sunday and
holidays 12noon-2pm and 5-7pm.

**Island of Tabarca**
Frequent ferries

**Vergel**
Safari Park
Open: daily.

**Villena**
Festero Museum
Open: during September celebra-
tions only.

Water Jug Museum
To visit, ☎ 80 05 71.

Castle
Open: enquire at the town hall.

Museum of Archaeology
Open: daily. If closed, and to inspect Treasury, apply to the police.

**Yecla**
Museum of Archaeology

Open: weekdays 9.30am-12.30pm
and 5-9pm.

Museum of El Greco Reproductions
Open: weekdays 9.30am-12.30pm
and 5-9pm.

## Tourist Information Offices

**Alcoy**
Av Puente San Jorge 1
☎ 33 28 57

**Alicante**
Explanada de España 2
☎ 21 22 85

**Cartagena**
Pl Castellini 5
☎ 50 75 49

**Denia**
Patricio Ferrandiz
☎ 78 09 57

**Elche**
Passeig de l'Estació
☎ 45 27 47

**Lorca**
López Gisbert
☎ 46 61 57

**La Manga del Mar Menor**
Pl de Bohemia
☎ 56 37 24

**Murcia**
Alejandro Seiquer 4
☎ 21 37 16

**Orihuela**
Francisco Diez 25
☎ 30 12 85

**Santa Pola**
Pl de la Diputación
☎ 41 49 84

# Index

# ACCOMMODATION AND EATING OUT

Of all the different types of accommodation available in Spain, the best-known are undoubtedly the *paradores*, a nationwide system of comfortable, well-equipped hotels run by the State and situated less than a day's drive apart. Visitors can tour the entire country, staying for the most part in historic palaces, castles and convents. To avoid leaving any awkward gaps in the chain they have been augmented with new hotels in areas where the existing accommodation was either very limited or not entirely suitable. There are some eighty *paradores* in all, the most elaborate being the most expensive, but all of them are guaranteed to provide first class amenities, excellent service and interesting traditional menus.

Apart from the *paradores*, the hotels range from luxurious establishments down to the basic variety which may well not have any private bathrooms or public lounges and almost certainly no lift. The *hostales* are also star-rated but usually correspond to hotels in the grade below, while the term *residencia* indicates that there is no dining room although they may provide breakfast and occasionally have a cafeteria. All the hotels and *hostales* are government controlled and have blue plaques at the main entrance giving their official status. A list of prices must be displayed in the lobby so it is possible to see at a glance if a room has a bath or only a shower. It is a good idea to look before you book in case there is some hidden drawback, such as windows opening onto a busy road. All except one-star *hostales* have heating installed and frequently provide extra blankets.

In the unlikely event of any serious difficulties, guests can always ask for the complaints book, or *libro de reclamaciones* and all entries must be shown to the authorities immediately. This means trouble for the proprietor so the management will usually prefer to put things right and so avoid an official black mark. Unless otherwise stated, the prices are for two people sharing a double room. Anyone on their own will pay more than 50 per cent of the price but if a third bed is available it will only cost about one third more. Many hotels make reductions for young children but as this is at the discretion of the management it is necessary to agree the terms in advance. Breakfast is nearly always extra and 6 per cent VAT is added to the overall bill. Guests who have to watch the *pesetas* should remember this and pay for drinks rather than ask for them to be charged to the number of the room.

Some of the larger towns and established holiday resorts provide furnished accommodation which may be either a villa or an apartment.

## Currency and Credit Cards

The Spanish currency is the *peseta* and the coins in use are 1, 5, 10, 25, 50, 100 *ptas*, augmented by 1,000, 2,000, 5,000 and 10,000 denomination notes. In street markets and out-of-the-way places the prices may be given in *duros*, which is a 5 *peseta* piece, or *notas*, indicating 100 *pesetas*.

Any amount of foreign currency may be taken into Spain but only limited amounts of foreign currency taken out again unless it can be proved that the excess was imported initially. As the exact amounts concerned may vary it is wise to get expert advice if quite large sums are involved. Most banks will change money and cash travellers cheques and Eurocheques, giving a better rate than the average hotel.

One or more of the major credit cards such as Access, American Express and Visa, are usually accepted by the larger hotels and restaurants, especially in cities and established tourist resorts, but even if the relevant logo is displayed in the window or at the reception desk it does no harm to confirm this in advance. Some garages in the cities and on the main highways also take credit cards but very few are prepared to accept them, nor will the majority of supermarkets. Banks displaying the logo concerned will usually pay out a reasonable sum against a credit card provided it is backed up by some form of identification. It should be remembered that in rural areas the use of credit cards may be infrequent or even non-existent.

## Restaurants and Bars

Mealtimes in Spain differ from those in many other countries. The gap between lunch and dinner is bridged by *tapas* bars where a whole variety of dishes of the hors d'oeuvre type are served with the drinks. It is possible to sample a *porcion*, or small helping, of any that look appetising and return for a second helping or a *racion*, a larger quantity, if you are still hungry. One of the advantages of *tapas* bars and cafés is that they are open all day and will supply something to eat at almost any time. The Spaniards themselves prefer to linger over lunch at around 1.30pm or 2pm, pop into a bar when the sun goes down and start thinking about dinner at 10pm or 11pm. However there is an increasing tendency for restaurants to open at 8.30pm or 9pm to accommodate their foreign visitors. There are also cafeterias where coloured photographs of *platos combinados* or combination plates, such as hamburgers and chips solve the language problem. Except in the case of international type restau-

318 Off The Beaten Track: Spain

rants it is better to choose a busy place than an empty one and sample the local dishes. The *menú del dia* or menu of the day, usually consists of three courses and is almost invariably better value for money than à la carte. The bill of fare is always displayed outside the door so it is easy to see in advance what is on offer and how much it will cost. Visitors who are determined not to eat anything out of the ordinary will find plenty of familiar dishes in dozens of little cafés that cater for tourists.

## Telephone Services

Direct calls can be made from all the provincial capitals, large towns and established tourist resorts. To telephone Spain the international dialling codes to add are: from the USA and Canada 011 34, UK 010 34 and Australia 0011 34. When making an international call remember to delete the first number from the area code when dialling. The central telephone offices (*telefonica*) in the larger towns have metered booths where you talk first and pay afterwards plus a percentage added for the service but this is still less than the surcharge imposed by most hotels.

## Tipping

Hotels and restaurants automatically include the equivalent of VAT in their bills and most of them also add a service charge. However it is as well to confirm this, especially in out-of-the-way places, and it is customary to leave a small tip anyway unless the food or the service has been unsatisfactory. Anyone who provides a personal service, such as cloakroom attendants, guides, porters and usherettes expect a gratuity and so do taxi drivers when the amount should be about 10 per cent to 12 per cent of the fare.

## Tourist Information Offices

Many large towns and holiday resorts on the costas have both Tourist Information Offices and Centres of Touristic Initiative. Where neither is available it is usually possible to get advice from the town hall during working hours. The main national tourist offices are:

**UK**
Spanish National Tourist Office
57/58 St James Street
London SW1A 1LD
☎ (071) 44 17 499 0901

**USA**
Spanish National Tourist Office
665 Fifth Avenue
New York
NY 10017
☎ (1212) 759 8822

**Canada**
Spanish National Tourist Office
60 Bloor Street West
Suite 201
Toronto
Ontario M4W 3B8
☎ 1416 961 3131

It may well be worth contacting local regional tourist boards for accommodation and other details. Some countries are better organised than others, but regional offices are more likely to be used to such requests. Tourist offices are listed in the Further Information section at the end of each chapter.

## Accommodation and Eating Out

❀❀❀  Expensive
❀❀   Moderate
❀    Inexpensive

### Chapter 1 •
### Aragonese Pyrenees

#### Accommodation

**Ainsa**
*Mesón de L'Ainsa* ❀
Sobrarbe 12
☎ 974 50 00 28

*Dos Rios* ❀
Avenida Central 2
☎ 974 50 00 43 No restaurant.

**Barbastro**
*Rey Sancho Ramírez* ❀
1km (½ mile) down the N240 towards Huesca
☎ 974 31 00 50

*Palafox* ❀
Corona de Aragón 20
☎ 974 31 24 61 No restaurant.

**Benasque**
*Monte Alba* ❀❀
6km (4 miles) from the town
☎ 974 55 11 36
Closed mid-April to late June and mid-September to Christmas.

*Aneto* ❀
Carretera Anciles 2
☎ 974 55 10 61

**Bielsa**
*Parador Monte Perdido* ❀❀
14km (9 miles) in the Valle de Pineta
☎ 974 50 10 11

*Carretera de Ainsa* ❀
☎ 974 50 10 08
Closed November to March.

**Huesca**
*Pedro I de Aragón* ❀❀
Parque 34
☎ 974 22 03 00

*Sancho Abarca* ❀
Plaza de Lizana 13
☎ 974 22 06 50

**Jaca**
*Gran Hotel* ❀❀
Paseo del General Franco
☎ 974 36 09 00

*Ramiro* ❀
Carmen 23
☎ 974 36 13 67

**Torla**
*Edelweiss* ❀
Avenida de Ordesa 1
☎ 974 48 61 73

*Bujaruelo* ❀
Avenida de Ordesa
☎ 974 48 61 74
Closed mid-January to mid-March.

### Eating Out

**Ainsa** ❀
*Bodegas del Sobrarbe*
Plaza Major
☎ 974 50 02 37
Open: mid-March to mid-October.

**Barbastro**
*Flor* ❀
Goya 3
☎ 974 31 10 56

**Benasque**
*La Parrilla* ❀
Carretera de Francia
☎ 974 55 11 34

**Huesca**
*Navas* ❀
San Lorenzo 15
☎ 974 22 47 38

*El Bearn* ❀
8 ½km (5 miles) on the N240
☎ 974 26 02 86
Closed Mondays.

**Jaca**
*La Cocina Aragonesa* ❀
Cervantes 5
☎ 974 36 10 50

*El Rancho Grande* ❀
Del Arco 2
☎ 974 36 01 72
Closed Mondays.

### Chapter 2 •
### Picos de Europa

#### Accommodation

**Cangas de Onis**
*Ventura* ❀
Avenida de Covadonga 3
☎ 985 84 82 00

**Cosgaya**
*Del Oso* ❀
☎ 942 73 04 18

*Mesón del Oso* ❀
☎ 942 73 04 18 No restaurant.

**Covadonga**
*Pelayo* ❋❋
☎ 985 84 60 00
Closed 20 December to
the end of January.

**Fuente Dé**
*Parador del Rio Deva* ❋❋
☎ 942 73 00 01

**Panes**
*Tres Palacios* ❋
Plaza Major
☎ 985 41 40 32

**Potes**
*Picos de Valdecoro* ❋
Roscabado
☎ 942 73 00 25

*La Cabaña* ❋
½km (1 mile) on the road
to Fuente Dé
☎ 942 73 00 50

*Eating Out*
**Cangas de Onis**
*La Cabaña* ❋
2 ½km (1½ miles) on the
road to Covadonga
☎ 985 84 82 84
Closed Thursdays.

**Covadonga**
*Hospederis del Peregrino* ❋
☎ 985 84 60 47
Closed late January to
late February.

**Panes**
*Casa Julián* ❋
9km (6 miles) on the road
to Cangas de Onis
☎ 985 41 41 79
With accommodation.

**Potes**
*Paco Wences* ❋
At the hotel Picos de
Valdecoro
☎ 942 73 00 25

*Chapter 3 •*
*Soria*
*Accommodation*
**Agreda**
*Doña Juana* ❋
Avenida de Soria 16
☎ 976 64 72 17

**Almazán**
*Antonio* ❋
Avenida de Soria 13
☎ 975 30 07 11
Closed Christmas to late
January.

**Berlanga de Duero**
*Hoz La* ❋
Carretera Postigo
☎ 975 34 31 69

**Medinaceli**
*Duque de Medinaceli* ❋
3½km (2 miles) on the N11
☎ 975 32 61 11
Closed early February to
early March.

**Santa Maria de Huerta**
*Parador Santa Maria de
Huerta* ❋❋
Between Medinaceli and
Calatayud
☎ 975 32 70 11

**Soria**
*Parador Antonio Machado* ❋❋
Parque del Castillo
☎ 975 21 34 45

*Mesón Leonor* ❋
Paseo del Mirón
☎ 975 22 02 50

*Viena* ❋
Garcia Solier 5
☎ 975 22 21 09 No restaurant.

*Eating Out*
**El Burgo de Osma**
*Virrey Palafox* ❋
Carretera Universidad
☎ 975 34 02 22
With accommodation.

**Medinaceli**
*Hostal Medinaceli* ❋
Portillo
☎ 975 32 61 30
Closed mid-November to
mid-December.With accom-
modation.

**Soria**
*Maroto* ❋❋
Paseo del Espolón 20
☎ 975 22 40 86

*Mesón Castellano* ❋
Plaza Major
☎ 975 21 30 45

*Chapter 4 •*
*Serranía de Cuenca*
*Accommodation*
**Beteta**
*Los Tilos* ❋
☎ 966 31 80 97

**Cuenca**
*Torremangana* ❋❋
Carrero Blanco 4
☎ 966 22 33 51

*Alfonso VIII* ❋
Parque San Julián 3
☎ 966 21 25 12

*Cueva del Fraile* ❋
7km (4 miles) on the road
to Palomera
☎ 966 21 15 71

*Posada de San José* ❋
Julian Romero 4
☎ 966 21 13 00 No restaurant.

**Una**
*Agua-Riscas* ❋
Egido 17
☎ 966 28 13 32
Closed most of January.

*Eating Out*
**Cuenca**
*Figón de Pedro* ❋
Cervantes 13
☎ 966 22 68 21
Closed Sunday evenings.

*Taverna de Petro* ❀
Calle de los Tintes

*Baviera* ❀
Calle Hurtado de
Mendoza

## Chapter 5 •
## The Ebro Crescent

### Accommodation

**Alcañiz**
*Parador La Concordia* ❀❀
Castillo de los Calatravos
☎ 974 83 04 00

*Meseguer* ❀
Carretera de Castellón
☎ 974 83 10 02

**Alhama de Aragón**
*Bain Termas Pallarés* ❀
General Franco 20
☎ 976 84 00 11

**Amposta**
*Montsiá* ❀
Avenida de la Rápita
☎ 977 70 10 27

**Calatayud**
*Hotel Calatayud* ❀
2km (1 mile) along the N11
☎ 976 88 13 23

*Fornos* ❀
Paseo Cortés de Aragón 5
☎ 976 88 13 00

**San Carlos de la Ràpita**
*Miami Park* ❀
Avenida Constitución 33
☎ 977 74 03 51
Closed mid-January to
mid-March.

*Juanito* ❀
At Playa Miami
☎ 977 74 04 62
Closed October to March.

*Plaça Vella* ❀
Arsenal 31
☎ 977 77 24 53

**Tortosa**
*Parador Castillo de la Zuda* ❀❀❀
☎ 977 44 44 50

*Tortosa Parc* ❀
Conde de Bañuelos 10
☎ 977 44 61 12
No restaurant.

### Eating Out

**Alhama de Aragón**
*Villa Robledo* ❀
1km (½ mile) along the N11
☎ 976 84 02 70

**San Carlos de la Ràpita**
*Fernandel* ❀
2km (1 mile) on road to
Valencia
☎ 977 74 03 58

**Tortosa**
*Racó de Mig-Camí* ❀
2½km (1½ miles) on road
to Simpática
☎ 977 44 31 48

## Chapter 6 • El
## Bierzo

### Accommodation

**Carracedo**
*Las Palmeras* ❀
☎ 987 56 25 05

**Ponferrada**
*Del Temple* ❀❀
Avenida de Portugal 2
☎ 987 41 00 58

*Madrid* ❀
Avenue de la Puebla 44
☎ 987 41 15 50

*Conde Silva* ❀
Avenida de Astorga 2
☎ 987 41 04 07
No restaurant but a cafeteria.

**Villafranca del Bierzo**
*Parador de Villafranca del
Bierzo* ❀❀
Avenida de Calvo Sotolo
☎ 987 54 01 75

*San Francisco* ❀
Place Generalísimo
☎ 987 54 04 65
No restaurant.

### Eating Out

**Cacabelos**
*La Moncloa* ❀
Cimadevilla 99
☎ 987 54 61 01

*Casa Gato* ❀
Avenida de Galicia 7
☎ 987 54 70 71

**Molinaseca**
*Casa Ramón* ❀
Jardines Angeles Balboa 2
☎ 987 41 82 73

**Ponferrada**
*Azul Montearenas* ❀
6km (4 miles) on the NV1
☎ 987 41 70 12

*Ballesteros* ❀
Fueros de León 12
☎ 987 41 11 60

**Villafranca del Bierzo**
*Casa Méndez* ❀
Place de la Concepción
With accommodation.

## Chapter 7 •
## The Rías Altas

### Accommodation

**Betanzos**
*Los Ángeles* ❀
Ángeles 11
☎ 981 77 12 13

**Carballo**
*Moncarsol* ❀
Avenida Finisterre 9
☎ 981 70 24 11
No restaurant.

**Ferrol**
*Parador de Ferrol* ❀❀
Plaza Eduardo Pondal
☎ 981 35 67 20

*Almirante* ❀
Maria 2
☎ 981 32 53 11

*Ryal* ❀
Galiano 43
☎ 981 35 07 99

**La Coruña**
*Finisterre* ❀❀❀
Paseo del Parrote 20
☎ 981 20 54 00

*Ciudad de la Coruña* ❀❀
Ciudad Residencial La
Torre
☎ 981 21 11 00

*Rias Altas* ❀❀
La Playa de Santa Cristina
☎ 981 63 53 00

*Riazor* ❀
Avenida Barrio de la
Maza 29
☎ 981 25 34 00
No restaurant but a cafeteria.

*Mar del Plata* ❀
Paseo de Ronda 58
☎ 981 25 79 62
No restaurant.

**Mondoñedo**
*Mirador de los Paredones* ❀
2km (1 mile) on the N634
☎ 982 52 17 00

*Hostal Montero* ❀
Avenida San Lázaro 7
982 52 17 51

**Ortigueira**
*La Perla* ❀
Avenida de la Penela
☎ 981 40 01 50
No restaurant.

**Ribadeo**
*Parador de Ribadeo* ❀❀
Amador Fernandez
☎ 982 11 08 25

*Eo* ❀
Avenida de Asturias 5
☎ 982 11 07 50

**Villalba**
*Parador Condes de Villalba* ❀❀
Valeriano Valdesuso
982 51 00 51

*Villamartin* ❀
Avenida Tierra Llana
☎ 982 51 12 15

**Viveiro**
*Las Sirenas* ❀
Covas Beach
☎ 982 56 02 00

*Tebar* ❀
Las Sirenas
Avenida Nicolás Cora
Montenegro 70
☎ 982 56 01 00
No restaurant.

## Eating Out
**Betanzos**
*Casanova* ❀
Plaza García Hermanos 15
☎ 981 77 06 03
Closed October.

*La Casilla* ❀
Avenida de Madrid 90

**Camariñas**
*La Marina* ❀
M. Freijo 4
☎ 982 73 60 30

**Carballo**
*Chochi* ❀
Perú 9
☎ 981 70 23 11

**Corcubion**
*Dona Ximena* ❀
Simón Tomé Santos 24
☎ 981 74 74 22

**Ferrol**
*Pataquiña* ❀
Delores 35
☎ 981 35 23 11

*O'Xantar* ❀
Real 182
☎ 981 35 51 18

**La Coruña**
*Coral* ❀❀
Estrella 2
☎ 981 22 10 82

*El Gallo de Oro* ❀❀❀
12km (7 miles) away at
Arteijo, on C552
☎ 981 60 04 10

*El Rápido* ❀
Estrella 7
☎ 981 22 42 21

*La Marina* ❀
Avenue de la Marina

*La Granja* ❀
Plaza Maria Pita

**Ribadeo**
*Mediante* ❀
Plaza de España 8
☎ 982 11 01 86
With accommodation.

*Oviedo Bar 1* ❀
Amando Pérez 5
☎ 982 11 00 35

**Viveiro**
*Nito* ❀
Playa de Area
☎ 982 56 09 87

## Chapter 8 •
## The Western Marches

### Accommodation

**La Alberca**
*Las Bateucas* ❀
Carretera de las Batuecas
☎ 923 43 70 30

*Hostal Paris* ❀
San Antonio
☎ 923 43 70 56

**Béjar**
*Colón* ❀
Colón 42
☎ 923 40 06 50

*Comercio* ❀
Puerta de Avila 5
☎ 923 40 02 19

**Caminomorisco**
*Pension Abuelo* ✷
Carretera de Salamanca
☎ 923 43 61 14

**Ciudad Rodrigo**
*Parador Enrique II* ✷✷
Plaza del Castillo 2
☎ 923 46 10 50

*Conde Rodrigo* ✷✷
Plaza de San Salvador 9
☎ 923 46 14 04

**Coria**
*Los Kekes* ✷
Avenida Sierra de Gata 49
☎ 927 50 09 00

**Jarandilla**
*Parador Carlos V* ✷✷✷
☎ 927 56 01 17

**Plasencia**
*Alfonso VIII* ✷✷
Alfonso VIII 34
☎ 927 41 02 50

*Real* ✷
1½km (1 mile) on road to
Salamanca
☎ 927 41 29 00

*Eating Out*
**La Alberca**
*El Castillo* ✷
Carretera de Mozarraz
☎ 923 43 74 81
With accommodation.

**Béjar**
*Tres Coronas* ✷
Carretera de Salamanca 1
☎ 923 40 20 23

**Ciudad Rodrigo**
*Casa Antonio* ✷
Gigantes 8
☎ 923 46 00 22
Closed most of September.

*Estoril* ✷
Travesia Talavera 1
☎ 923 46 05 50

**Plasencia**
*Florida* ✷
Avenida de España 22
☎ 927 41 38 58

# Chapter 9 •
# Extrema-dura &
# Huelva

*Accommodation*
**Almendralejo**
*Espronceda* ✷
Carretera de Sevilla
☎ 924 66 44 12

*Los Angeles* ✷
Macarena 2
☎ 924 66 06 33

**Aracena**
*Sierra de Aracena* ✷
Gran Via 21
☎ 955 11 07 75

**Ayamonte**
*Don Diego* ✷
Ramón y Cajal
☎ 955 32 02 50
No restaurant.

**Badajoz**
*Gran Hotel Zurbarán* ✷✷✷
Paseo Castelar 6
☎ 924 22 37 41

*Rio* ✷✷
Avenida Adolfo Diaz
Ambrona
☎ 924 23 76 00

*Hostal Menacho* ✷
Abril 12
☎ 924 22 14 46

**Cáceres**
*Parador de Turismo* ✷✷
Ancha 6
☎ 927 21 17 59

*Extremadura* ✷✷
Avenida Virgen de
Guadalupe 5
☎ 927 22 16 00

*Goya* ✷
Plaza General Mola
☎ 927 24 99 50

**Don Benito**
*Veracruz* ✷
Carretera de Villanueva
at 2½km (1½ miles)
☎ 924 80 13 62

**Guadalupe**
*Parador Zurbarán* ✷✷
Marqués de la Romana 10
☎ 927 36 70 75

*Hospederia del Real
Monasterio* ✷
Plaza Juan Carlos
☎ 927 36 70 00

**Huelva**
*Luz Huelva* ✷✷✷
Avenida Sundheim 26
☎ 955 25 00 11
No restaurant.

*Tartesso* ✷
Avenida Martin Alonso
Pinzón 13
☎ 955 24 56 11

**Isla Cristina**
*El Paraiso* ✷
Camino de la Playa
☎ 955 33 18 73

**Mazagón**
*Parador Cristóbal Colón* ✷✷
6½km (4 miles) on road
to Matalascañas
☎ 955 37 60 00

**Mérida**
*Parador Via de la Plata* ✷✷
Plaza de la Constitución 3
☎ 924 31 38 00

*Emperatriz* ✷
Plaza de España 19
☎ 924 31 31 11

**Punta Umbria**
*Ayamontino* ✷
Avenida de Andalucia
☎ 955 31 14 50

**Trujillo**
*Parador de Trujillo* ❋❋
Plaza de Santa Clara
☎ 927 32 13 50

*Hostal Pizarro* ❋
Plaza Major
☎ 927 32 02 55

**Zafra**
*Parador Hermán Cortés* ❋❋
Plaza Corazon Maria
☎ 924 55 02 00

*Huerta Honda* ❋
Lopez Asme 32
☎ 924 55 08 00

**Eating Out**

**Almendralejo**
*Danubio* ❋
Carretera de Sevilla
☎ 924 66 10 84

**Aracena**
*Casas* ❋
Colmenetas 39
☎ 955 11 00 44

*Venta de Aracena* ❋
Carretera N433
☎ 955 11 07 62

**Ayamonte**
*Restaurante Barbieri* ❋
Paseo de la Ribera

**Badajoz**
*El Tronco* ❋
Muñoz Torrero 16
☎ 924 22 20 76

*El Sótano* ❋
Virgen de la Soledad
☎ 924 22 00 19

**Cáceres**
*Atrio* ❋❋
Avenida de España
☎ 927 24 29 28

*Hosteria El Comendador* ❋
Ancha 6

**Guadalupe**
*Cerezo* ❋
Gregorio López 20
☎ 927 36 73 79
With accommodation.

**Huelva**
*La Muralia* ❋
San Salvador 17
☎ 955 25 50 77

**Mérida**
*Nicolás* ❋
Félix Valverde Lillo 11
☎ 924 31 96 10

*Borroso* ❋
(Pedestrian) St Eulalia
Off the Plaza España

**Trujillo**
*Mesón La Troya* ❋
Plaza Major 10
☎ 927 32 13 64

*Mesón La Cadena* ❋
Plaza Major 8
☎ 927 32 14 63
With accommodation.

## Chapter 10 •
## Seville and Córdoba

### Accommodation

**Carmona**
*Parador Alcázar del Rey
Don Pedro* ❋❋❋
☎ 95 414 10 10

**Córdoba**
*Meliá Córdoba* ❋❋❋
Jardines de la Victoria
☎ 957 29 80 66

*Parador de la Arruzafa* ❋❋❋
3½km (2 miles) on the road
to El Brillante ☎ 957 27 59 00

*Los Gallos Sol* ❋❋❋
Avenida Medina Azahara 7
☎ 957 47 32 34

*Marisa* ❋
Cardenal Herrero 6
☎ 957 47 31 42 No restaurant.

*Hostal Seneca* ❋
Calle Conde y Ligue 7
☎ 957 47 32 34

**Écija**
*Ciudad del Sol* ❋
Carretera N IV
☎ 95 483 03 00

*Astigi* ❋
Apartado 24
☎ 95 483 01 62

**Pozoblanco**
*Los Godos* ❋
Villanueva de Córdoba
☎ 957 10 00 22

*San Francisco* ❋
2km (1 mile) on road to
Alcaracejos
☎ 957 10 14 35

**Seville**
*Alfonso XIII* ❋❋❋
San Fernando 2
☎ 95 422 28 50

*Tryp Colón* ❋❋❋
Canalejas 1
☎ 95 422 29 00

*Doña Maria* ❋❋
Don Remondo 19
☎ 95 422 49 90
No restaurant.

*Hispalis* ❋❋
Avenida de Andalucia 52
4½km (3 miles) on road
to Málaga
☎ 95 452 94 33

*Simon* ❋
Garcia de Vinuesa 14
☎ 95 22 66 60

*Hostal Residencia Goya* ❋
Mateos Gago 31
☎ 95 421 11 70

*Hostal Atenas* ❋
Caballerizas
☎ 95 421 80 47

## Eating Out

**Carmona**
*El Molino* ❀
On the road to Seville

**Córdoba**
*El Caballo Rojo* ❀❀
Cardenal Herrero 28
☎ 957 47 53 75

*El Churrasco* ❀
Romero 16
☎ 957 29 08 19

*El Aguila* ❀
Calle Conde y Luque

**Osuna**
*Mesón del Duque* ❀
Plaza de la Duquesa 2
☎ 95 481 13 01

**Seville**
*Egaña Oriza* ❀❀❀
San Fernando 41
☎ 95 422 72 11

*Mesón del Moro* ❀
Calle Mesón del Morro,
in Santa Cruz

*Rio Grande* ❀❀
Betis
☎ 95 427 39 56

*Las Duendes* ❀
Calle Quintero

## Chapter 11 • Jaén

### Accommodation

**Andújar**
*Don Pedro* ❀
Gabriel Zamora 5
☎ 953 50 12 74

*La Fuente* ❀
Vendederas 4
☎ 953 50 46 29

**Baeza**
*Juanito* ❀
Paseo Arca del Agua
☎ 953 74 00 40

*Comercio* ❀
San Pablo 21
☎ 953 74 01 00

**Bailén**
*Parador de Bailén* ❀❀
☎ 953 67 01 00

*Motel Don López de Sosa* ❀
On the NIV
☎ 67 00 58

**La Carolina**
*La Perdiz* ❀❀
On the NIV
☎ 953 66 03 00

*La Gran Parada* ❀
On the NIV
☎ 953 66 02 75
No restaurant.

**Cazorla**
*Parador El Adelantado* ❀❀
26km (16 miles) from
Lugar Sacejo
☎ 953 72 10 75

*Sierra de Cazorla* ❀
2km (1 mile) on Carretera
de la Sierra
☎ 953 72 00 15

*Mirasierra* ❀
36km (22 miles) on the
road to El Tranco
☎ 953 72 15 44

**Jaén**
*Parador de Santa Catalina* ❀❀❀
5km (3 miles) in the
Castillo de Santa Catalina
☎ 953 26 44 11

*Condestable Iranzo* ❀❀
Paseo de la Estación
☎ 953 22 28 00

*Los Cazadores* ❀
Paseo de la Estacion 51
☎ 953 25 21 42

**Linares**
*Anibal* ❀❀
Cid Campeador 11
☎ 953 65 04 00

*Victoria* ❀
Cervantes 7
☎ 953 69 25 00
No restaurant.

**Marmolejo**
*Balneario* ❀❀
Calvario 101
☎ 953 54 00 00

**Úbeda**
*Parador Condestable
Dávalos* ❀❀❀
Plaza Vazquez de Molina 1
☎ 953 75 03 45

*Consuelo* ❀
Ramon y Cajal 12
☎ 953 75 08 40

*La Paz* ❀
Andalucia 1
☎ 953 75 08 48
No restaurant.

### Eating Out

**Andújar**
*Caballo Blanco* ❀
Monjas 5
☎ 953 50 02 88

**Baeza**
*Sali* ❀
Juanito, on the road to Úbeda
Pasaje Cardenal Benavides 15
☎ 953 74 13 65

**Jaén**
*Jockey Club* ❀
Paseo de la Estación 20
☎ 953 25 10 18

*Restaurante Nelson* ❀
Paseo de la Estación 33

**Linares**
*Mesón Campero Pozo
Ancho 5* ❀❀
☎ 953 69 35 02

*Mesón Castellano* ❀
Puente 5
☎ 953 69 00 09

**Úbeda**
*Cusco* ❋
Parque Vandelvira 8
☎ 953 75 34 13
Closed Sunday evening.

*Volga* ❋
Granada 4
☎ 953 75 11 88
Closed Mondays and
August.

# Chapter 12 •
# Ciudad Real and
# Albacete

## Accommodation

**Albacete**
*Los Llanos* ❋❋❋
Avenida Espana 9
☎ 967 22 37 50 No restaurant.

*Parador La Mancha* ❋❋
☎ 967 22 94 50

*Albacete* ❋
Carcelén 8
☎ 967 21 81 11

**Almagro**
*Parador de Almagro* ❋❋
Ronda de San Francisco
☎ 926 86 01 00

*Don Diego* ❋
Bolaños 1
☎ 926 86 12 87

**Alcázar de San Juan**
*Ercilla Don Quijote* ❋
Avenida de Criptana 5
☎ 926 54 38 00

*Barataria* ❋
2km (1 mile) on road to
Herencia
☎ 926 54 06 17

**Almansa**
*Los Rosales* ❋
Carretera N430
☎ 967 34 07 50

**Ciudad Real**
*Santa Cecilia* ❋❋
Tinte 3
☎ 926 22 85 45

*Castillos* ❋
Avenida del Rey Santo 8
926 21 36 40

**Daimiel**
*Las Tablas* ❋
Virgen de las Cruces
☎ 926 85 21 07

**Puerto Lápice**
*Aprisco* ❋
Carretera NIV
☎ 926 57 61 50

**La Roda**
*Hostal Molina* ❋
Alfredo Atienza 2
☎ 967 44 13 48

**Santa Cruz de Mudela**
*Santa Cruz* ❋
Carretera NIV
☎ 926 34 25 54

**Valdepeñas**
*Meliá El Hidalgo* ❋❋
7km (4 miles) on the NIV
☎ 926 32 32 50

*Cervantes* ❋
Junio 6
☎ 926 32 36 00

# Eating Out

**Albacete**
*Nuestro Bar* ❋
Alcalde Conangla 102
☎ 967 22 72 15

*Las Rejas* ❋
Dionisio Guardiola 9
☎ 967 22 72 42

**Alcázar de San Juan**
*Casa Paco* ❋
Avenida Alvarez Guerra 5
☎ 926 54 10 15

*La Mancha* ❋
Avenida de la
Constitucion
☎ 926 54 10 47

**Almagro**
*Meson El Corregidor* ❋
Plaza Fray Fernando
Fernández de Córdoba
☎ 926 86 06 48

**Ciudad Real**
*Miami Park* ❋
Ronda Ciruela 48
☎ 926 22 20 43

*Casablanca* ❋
Ronda de Granada
☎ 926 22 59 98

**Puerto Lapice**
*Venta del Quijote* ❋
El Molino 4
☎ 926 57 61 10

# Chapter 13 • Cádiz

## Accommodation

**Algeciras**
*Reina Cristina* ❋❋❋
Paseo de la Conferencia
☎ 956 60 26 00

*Guadacorte* ❋❋
7½km (5 miles) on the N340
☎ 956 66 45 00 No restaurant.

*La Posada del Terol* ❋
At the Playa de Palmones
☎ 956 67 75 50

**Arcos de la Frontera**
*Parador Casa del Corregidor* ❋❋
Plaza de Espana
☎ 956 70 05 00

*Los Olivos* ❋
San Miguel 2
☎ 956 70 08 11
No restaurant.

**Barbate de Franco**
*Sevilla* ❋
Padre Lopez Benitez 12
☎ 925 43 23 83

**Cádiz**
*Atlántico* ✺✺✺
Duque de Nájera 9
☎ 956 22 69 05

*Espana* ✺
Marquez de Cadiz 9
☎ 956 28 55 00

*Imares* ✺
San Francisco 9
☎ 956 21 22 57

**Castellar de la Frontera**
*La Almoraima* ✺✺
8km (5 miles) from the town
☎ 956 69 30 50

**Chipiona**
*Cruz del Mar* ✺
Avenida de Sanlúcar
☎ 956 37 11 00

**Conil de la Frontera**
*Don Pelayo* ✺
Carretera del Punto 19
☎ 956 44 02 32

**Grazalema**
*Grazalmena* ✺
☎ 14 11 36

**Jerez de la Frontera**
*Jerez* ✺✺✺
Avenida Alcalde Alvaro
Domecq 35
☎ 956 30 06 00

**Avenida Jerez**
*Avenida Alcalde Alvaro* ✺✺
Domecq 10
☎ 956 34 74 11
No restaurant but a cafeteria.

*Virt* ✺
Higueras 20
☎ 956 32 28 11
No restaurant.

**El Puerto de Santa Maria**
*Monasterio de San Miguel* ✺✺✺
Larga 27
☎ 956 86 44 00

*Melia Caballo Blanco* ✺✺
Avenida Madrid 1
☎ 956 86 37 45

*Los Cántaros* ✺
Curva 2
☎ 956 86 42 40
No restaurant but cafeteria.

**Rota**
*Playa de la Luz* ✺
Avenida Diputación
☎ 956 81 05 00

**Sanlúcar de Barrameda**
*Tartaneros* ✺
Tartanerous 8
☎ 956 36 20 44

**Sotogrande**
*Sotogrande* ✺
Carretera N340
☎ 956 79 21 00

**Tarifa**
*Balcón de España* ✺
La Peña 2
☎ 956 68 43 26
Closed November to March.

*La Ensenada* ✺
9 ½km (6 miles) on road
to Cádiz
☎ 95 664 36 37

**Vejer de la Frontera**
*Convento de San Francisco* ✺
La Plazuela
☎ 956 45 10 01

**Zahara de la Sierra**
*Marqués de Zahara* ✺
San Juan 3
☎ 956 13 72 61

**Zahara de los Atunes**
*Atlanterra Sol* ✺✺✺
4km (2 miles) on road to
Atlanterra
☎ 956 43 27 00

**Eating Out**

**Algeciras**
*Encajuan* ✺
On the N430
☎ 956 66 45 00

*Iris* ✺
San Bernado 1
☎ 956 65 58 06

*Marea Baja* ✺
Trafalgar 2
☎ 956 66 36 54

**Arcos de la Frontera**
*El Convento* ✺
Maidonado 2
☎ 956 70 23 33

**Barbate de Franco**
*Gadir* ✺
Padre Castrillón 15
☎ 925 43 08 00

**Cádiz**
*El Faro* ✺
San Felix 15
☎ 956 21 10 68

*Achuri* ✺
Plocia 15

*1800* ✺
Paseo Maritimo 3
☎ 956 26 02 03

**Chipiona**
*Mesón La Barca* ✺
Avenida de Sanlúcar
☎ 956 37 08 51

**Jerez de la Frontera**
*El Bosque* ✺✺
Avenida Alcalde Alvaro
Domecq
☎ 956 30 33 33

*Mesón La Cueva* ✺
10½km (6½ miles) on the
N342

*Gaitán* ✺
Gaitán 3
☎ 956 34 58 59

*Venta Antonio* ✱
6km (4 miles) on the
Carretera de Sanlucar de
Barrameda
☎ 956 33 05 35

**El Puerto de Santa Maria**
*Alboronia* ✱✱
Santo Domingo 24
☎ 956 85 16 09

*El Resbaladero* ✱
Aurora 1
☎ 956 85 68 53

*El Faro del Puerto* ✱
Carretera de Rota
☎ 956 87 09 52

**Rota**
*Bodegón la Almadraba* ✱
Avenida Diputación 150
☎ 956 81 18 82

**San Fernando**
*Venta de Vargas* ✱
Carretera NIV
☎ 956 88 16 22

**Sanlúcar de Barrameda**
*Mirador Doñana* ✱
Bajo de Guia
☎ 956 36 42 05

*Casa Bigote* ✱
Bajo de Guia

## Chapter 14 •
## Málaga

### Accommodation

**Alora**
*Alondra* ✱
Mola 56

**Antequera**
*Parador de Antequera* ✱✱✱
Paseo Garcia de Olmo
☎ 952 84 02 16

*Molino de Saydo* ✱
12km (7 miles) on N334
☎ 952 74 04 75

**Benalmádena**
*Torrequebrada* ✱✱✱
Carretera N340
☎ 952 44 60 00

*Riviera* ✱✱
Avenida Antonio
Machado 49
☎ 952 44 12 40

*Villasol* ✱
Avenida Antonio
Machado
☎ 952 44 19 96

**Estepona**
*Atalaya Park* ✱✱
On road to Málaga
☎ 952 78 13 00

*Buenavista Paseo Maritimo* ✱
☎ 952 80 01 37

**Fuengirola**
*Byblos Andaluz* ✱✱✱
5km (3 miles) on road to Coin
☎ 952 47 30 50

*Angela* ✱✱
Paseo Maritimo in Los
Boliches
☎ 952 47 52 00

*Mare Nostrum* ✱
On road to Cádiz
☎ 952 47 11 00

**Málaga**
*Parador de Gibralfaro* ✱
☎ 952 22 19 03

*Avenida* ✱
Alameda 5
☎ 952 21 77 29

*Castilla* ✱
Córdoba 5
☎ 952 22 86 37

**Mijas**
*Mijas* ✱✱
Urbanizacion Tamisa
☎ 952 22 86 37

*Novotel* ✱✱
Carretera de Fuengirola
☎ 952 48 64 00

**Nerja**
*Parador de Nerja* ✱✱
Playa de Burriana
☎ 952 52 00 50

*Nerja Club* ✱
Carretera N340
☎ 952 52 01 00

*Balcón de Europa* ✱
Paseo Balcón de Europa
☎ 952 52 08 00
No restaurant.

**Rincón de la Victoria**
*Rincón Sol* ✱
Avenida del
Mediterráneo 24
☎ 935 40 11 00
No restaurant but a cafeteria.

**Ronda**
*Reina Victoria* ✱✱
Dr Fleming 25
☎ 952 87 12 40

*Polo* ✱
Mariano Souvirón 8
☎ 952 87 24 47

*El Tajo* ✱
Cruz Verde 7
☎ 952 87 62 36
No restaurant but a cafeteria.

**San Pedro de Alcántara**
*Golf Hotel Guadalmina* ✱✱
Carretera N340
☎ 952 78 14 00

**Vélez-Málaga**
*Dila* ✱
Avenida Vivar Téllez 3
☎ 952 59 39 00
No restaurant.

### Eating Out

**Antequera**
*El Faro* ✱
7km (4 miles) at Cruce de
la Vega
☎ 84 03 67

**Benalmádena**
*La Rueda* ❀
San Miguel 2
☎ 952 44 82 21

**Estepona**
*Le Soufflé* ❀❀❀
11km (7 miles) on road to
Málaga
☎ 952 78 62 89

*Robbies* ❀
Jubrique 11
☎ 952 80 21 21

**Frigiliana**
*El Jardin* ❀
☎ 253 31 85

**Fuengirola**
*Ceferino* ❀❀
Rotonda de la Luna
☎ 952 46 45 93

*Monopol* ❀
Palangreros 7
☎ 952 44 47 48

*Brava* ❀
Avenida Ramón y Cajal

*Djakarta* ❀
Trinidad 4

**Málaga**
*Antonio Martin* ❀
Paseo Maritimo
☎ 952 22 21 13

*Taberna del Pintor* ❀
Maestranza 6
☎ 952 21 53 15
Closed Sunday

*El Rumblar* ❀
At Churriana
Carretera de Coin 44
☎ 952 43 50 60
Closed Sunday night,
Monday and during
October.

**Manilva**
*Macues* ❀
Puerto de la Duquesa
☎ 952 89 03 95

**Mijas**
*Valparaiso* ❀❀
On road to Fuengirola
☎ 952 48 59 96

*El Padrastro* ❀
Paseo del Compás
☎ 952 48 50 00

**Nerja**
*Rey Alfonso* ❀
Paseo Balcón de Europa
☎ 952 52 01 95

*Casa Luque* ❀
Plaza Cavana 2
☎ 952 52 10 04

**Puerto Banús**
*Taberna del Alabardero* ❀❀
Muelle Benabola
☎ 952 81 27 94

*Cipriano* ❀
Edificio Levante
☎ 952 87 10 90

**Ronda**
*Don Miguel* ❀
Plaza de Espana 3
☎ 952 87 10 90

*Pedro Romero* ❀
Virgen de la Paz 18
☎ 952 87 10 61

*Alhambra* ❀
Pedro Romero 9
☎ 952 87 69 34

**Torre del Mar**
*El Jardin* ❀
Paseo Maritimo de Levante
☎ 952 54 06 36

*Carmen* ❀
Avenida de Andalucia 94
☎ 952 54 04 35

*Chapter 15* •
*Granada and*
*Almería*

**Accommodation**

**Aguadulce**
*Satélites Park* ❀
☎ 951 34 06 00
Closed November to March.

**Almería**
*Gran Hotel Almeria* ❀❀
Reina Regente 8
☎ 951 23 80 11
No restaurant.

*La Parra Bahia de Palmer* ❀❀
Bahia de Palmer

*Indálico* ❀
Dolores Sopeña 4
☎ 951 23 11 11
No restaurant but a cafeteria.

**Alhama de Granada**
*Balneario* ❀
3km (2 miles) on
Carettera de Granada
☎ 958 35 00 11

**Almuñécar**
*La Najarra* ❀
Guadix
☎ 958 63 08 73

*Goya* ❀
Avenida de Europa
☎ 958 63 05 50

**Baza**
*Venta del Sol* ❀
Carretera de Murcia
☎ 958 70 03 00

**Granada**
*Parador de San Francisco* ❀❀❀
In the Alhambra
☎ 958 22 14 40

*Alhambra Palace* ❀❀❀
Peña Partida
☎ 958 22 14 24

*Kenia* ❋
Molinos 65
☎ 958 22 75 06 No restaurant.

**Guadix**
*Carmen* ❋
Carretera de Granada
☎ 958 66 15 11
No restaurant but a cafeteria.

**Lanjarón**
*Miramar* ❋
Avenida Gereralísimo
☎ 958 77 01 61

*Royal* ❋
Avenida de Andalucia
☎ 958 77 00 08

**Loja**
*La Bobadilla* ❋❋❋
21km (13 miles) off the
Carretera N342
☎ 958 32 18 61

*Del Manzanil* ❋
Carretera de Granada
☎ 958 32 17 11

**Mojácar**
*Parador Reyes Católicos* ❋❋
Carretera de Carboneras
☎ 951 47 82 50

*El Moresco* ❋
Mirador de la Puntica

*El Puntazo* ❋
Carretera de Carboneras
☎ 951 47 82 29

**Motril**
*Costa Andaluza* ❋
Islas Bahamas 59
☎ 958 60 56 05

**La Rábita**
*Los Conchas* ❋
☎ 958 82 90 71

**Salobreña**
*Salobreña* ❋
Carretera de Málaga
☎ 958 61 02 86

**Santa Fé**
*Santa Fé* ❋
Carretera N342
☎ 958 44 11 11

**Sorbas**
*Sorbas* ❋
Carretera N340
☎ 951 36 41 60

**Sierra Nevada**
*Parador Sierra Nevada* ❋❋❋
☎ 958 48 02 00

*Meliá Sierra Nevada* ❋❋❋
Plaza Pradollano
☎ 958 48 04 00
Closed May to November.

*Santa Cruz* ❋
On road to Granada
☎ 958 47 08 00

**Vera**
*Terraza Carmona* ❋
Manuel Jiménez 1
☎ 951 45 01 88

*Arga* ❋
2km (1 mile) on road to
Murcia
☎ 951 45 14 01

**Vélez Rubio**
*Hostal Jardin Casa Pepa* ❋
Carretera de Murcia
☎ 951 41 01 06

## Eating Out

**Aguadulce**
*Cortijo Alemán* ❋
Área Playasol
☎ 951 34 12 01

**Almería**
*Ánfora*
González Garbin 25
☎ 951 23 13 74

*Imperial* ❋
Puerta de Purchena 13
☎ 951 23 17 40

**Almuñécar**
*Chinasol Playa* ❋
Playa San Cristóbal
☎ 958 63 22 61

*Los Geranios* ❋
Plaza de la Rosa
☎ 958 63 07 24

*Cotobro Playa* ❋
Bajada del Mar
☎ 958 63 18 02

**Granada**
*Horno de Santiago* ❋❋
Plaza de los Campos 8
☎ 958 22 34 76

*Colombia* ❋
Antequeruela Baja 1
☎ 958 22 74 33

*Sevilla* ❋
Oficios 12
☎ 958 22 12 23

*Ruta del Veleta* ❋❋
6km (4 miles) on the
Carretera de Sierra Navada
☎ 958 48 61 34

*Cunini* ❋
Pescaderia 9
☎ 958 26 37 01

*China* ❋
Pedro Antonio de Alarcón 23
☎ 958 25 02 00

**Motril**
*La Caramba* ❋
Avenida de Salobreña 19
☎ 958 60 25 78

**Roquetas de Mar**
*Al-Baida* ❋
Avenida Las Gaviotas
☎ 951 33 38 21

*La Colmena* ❋
Lago Como Edificio
Concordia 1
☎ 951 33 35 65

**Salobreña**
*Salobreña* ❀
On the Carretera 340
☎ 958 82 88 29

**Chapter 16 •**
**Murcia and Alicante**

**Accommodation**

**Los Alcázares**
*Corzo* ❀
Avenida Española 8
☎ 968 57 51 25

**Aguilas**
*Stella Maris* ❀
Playa de las Delicias
☎ 968 41 00 97

**Alcantarilla**
*La Paz* ❀
On Carretera N340
☎ 968 80 13 37

**Alcoy**
*Reconquista* ❀
Puente de San Jorge 1
☎ 96 533 09 00

**Alicante**
*Meliá Alicante* ❀❀❀
Playa de El Postiguet
☎ 96 520 50 00

*Palas* ❀❀
Cervantes 5
☎ 96 520 92 11

*Cristal* ❀
López Torregrosa 11
☎ 96 520 96 00
No restaurant.

*Europa* ❀
Avenida de Denia
☎ 96 526 12 55

**Altea**
*San Miguel* ❀
Generalísimo 65
☎ 96 584 04 00

**Benidorm**
*Gran Hotel Delfín* ❀❀❀
Playa de Poniente La Cala
☎ 96 585 34 00

*Don Pancho* ❀❀
Avenida del
Mediterràneo 39
☎ 96 585 29 50

*Bilbaino* ❀
Avenida Virgen del
Sufragio 1
☎ 96 585 08 04

**Calpe**
*Hostal El Parque* ❀
Portalet
☎ 96 83 07 70

*Marysol Park* ❀
1km (½ mile) in Marysol Park
☎ 96 583 22 61

*Venta La Chata* ❀
4½km (3 miles) on
Carretera de Valencia
☎ 96 583 03 08

**Cartagena**
*Los Habaneros* ❀
San Diego 60
☎ 968 50 52 50

*Cartagonova* ❀
Marcos Redondo 3
☎ 968 52 00 00

**Elche**
*Huerto del Cura* ❀❀
Porta de la Morera 14
☎ 96 545 80 40

**La Manga del Mar Menor**
*Galúa Sol* ❀❀❀
Gran Via
☎ 968 56 32 00

**Murcia**
*Rincón de Pepe* ❀❀
Plaza Apóstoles 34
☎ 968 21 22 39

*Conde de Florida Blanca* ❀❀
Corbalán 7
☎ 968 21 46 26 No restaurant.

*Hispana 1* ❀
Traperia 8
☎ 968 21 61 52

**Santa Pola**
*Pola Mar* ❀
Playa de Levante 6
☎ 96 541 32 00

*Patilla* ❀
Elche 29
☎ 96 541 10 15

**San Pedro del Pinatar**
*Neptuno* ❀
Generalísimo 6
☎ 968 18 19 11

**Sax**
*Hostal El Molino* ❀
Jaime 1
☎ 47 48 42

**Torrevieja**
*Fontana* ❀
Rambla Juan Mateo 19
☎ 96 571 41 11

*La Cibeles* ❀
Avenida Dr Gregorio
Marañon 26
☎ 96 571 00 12

**Villajoyosa**
*Montiboli* ❀❀❀
3km (2 miles) Carretera
de Alicante
☎ 96 589 02 50

**Eating Out**

**Alcantarilla**
*Mesón de la Huerta* ❀
Carretera N340
☎ 968 80 23 90

**Alcoy**
*Lolo* ❀
Castalla 5
☎ 96 533 69 42

**Alicante**
*Delfin* ❀❀❀
Explanada de España 12
☎ 96 521 49 11

*Dársena* ❀
Muelle de Puerto
☎ 96 520 75 89

*Quo Vadis* ❀
Plaza Santisima Faz
☎ 96 521 66 60

*Auberge de France* ❀
Finca Las Palmeras
☎ 96 526 06 02

**Altea**
*Monte Molar* ❀❀❀
3½km (2 miles) off
Carretera de Valencia
☎ 96 585 44 68

**Benidorm**
*Tiffany's* ❀❀
Avenida del Mediterráneo
☎ 96 585 44 68

*Caserola* ❀
Bruselas 7
Rincón
☎ 96 585 17 19

*Alcázar* ❀
4km (2 miles) on the
Carretera de Pego
☎ 96 587 32 08

*Casa Modesto* ❀
Cala Finestrat
☎ 96 585 86 37

**Calpe**
*Los Zapatos* ❀
Santa Maria 7
☎ 96 583 15 07

*El Bodegón de Calpe* ❀
Delfin 6
☎ 96 583 01 64

*Viñasol* ❀
9½km (6 miles) on
Carretera de Moraira
☎ 96 573 09 72

**Elche**
*Enrique* ❀
Empedrat 6
☎ 96 545 15 77

*La Masía de Chencho* ❀
4km (2 miles) on
Carretera de Alicante
☎ 96 542 05 16

**Guadalest**
*Xorta* ❀
Carretera de Callosa de
Ensarri
☎ 96 588 13 87

**La Manga del Mar Menor**
*Tropical* ❀❀
Gran Via-Pol
☎ 968 14 03 45

*Borsalino* ❀
Edificio Babilonia
☎ 968 56 31 30

**Murcia**
*Rincón de Pepe* ❀❀❀
Plaza Apóstoles 34
☎ 968 21 22 39

*Los Apóstoles* ❀❀
Plaza de los Apóstoles
☎ 968 26 69 73

**Santa Pola**
*Miramar* ❀
Avenida Perez Ojeda
☎ 96 541 10 00

*Varadero* ❀
Playa del Varadero
☎ 96 541 17 66

*Maria Picola* ❀
3km (2 miles) on
Carretera de Elche
☎ 96 541 35 13

**Torrevieja**
*Miramar* ❀
Paseo Vista Alegre 6
☎ 96 571 34 15

*La Tortuga* ❀
Maria Parodi 1
☎ 96 571 09 60

**Villajoyosa**
*El Panchito* ❀
Avenida del Perto 46
☎ 96 589 28 55

*El Brasero* ❀
Avenida del Puerto
☎ 96 589 03 33

# A Note To The Reader

The accommodation and eating out lists in this book are based upon the authors' own experiences and therefore may contain an element of subjective opinion. The contents of this book are believed correct at the time of publication but details given may change. We welcome any information to ensure accuracy in this guide book and to help keep it up-to-date.
Please write to The Editor, Moorland Publishing Co Ltd,
Moor Farm Road, Airfield Estate, Ashbourne, Derbyshire,
DE6 1HD, England.

American and Canadian readers please write to The Editor, The Globe Pequot Press, 6 Business Park Road, PO Box 833, Old Saybrook, Connecticut 06475, USA.

MPC

# Discover a New World
## with
## *Off The Beaten Track* Travel Guides

### Austria
Explore the quiet valleys of Bregenzerwald in the west to
Carinthia and Burgenland in the east. From picturesque
villages in the Tannheimertal to the castles north of
Klagenfurt, including Burg Hochosterwitz. This dramatic
castle with its many gates stands on a 450ft high limestone
cliff and was built to withstand the Turkish army by the
man who brought the original Spanish horses to Austria.

### Britain
Yes, there are places off the beaten track in even the more
populated areas of Britain. Even in the heavily visited
national parks there are beautiful places you could easily
miss — areas well known to locals but not visitors. This book
guides you to such regions to make your visit memorable.

### Greece
Brimming with suggested excursions that range from
climbing Mitikas, the highest peak of Mount Olympus, the
abode of Zeus, to Monemvassia, a fortified medieval town
with extensive ruins of a former castle. This book enables
you to mix a restful holiday in the sun with the fascinating
culture and countryside or rural Greece.

### Italy
Beyond the artistic wealth of Rome or Florence and the hill
towns of Tuscany lie many fascinating areas of this ancient
country just waiting to be discovered. From medieval towns
such as Ceriana in the Armea valley to quiet and
spectacular areas of the Italian Lakes and the Dolomites
further to the east. At the southern end of the country, the
book explores Calabria, the 'toe' of Italy as well as Sicily,
opening up a whole 'new' area.

# Germany
Visit the little market town of Windorf on the north bank of the Danube (with its nature reserve) or the picturesque upper Danube Valley, which even most German's never visit! Or go further north to the Taubertal. Downstream of famous Rothenburg with its medieval castle walls are red sandstone-built villages to explore with such gems as the carved altar in Creglingen church, the finest work by Tilman Riemenschneider — the Master Carver of the Middle Ages. This book includes five areas in the former East Germany.

# Portugal
Most visitors to Portugal head to the Algarve and its famous beaches, but even the eastern Algarve is relatively quiet compared to the more popular western area. However, the book also covers the attractive areas of northern Portugal where only the more discerning independent travellers may be found enjoying the delights of this lovely country.

# Scandinavia
Covers Norway, Denmark, Sweden and Finland. There is so much to see in these countries that it is all too easy to concentrate on the main tourist areas. That would mean missing so many memorable places that are well worth visiting. For instance, there are still about sixty Viking churches that survive in Norway. Alternatively many private castles and even palaces in Denmark open their gardens to visitors. Here is your guide to ensure that you enjoy the Scandinavian experience to the full.

# Spain
From the unique landscape of the Ebrodelta in Catalonia to the majestic Picos d'Europa in the north, the reader is presented with numerous things to see and exciting things to do. With the mix of cultures and climates, there are many possibilities for an endearing holiday for the independent traveller.

# Switzerland

Switzerland offers much more than the high mountains and deep valleys with which it is traditionally associated. This book covers lesser known areas of the high mountains — with suggested walks in some cases. It also covers Ticino, the Swiss Lakeland area near to the Italian Lakes and tours over the border into the latter. In the north, the book covers the lesser known areas between Zurich and the Rhine Falls, plus the Lake Constance area, with its lovely little towns like Rorschach, on the edge of the lake.

*Forthcoming:*

# Northern France
# Southern France

Touring the ancient fishing port of Guethary, hiking in the Pyrennees and visiting the old archway in Vaucoulers (through which Joan of Arc led her troops), are just a few of the many opportunities these two books present.

# Scotland

Heather-clad mountains, baronian castles and magnificent coastal scenery, all combined with a rich historical heritage, combine to make this an ideal 'off the beaten track' destination.

# Ireland

Ireland not only has a dramatic coastline, quiet fishing harbours and unspoilt rural villages, but also the natural friendliness of its easy-going people. *Off the Beaten Track Ireland* will lead you to a memorable holiday in a country where the pace of life is more relaxing and definitely not hectic.